FAMILY THERAPY

FAMILY THERAPY

John Elderkin Bell

Veterans Administration
Stanford University School of Medicine
University of California, San Francisco
Palo Alto Medical Research Foundation

JASON ARONSON New York London

FOR ELISABETH, MY LOVE,

AND

COLIN, OUR SON

Library of Congress Cataloging in Publication Data

Bibliography; index.
1. Family psychotherapy.   I. Title.
[DNLM: 1. Family therapy.   WM430 B433f]
RC488.5.B45   616.8'915   74-22276
ISBN 0-87668-114-3

First Edition 1975
Copyright © 1975 Jason Aronson, Inc.

Preface

This book contains much material I did not intend for print. I am one who has kept pushing on to new experiences and ideas, and this is still the orientation in my life. It has always seemed like marking time to prepare material for print and it brought back painful memories of school classes in "composition," never one of my areas of interest or accomplishment. I always worked hard to polish manuscripts when I hesitantly decided to submit them for publication, and my wife was nearby for a discerning critique.

It has been more my custom to report ongoing work in lectures, sometimes written in advance, and usually prepared with attention inwardly for how they might sound. Frequently, the only record of what I said was on tapes that someone had made during the course of a workshop, address, or seminar. To suggest that others might now want to hear my words I have only recollections that audiences once heard them. I ask you to listen to this book then—this will more nearly reproduce the circumstances under which most of its contents were made public before.

Many of the things I spoke were expressed in rather absolutist ways. I did this deliberately for the sake of clarity in my presentations, but I may have created an impression that there is only one way of working with families. What I said were distillations out of my own experiences, learned often by facing inadequacies in my self and pain in others. Perhaps in the hands of someone else these difficulties could have been avoided. Alternate ways and variations on the things I tried might have been better. If then you find that I have carried over here a tone that still sounds doctrinaire, remember that those who heard me speak had the opportunity to challenge me in discussion periods.

Since we do not know yet the full possibilities among techniques for helping families, may I encourage you to challenge my ideas and my methods, invent new ideas about people's problems, and experiment with all manner of ways to help the whole family together. Most especially, turn away from old judgmental prejudices against parents; reject such comments as "This child's parents must have been in a colossal mess to produce this bad sheep!" That is not a family idea; when one carries the implication of responsibility for a black sheep back to others in a family, one is using an individual-oriented approach. Let us look at the family as a family, look at pathology in this integrated group, see how the group uses a black sheep to perpetuate itself and its activities. Let us get away from thinking of parents as evil. Let us abandon thinking of all child patients as victims of their parents, or of circumstances. Let us remember that children do terrible things to parents, and, whenever we have a disturbed individual in a family, the whole family is probably embroiled in the problem. Let us remove from our thinking any bias against involving fathers in treatment. Let us get away from fixed ideas that adults are inflexible and unready to change; even with patterns that are more fixed than among their children, adults have potentialities for change that are not thought of when we are looking only for pathology; they can change and in major ways. They have a non-pathological side where readiness to change comes from, and family therapy works with the strengths among all the family members.

Meanwhile, as you are listening to this book, I will be busy with new enterprises—training physical therapists and other medical personnel at Stanford to work with families, developing new ways to relate families and the community to long-term patients in the Palo Alto Veterans Administration Hospital, conducting a demonstration of a new concept in the rehabilitation of long-hospitalized patients, and seeking the chance to test out in practice other new ways to work with families.

Contents

Part Two: Refinements and Reflections

An Extended Perspective, Four Definitions of Family,
Family Group Theory, Pathology and Change, Acute
Symptoms, Concomitants of Chronicity, Family Therapy
as a Mechanism
For Change, The Nature of Family Changes,
Summary

A New Angle of Vision, The Vexing Theory of Insight,
Interpretation in Family Therapy, Preferred Theories, A
Derivation for
Individual Therapy

The Therapist's Intent, Working with a Family, Working
with a Group, Working as a Therapist

Part Three: Extensions

Pathology as a Circular Process, Symptoms as Expressions
of Family Growth, Disorder as Family Rigidity, Disorder

and Family Dynamics, Functions of Symptoms,
Differentiation Among Disorders, Family Sub-Systems

The Theme, The Issues, Family Tension,
Interinstitutional Tension, Tension in the Community
and Beyond

Why Family Therapy?, Shall we Abandon Individual
Treatment?, Problems with Family Treatment, Statutes
and Tradition, Family Boundaries, Therapist's Contract,
Roles for Other Specialists, Therapy Goals, Family,
Offender,
and Institution

Sources of Data About a Marriage, Affecting the Marital
Relationship

Part Four: Expansion

Family Therapy as a Technology, Family Therapy in New
Settings, Prevention of Family Problems

Part One

BEGINNINGS

Chapter I

Family Group Therapy
—A New Treatment Method
for Children

W hen I was in London in 1951, a casual remark of Dr. John Sutherland to the effect that Dr. Bowlby of the Tavistock Clinic was experimenting with group therapy with families, stimulated my interest in studying some of the potentialities of this method for the treatment of behavior problems in children. [1] To my knowledge there were no other precedents to fall back on in applying the method than an article by Bowlby (1949), where he discussed the occasional use of a group meeting with the whole family as an adjunct to individual therapy. [2] My intent was, however, to use family group therapy as the sole method of treatment. [3]

The results with seven initial groups seen over the past one and one-half years have been sufficiently promising that I feel the technique has wide applicability. It is able to bring dramatic, and often speedy improvements in family living and direct changes in the maladapted behavior of children. My time has been limited, so that I have never been able to carry more than three groups at one time, holding weekly conferences with each. It takes long years to accumulate experience at this rate. I feel that I have now learned enough of the course that treatment takes, and the errors one is likely to make that I am ready to share my preliminary findings with others. [4]

In beginning this treatment I had in mind that it would need to be based on talking, and thus that it would not be adapted to very young children. From theoretical knowledge, developmental studies, and prior experience in individual therapy with children, I assumed that a lower age limit might be about nine years of age, perhaps higher in the cases of children with limited ability or severe emotional blocking.

Three of my family groups have included eight-year old children. In one instance the group consisted of a stepfather, mother and eight-year old girl. It is still too early to assess whether the outcome was satisfactory. At the moment I have reservations about it, but more on the basis of limitations of the parents than because of the inability of the child to participate effectively. The other family with an eight-year old consists of four children, two girls, fourteen and nine, the eight-year old, a boy, a five-year old boy, Peter, and their parents. Initially I excluded Peter, the five-year old. The other three children kept constantly referring to him, making such comments as "How can we solve the family problems if Peter is not here?" "He's one of the family and if we decide anything he won't know what it is." I invited Peter to the third session, and he remained with us for three months of conferences. I put out play material for him. It became increasingly obvious that the eight-year old felt that Peter's presence was justification for his isolating himself from the group seated around the table. So finally it was decided that Peter should stay home. Since that time the eight-year old has engaged actively in the group discussions, seemingly identifying himself with the older members of the group and attempting to hold his own on a verbal level. Therapeutic progress has been rapid since Peter left. In the third family, the eight-year old is functioning mentally on a high level and no communication problems have arisen.

Since this technique is a verbal one, its use is probably contraindicated with the most withdrawn children. This has not yet been tested. I am not prepared to rule out cases with major personality difficulties. Certainly some of those cases with which I have dealt have had serious problems, and the changes that have been wrought do not appear to be superficial. For example, in the case of an adopted girl of thirteen years of age, the referring symptoms were inability to play with the other children in the neighborhood, uncontrollable behavior at home with much lying, outbursts of temper, and sullen withdrawal from family activities and a school maladjustment so severe that she was being faced with expulsion. It became evident that the girl was strongly identifying herself with a rather rigid and hostile father and with her older brother, a son of the parents. Over the year and a half of treatment we saw her identification shift toward the mother, with a consequent adoption of feminine patterns of behavior and the disappearance of the symptomatic masculine traits. Central to this change was the releasing of the girl from clinging dependence on the mother, and from inhibition of expression of hostility to her father. It was not long after the girl was openly telling her father how angry he made her and how she had to lie to protect herself from his irritability that her total adjustment showed the dramatic changes, not only at home but also at school where she is doing acceptable work and no longer is a behavior problem.

My method has evolved into the following program:

THE INITIAL INTERVIEWS

A beginning is made by a joint conference with the father and mother. This is for the purposes of securing the parents' story of the problems the child is facing, the history of the development of the child, and for interpreting to them the method that will be used. In this initial interview I tell the parents that I will serve as a kind of referee, whose job is to see that everyone gets a chance to take part in the discussion, and that I will especially support the child because it is necessary to win his confidence that it is safe and desirable for him to express himself freely. I warn the parents that the child will probably be demanding of changes in his routine at home, that I will not make decisions for them about how the family is to be run, but that I would feel it helpful for them to go along with making feasible changes, especially at the beginning, even though these may be somewhat inconvenient for them. I prepare the parents also for the child's hostility, since the earliest expressions of the child are usually hostile. I reassure them that the more the hostility is expressed the more we may expect expressions of affection and willingness to adapt on the part of the child. I also assure the parents that they will have a chance to express their real feelings, problems, and wishes for the family in the conferences, since the goal of the treatment is the development of new and better communication among all members of the family, but that at the beginning it is more helpful to set the stage for the children to speak freely by their keeping somewhat in the background.

Up to now the parents' response to the first interview has been enthusiastic. This may be partly because of a feeling of relief that something is to be done to help them with their problems, but I feel that it relates to the method of treatment, also. For one thing, I have heard several express a conviction that this method seems to them a natural approach to treatment. I believe various attitudes underlie this spontaneous expression of enthusiasm for the approach.

First, a deep longing for a closer family bond. That this grows out of primary biological relationships, reinforced by the fundamental tradition of the family as a basic unit in our culture is not a sufficient explanation for this longing. Psychology has emphasized enough in recent years the responsibility of parents for children's problems that they nearly always feel considerable personal guilt when the family does not function well. Treating the whole family as the problem has the effect of recognizing the responsibility of everyone in the family for the problem. Blame is no longer directed against one individual, but the difficulties are recognized as a misfortune of the whole group.

Second, suspicion about treatment is reduced. In the more common approach to treatment, where mother is seen separately from the child, and father is seldom a part of the therapeutic relationship, it is inevitable that there will be curiosity, suspicion, and jealousy of the relations that are established. This will show itself in various forms of resistance that must be dealt with for the effective progress of the therapy. Within family group therapy there is an immediate reassurance that whatever happens will be common knowledge. This has some negative aspects as far as the treatment is concerned, but has been verbalized by parents who have previously been working in individual therapy as a desirable aspect of this approach.

Third, the immediate advantages of the father's participation in therapy. This should be self-evident. In my experience with this approach, I have not found fathers reluctant to take part—not nearly as reluctant as when they are approached for individual therapy. I have been somewhat surprised that they are even willing to go to considerable lengths to rearrange business schedules, to postpone getting home for dinner after the day's work, to make somewhat complicated transportation plans so that the members of the family can be picked up from home, school, dental appointments, dancing classes, and so on, and brought to the therapy hour. I may have been dealing with a selected group of fathers, but my experience is that they get into the spirit of the therapy often more rapidly than the mothers. This may be because mother feels she has been carrying the major share of the burdens of the child's disturbance and is relieved of this heavy responsibility by father's active participation in the treatment. At least mothers have made comments to this effect within the family conferences.

After the practical details of the treatment hours have been worked out with the parents, the first session with the family as a whole is scheduled. At this first session I tell the children that I have talked with their mother and father and that we are getting together because they feel the family is not as happy as it should be. I aim to structure the situation by including the following in my comments during the first session. I recognize, first, that grownups are big, strong, sometimes bossy, and often fail to understand children. As a result they sometimes so run the family that the children are afraid to talk about their real feelings and real wishes. Second, that this therapy is a unique situation in that I am a grownup who is here to make sure that each child gets a chance to talk about the things that seem to him to make the family unhappy. Third, that I am on the children's side, as indeed the parents really are, but that parents sometimes don't know how to take the children's side best, and that we can help them here to understand what the children feel and want. Fourth, that their mother and father really want to change things so that the children will be happier and be able to have more say in how the family is to be run. Fifth, that I am to see that everyone gets a chance to talk about important things and to work out together the plans for the family, but that I am only an umpire or a referee. I will not make decisions for the family.

The rationale behind this orientation is manifold. I want the child to feel that he has support for expressing his own point of view and encouragement for his own efforts to grow, to take responsibility and to experience freedom for self-direction. I want the child to sense that the feelings he harbors toward the parents are worth talking about and desirable to talk about, even if they are negative feelings. I want the parents to recognize that I am not assuming control of the family, that it remains within the family, and that I am not an advice giver but an interpreter of the family relationship. This has special relevance for the fathers, who may be easily threatened, experience has shown, if the the therapist is active in directing family affairs. I want the family, and especially the children, to know that it is by talking that we hope to work. That the child usually grasps this quickly was illustrated by Michael, a ten-year-old, who moved his chair right over next to mine as I was speaking and said "Good. Now we can have a war! (bang, bang, bang)."

THE CHILD-CENTERED PHASE

After the orientation statement has concluded I encourage the child to tell us what he thinks makes the family unhappy. By my attitude I discourage the parents from too much speaking at the beginning. If they talk at this time they usually are full of complaints about the behavior of the child, and I do not wish to set up the therapy as a reinforcement of their authority. It frequently takes considerable time during the first hour to help the child to speak. I keep reassuring him that he does not need to speak until he feels ready, that he will not be punished if he does not speak, and that his parents have promised to rearrange things to make the family better for him.

All the children have begun by pointing out annoyances connected with the rules and routine of living—perhaps they can't stay up to see a favorite T.V. program, or Dad won't play games, or Mother nags about their getting out for school in time, or the allowance is not sufficient. I try to deal with these concrete issues as they come up, by asking how the child would propose to solve the problem. Sometimes he demands complete acceptance of his solution by the parents, sometimes he is ready to work out a compromise, but at the beginning I hope the parents will go as far as the child wishes. I usually leave the way open for future consideration of the issue by saying we can see how it works and if anyone needs to talk about it later, we can bring it up again. The speed of movement in therapy at this point depends on the willingness or ability of the parents to readjust the family to fit in with the child's wishes. If they go along readily the child exhausts his demands in a few weeks and the therapy enters the next stage.

THE PARENT-CENTERED PHASE

The next major period of the therapy begins when the child gets to the point of saying, "Everything is going good." Then the parents enter the picture actively. They begin to complain about ways in which the child irritates them, worries them, and so on. Often this is initiated by talking about difficulties at school or in the community rather than in the home. I bring the center into the home by interpretation that we can do little in the conferences about those things that take place outside the home and that often these difficulties are signs of disturbances in the home. Considerable hostility in the parents builds up in the first therapy stage. The explosion of this hostility creates a delicate situation, for it is important to permit the parents to express this feeling and yet to protect the relation of the therapist with the child. Three methods of handling this are used:
    a. Stating that the child will and must have his say too;
    b. Interpreting to the parents the normalcy of a child's behavior when it is appropriate for his age. Gesell's and other developmental studies are handbooks for this therapy;
    c. Helping the child to express his point of view regarding the complaints by interpreting that he must have his reasons for acting this way.
The consequence of this parental explosion is defense on the part of the child—defense which usually takes the form of counterattack and frequently the expression of hostile feelings that have been re-

pressed, the recall of incidents that have never been spoken of with the parents, the expression of fears that account for the behavior, and the telling of episodes at school and elsewhere that contribute to the difficulties in the home. For example, when Michael's parents complained about his seemingly irrational difficulties in leaving home, driving in the car, and being separated from the mother, Michael recalled an incident that took place when he was three and that he had never before mentioned to his parents. He was driving toward home with his mother, and was misbehaving in the car. About three blocks away from home the mother's patience could not contain itself and she stopped the car, put Michael out, and told him to walk home, which he did. On one other occasion, when the family was driving to New York City, the parents threatened to put him out of the car. For six or seven years after these episodes Michael was car-sick, and thoroughly disagreeable whenever the family went driving. But after telling this he traveled happily and without car-sickness for six weeks throughout the country with his family. He carried everywhere a signed affidavit from his parents that they would not throw him out of the car; and his demand for the affidavit was accepted without question by the parents.

Through the weeks of this parental complaint and child's defense emerges deepening understanding on the part of all regarding the nature of the emotional bonds between the various members of the family and the nature of the forces that determine behavior. In spite of the attack, recrimination, bitterness, and not infrequent tearfulness, during the conferences at this stage, life goes more smoothly at home. The intense catharsis of negative feeling in the conferences does not carry over, for the most part, to the home. It appears that in the home there is increased tolerance and mutual planning and carrying out of the joint living of the family—punctuated by the occasional explosion. Often when the hostility gets most intense we have the bonds between the members of the family strengthened as for instance when Mickey, an 11-year old who had threatened to run away from home three weeks earlier, said during a particularly tense conference: "But I don't want to run away any more. I love you too much." But it is not only the children who provide these positive feelings. Parents at this stage often say to the child, "Now I realize how wrong I have been." Or "I guess the real problem is not with you but with us."

The parent-centered stage of the therapy develops into concern with the parent's problems. This takes various forms. In one instance the therapy was concluded at this point, I believe with excellent therapeutic results, although I would have been more content if there had not been a sudden break.[5] I attribute the termination to my error in management. The week before I had seen the mother and the two children without the father who was tied up in a business deal from which he could not get free. In this session I had permitted all three to bring out floods of resentment against the father. Next conference, when it could not help but be apparent to the father what the content of the previous session had been, he reacted with intense fury, and this was the last time I met the family. I learned from that not to see a part of a family group. If one member cannot come, we postpone the session. The only exception to this rule is when it is preplanned in a conference of the whole family for me to see alone one or more members, as for instance the parents, which I find is sometimes necessary. After such a conference I make a brief report to the whole family on the content of what we have talked about. In the case of the family that broke off the contact, I have happened to meet informally each of the members of the family since that time. Each one reports striking improvement in the family. Even the father has greeted me warmly but with some underlying tension that I attribute to continuing hostility to me. I am sure this is in part hostility toward the wife and two children displaced on to me. Therapeutically it appears good for the father to have me as a scapegoat, although I would have preferred to see this treatment go into the final stage that has been characteristic of the other groups that have terminated.

THE FAMILY-CENTERED PHASE

Normally the final stage has been marked by the following:

Disappearance of many of the referral symptoms. Not all disappear since some of them are now reinterpreted by the parents and lose their disturbing effect;

The appearance of laughter in the conferences, frequently growing out of the parents laughing at themselves;

The reporting of incidents during the week when the whole family worked together to resolve a problem that had arisen; or,

Incidents in which the family engaged pleasurably in some
mutual activity;

The volunteering of the child to take on necessary chores for the
family;

The spontaneous expression of the feeling that the family life is
going so well that the conferences are no longer necessary. "I guess
we can manage ourselves now without you."

In this brief account I have not perhaps made clear enough the
role that interpretation plays. I am more active than being simply a
listening referee. At each of the four stages interpretation is necessary. At the beginning I must interpret and reinterpret my role in the
group. Before the therapy can proceed I have often to interpret to the
family the resistance of the child to participation. As therapy centers
more and more on the child occasionally it is necessary to interpret to
the parents what appears to be the basis of the child's resentment
about routines and rules. At this level I have also to reinterpret my
own relationship to the family, for the parents often persist in trying
to make me an ally against the children. At the third level when the
parents begin to become vocal, I have to verbalize the feelings and
reactions that are being engendered in the group, and something of
their historical and current basis. When the parents are facing their
own problems I find myself pointing out parallels between their own
childhoods and the experiences of their children, the ways in which
their childhood experiences have contributed to their present difficulties, and the effects of their communications on the children. I
have often to point up that the child's increasing knowledge of the
parents is not to be feared. In the final stages I play a role in pointing
out what is now the mode of communication in the family and its
consequences. At this time usually comes also a recapitulation of
what has happened through the various stages of the treatment.

It is only appropriate that I should also mention some of the
limitations to this method that I have encountered or that are potentially present.

1. Limits on age. The families I have worked with have included children from 8 to 16 years of age. I am relatively certain I could not use this method with younger children. I believe the age level could be extended upwards, as long as the family is living together as a unit. This might mean that it would be effective with younger hospitalized patients, but I do not know.

2. Time is a crucial and sometimes a limiting factor. I have found it helpful to have a somewhat flexible schedule. Since all members of the family group apparently need to be present, some allowances have to be made for demands on members of the family as well as for sickness. Since I have only seen families on a weekly basis, and a conference missed produces a long interval, I have set up a basic conference time and made temporary adjustments as necessary, keeping in mind the goal of as much continuity as possible. As with any therapy, the overall duration of treatment varies. My longest series has been one and one half years, my shortest two months.

3. Limits of economic and cultural background. These are unexplored questions. My families, with one exception, have been from the middle class. The parents have had above average education and ability. The one exception was that of a house painter and his family. For them the technique needed considerable modification. I do not know whether this was personal to the family or a general condition of work with groups where lower intelligence, education, and different mores apply.

4. Limits on level of parental adjustment. I would say that in two of my families the parents were badly adjusted to one another, but that in neither case were the difficulties such that separation was imminent. If we had a more serious disturbance between the parents I do not know how the therapy would work. With one family it was necessary to discontinue work with the whole family group for a period in order to work with the parents alone. I believe the family conferences brought home to them, in a way that would not have been otherwise possible, their own need of help. I am not sure, however, that this could have been accomplished without a basic desire on the part of the parents to hold their marriage together.

5. Technical limits. I have been conscious during my work of complexities in family adjustment beyond those revealed by individual therapy. This makes this method singularly appropriate as a

research tool. As an example of an insight that has been made plain to me through work with two of the families, I have observed how rejection by one parent is in many ways equivalent to rejection by both parents. Joan, an 11-year old adopted girl, put it this way: "Daddy doesn't love me like he does Margaret (her older sister) and even when mummy does nice things for me I am always afraid that she won't love me either." It is quite evident that the mother really prefers Joan but even her warm affection occasions anxiety and not security in Joan. This has been evident as a pattern in one other case, and I was not previously sensitized to this as a familial pattern. Maybe all the observations that I make have been recorded in the literature, but I keep running into relations that I would not have anticipated. These I find new to evaluate, to interpret, to understand, and sometimes I am not prepared to deal with them. Maybe with more experiences I shall not be as surprised as I sometimes find myself—and I hope my technical proficiency will improve.

In many issues the best method of handling them is not plain. I sense that detailed normative data on family adjustments, similar to those available about child development, would be of great practical value. Many normative issues regarding family life and adolescence emerge, which need to be dealt with specifically rather than by the generalities that characterize much of our present knowledge. Through such a therapeutic technique as this we may be able to deepen our understanding of adolescent behavior in relation to the family. In recent years child psychology has so stressed the young child, the pre-school period, that we have not progressed far beyond the insights of G. Stanley Hall and the workers of his era into development during the pre- and post-pubertal years. Family group therapy offers a tool for analysis of one of the most crucial segments of life during this period.

Chapter II

The McAndrew Family

To find an adequate treatment method for the disturbed adolescent is one of the major problems in psychotherapy. Conducting therapy with persons of this stage has been so difficult that many have said we should not try to treat adolescents, and that when a child has reached 10 or 11 years of age we should modify his situation but postpone the attempt to do psychotherapy with him until he becomes an adult.

I have for many years been troubled by this defeatist attitude toward psychotherapy with the adolescent, partly because at his developmental stage the need for help is so patently demonstrable and acutely felt, and partly because the difficulties in treatment may have arisen from inadequate understanding of him, and thus from our using unsuitable approaches. The tendency to attribute the causes of success or failure in development to a person's experiences in the preschool period has centered study on that period and withdrawn attention from the study of adolescence. In no area of psychological concern has there been less imagination applied to the development of techniques for study. Since the application of the questionnaire by G.

Stanley Hall no other method of observation has attained comparable importance, although projective techniques have been applied occasionally. The paucity of knowledge and theory about the adolescent faces us most clearly when we are placed in the position of trying to help him. Unfortunately we do not even have the clinical opportunity to gain insights into adolescence comparable to those that child analysis and play therapy have provided into childhood.

It is not through lack of trying psychotherapy that we have failed with children in this developmental stage. Psychoanalysis, which has had notable success in a few reported cases, has not proved, in general, a very useful method for this age. In most instances the ambivalence of the adolescent toward the therapist, as toward all adults, has made it difficult for the therapist to establish and maintain a therapeutic relationship within which the adolescent could examine his own difficulties and learn to adapt in new ways. The modifications of psychoanalysis in which the therapist has become more directive, more of a reality figure for the patient, have been reported to be more effective. But apparently the success has not been sufficient to encourage widespread adoption of this approach. Therapy with groups of adolescents, which has been utilized more and more commonly of late, has been advocated as a therapy of choice for their age. Complementary groups composed of the parents of adolescents have been urged as desirable supplements to the adolescent groups. These and similar approaches have not filled the need for effective therapeutic method, for in many cases the results they have produced have been less than gratifying.

It was against this background of some urgency that the method of treatment I called "family group therapy" was developed.

Family group therapy is an effort to effect behavioral and attitudinal changes within a total family through a series of conferences attended by the parents, the children, 9 years of age and older, and the therapist. In most instances the conferences are initiated through referral of a child who is disturbed, but from the beginning the therapeutic goals are family-centered rather than child-centered. The primary intent of the therapist is to accomplish a modification of the functioning and structure of the family as a group. It is assumed that as a consequence modifications will be effectuated secondarily in the situation of individuals within the family. The method of the therapy emerges, then, from the one basic assumption differentiating it from individual therapy: *the family is the unit to be treated.*

It is important to stress that in this method the family is not regarded as an assembly of individuals, but is recognized as a biological and social unit. One must keep in mind that here no child or parent is under treatment as an individual. Whereas in individual therapy the emphasis is on the unique person, in family therapy specific attention to the individual as an individual is to be avoided as much as possible. The problem for which the family is accepted for treatment is to be thought of as a problem of the family, not as a problem of the child. Those who are accustomed to individual therapy may find the shift to emphasis on the family as a unit a difficult change in orientation.

In the conferences the therapist relates himself to the family. Individual participants will attempt to break this rapport with the group and involve the therapist in relationships with themselves as individuals. The therapist must prevent the establishment of such ties, for the efforts of individuals to possess the therapist to the exclusion of the other members of the family constitute a major form of resistance to the therapy. This expression of resistance is discussed and illustrated later (pp. 52 to 58).

Specifically, emphasis on the family means that the problem for which the family comes to treatment, usually a difficulty with one of the children, must be accepted not as the symptom of an individual's disturbance but as a symptom of disrupted relationships in the family. The hypothesis that lies behind the therapy for both child and parent in the traditional clinic, namely, that where there is a disturbed child there are disturbed parents, is reinterpreted. The hypothesis is now made that where there is a disturbed child there is a disturbed family. This leads to a series of theoretical consequences culminating in the conclusion that all members of the family contribute to the disturbance. Whereas etiologically it may be true that the parents were disturbed first, in the present they are not judged individually as either more or less responsible for the disturbance than others in the family. Thus it is not important to try to decide whether this parent is good or that parent is bad. What each parent and each child may be is the result of the family totality. It is no more useful to say the parents are responsible for the child's difficulties than to say the child is responsible for the parents' problems. To continue to think in traditional terms will handicap the therapist, who must learn to think of the family as an organic unit.

Functionally, then, the symptom is thought of as the product of a disruption in family interaction, most usually a breakdown in intrafamily communication, and not as the product of intrapsychic conflicts. From this point of view conflicts within the individual become the end results rather than the causes of disturbance. The normal interpretation of what is symptomatic is thus modified.

Practically, the impact of this shift in thinking may be illustrated by the therapist's approach when the parents begin to complain about the behavior of the child. The therapist takes the standpoint that there must be "good" reasons why the child does what he does, and that the understanding of these reasons is one step toward helping the whole family to function better. The behavior of the child that disturbs the adults may at the same time be assumed to be a complement to the behavior in the adults or other children that demands the problem behavior from the child. The child may not always be able to verbalize the reasons why he reacts as he does, but often he can state specifically the factors in the family that precipitate his behavior. In other instances the child, failing to understand why the parents are distressed, may defend his behavior. Often this defense is justifiable, since the child has recognized correctly that he is functioning as his age mates do. Sometimes the parent is revealed as casting the child into the role of the "disturber," just as others in the family are reacted to as the "good," the "model," the "lovable," the "baby," the "easy one," and the like.

A further implication of the basic assumption relates to the goals of the therapy. The goals may represent the values of the therapist, but it is more likely that they emerge primarily from the matrix of cultural norms established within the subculture of which the individual problem family is a part. Consciously the therapist seeks to improve the means by which interaction may take place within the family. This is at least a twofold process: first, of releasing the respective members of the family from inhibition about the expression of feelings, wishes, ideals, goals, and values, and second, of developing new forms of expression to channel the interpersonal communication. To increase spontaneity is only one side of the picture; the other is to pattern the more spontaneous activities so that the perpetuation of activities that are helpful to the family's purposes is facilitated and the change of interactions that may retard the needed growth of family life is accomplished. We can say, then, that both release and discipline are goals of the therapy.

The explanation of why the ambivalence of the adolescent toward his parents does not interfere with therapeutic progress may rest in the fact that the treatment situation provides the adolescent with opportunities both to express his ambivalent feelings and to learn to express them in a controlled manner. In a sense we could say that the adolescent's ambivalence is used for the therapy instead of against it. The treatment moves toward more complete communication about the range of experiences within the family. Further, the analysis of the modes of communication, their modification, and the development of new modes give increased possibility for control of intrafamily communication. The increase in the number of patterns of communication, the development of greater awareness of them, and the more conscious choice of seemingly appropriate patterns is what is meant by discipline.

A further goal of the therapy is to make the family conscious of the roles that the various members play in relation to one another. It might be expected that changing these roles would be a major aim, but that is not necessarily so. Many of the forms of behavior that grow out of the roles appropriated by the members of the family are desirable to the family and to the individuals in the family, who must retain the option of continuing or discarding these roles. The option will be taken up by the family as a whole as well as by the individuals who have assumed the roles, while the therapist avoids passing judgment on the behavior of members of the family. As a consequence, some families have accepted and continued types of behavior that other families have worked hard to eradicate. For example, in one family the studiousness of a very bright 11-year-old son was thought to be a problem. The family worked to help the boy find his place in social groups and to become a "more rounded person." Another family, with an equally bright 13-year-old son who was also exceedingly studious, worked to develop his studiousness and to insure the conditions under which it might be promoted. The therapist in each of these situations functioned as an interpreter of family interactions and the roles played by family members, but not as an arbiter passing upon the value of the roles.

The climate offering freedom for the development of the most satisfactory complex of family roles seems to require consciousness by the family of the impact that each member has on each other member. When there is sufficient exploration of these interactions there may also be common exploration of the effects that modifications in the roles might have on the family and the individuals in it. This exploration makes for the possibility of greater flexibility in the individual and social behavior in the family. A common and significant occurrence during the therapy is that stereotyped generalizations about each other are abandoned. This appears to be not only a change in manner of speaking but also an actual change in attitude, as far as can be judged by the ways in which members of the family deal with one another.

A third goal is to demonstrate to the family its essential unity and thus the mutual interdependence of each with the other and with the family as a whole. The strength of the cohesive forces within most families makes it seem natural to both the parents and the children that the family should examine its status and rethink its fortunes in the family therapy conferences. In spite of the tacit recognition of these bonds, the members of a disturbed family are more likely to be aware of the divisions, the tensions, and the hostilities they experience with one another and of their symptomatic expression. In the course of the therapy there is a reaffirmation of the meaning of the family to each. While this may be thought of as a consequence of the therapy, since for the most part it is to be found in the final stages, it is also true that it is a factor in bringing about therapeutic progress. The verbalization of positive ties in the family speeds the reconciliation of differences, but apparently this occurs only when there is an opportunity to express the full range of feelings engendered in family life. Emphasis upon the positive links between the members of the family without a comparable expression of the negative feelings appears to increase anxiety, rage, and the intensity of symptoms.

PATTERN OF THE TREATMENT

Now let me trace the overall pattern of the treatment as it progresses. The sessions with the family are held once a week, although there is no particular magic in this schedule. The first session is held with the father and mother alone. The children and the parents come to all succeeding sessions.

I have thought of the therapy as developing through several stages[1]:

1. The treatment begins with an orientation phase. Two orientation interviews are held: one with the parents alone, as mentioned above; and the other with the whole family present, at the first conference attended by the children.

2. Treatment proceeds into a child-centered phase. During this period the child is held in the center of the family group, and he is given the chance to air his complaints and to suggest the changes in family procedure that he would regard as desirable.

3. The parent-child interaction emerges next. This phase is characterized by an examination of the dimensions of the parent-child relationships, especially of much previously unverbalized emotion associated with the ways in which the child experiences the parents and vice versa.

4. The center of therapy shifts to the father-mother interaction. In the presence of the children, toward the later stages of the treatment, the parents begin to discuss openly their own emotional inter-relationships and problems. This is the forerunner of the last stages of the therapy.

5. As the parents approach resolution of their difficulties, emphasis gradually shifts to the sibling interaction, a stage in which the relationships between the children in the family are subjected to examination.

6. Finally, we observe what has been called the family-centered phase. In this concluding stage, there is evidence of two forms of family functioning: family activity in which all members of the group participate according to the commonly accepted and generally approved roles for each; and family support for each member in the activities that take him away from the family into independent spheres of action, for instance, business, school, clubs, and friendships.

The question may be raised legitimately as to whether this development is a pattern imposed on the treatment by the therapist or is a sequence that grows out of the natural development of family interaction in such a setting. Of course the answer must recognize the inseparability of these two aspects of the treatment. It is my impression that the pattern I have described is based on my observations of what took place with the first few families treated. But by that time the techniques for handling the treatment situation already had been thought through and were in the process of being refined. There appears to be a certain external justification for the present method. The attention to the children at the beginning accords with parental expectations when they bring a child for treatment and with their anticipation that it will be necessary to deal at an early stage with the communication difficulties of the children. The possibility of altering the sequence by modifications in the orientation for the parents or for the children might be investigated. The present sequence should not be sought so rigidly as to preclude adaptations to immediate circumstances that would promote the speed or success of treatment.

The McAndrews

Detailed examination of the various stages through which the therapy progresses is illustrated from the record of a single case, one that was completely recorded and transcribed.[2] It may be well, then, to give a brief introduction to the case, that of a Scottish family with whom I worked when I was teaching at the University of Edinburgh in 1955. Eleven sessions with this family, here called by the pseudonym, "McAndrew," were held in Edinburgh in the spring of 1955. The family consisted of father, mother, a boy, "Sandy," aged 13, and a girl, "Jean," aged 9. The father was a skilled laborer in a publishing firm, and the mother was an attendant in a checkroom.

The McAndrews were well known to the staff of the local child-guidance clinic, whose contacts with the family went back to the summer of 1952, when the mother and father appeared for an intake interview with the psychiatric social worker. The problem was their daughter, Jean, then 6 years old and described by her mother as "irresponsible, forgetful, disobedient, and careless, noisy in public; she monopolizes the conversation at the table; she always has to be hustled; she is interested in the present moment only and heedless of what she has done or what she is to do; she leaves toys lying about, loses them, is untidy and a nuisance; she has always required a lot of persuasion to eat; she is constipated; she does not seem to care deeply for anything that is said to her."

Of that interview, the social worker noted: "The mother spoke most of the time, at great pressure, and veiling only thinly her aggression to the patient and to the social worker. She speaks kindly of the elder child, Sandy (aged 10), and contrasts him with the patient." The father appeared to be of an easy disposition, much more reasonable than the mother, and anxious to ease the pressures being put on Jean.

During the 3 years between their first appearance at the clinic and my work with the McAndrews, the mother had 33 interviews with the psychiatric social worker and attended a mothers' therapy group seven times. Jean had 24 interviews with a psychiatrist and 3 interviews, for testing purposes, with a psychologist. In the judgment of the clinic staff, this considerable amount of individual treatment had failed to produce any noticeable changes in the symptoms or personality structures of these three members of the family. The father had not been in treatment.

Jean scored above average on all intelligence tests and probably would be in the "superior" category. Her brother had a Terman-Merrill I.Q. of 158, and his school performance supported these findings. He stood first in his grade in the highly competitive atmosphere of one of Edinburgh's finest boys' schools, which he attended by virtue of a scholarship.

Sandy was on the pedantic side. For example, at his first session of family therapy he complained: "Whenever we're left on our own and I catch Jean doing something which she's not supposed to, I give her a—I tell her that she's not supposed to do that, but she won't recognize me as somebody who's got more experience in such things than she has. And, well, she's *rather reluctant* to do as I suggest to her, with the result that Mum and Dad are *disinclined* to leave us on our own."

The key to Sandy's personality and his role in the family was given in the same interview, when he said: "I think that Mum and Dad are very fair, but it only rests upon my shoulders. If I'm a good boy, well, they'll be good to me, and it works out that way. But when I'm in a bad mood, they become cross with me, which is quite fair."

The story with Jean was different. In the first session, which, as

I have said, is always with the parents alone, the mother supplied the following history: "I started to bring Jean here when she was 6 . . . she was entirely irresponsible and by this time I was beginning to fear that there was something mentally wrong with her." The irresponsibility described by the mother consisted of failing to come straight home from school so she could go to dancing class or to a medical appointment. "We came pretty regularly to the clinic week after week, but there didn't seem to be any improvement, and it sort of tapered off."

Now, at 9 years of age, the mother went on, Jean had the following problems: "She wants to talk all the time. She's irresponsible. She has so much that she wants to talk about, to speak about, that she must get it all out. . . . She doesn't have staying power . . . every day she wants to be something different—one day she wants to be a singer like Doris Day, and another time she's been seeing some dancer and she wants to be a dancer—or a trapeze artist, but all the time the star that everybody'll notice. . . . She doesn't make friends well, she won't play . . . and she has been *dreadful* with her food . . . it doesn't matter what I put out to her, there's an argument. . . . She's a very callous, thoughtless child. She can say some very cruel, unthinking remarks. . . . She can't bear to be ignored and left out of the conversation."

The father summed up Jean's situation: "She would respond to very modern treatment (laughing)." He also stated: "She's curbed and curbed and curbed, and she seems to be getting all mixed up."

Quotations from the McAndrew record highlight the interactions that involved Jean and may give the impression that Sandy was not participating. Although this was far from the case, it is true that Sandy was less active verbally than the mother and Jean.

With this brief introduction, then, we are ready to turn our attention to the specific steps in the family treatment method.

First Conference

The stage is set for the family conferences in the first interview, which is attended by the mother, the father, and the therapist. This first session serves three main purposes: (*a*) to work out the practical details of time, frequency of interviews, and fees (if any); (*b*) to obtain a picture of the problem the parents see in the child and some background information; and (*c*) to acquaint the parents with some aspects of the therapy method.

ARRANGING FOR THERAPY

When a parent, usually the mother, seeks an appointment to discuss a child's difficulties, the therapist arranges to have both parents come to the first interview. Some mothers have demurred, protesting, "My husband would never come." Quiet insistence that it is necessary to see both parents and recognition that the mother might like to talk it over with her husband before making the appointment have usually resulted in the immediate arrangement of an appointment. Once or twice a mother has called back later, after talking with her husband, to schedule the first hour. It has never been necessary for the therapist to refuse to make an appointment unless both parents would come, that is, to refuse as a means of bringing pressure on them to come. If, however, one of the parents should prove uncooperative it would probably be advisable to refer the child to someone else. It has been suggested that the success in family therapy may be related to the willingness of both parents to participate right from the beginning.[3] Though this has not been tested, it may have some validity. We shall have to wait until cases have been undertaken in which one of the parents has come under strong protest before we can confirm or negate the suggestion.

The thought that fathers will be reluctant to attend the sessions may come naturally to the mind. The general experience in most child guidance clinics would suggest this might be so, partly because there are practical difficulties in the way of scheduling appointments for a father. It may be, however, that the assumption he will not come sometimes so colors the way a worker approaches a father that he gets the impression his attendance is not especially important to his child's treatment. It has certainly been true that the fathers in the families with which I have worked have been willing to make considerable adjustments in order to clear suitable hours for the therapy. In fact, in spite of the practical difficulties, the fathers have manifested a certain eagerness that suggests they may have been pleased to be included in the therapy.

There may be a willingness to come for the family conference kind of therapy that would not be present if we were asking the father to have private interviews with a caseworker. It was true with the McAndrews, for example, that the father was most cooperative right from the beginning. Since Friday night was unsuitable for the therapist but was also the only night when both father and mother were not working, a mutually convenient therapy hour was not easy to arrange. After considerable discussion and not a few long pauses, Mr. McAndrew suggested that he work late on Friday night and free one of the other nights—the plan that was finally made. He also countered a protest from his wife against planning the hour for a time that would require postponing the supper by affirming that coming directly from work at this hour would be best. This positive approach to scheduling the sessions was not exceptional, but customary, among fathers asked to participate in family therapy.

It may even facilitate the therapy if the situation occasions a demand on the father's time, in much the same way that the payment of a fee may promote progress in psychotherapy. When wage-earners who would not hesitate to make arrangements to be released from work in order to take their children to a medical clinic for attention to a physical illness show reluctance to do the same for the sake of their children's emotional health, the fault may rest with them. But here again we may question how much this may be a response to the therapist's lack of confidence in his own approach. Just as some therapists have to work through to a realistic attitude about demanding fees for their work, some will have to achieve comparable realism about requiring a patient to give of his time. Recognizing the father as a participating member of the family group and, therefore, expecting his collaboration in the therapy are necessary prologues to family therapy. Such experience as has been built up so far would seem to indicate that fathers will come for treatment with their families.

CASE HISTORY AND ITS USES

Using part of the first interview to obtain the parents' summary of the presenting problem and its history follows the common pattern for first interviews. It fits in with the parents' expectations and eases them into the relationship with the therapist.

For the purposes of family group therapy, the information obtained in this initial session is not crucial, unless there is suspicion of an organic basis for a child's disturbance and the therapist wishes to determine the fact before seeing the child. By mentioning this special case I do not wish to imply that I would regard the presence of demonstrated organic causation for a child's symptoms as a contraindication for family group therapy. On the contrary, I believe a family that includes a brain-damaged child might profit from this therapeutic approach provided the child can speak without major difficulty.

But in general, the kind of information that can be obtained in the intake process is of less value to family group therapy than to individual treatment. If diagnosis of the family as a group were feasible, then extremely pertinent information could be developed. That is, if the communication, decision, and action processes of the group as a unit could be studied before the beginning of treatment, it can be presumed that the findings of such a study would be helpful. Methods for diagnosis of this nature are not now at hand. I do not wish to discount the value of the case history, medical evaluation, psychological and psychiatric examination, or other diagnostic methods. They are exceedingly important as precursors to individual treatment. In family therapy they are less relevant. The significant data for the operation of family therapy relate to the interactional life of the family—not just what is seen by individual family members (which may be discovered in intake sessions), but what occurs in the group life of the family.

Indeed, the method I present for initiating family therapy would have to be modified in a clinic or social agency where the intake procedure requires individual interviews, or testing, or both. It is essential that the professional person who carries the family in treatment have no contact with family members as individuals before beginning the treatment. Even a minimal relationship between the therapist and one individual member of the family, such as might be established in an intake interview or during psychological tests, obstructs the development of the very different relationship requisite to dealing with the whole family. [4] Thus, as considerable experience has shown, it is still less advisable for a therapist who has had one family member in individual therapy to attempt a shift to family group treatment by bringing together the rest of his patient's family.

On the other hand, one value to family group therapy of the first interview with the parents alone is that it provides the therapist with an opportunity to compare what is expressed when the child is not present with what is stated directly to the child on later occasions. For example, the problem of enuresis was the central concern of one mother and father who brought their 11-year-old daughter in for treatment. The parents discussed this openly in the initial interview, but they never mentioned it in the family sessions. Only after the treatment had terminated did the mother confirm the therapist's suspicion that the enuresis had cleared up meanwhile. Some issues that are not verbalized in the family conferences may be talked about at home. Others may not be mentioned to the child but simply remain as part of the parents' apperception of the child. Such apperceptions may, of course, be communicated to the child by other than verbal means. For instance, attitudes toward a child's handicap may never be verbalized, and yet the child may be aware of the varying attitudes the parents hold toward the handicap. Perhaps he gains this awareness from the parents' gestures, from the emotional content of situations, or by analyzing the parents' behavior.

Our knowledge of levels of communication and of the content that is communicated at various levels within the family is scanty. Since family therapy is a therapy of the communicative process, it is important to think of this aspect of family life. The contrast between what happens at the first interview and what happens later provides some insights into the dimensions of family communication.

Occasionally, the information provided by the parents in the first interview is used to modify the treatment situation in later conferences. At one point in the third interview with the McAndrew family, after there had been a great deal of discussion of the boy's request that his bedtime be made later so he could play longer with his friends and of the girl's wish for an increase in her allowance, Mr. McAndrew said:

Father: "Well, I'm afraid I think it's trivial. It [the discussion] has no real bearing on the family life at all. We haven't been living too harmoniously for a while. I mean an increase in pocket money won't make much difference in that."

After both the girl and the boy had expressed their points of view, that the pocket money and the bedtime were important, the father continued:

Father: "Is there not a danger when we come here that the children will just be inclined to think, 'If I ask for this, I'll get this' and 'ask for that, and get that.' And it's rather one-sided."

Because of the need to maintain the father's authority in the family and yet to build up the confidence of the children that matters they considered important could be discussed profitably, the therapist at this point felt it necessary to recall some of the content of the first interview, when the parents had visited without the children. He said to the children:

Therapist: "Now I can remember when your Mum and Dad were here without you, that one of the things they told me was that at one time they were a little worried because Sandy wasn't playing very actively with the boys in the community. And they hoped that you (to Sandy) would find more pleasure in playing with the boys. And, in a way, this is something you wanted for yourself, too, because you wanted the opportunity to be out and play with the boys. Now, I wonder if you get this chance to play and find out that you're getting along even better than you have been before with the neighborhood gang, if actually this won't make you feel happier."

The effect was to direct the conversation to what would help the boy in his friendships, allowing him to talk about the need for golf clubs and a bicycle. It also led to a positive approach on the part of the father:

Father: "It would be easy enough to get him some clubs—you can get old clubs quite cheaply. The trouble was that I think a year ago I gave away a set of old clubs that I think we have discarded. I have two midirons to begin with, and I could get one or two others."

Mentioning the content of the first interview provided a new frame of reference for the discussion and helped to ward off further expression of the parents' hostility toward the children at a time when the relationship of the children to the therapeutic situation was scarcely clear enough to risk hearing criticism from their father and mother. Fortunately, reminding the children that the therapist knew about them from the parents did not seem to trouble them, perhaps because what was recalled related to the parents' desire to help the boy as much as to a complaint about him. This use of information from the first interview is relatively unusual and was only made here because the center had shifted from the children to the parents at too early a stage in the therapy. It was effective in reminding the father and mother of the children's priority in the therapy situation, which had been pointed out to the parents during the first interview as part of the orientation I shall now describe.

ORIENTATION TO THE THERAPY

The second part of the first interview is devoted to interpretation of the therapy method for the parents. Perhaps direct quotation from the McAndrew interview gives the best indication of how the orientation can be made.

To explain his association with the family's immediate situation, the therapist had said at the beginning of the interview:

Therapist: "I have been working for quite a while with families—getting the whole family together, where there is one member who doesn't seem to be getting along too well, and in the whole family group talking over with the various members of the family, the children and the parents, what it seems to be that makes the family an unhappy place for the little girl, or the boy. And this seems to have been a pretty effective way of bringing about changes in the situation for the child."

About two-thirds of the way through the interview the therapist interrupted the discussion to explain how the family sessions would be conducted:[5]

Therapist: "I think I should tell you a little bit about what we're going to do together. Next time we meet I hope that Sandy and Jean will come along. And at the beginning, I think it would be best if you would, if you could, help them to sort of tell us what seems to be the difficulty as they see it."

Mother: "Yes."

Therapist: "Jean may eventually be able to tell us what are the problems that make her act as she does. Of course this maybe isn't up on the top of her mind. It may be buried down, and we may have to work for a while in order to really find out what the difficulties are.

But at the beginning, I would like to give her a chance, especially, to talk and to tell us what she feels might be wrong with the family. But, I also want Sandy in on it, because I don't want him to feel that this is just for Jean alone, but that he is also a part of the family."

Father: "Yes."

Therapist: "And we'll see what Jean has to tell us. Now, if she's like the other youngsters that I've known in this situation, she'll begin to complain about all sorts of little rules and regulations and things like that about the family life. This is sort of the way the youngsters test out how freely they can talk about things."

Mother: "Yes."

Therapist: "I don't know whether you have television or not."

Mother: "No."

Therapist: "Well, television is one of the things that creates lots of difficulties for families that have it. But I'm sure that there are little things that she'll complain about. Maybe it's going to bed; maybe it's something—"

Mother: "Food—"

Therapist: "—to do with food. I don't know what it will be, but she will have complaints. And I assume that once she begins to tell us how she feels about the family that she'll bring out quite a few of these complaints. Now, it is important to give her, and Sandy, the feeling that if they talk about things that they feel about the family, what they say is taken seriously."

Father: "Yes."

Therapist: "Because if we want finally to find out what's troubling Jean, we have to take seriously the little things that she'll say at the beginning, so that she can feel that we're really wanting to understand her, really wanting to get down to the bottom of it. And one of the things that makes youngsters feel that their remarks are being taken seriously, is to make changes in accordance with those remarks. And so, for the first few weeks, if it's feasible, it would be very helpful in freeing Jean so she can get to the point of telling us the things that are troubling her, if the little changes that she wants could be managed. Now, not all of them could be managed. I mean she may want to stay up until midnight—"

Mother: "Yes."

Therapist: "—and this might injure her health and wouldn't seem to be a desirable thing. And so, it may not be possible to go along with everything she wants."

Mother: "No."

Therapist: "But insofar as it's feasible, it would be helpful to make the changes that she asks for—and if possible and not in conflict—the things that Sandy wants to make different, the changes that he wants too. Now, this is only temporary. I mean some of the things that Jean may ask for will be inconvenient and won't be pleasant for you, but it's only a temporary kind of thing. It's only to help her to get to the point of having confidence that we really mean what we say, when we say that we want to listen to what she feels is important. And any change that's made in the family is only a temporary change. Eventually, we'll probably want to come back and talk these things over again. Now, my prediction is that if we listen to the things that Sandy and Jean have to tell us about, and make changes, it won't be so very long before Jean will be saying, 'Everything's going good.' And everything won't be going good, but as far as—"

Mother: "Yes."

Therapist: "—she feels about it, everything will be going good, because the changes that she has wanted will have been made. But you will know, probably, that things aren't right yet. And when she gets to this point of saying that she feels that things are going all right, then is the time we want to hear what you have to say about what she is doing—the things that are troubling you about how she acts."

Father: "Certainly."

Therapist: "At the beginning it's not very wise to have you tell us too much about what troubles you. It's better to postpone that. That'll come in a little while later. At the beginning, we would like to know what troubles Jean."

Mother: "Yes."

Therapist: "And then, later on we'll hear what troubles you about her. Now when you begin eventually to complain about her, to tell us the things that are wrong—with her sitting here—this is the time we really will find out what's bothering her, when she will begin to give us her real reasons why she acts as she does. So that eventually we'll work through to an understanding. The course of it will go like this:

Jean and Sandy will tell us things they think are wrong with the family. If possible things will be readjusted within the family to accord with what they wish. Eventually they'll get to the point of saying things are going good. And once that happens then we'll really begin to get to a knowledge of what's troubling Jean. Now, how long this will take, I can't predict. But at the beginning, when we get together as a family, we'll listen mostly to the youngsters."

Father: "Will we be present all the time?"

Therapist: "Yes, of course—the whole family will be together. And I'll be here as a kind of umpire. I'm not going to be one to make decisions for you. I mean I'm just an outsider. The family is yours, and the decisions that are made are your decisions. But I'll be a kind of referee, as it were, and at the beginning, especially, I'll try to help Jean and Sandy to tell us the things that are troubling them. I'm going to talk, not about Jean being a problem, not about Sandy being a problem, but about the family being an unhappy place—"

Mother: "Yes."

Therapist: "—to grow up in."

Mother: "Yes."

Therapist: "For some reason it's unhappy for Jean and we'll see what we can do about finding out why. Now, some of the things that Jean will say may be new to you, and some of them may be pretty harsh. I've had youngsters say dreadful things about their mothers and fathers—things that they have felt but have never said before. And some of the things that Jean may say may cut pretty deeply."

Mother: "Yes."

Therapist: "And Sandy too—although he's been a very placid and easy-going boy—he may have something stored up inside himself we don't know about."

Father: "Oh yes."

Therapist: "And it's pretty tough to hear your youngsters say harsh things about you, especially when somebody is sitting here listening to what's going on. There may be moments when it won't be easy—"

Mother: "Yes."

Therapist: "—for you. And we may have some times when our feelings are pretty upset. This we just have to live through."

Mother: "Yes."

Therapist: "Because it's part of the process of finding out—"
Mother: "Yes."
Therapist: "—what's troubling the children."
Father: "Yes, yes, I understand."

The preceding explanation includes the elements of orientation that it has been found desirable to state. They may not always be given in the same order or the same language; they may come out as responses to questions rather than as a formal statement. Whatever the form used, the following points are covered:

1. The therapy will proceed in a setting where the whole family is together with the therapist.

2. The therapist will remain somewhat as an outsider. The term "umpire" or "referee" is especially useful because the function of a referee in a game is analogous, in so many ways, to the therapist's functions.

3. One main function of the therapist will be to assure that everyone has a chance to speak in the discussions, and with respect to this function, the therapist will support the children, especially at the beginning, so that they can build up confidence to speak.

4. The children, particularly at the beginning, will demand changes in their routines at home. Whether such demands are met will depend on the parents' decisions. The therapist will not make decisions nor give advice about how the family is to be run. Progress of the therapy at the start, though, will depend on making the changes the children require, insofar as these are feasible.

5. The children will show anger, and such anger may be expressed harshly; it may seem unjustifiable to the adults. It is necessary to hear this anger before more positive feelings will emerge.

6. The parents will have their chance to express their feelings, their problems, their wishes later on. At the beginning, it will be better if they let the children do the speaking.

7. The goal of the treatment is better understanding and communication among all the members of the family. [6]

Jean and Sandy—Child-Centered Phase

As soon as the family assembles for the second session, an important early phase of the therapy is under way. This period may be called the child-centered phase, for the intent of the therapist is to concentrate on his relationship with the children. The purpose is to build a sufficiently strong rapport with them that they will be able to withstand the later explorations of family relationships, especially those launched by the parents with criticism of the children.

Much of what was said to orient the parents is repeated when the children come with their parents to the second session. For several reasons, the therapist centers his attention on the children at this session, just as he had focused on the parents at the preceding interview.

First, it is necessary to counsel the children about the purposes and methods of the treatment. They are told that the therapist and the parents have talked together and that the parents have reported the family is not as happy as it should be. A number of weekly treatment conferences will be held so that each person may talk over with the others in the family his reasons for feeling the family is not happier, and each may offer his suggestions for improving the situation.

Second, it is essential to give the children a sense of having at least an equal voice with their parents in the sessions. The therapist indicates that in families he has known, the children frequently do not have enough chance to take part in planning for the family, and this causes some unhappiness. The therapy situation may be a new one for the children, for in it they will be certain of having a chance to speak. They are assured that their parents approve and have promised to listen and not to punish them for whatever they say. This is an orienting statement for the parents, to reinforce earlier instruction, as well as a statement for the children to interpret the conditions under which speaking will occur.

It is important, also, to lay the foundations of confidence for the children that talking about the changes they would like in their family can help to produce the changes. For the children not only are assured of a chance to advance their own ideas, but are also told their parents have expressed a willingness to change life at home to make it more satisfactory for them.

Finally, the dimensions of the children's relationship with the therapist must be defined, just as the parents' relationship to him was spelled out in the preceding interview. The children must understand that he is not preempting a parental role for himself—he will not make decisions or give advice, but he will strive to provide equal opportunities to participate for all members of the family.

ORIENTATION FOR THE CHILDREN

The manner of presenting this orientation can be illustrated with quotations from the beginning of the second interview with the McAndrews. Frequently the orientation is made in a more piecemeal fashion, because the members of the family, especially the children, respond to the therapist's encouragement to find their voices and interrupt the flow of speech. It is not possible to reconstruct the therapist's reasons, if indeed they were ever conscious ones, why it seemed more appropriate to give this orientation in a long and uninterrupted sequence:

Therapist: "Well, I'm going to tell you a little bit about why we are all here together, and first of all I wanted you to know that I have talked with your mother and your father last week. They came up to see me. And they were telling me that the family wasn't too happy, and that there were things about the family that really worried them. And we never like to hear this about a family. Of course there are lots of good things about your family, like there are about everybody's families, but some things aren't too happy. And so we decided that we'd all get together and talk about the family, just to see if we couldn't figure out some ways to make it a better family for everybody. Now I know a lot of boys and girls, and I know that in families lots of times Mummy has lots to say, Daddy has lots to say, and the boys and the girls don't get as much chance to say what they really want to say as they'd like. At least some families that I know about are like that. And lots of times, boys and girls get the feeling that when they want something in the family, nobody takes them very seriously. So that's why I'm here. You see, we're going to talk about the family, and we want everybody to help out by telling how they think it can get to be a better family and a happier family. And I'm going to be a kind of umpire, a referee. I'm here to see that everybody gets a chance to talk, and that when somebody is talking, everybody else is listening and paying attention to what's being said.

"And when I was talking with your Mummy and Daddy last week, we talked over the fact that there might be some changes that you [Jean] would like to have made in the family, and you, Sandy, would like to have made. And they have promised that they'll make as many changes as possible to fit in with the things that you feel will make the family a better family. So we're going to be getting together on Tuesdays from six to seven for at least a few weeks while we talk over the family and see what we can do to make it a better place for everybody.

"Now I also told your Mummy and Daddy last week that I wasn't going to make up any rules for the family, or decide how things should be run in the family. This is something that really has to be talked over with everybody, and I'm just here to make sure that everybody gets a chance to say the things that are really on his mind. But the way in which changes are made, rules are made, and so on, that has to stay with you, and you, and you. You're the family, and I'm just a sort of outsider.

"I'm a grownup who is here especially to be on your side [Jean], and to be on your side [Sandy], because I want to help you to get a chance to say what you feel about the family, about how things should be run.

"So we're going to talk about the family and the things that make it less happy than we'd like to have it, and what we can do to make it a better family. And I don't know who'd like to start, but I think it would be fine if we heard, really, from Sandy or Jean about what they feel would make the family a better family, because maybe they're the ones whose ideas don't get talked over as much as they should."

As might be expected it takes a while to help some children reach the point where they feel they may speak, even haltingly. Spontaneity was not evidenced by the McAndrew children. After a long pause at the conclusion of the therapist's statement, the mother said:

Mother: "Well, I don't understand Jean taking all this time to talk."

Jean at this point developed a need for a handkerchief, a device she was to use later when the mother was especially critical of her. After the handkerchief had been produced and some time had elapsed, the therapist asked:

Therapist: "What do you think about the family, Jean?"

Jean: "I'd sooner that Sandy began."

Sandy was asked how he would feel about that:

Sandy: (snickering) "I don't dare."

As their feelings of strangeness in the therapy situation were recognized, as they were reassured that there was no hurry and they could choose when and how they wished to speak, and as it was pointed out how their hesitation was like that of most boys and girls at the beginning, they were soon talking along. Jean began:

Jean: "What about trying to understand each other and then we could know what each other felt, and then try to know it . . . I just feel that they don't all understand each other so much or there'd be much more happiness in the family."

Jean's suggestion might provide a general theme for family therapy. The aim proved to be as difficult to accomplish with the McAndrews as with other families. Jean was soon off this elevated level of discourse and on to a more earthy plane—talking about how she didn't like her elder brother to boss her and how she felt she was "getting an awful shortage of money" when he got two shillings and she got threepence.

For his part, Sandy was busy telling us: "If I'm a good boy, well, they'll be good to me, and it works out that way."

As if to reinforce this idea, Mother at this point added: "There's one thing you would like different, Sandy, and that is your bedtime changed." His bedtime was changed during the next week, but Sandy was dismayed to find himself too sleepy to take advantage of it.

In general, the therapist tries in this phase to direct the children's attention to concrete problems and recommendations, especially at the beginning when the younger members of the family are being helped to take part freely. Talking about specific occasions when the family has been troubled or the child himself has felt unhappy seems preferable to talking in generalities.

For example, Jean said: "Sometimes I feel that I shouldn't really be checked by things that I am checked by . . ." meaning that she was stopped from doing things when she felt she had good grounds for doing them.

It seemed well for the therapist to say, then: "Can you tell us a time when you noticed that you thought you had good reasons and they didn't understand it?

This led to a rather typical reply. Jean told about how an aunt had stopped her talking, when Jean was going to thank her for some perfume that had been put on a hankie. The typical element was the mention of an episode involving persons other than those in the immediate family. Sometimes it is a teacher, a neighbor, a storekeeper, or as with Jean, a relative outside the home.

After a short time, the therapist directed the conversation to the immediate family, when he asked Jean: "How about your Mummy and Daddy and Sandy? Do you feel that they understand the good side of it that you see?" As would be expected, she next talked about Sandy, and then with some further support was telling about her annoyance at her Mother's always telling her to "get on with it" at mealtimes.

The emphasis on concrete illustrations, rather than on general statements of problems, leads into the discussion of concrete steps the family could take to prevent the recurrence of such difficulties. The desired focus is on action[7]—action that the child has experienced as hurtful, and action that would prevent such injuries. It seems to be easier at the beginning for the family as a whole to discourse about real things done and to be done. Before the end of the second session in almost all cases, the children have talked about specific actions within the family. The therapist attempts to facilitate the movement of discussion to this level as rapidly as possible.

It must not be imagined that the child will move immediately into rapport that gives him the confidence to raise any concerns he may have on his mind regarding the family. The center of the discussion may shift very rapidly back into extrafamilial situations. It is essential that the therapist make the family conscious of this form of resistance to the progress of the treatment. In the early interviews it may be assumed, generally, that discussion of activities outside the home is a form of evading discussion of events, feelings, and interactions occurring in the family.

About two-thirds of the way through the second session with the McAndrews, the following interchange initiated this kind of shift to an extrafamilial matter:

Therapist: "Do you feel, in a way then, Jean, that you're in the worst position in the family?"

Jean: "Yes, well since I'm the, what's the word, the youngest in the family, it doesn't feel very, it feels very strange to me, for everyone seems to be doing, to tell me what to be doing instead of telling everybody else what to do."

Therapist: "Yes, yes. And that's something that the youngest in the family usually feels, because there are just so many older people around to boss, and not very many who listen."

Jean began to talk about how she felt her mother was on the side of a little girl at school from whom Jean had borrowed a pencil. There had been a tussle as to whether she had returned it or not. Jean had hoped to get sympathy and understanding from her mother when she had told her about this difficulty with the little girl. It had not been forthcoming; instead, the mother had taken the point of view that Jean should have taken her own pencil to school. But soon the emphasis in her report shifted from what this meant in the mother-daughter relationship to what had actually happened at school, whereupon the therapist stepped in:

Therapist: "Well now, Jean, we can't really do anything here about what goes on in school, but here we can do things about what goes on in the family."

Jean: "Yes, I know."

Therapist: "Now the part of this story you just told us that is about the family is where you felt your mother was on the side of the little girl instead of being on your side."

Jean: "Yes. She's never seen the wee girl. That's what I don't understand about it."

One minute later, though, the talk was again about the little girl at school. At this point the therapist may have mishandled the situation. Having failed by direct means to keep the discussion centered in the family, he redirected it to the more general issue of being bossed, with which the talk of school had been initiated. An extremely common form of resistance then ensued, although it was rather more politely expressed than is usual:

Jean: "Well this is only about one of the times that I remember ever having been allowed to talk to anybody before so much as this, and I feel that I'm taking more than my share."

In retrospect it is easy to see that here a problem had been raised which was touched with such strong feeling that Jean had become frightened at having brought it up. Had such an occurrence taken place in later therapy conferences, it might have been appropriate for the therapist to mention the fact and go on to examine it. But in a first contact with the whole family, where already so much had been expressed by Jean, it seemed better to accept the level already attained and permit another member of the family to express himself. Fortunately Sandy wanted to speak, and the silence that might have impelled the parents to join in did not ensue.

In the third session, Sandy brought up for discussion a similar extrafamilial matter. It also touched on child-parent relationships, but it concerned people outside the immediate family in such a way that the difficulty described could not be wholly resolved within the family. Sandy complained that because the parents played bridge with his grandmother all day during the occasional family visits to her, the children felt excluded from their grandmother's company. Again, but only after a rather full exploration of what was involved, it had to be pointed out that nothing could be done about this, because grandmother wasn't taking part in the conferences—an interpretation that led to the discussion of "bedtimes," "pocket money," and other topics related to the immediate child-parent interaction.

PARENT PARTICIPATION

As much as possible, the parents are discouraged from talking. In his posture and gaze, in the direction of his comments, and in the support he offers, the therapist places himself in relation to the children. The parents are not completely ignored—they cannot be—but they are expected to listen rather than talk.

For instance, at the beginning a parent may urge the children to talk. Mr. McAndrew said:

Father: "Don't be afraid to speak, son, you know. We'll be glad to listen to anything you say, and there won't be any repercussions about it."

And shortly after, Mother said to the therapist:

Mother: "Well, perhaps if you asked some questions you'd get what you needed to understand."

In order to free the children, the therapist must either prevent or quickly put an end to such parental domination, even if it seems to be well intentioned, as it did here.

In this instance, Jean volunteered a 20-minute report on what she felt was wrong for her in the family immediately after the therapist rejected the mother's suggestion with the following statement:

Therapist: "Well, I think that probably if Jean and Sandy are like most girls and boys that I've known before, they do have some ideas about things that they'd like to see different in the family. But it just takes a little while to sort of get up courage to talk about them. And so we can just take our time, and when these ideas are ready to come out, they'll come out all right."

In this phase of treatment, if the mother and father bring up some criticism of the children or refer to some occasion when they felt the children created trouble, the therapist ignores it. If, however, a parent is insistent on being heard, as soon as possible the therapist will urge hearing the child's side of the story. On occasion it has been necessary to ask the parents, "Have you spoken to the child about this before?" (It is the usual case for the parents to complain at this time about what has been constantly and vocally criticized.) When the parent agrees and it is then discovered that talking about it has produced no appreciable difference in the child's behavior, the parents may be encouraged to try a new approach. The therapist may say, "Well, since this has not worked very well before, perhaps we should try a way of changing things about."

If at this stage of the therapy the parents deflect attention from the children by engaging one another in an interchange, it must be gently discouraged. For instance, Mrs. McAndrew began to disagree with her husband about Sandy's bedtime. Father said:

Father: "I think it should be more on an elastic basis. If he's going out and playing he's bound to get more tired and get to sleep quicker. If he's indoors all night, he won't be getting sleepy at all. But if you're running about in the open air you're bound to be more tired. I think his bedtime should fluctuate."

Mother: "Yes, but then you're maintaining that if he's out playing he's needing his bed by half-past-eight, but if he's out playing he's not wanting to come in by half-past-eight."

Father: "No, I don't think he'd be too late, and I don't think he'd have any worry getting to sleep."

The therapist did not comment on this exchange, but did wel-

come Jean's following it with, "I'd like to read a bit in bed, too . . ."
Had she not spoken up, it might have been necessary to intercede
with further encouragement to the children to speak.

When, however, the parents amplify what the child has been
saying, bringing out more fully what the child has been seeking to
convey, they are encouraged to speak. If the therapist suspects from
any of the child's reactions that the parents have twisted a story in a
way the child did not intend or would not welcome, he can return the
initiative to the child by asking, "Is that what you were going to tell
us?" or, "Is that what you meant?"

For another thing, the parents are encouraged to try changes
suggested by the children. They can be reminded of the suggestion
made to them during the previous interview that they agree to such
changes, or the therapist can speak as though it were taken for
granted that the changes would be made. If the parents balk at actual
commitment, the therapist may even urge that the children's requests be tried out on a tentative basis. This last approach is made
easier if one or the other of the parents shows willingness to change,
but the therapist does well to remember that whether he presses both
parents or supports one against the other, he is building hostility in
the parents which will and must come forth at a later time. The final
decision regarding what is to be done must rest with the parents. The
formula, "Of course you must decide, but it would help us along if
you could see your way to trying out this change," is frequently used.
It protects the authority of the parents and helps them to see the
relationship of their actions to the progress of the therapy.

The end of the child-centered phase is indicated by the children
themselves. The first sign is that requests for changes cease. For
example, at the beginning of the fourth interview, Sandy said, "For
me I don't find anything wrong . . . I have no complaint. I'm quite
happy." Jean, for her part, said, "I think we're just quite happy as it
is. There is nothing much that can be altered except what we have
already done."

After the children have reached the point of requiring no further
shifts in family arrangements, they usually indicate that they are
ready to talk about their hostility to their parents. This may come in
response to attack by a parent, or it may be started by the child. Here

the character of the therapy so changes that we can see the emergence of a new phase, one we have called the parent-child interaction.

Summarizing the child-centered phase, which begins in the first session attended by the whole family, we can say that its goals are to orient the children to the therapy and to begin to build up a situation within which they can feel safe enough to express their wishes, feelings, and insights. Attention is focused by the therapist on the children rather than on the parents, since it is assumed that there will be greater difficulties in self-expression for the children than for the parents. In a recent and exceptional case, however, where an extremely intelligent and verbal 14-year-old boy had been permitted by his parents to dominate family life, including all conversation, the first sessions had to be structured so as to help the father to speak freely. Normally the parents are discouraged from speaking so that their authority and hostility do not dominate the conferences, thereby freezing the children.

Parent-Child Interaction

While the child-centered phase involves the parents in acceding to the wishes of the children, it may scarcely be described as involving a true parent-child interaction. The relationship at the beginning is a contrived one, occasioned by the therapist for the needs of the children and of the therapy. It becomes increasingly clear that the requests made by the child are about issues that do not figure largely in the overall pattern of the family life, no matter how relevant they seem at the moment to the child. Often all the child himself asks is a hearing on these matters. It does not always seem urgent for him to press for change. Thus from the viewpoint of the total therapy, the child-centered phase may be regarded as a warming-up period that comes to a close when the children bring forth no further demands.

The termination of these requests may be thought of as a token of the readiness of the children for a more spontaneous type of interaction within the therapy. In most cases it is a parent who begins this interaction. One mother, for example, responded to her girl's saying that all was going well by bursting out, "Well, I don't think things are going well!" and then she brought out a list of complaints about how her little girl fought with the neighbor children, was "absolutely impossible in the house," couldn't be trusted with the baby, and so on. The heat with which the mother spoke is typical of what happens at this stage. Part of this hostility may be generated during the child-centered phase, when the parents are required to remain in a submissive position. Most of it, however, would seem to be related to difficulties of longer standing.

Quite frequently the offensive of the parent opens with complaints about the symptoms for which the child was originally referred. In three cases, where the symptoms were stuttering, enuresis, and asthma, no complaint of the symptoms was made. On the other hand, where the difficulties were what the parents regarded as misbehavior—rebelliousness, lying, destructiveness, and the like —anger about the symptoms was always expressed. The vocal parent usually tries to draw the other parent in as support.

In the McAndrew family it was Jean who brought about the beginning of the parent-child interaction. At the start of the fourth interview, she said: "I'm afraid I don't find much point in coming here. I think we're just quite happy as it is. There is nothing much that can be altered except what we have already done." But before she had finished speaking she had begun to talk about flying into a temper inside the house. Then took place a typical beginning to the parent-child interaction.

Jean: "I am enjoying myself a lot better than I used to. And I find that, if I try to be outside as well as inside—not get into a hot temper as I'm doing more or less inside the house. But outside the house I find I can just let it go free, because I don't find anything to make me into a hot temper. And I even enjoy myself a lot more when I don't get worked up."

Therapist: "There are things in the house that give you a hot temper, is that it?"

Jean: "Sometimes I have no reason, but most times in fact I just suddenly fly into a fury—just feel I need to go mad."

Therapist: "There must be some reason, isn't there?"

Jean: "Well, maybe something has happened that I haven't been too happy about."

Almost as though it were foreordained, the mother then entered the discussion, and it went on:

Mother: "Well, this business of me insisting on you wearing your coat when you go out to play. This sends her into one of her hot tempers (giggle) as she calls them, because I don't know whether you know the expression 'Ne'er cast a cloot till May's oot'?"

Therapist: "Yes."

Mother: "And it very much applies. Today is just positive proof. And it so happened in one of our Sunday papers there was a doctor writing an article that his surgery was full of mothers with children with streamimg noses and cóughs just because at the first blink of sunshine they have shed their coats and their woollies and all the rest of it. So Jean, whenever she sees the sunshine, she wants to discard everything."

Jean: "Oh, no, I don't!"

Mother: "I won't allow it and she gets pretty mad at this."

After an interruption to find a handkerchief, Jean said, "My own side is that . . ." and she told a long tale of wishing to wear a light coat ("It gets me into a bit of a puggy when I'm not allowed to wear anything but my napcoat") and of wishing some say in deciding what coat would be appropriate—a story that included such statements as: "Mum's sort of like that wee girl that has a wee curl—'when she's nice, she is very, very nice; but when she is bad, she is—a bit —horrid,' I'm afraid."

As might be expected, Mum could take only so much of her daughter's talking in this manner. Soon she was defending herself by interposing, "Very well, don't mind me!"; giving her own point of view and adding, "That's not defense, it's an explanation"; interpreting how the tantrum looked to her, "We don't start off with *me* being angry"; explaining how it was only on grounds of health that she was concerned; asserting her authority, "She's going to wear what I tell her"; and blaming Jean, "She just doesn't like to be crossed."

BALANCED EXPRESSION

The basic technique at this stage of the therapy is to permit both sides—parent and child—an equivalent opportunity to express themselves. The assumption is that behind the annoying and disturbing behavior there are good and sufficient reasons, which, if they could be understood, would change the evaluation of the behavior. This applies to both the parents and the child. It is further assumed that

the primary cause of the disturbing behavior is within the family
relationships, although events that take place outside the home may
contribute. As I pointed out in the preceding chapter, the explanation or justification of behavior by pointing to supposed causes outside
the home is most often an evasion of unpleasant aspects of relationships inside the family. Allowing discussion of these extra-family
problems at this stage postpones the progress of the parent-child
interaction.

Delicate handling is needed at this level of the discussion to keep
the parent's explosion of hostility from breaking the child's security
in the therapy conferences. The mother's or father's right to speak
openly has to be respected, but at no point should a parent be permitted to undermine the confidence a child has gained during the preceding phase of treatment that he may express his own point of view
with impunity. It is in keeping this balance that the therapist helps
the family to new perspectives on parent-child interaction.

In the McAndrew case, the mother was very strong in voicing
blame of Jean, and it was not surprising that the discussion reached a
point where Jean began to fear the consequences of continuing to
speak:

Jean: "I just wanted to kick out my arms and legs."

Therapist: "You have the feeling that it's especially your mother
that makes you feel this way."

Jean: "Yes, it's the way she looks at me, glares at me with her eyes
sometimes that gets me rather frightened of her."

Therapist: "Is that so? How do you mean, frightened?"

Jean: "Well frightened to do anything more."

Therapist: "You're frightened that she'll . . . what would happen?"

Jean: (giggles) "I'd rather Mum said that."

Mother: "It's you that's frightened."

Therapist: "What are you frightened will happen, Jean? What do
you feel will happen?"

Jean: "I'd rather not say."

Mother: "Of course you say."

By this time the balance between the mother and daughter had
become weighted too heavily on the mother's side. The therapist
therefore stepped in to ease Jean's fear of the immediate situation,

which, it was assumed, had led her to talk about being frightened. Within the next 2 minutes the therapist made three different comments designed to alleviate her fear. First he attempted to put into words what Jean might be unwilling to say, and to lead her to talk:

Therapist: "You feel that your mother will hurt you, or . . . ?"

Jean: "Well, she'll get into an awful . . . I'll get an awful row for it. I feel I'd rather not get that because when I get a row it really is a row."

Her hesitation and change of person indicated a further need for help toward free expression, so in his second try the therapist interpreted the identity between Jean and her mother:

Therapist: "Well, you know one thing that strikes me as you talk is that you and your Mum are doing the same thing."

Jean: "What do you mean?"

Therapist: "That you get your temper up and your Mum gets her temper up."

Jean: "It's really her first (giggles) . . ."

Therapist: ". . . there seems to be a lot of anger with you and your mother."

Jean: "Just passed on from me. It's just the way she looks her eyes at me. It just makes me back away again. Dr. Bell has not saw how you sometimes did it Mum. I'm sure he'd understand."

Jean's calling on the therapist's authority was still further indication that she was having difficulty in expressing her point of view openly. The therapist's next comment was intended to relieve some of her guilt:

Therapist: "I'm not surprised that you and your Mum have some feelings of being cross at one another. Because you know in most families where there is a girl, the little girl and her mummy have a lot less easy feeling with one another than for instance the little girl would have with her daddy."

Jean picked up the suggestion with alacrity, interrupting, to say:

Jean: "Mummy I've thought of something."

Therapist: "Won't you go ahead, Jean? You were going to say something."

Jean: "Sandy and I have decided we have just got two perfectly good parents. Dad is the one that is the softie and Mum is exactly the opposite. Well, when you're nice Mum—."

Mother: "Very well, don't mind me!"

Jean: "I was going to say that Dad's just . . . Mum is more often angry, I'm afraid, than you are very very nice (to Father), and Dad is more often very very nice than he is angry, so we have decided we are rather lucky with our parents. I wouldn't like to be spoiled by both of them and I wouldn't like them both to be hard—we have just got a decent pair of parents, and yet I sometimes feel that Mum is a bit rotten at times."

During the last few minutes the mother's anger had been rising. After she had brought forth another statement in defense of herself, the therapist felt it time to permit her to express some of her feeling. In view of later developments, this was an error in judgment. Mother took full advantage of the opportunity, railing against Jean for several minutes in the following manner:

Mother: "You see, immediately I cross Jean she flares up, she goes into a tantrum and into a huff. She puts on the most awful face and this does make me mad. So sometimes she beats it out the road, you know, before the volley comes; sometimes she doesn't. But we don't all get into furious tempers and that sort of thing, as Jean—at least I don't think so—Jean fears. I think there is some ground in it, granted, but I'm not really (giggles) the terror that she makes me out to be . . . ."

When the chance was given Jean to express her side of the issue again, it became obvious that there had been a misjudgment in handling, for Jean began to fiddle with a pencil and a handkerchief, and to look away. When she was asked for her comments on what her Mother had been saying, she replied:

Jean: "Please, I haven't got anything to say."

Mother: (with annoyance) "Put your pencil away and your handkerchief somewhere and pay attention to what is going on, please."

Jean: "I can't find anything to say about what Mum has been saying."

Once again it was going to be necessary to support Jean in expressing her point of view, for she was much less open, now, and spoke in a self-blaming way:

Jean: ". . . I just feel I have just made the whole place a rotten place. You see I'm like a girl I once read in a book about—make bushels of good resolutions in a week and never get the chance to keep them—yet when the chance comes, I never keep them."

Trying to relieve Jean's guilt and enlarge her perspective so that she might interpret her own behavior in a broader way, the therapist introduced the idea that she was identifying with her mother:

Therapist: "Do you know one good thing about this—this may sound very funny—but you talk about your mummy losing her temper and how you lose your temper too. You know one good thing about this is it tells me that I think you are trying to be like your mummy. And it is right that a girl should try to be like her mummy. And sometimes it is really the way the little girl tries to be like her mummy that annoys her mummy so much."

Jean: (giggles)

Therapist: "And this is because sometimes mummies don't like themselves and so when they see themselves in their little girls they don't like what they see. Now I don't know whether it is a good thing for you both to be getting in tempers like this, but I do see this, that in a way you are trying to be like your Mum."

Mother: "I quite agree with what you say."

Jean: "Well, I don't find that I am trying to be exactly like you . . . I just go as I like to . . . I don't try to be like Mum,—well, I suppose in a way, in some things, that I am doing it unconsciously, but I don't actually, well, say: 'Mum does this, so I'll do this.' "

Apparently, interpreting Jean's identity with her mother supported Jean, for she went on to say:

Jean: "I find that I am just, well, as I would like to be."

But this brought forth a renewal of the attack on Jean:

Mother: "Jean just seems naturally to resent any opposition and I resent that."

So once more the therapist sought to help Jean express her point of view:

Therapist: "Well now, Jean, you have your good reasons for feeling this resentment about opposition. We should know so we can understand what your good reasons are for resenting this. You see, it isn't something that just happens without good reasons behind it."

At the time it was not anticipated that Jean would interpret "good" in an ethical sense rather than in the intended sense of "personally justifiable," which raises a point worth discussing. It is essential to give special attention in this therapy to the words used and the meanings attributed to them. This is so, of course, in all types of therapy, but here there are communication difficulties beyond those that would be encountered in individual therapy. For one thing, the children may not have as fully developed language resources as the adults present may assume. On the other hand, one of the devices often used by the parents to exclude the children from the group is speaking with vocabulary beyond the children's comprehension.

The exchange with Jean shows that even when the therapist uses simple words he may not transmit his meaning to children. In his attempt to support Jean in the expression of hostile feelings toward her mother and relieve her guilt, his unfortunate use of the word "good" defeated his purposes. For Jean's understanding of "good reasons" in ethical terms rather than in the intended meaning of "reasons important to her" appeared to sustain her sense of guilt:

Jean: "Well, it's really all my own fault, this. There's no reason behind it. Well I suppose there is a very sly reason, that I want to work everyone into a puggy so the next time they don't want me to be angry and get them angry, so they just give me what I want."

Therapist: "You mean that that is one of the ways which you have to use in order to get what you want? Is that what you mean?"

Jean: "I'm afraid it is rather sleekit of me, but I'm afraid it is rather that way. I mean, when it doesn't come out to suit me, I just do it all over again."

Although Jean returned to the altercation with her mother about which coat she should wear, she remained on the defensive:

Jean: "You see, after I do it, I feel rather silly, and the next time comes and I do exactly the same again. I feel afterwards, I say to myself, I was very silly and I shouldn't have done it . . . Yet when the next time comes, as I say, I'm exactly the same. And it all starts over again. So thinking that to myself afterwards isn't much good to me at all."

Again the therapist sought to release Jean so she could express the anger she had begun to talk about earlier:

Therapist: "I wonder if there isn't some reason why it's important to get mad at your mother? Some reason that's really beyond whether she says you can go out with your coat or not go out with your coat. I wonder if there isn't some reason that goes beyond it, because it seems that every time you come to this kind of situation there's a lot of anger all ready to burst out, beyond what really comes up just because she says no."

Jean: "Well, yes, I suppose there is, but—there's probably a lot of anger inside me, but I don't actually, I'm not very conscious of what it's, that it's there. It just mingles with the anger because Mum says no, and it all comes out worse than it should be at all."

Up to this point we have seen an example of the usual form the parent-child interaction takes. If the therapist had exposed what was happening in this fourth session by explaining to the family how the interaction between Jean and her mother led to guilt on Jean's part when she expressed negative feeling against her mother, and how guilt drove Jean to self-condemnation in the place of anger against her mother, what happened next might have been prevented. But the explanation had not been made, and because it had not, the interview veered dramatically in a new direction.

EXAMPLE OF RESISTANCE

What occurred was a form of resistance to the therapy. We shall examine its manifestastion in the McAndrew case in detail, for parallels occur at some stage in the treatment of almost every family. Furthermore, the therapist's way of dealing with this form of resistance in the McAndrew case is typical of the approach that has proved best when individual members try to prevent the therapist from dealing with the total family, from achieving the therapeutic goal of balanced opportunities for self-expression.

Resistance had undoubtedly been developing during the earlier part of the McAndrews' fourth interview, but it was openly manifested immediately after the statement by Jean that I am about to quote. She was relating what had apparently been a confidence she had given her mother in a long private talk on the preceding Sunday. The fact to note is that in the telling, she plainly revealed what was subsequently treated as her "secret," a fact supporting my interpretation that what happened next in the interview was a form of resistance.

Jean: "Yes, I'm afraid I was usually having a heavy conscience *because I used to tell lies,* I'm afraid. But I don't now because

Mummy says she'll never trust me again if I do tell—if she finds out one time that I do, have told her a lie. And well that just comes to the point that I've told lies, I've got a heavy conscience . . . and I'm so used to my heavy conscience that I just feel cowardly, afraid to do anything naughty, and that prevents me from doing it, and yet keeps me with a heavy conscience all the time."

Jean's confession of her "heavy conscience" brought her mother to her defense:

Mother: "This is something I would like to discuss with you in private, Dr. Bell. Do you think the children would maybe go down to the waiting room for a while until we have a little chat about it?"

Now the mother was taking Jean's part. It was notable that when Jean desisted from expressing anger against her mother and took a self-condemnatory role she won defense from her mother. Thus acceptance of the mother's proposal of a private conversation would have been to yield, indirectly, to her authority over Jean and to her desire that Jean be prevented from showing her hostile feelings.

The therapist attempted to restructure the situation as a family situation:

Therapist: "Well, I'm wondering whether we really should talk about things in private. After all we are here to sort of talk these things all out in public. And I think it might be better if we could talk it out with everybody."

The compact between the mother and Jean was emphasized by Jean:

Jean: "Well, I don't feel too bad about going down to the waiting room, if Mum feels it should be a private conversation between Mum and Dad and yourself, Dr. Bell."

The therapist took a somewhat stronger tone:

Therapist: "You see, it's important, though, since we are here to talk not really about Jean or Mrs. McAndrew or Sandy or Mr. McAndrew, as individuals, but about the whole family, that we keep things all in the family. This is important. And for this reason I said to your mummy and daddy that we might on occasion . . . meet as individuals . . . but that the only way in which we could do this would be for us to talk about it first, and then for me to report back afterwards what we had talked about.[8] Because I want everybody to know what the reasons are and to understand what the feelings are in the family. I wonder if part of what you want to tell me couldn't actually be said right here?"

Mother persisted, however:

Mother: "No, I don't think it is advisable, Dr. Bell. I'd rather speak to you in private about this matter . . . You can do what you like with it afterwards, what you think fit, but I don't think it is something that should be discussed before the children."

An open rebuff to the mother by the therapist would have been as undesirable as yielding to her desire to shift the basis of the therapy away from the family. The therapist decided to indicate the availability of other therapists for individual consultation:

Therapist: "If there are things which are important for you to talk over with somebody privately, then I can arrange for somebody here at the clinic to work with you, talking things over privately. The things that we are to talk over are the things that could be talked over in the group as a whole."

But the mother continued to press for the private session:

Mother: "It's just the effect that it might have on Jean that I was thinking about, but I feel that it might enable you to get to the root cause of the trouble more quickly, but . . ."

The therapist next reviewed all that Jean had talked about during the session, pointing out how much she had already said that was important. But Jean urged her mother and father to let her leave. In this she had her mother's support. The therapist continued to emphasize the necessity for the total family approach:

Therapist: "If it would embarrass Jean, we'll wait, and maybe if sometime she feels it won't embarrass the whole family then we can talk about it. But we'll talk about things here at the moment that you (to Jean, and then to the others) feel can come out in front of everybody . . . In other words we won't try to bring out yet things that we would feel would be terribly embarrassing to discuss."

The extent of the identification between Jean and her mother at that moment was indicated by Jean's picking up the mother's theme:

Jean: "Well, you see, I would like Mum to talk it over with you. But you see the thing is that I don't think Dad quite understands it all. It has been mostly between Mum and myself. And I'd like her to talk it over with you. Because I feel it would do me good for what you maybe said about it afterwards. I could maybe get some benefit from it. I would rather that I didn't hear it, the way Mum put it. I would like her to talk it over with you, not because it is her that wants to do it. I feel that I might benefit from it if it was talked in private."

Therapist: "Yes. Well do you think that what you have on your mind, what your mummy is thinking of, is something that you would hope that Sandy and your daddy would understand?"

Jean: "Well, as I said, it has just been going on between Mum and myself. Well, lots of times when I've been naughty I've wanted to cry and sit on Mum's knee and talk over things I have done and say I was sorry and all that sort of thing. I'd like Mum to talk it over with you and Dad, because I feel I might benefit from it in a way. It might help me—my conscience to be cleared—and therefore I'm afraid that wouldn't only help me but it would help Mum as well to have, to lead a much happier life—instead of me cowering away all the time because I had a guilty conscience, and yet I couldn't think of what I had done wrong. I might benefit and it might help me to have a clear conscience. And yet, as I say, I'd feel a little bit embarrassed to face Dad and you when Mum is telling it—I would like her to talk it over with you."

As the therapist kept on pointing out how the end result would have to be the discussion of the mother's and Jean's private revelations in front of Sandy and her dad, Jean repeated over and over her desire that her mother talk alone with the therapist. Once again it was necessary to indicate that private therapy could be arranged with another therapist:

Therapist: "If it is important for you to talk with somebody else so that you can get your conscience clear, and talk with somebody privately, I can arrange that here, but not with me. You see I'm here to hear about what goes on in the family and not just to hear about those things which are private to you as individuals—that you can't talk about in front of the other members of the family."

Finally, after several more minutes of discussion, the mother said:

Mother: "Well, there's no alternative than just to discuss it here. (Long pause . . . to Jean) Are you ready?"

Jean: "I'd still rather leave the room."

Mother: "What do you think, Dr. Bell? Should we leave it alone?"

Therapist: "It's up to you, it's up to you."

The usefulness of this firm insistence on open family discussion was indicated by the next development: the father, who had been almost completely silent for the whole interview, began to speak. Had the therapist acceded to the wishes of the mother and Jean for private discussion, the father would have felt excluded and displaced by the therapist. Although he had been silent, he had still been an active participant in the group session. Silence is a role, an active influence in the session, and the therapist would have implied a criticism of the father's role if he had permitted the father to be disestablished.

Father: (to Jean) "Is it something that is all past and done with now?"

Mother: "Yes."

Jean: "Yes. Well, that's what, these are the things that make me embarrassed—when it's all past and done with and it's brought up again."

Father: "You shouldn't be embarrassed about it."

Mother: "You come and sit up [on her lap] and tell Dr. Bell about it, eh? Come on."

Jean: "No."

Mother: "Come on."

Therapist: "Well, Jean, when you are ready you can talk about it. It may not be today, and it may not be next week. (Perhaps this suggested the timing that Jean used, for she spoke about her "secret" the session after the next.) You may feel that later on you can talk about it very easily. It's just that we don't want you to feel that you have to say anything at any time, but only when you feel that it's important and going to help you and the family."

Jean: "Well, I feel that I'll never want to discuss what I've been doing lately—well not lately but before—and I'll never want to hear anybody talking it over or to say it myself. I would rather leave the room if Mummy is going to talk about it, and I would rather she did."

Father: "We've all been naughty before, Jean. I can remember many naughty things when I was a boy."

Therapist: "Then maybe you could tell us about some of those memories."

Jean: (giggles)

Father then told of stealing when in the company of a group of boys—something that he had never told his own father or mother —and ended with, "Grandma doesn't know about that."

Jean: "Does she not? Well I feel I'd rather she did know because it even gives me a guilty conscience to know that even one of my parents, or even Sandy, has done some thing he shouldn't."

Jean followed up this reference to her guilty conscience by renewing her request that mother tell about what was on her (Jean's) mind, but this time she proposed that she step out so her mother could tell the whole group. The therapy hour ended before discussion of her suggestion could be completed, and the request for private sessions was not presented at any subsequent meeting.

Two weeks later, in the sixth family session, Jean permitted her mother to bring out her "secret," that "Jean for many years has told lies." That Jean herself had told the secret midway in the fourth interview had been forgotten, or suppressed, or had never been caught by the family. At the time, apparently, it was more important to the family to test once again the limits of the therapist's role and functions—in this case, the extent to which he would respond to the mother's attempt to take over the direction of the conferences and to break up the family group; the extent to which he would permit a distinction between the parts that the adults and the children would be allowed to play in the conferences; the extent to which he would allow himself to replace the father in the mother's eyes; the extent to which he would sponsor an alliance between mother and daughter that would exclude father and son.

In everyday family life, the exclusion of some family members from intimacies between others and the splitting of the family into camps are common methods of structuring family interrelationships. But resort in family therapy sessions to these customary divisive maneuvers represents a resistance to the new ways of relating demanded by the therapist and the conference situation. The old ways are not necessarily inappropriate in ordinary family life. Used in the conferences, however, the old ways are attempts to remove into a private realm what the therapist needs to be able to see; thus they constitute resistances to the rules and procedures he has established as part of the therapeutic method.

In other families, comparable resistance to the therapy has shown itself in a number of ways. For example, part of the family arrives early or lingers after a conference to talk with the therapist, tries to carry on private sessions by telephone, writes lengthy letters to the therapist, or fails to bring one or more members to a conference. It is important to discourage such private contacts. Letters may have to be read at the family conference, parents may have to be told they may not discuss matters over the telephone, or a session may have to be postponed if a family member does not appear. Otherwise the progress of the therapy will be slowed down.

The fact that resistance to the therapy often takes the form of attempts to isolate segments of the family from the therapist carries an implication for the usual situation in child guidance, where only a part of the family is seen: the building of what is interpreted as a positive transference between a family member and a therapist may increase the resistance within a family to dealing with and solving family problems. Thus the development of a strong tie between a mother or a child and the therapist may defeat rather than assist the therapy by having the effect of isolating other members of the family from the patient. The failure of individual therapy in the cases of Mrs. McAndrew, Jean, and Sandy, for example, can be attributed partly to this effect. It would seem that failure to include the father in the therapy tended to preserve the status quo in the family. The dramatic changes that took place when family therapy was instituted can be attributed, at least in part, to the father's no longer needing to react to isolation from the therapy being received by his children and his wife.

RETURN TO PARENT-CHILD INTERACTION

With the McAndrew family the parent-child phase continued through the fifth interview, which began with the mother's criticizing Jean for creating many problems about eating:

Mother: "Well, she's an awful bag of mystery in that respect because what's the ideal dinner to her one day, I give it to her one week later—she doesn't want it!

(Later) "I think the main trouble is that she must draw attention to herself—she can't be anything but the focal point of the conversation. You see, Sandy can't have a conversation with anyone without Jean chiming in, and so that I think if she can't get attention any other way she will get it this way, fussing with her food. And I mean we have had some most unpleasant scenes over this and it still doesn't stop her. We have told her that she spoils our lunch every day."

During almost the whole of the interview the mother pursued this theme, describing it, elaborating it, repeating it with new emphases, exposing the intensity of the resentment enveloping it. Since these complaints were not new to Jean, their reiteration provided an excellent opportunity to see how she defended against the mother's fury, which at times approached hysteria.

The verbal report of the fifth interview indicates that Jean used a variety of devices to ward off the attack:

A kind of mocking of the therapist: "Oh, I sometimes laugh at what I used to say—when I do something I shouldn't—'There's no good reasons.' I say to Sandy afterwards: 'I really could have howled with laughter if Mum had come and asked me what my good reasons were.' Some things I do there are no good reasons for—I just laugh at the thought of it."

Emphasizing the physical nature of her difficulties: eating what she didn't like made her "boke" (gag) and pills (prescribed recently by the family physician) before meals rid her of pain.

Accepting the fact of the difficulty but denying she could approximate any rationale for her behavior: "The fact of the matter is that I don't know why I do create trouble."

Giggling, which greatly annoyed her mother.

Beginning to say something and then forgetting what she was to say.

Accusing her mother of having said things which made her take offense. At one point she referred to how offended she was that her mother had called her a "nuisance." Mother denied she had ever used the word.

Deflecting the attack by pointing to Sandy's misbehavior (loud noises) and the way this annoyed her, and to Sandy's responsibility for removing the annoyance.

Sighing and saying in a resigned way, as the mother began a fresh attack: "Here we are again!"

This range of verbal defenses was carried on in the setting of what was probably more significant behavior, her general attitude. Observing her facial expressions one would have said that Jean was unconcerned. She looked around the room, smiled, glanced out the window, and registered very little evidence of being interested in the discussion, though her verbalizations were always to the point. One would have said from her face that she regarded all the business about dinner as an old, old story that had begun to pall and required only an occasional protest. In fact, Jean said at several points that what her mother was saying had nothing new in it for her.

It was not easy to understand, let alone explain, what was taking place during the fifth interview. One had the sense that the mother was engaged in a most intense outpouring of feeling, almost to the point where she might lose control. Frequently her voice rose so in pitch and intensity that she was nearly screaming. One also felt that Jean was protecting herself strenuously with well-practiced mechanisms for warding off her mother. But if one analyzes the interview just in these terms one misses the meaning of what was transpiring.

Since the family meets together to engage in the mutual task of analyzing its difficulties and of deepening intrafamilial communication as a step toward solution, we ask what the fifth interview contributed by way of an interpretation of the family problem. The mother was vigorously telling us the way Jean's behavior contributed to family difficulties. But Jean's indifference, punctuated only occasionally by defensive interruptions that seemed to egg the mother on, also told us that the perpetuation of the dinnertime crises may have had functional value for the family. It was the product of a particular set of pressures within the family. It was, in a way, an achievement as well as a problem, a solution as well as a symptom. The question may well be asked, as it was in the next interview, why the mother, Jean, the father, and Sandy wanted these dinnertime rows to persist. The silence maintained by Sandy and his father throughout the interview was also a comment on what the mother was saying so strongly. Their mode of participation implied their advocacy of the mother's role as an aggressive, irritable, domineering, and criticizing figure as well as of Jean's role of indifference and occasional defense. Here was a phase of this family's life and communication. Though he did not do so then, it might have been appropriate for the therapist to verbalize the nature of this interaction.

Two other occurrences in the fifth interview called for the therapist's attention and response. One was Jean's persistent talk about Sandy's making noises that "annoyed" her, and the other was Jean's nonverbal behavior before and during this talk.

She diverted the discussion from the lunch hour with her complaints of Sandy's noises. The mother protested:

Mother: "I'd still like to know her reason for the fuss at lunch. And this business of Sandy making noises that annoy her, well I think that perhaps that is infinitesimal compared to this, daily, around the dinner table."

But several minutes later Jean was back to mentioning how Sandy troubled her. Again mother rebuked Jean:

Mother: "Well, you are getting away from the dinnertime, Jean."

Therapist: "Not really. There is some connection here, too, between Sandy and this matter of the difficulty of the dinnertime."

Mother: "Sandy is not in at dinnertime."

Therapist: "There is some connection inside Jean, because when we bring up the matter of what her good reasons are she talks about Sandy."

At the end of the interview, after mentioning Sandy several times, Jean returned to the theme. In her final comment, she was again relating the importance to the family problems of her rivalry with her brother:

Jean: "Well, I'm maybe taking this off the subject, but the noises—well. Sandy doesn't take any interest in his mouth organ. Well I have got his old one, and he has got a beautiful new one. And I feel that if he would use that new one, I could join in. Well he never uses it, so I don't think there is any point in him making noises that I don't like. And I don't see any point in him having a mouth organ, whereas I'd very much like his big one. It's really a grand mouth organ, and he never uses it. He just makes noises that I don't like."

That this had a symbolic reference to sexual fantasy was demonstrated by the context within which it appeared. All during the session Jean had been patting and stroking her body. She was wearing a dress with pocket-like openings on the sides and almost all of the time she sat with a hand inside her skirt. Once or twice her mother pulled her hand away, but it soon returned. Just before she spoke about the mouth organs, the therapist had said:

Therapist: (to Jean) "I think you have been telling me something today. And that's that you have been holding yourself with your hands inside your skirt. And I think you have been telling me something today you wanted to tell the whole group about—with your hands. You see sometimes we talk with our hands and sometimes we talk with our mouths. Now I don't know what it is that you have been telling me with your hands, but it has been something about this part of your body down here. And it is of some interest to me that you were talking about tummy aches and about food and so on and that you also were telling me about your body with your hands. We haven't time now, since our time is up, to try to get some of these things in words that you have been telling me with your hands, but I wanted you to know that I noticed it."

The compulsive movement and the talk of mouth organs were significant as indications that solution of the family problem would require exploration of other relationships than just that between Jean and her mother. Jean herself had been telling us this, mostly indirectly, during the fifth interview.

At the beginning of the sixth interview, she chose another method to communicate that there was more to be said on the difficulties than she could put into words. She began:

Jean: "I understand that the talking point tonight is the dinner."

Mother: "Well she finds now that she has got a sore mouth."

Jean: "Toothache."

After recommending a visit to the dentist, the therapist went on:

Therapist: "There may actually be physical pain, but it is possible too that the pain is a pain that starts in the feelings rather than with something wrong with the teeth. Because we do sometimes get pains that start because we don't feel right, something is making us angry or something like that, so we get to feel the pain . . ."

Jean: "Today I was just fairly rotten . . . I just wasn't feeling well at all. I wanted to go to bed as soon as I came home, in fact, and then I got this pain, this terrible pain in my head. Well it might have been something, as you say, because I wasn't pleased."

Therapist: "Pains come because you can't tell someone about how you really feel and so you have to have something to tell them about, and you tell them about pains . . . It may be that this has something to do with the problem at dinnertime that your mummy brought up last time."

Because Jean had indicated previously that the problem was a larger one than the dinner, and because she was evidencing many difficulties in verbalization, the therapist deflected the mother's pressure on her by introducing an interpretation:

Therapist: (to Mother) "I wonder whether there isn't something about this trouble at mealtime that sort of fits in with something that you want. It may seem strange that I might say you would want trouble at mealtime. But I couldn't help but wonder, because it has gone on for so long, if maybe, somehow, this wasn't fitting in with something that you, without really recognizing it, wanted—in other words that the trouble at mealtime was important for some reason or other—and if there weren't some things behind this that made it go on all this long time.

"You see when you were talking with us last week you really were saying some harsh things in a strong way against how Jean acts at the table. It sort of rolled off Jean's back. It didn't really upset her as you'd think it might upset her. And I have the feeling that maybe for a long time it hasn't upset Jean very much. (Jean laughs.) The question I then ask is: Why have you gone on, mad, putting up with this week after week after week, telling Jean how cross you are and so on, when it doesn't seem to do any good? I wonder if it doesn't fit in somehow with something that feels good either to you or your husband or to both of you."

Naturally the mother was surprised at this, and first she protested and attempted to justify herself. Finally she said with strong emphasis:

Mother: "I can assure you I hate this terrible row at mealtime."

Therapist: "I know. I wasn't suggesting that you didn't hate it. I know you hate it, I know it is painful and uncomfortable. But on the other hand there is something about it that suggests there are good reasons why you have not taken a firm enough stand to stop it."

This brought the parent-child interaction to an end in the McAndrew case. At this point the father began to speak, and from then on he continued to play a vocal role in the proceedings. In a typical way, the therapy moved to an analysis of the reactions between the father and mother, or what is called the "father-mother interaction."

Summarizing briefly the parent-child interaction, we have seen a demonstration of the way the child-centered phase leads into an emotional and verbal exchange between a child and a parent. In another family group, the parent-child interaction might be extended through the exploration of the relationships of other children with one or both of the parents. Throughout this exchange, the therapist strives to balance the opportunity for expression available to the child and to the parent. The balance sought is not only of time to speak or quantity of verbalization, but of emotional intensity as well. Thus a child's single remark may balance an hour of complaint on the parent's part, or vice versa. The therapist functions further to reduce guilt about verbalizing aspects of parent-child relationships; to handle resistances that may become attempts to restrict communication to exchange between the therapist and only a segment of the family; and to help in the analysis of the nature of the interrelationships between the various family members. Toward these ends, the therapist may seek to clarify the fantasies and feelings of the participants, to direct attention to the motivating factors underlying behavior, and to make interpretations that facilitate communication and help to develop insight into parent-child interrelationships.

Interaction between Mr. and Mrs. McAndrew

As treatment progresses, the center of discussion shifts to analysis of the father-mother relationship, which takes place in many different ways. When it is carried on outside the therapy conferences, as it sometimes is, the mother and father may refer only to the conclusions reached in their private discussions. In other instances, at the family conferences in the presence of the children, the parents explore their relations with one another.

The extent of the discussion in family conferences may far exceed expectations. In one family, sexual difficulties between the father and mother were mentioned openly during a discussion of symptoms in the children that related to sex. This was the only instance of open discussion, although it was obvious that sexual relationships between the parents had been referred to indirectly in other cases. It was usual for such problems to be explored at the level of the parents' feelings for one another rather than with reference to specific sexual acts. I mention here the extent to which parents go in revealing their difficulties with one another because several times other professional workers have asked me questions about it.

The parents may also inquire how much they should reveal to the children about the marital relationship. Since this question usually relates to the difficulties rather than to the gratifications in their relationship, the therapist responds that the children are probably aware of such difficulties as exist between the parents, although they may not know exactly what the difficulties are about. If the child has sensed the presence of trouble, it is usually a relief to him to hear an open discussion. It limits his fantasies about the parents' problems and reassures him. Also reassuring is the fact that in exposing their difficulties the parents are taking steps toward dealing with these differences. While it is not usually mentioned to parents, it has been observed that the child often finds identification with a parent easier when he learns about problems in which the parent is involved. The father's or mother's level of adjustment appears easier to attain when the godlike superiority attributed to a parent gives way before a more realistic appraisal of the range of human qualities—good and bad —embodied in the parent's character and behavior.

The relationship between the parents is a factor in the situation creating symptoms of disturbance in the child. This statement does not imply that there are always difficulties between the parents, nor that it is their problems that occasion the children's disorders. Family therapy has demonstrated that it is more true to say that the whole relationship, good and bad, between the mother and father, as well as the individual relations between each of the parents and each child, and the children's relations with one another, pattern a child's behavior. It is the web of interrelationships within the family that structures the child's conduct.

It is worth repeating that direct or implied judgment about whether the relationship between the father and mother is good or bad does not facilitate therapy. For instance, it is sometimes the *closeness* of the bond between the parents that circumstances disordered reactions in the children. Parents will sometimes say: "I don't know why our child should be like this. We [husband and wife] always get along well together." If one were to assume that problem children only occur when there are irregularities in the parental relationship, one might mistrust such a statement of the parents. This suspicion is, in fact, often communicated to parents by child therapists. Parental confusion and guilt follows, beclouding the state of affairs in the family. As a result the parents and children are directed away from attending to those family facts that need to be understood in order to keep the family in harmonious growth. This is not to say that latent hostilities may not exist and be conditioning factors in the situation of a child. It means, rather, that a wider range of influences than the *problems* between the parents exerts an influence toward disturbance in the child.

When parents have conflicts, however, they tend to assume that these conflicts are relevant to the children's problems. Thus in the course of family therapy the bearing of parental difficulties on the family will normally be explored. For example, Mr. McAndrew opened up the whole subject of the father-mother relationship in the sixth interview, when he responded to the therapist's questions as to why the dinner difficulties had been allowed to persist:

Father: "This business of the dinnertime, I'm afraid it has always brought up a certain amount of conflict—the only conflict that there is between my wife and I. That may be one of the hidden factors in it. I suggested just giving a spoonful of this and a spoonful of that —about as much as I thought you would give to a bird—taking it right to the other extreme, suggesting—I'm afraid my wife thinks it's a bee in my bonnet—that she always gives the children too much. I think they should get very much less, and if they are eager for more they can ask for it. And this has been a sort of skirmish all the time. Mrs. McAndrew expects me to really back her up, and sometimes I don't feel very strongly about it."

Responding to verbal recognition by the therapist that dinnertime was an occasion of difficulty not only with Jean but also between the parents, the father went on to describe his customary role in this triangular relationship between the mother, Jean, and himself:

Father: "Yes, I'm afraid I usually sit back and let it go at that."

Therapist: "But inside you have the feeling that you differ somewhat with Mrs. McAndrew about some of the ways in which things are done about dinner?"

Father: "Well I don't like to show that and yet sometimes I think Jean realizes that she would have more sympathy from me than she gets from her mother."

Therapist: "You have the feeling maybe that Jean keeps on with this with the feeling that maybe she will be able to get your sympathy."

Father: "Oh, she tries it many a time. Oh, it's a side look, just a little touch of the arm and things like that. Of course she doesn't get it."

Therapist: "She doesn't get it—but she may continue to have the hope of getting it."

With a somewhat anxious tone, the mother entered the discussion:

Mother: "We have always made it a rule that we uphold each other in front of the children. Whatever we say outwith of their hearing, we present a united front; and then discuss anything that we differ over outwith of their hearing."

After this remark, there was further exploration of the relationships between Jean and her mother and father, and later between Sandy and his parents. But father returned to the matter of his feeling about his wife, explaining how some of the difficulties in the family may have originated from his wife's working:

Father: "I'm afraid I blamed this working at night a lot—the rest of the staff here [at the clinic] don't put much credence on it, but I think they are wrong, definitely."

Now followed considerable self-justification from the mother, and also reference to the authority of the clinic. But father kept up his criticism:

Father: "Well, it left only one day in the week in which we could exist as a family, and that was Sunday . . . Very often Sunday was taken up with visitors, so for long periods we never existed as a family."

The statement apparently released some resentment in the children. Shortly after, as though the children were taking sides against the father, they opened an attack on him because he spent so little time with them and was always busy filling out his pool coupons. This put the father on the defensive until Jean and her mother brought out Jean's "secret"—how she had been telling lies.

The remainder of the sixth interview was spent in a lengthy discussion of Jean's lying, of the mother's insistence that Jean tell the truth ("I always tried to pound truth into them from their earliest days"), and of the rationale for not telling Jean certain facts ("She'd be going out and telling everybody all about it"). Finally, as an illus- tration of the latter, the mother told of a "little business" at the weekend.

Mother: "Well, my husband doesn't like flavorings—sage, curry—he can't stand any of these things. But I thought, 'Well, I do.' So I popped in a little sage, you see. Well he said, 'Oh, it was all right, you know,' with the implication that, 'Don't keep on doing it,' you see. You can do it once, but months will go by before we'll have any more sage."

The next day when she was making "minced patties" (hamburg- ers), because Jean had liked the sage the mother put it in again, letting Jean into her secret. When the father came home from golf- ing, Jean greeted him with, "Didn't you smell sage when you came inside?"

It was the end of the interview time, and the therapist closed the session with a suggestion:

Therapist: "I wonder if this isn't another of those things that can divide. Here's Jean knowing that you're on the sage side and Mr. McAndrew is on the non-sage side, and she brings this out in the open—almost as though she's doing it to make Mr. McAndrew feel cross with you."

Privately the therapist was noting that in telling this story the mother was somewhat on the offensive against her husband. Thus, the interview which had first exposed hostility of the father against the mother came to an end with the mother expressing some mild opposition to her husband.

Consequent to this most tentative reference to difficulties be- tween the parents, a striking change in the family affairs took place. Suddenly all difficulties disappeared. At the seventh interview, the parents reported that Jean had eaten well and was creating no dif- ficulties at dinnertime. Fighting between Jean and Sandy had stopped. The family had made an excursion on Sunday and had a pleasant time together. There was good humor and banter between the members of the family. So completely were the characteristics of a terminal interview evidenced in this session that it seemed as though the problems were solved and the therapy might be nearing a conclusion. Actually, though, in the light of what happened later, one saw that a kind of massive group repression was in operation. All negative feelings were submerged and only the positive were permitted to come forth.

The height of the father-mother interaction was reached at the eighth interview and immediately thereafter. The tension at the beginning of the interview was striking. No one would speak. Finally the mother commented: "A big silence!" but no laughter ensued. Everyone sat in glum silence, which was finally rent by a vigorous attack from the mother:

Mother: "Well I am going to state right here and now that there have been some very bad sessions at dinnertime this last week. I don't see that there is any improvement in that direction."

In her report of the difficulties the mother noted that some of the days of the past week had been trouble free. But, as if to emphasize the difficulties she had been having, she made the following statement in a bitter tone:

Mother: "Oh, well, the days that there isn't trouble far outnumber the days that there is trouble."

The striking thing about this statement was that the mother had made a slip (which was not drawn to her attention). The therapist responded to the tone of her voice:

Therapist: "And this week it seems to have been especially bad."

Almost immediately she made another slip:

Mother: "That's the funny bit, she keeps on saying to me that she hates me always chasing her up, but she doesn't do anything so as I don't have to chase her up. She says she's sick of it and I certainly am, but the cure I don't think is in her hands. All she has to do is eat up her dinner—it's as simple as that!"

Father: "Unless we [mother and father] start talking at dinnertime and she stops—we would maybe be nearer it."

And for the third time in succession, the mother made a slip:

Mother: "I have tried telling her to stop talking and have forbidden her to stop talking—I think that's terrible and it shouldn't be. There should be a little conversation at the table, surely, and it has got to the stage that if I forbid Jean to talk at her meals my husband doesn't talk either."

Jean broke in to tell how much she had enjoyed one occasion when her dad and mum had carried on a conversation by themselves during the dinner hour. Then the mother continued:

Mother: "What's the worst thing is that she gets us—she gets me so mad that I just haven't—I'm not in a mood for ordinary conversation, apart from the fact that I'm having my dinner and dishing up for the rest all at the same time."

The therapist suggested that perhaps the mother was perpetuating the difficulty as much as Jean, to which the mother replied:

Mother: "It's sort of admitting that I can't stop it, isn't it? In a way that I'm keeping on putting up with it all this time?"

Now attempting to respond to the mother's tone of voice, the therapist continued:

Therapist: "And it may be that you feel very helpless to stop it."

Slowly, and in a very depressed tone the mother replied:

Mother: "I do. I feel it has gone on for so long that nothing will make her eat her dinner. I feel there will never be a time in my life when I'll sit down at the table and enjoy my dinner, leaving all this out: 'Get on with it, Jean.' 'Eat your dinner, Jean.' 'Stop talking, Jean.' It's really disgraceful. I am sick of it, and yet I don't know what to do about it. I've spoken to her about it, she knows how I feel about it, but I'm coming to the conclusion that school dinners is the only solution. If I could make a dinner and say, 'Well, there won't be any trouble today!' that would be grand. But I haven't even that to fall back on."

Father brought out again his suggestion of small helpings, and he proposed a 2-week trial period. This precipitated an argument between the father and the mother. Mother claimed she had tried it. She had served Jean's dinner on a small tea plate. Father reminded Mother that he had said at the time it was a wrong idea because the helpings were the same size and looked all the larger on the small plate.

From talk about specific issues, the discussion moved on to the expression of more general attitudes. Mother made such points as:

Mother: "I am sort of the responsible one in the family—you don't have the responsibility in the house and therefore you don't need to worry about it!

"If he would tell her to get on with it, perhaps even if he spoke more firmly, she may take more notice of him speaking to her the way I do!

"He's rather inclined to laugh things off and the children don't understand derision when they hear it.

"He just sort of takes away all your authority by laughing it off."

Whereas the father was saying:

Father: "The reason for a lot of the scenes is the fact that Mrs. McAndrew can't just ignore a lot of these things.

"It's only a different method of approach to the same problem!

"I don't know—maybe if I did start shouting and forcing things a bit more—it's the unpleasant way of doing things! I suppose my way means that the children have to do more; they have to cooperate more with that method of approach."

Finally the mother brought out another aspect of the controversy as she repeated her idea of what should be done:

Mother: "I think that if my husband gave her a rough house, the same as I do, and let her see that he was hating it as much as I do, she would maybe understand it wasn't only her mother who is against this go-slow method, her father was against it, too. But he won't jog her on. Just—in fact he slows down his eating in order to, not to show her up, don't you?"

Father: "So you say."

Mother: "You know you do! He does, quite definitely! If he sees her going slow, then he slows down and it doesn't look so bad that he is still eating while she is still eating. While he could be finished long ago!"

Father: "That may have happened before, but it doesn't now."

Mother: "Not since last week!"

With no resolution of the difficulties in sight as the eighth interview ended, the therapist said to the mother and father:

Therapist: "The issue, as it has been sharpened, has revealed that the solution Mr. McAndrew sees, you see as a difficulty; and the solution that you see, Mr. McAndrew sees as a difficulty—and here is the problem."

The ninth interview brought the father-mother interaction to a conclusion. Father began this session by saying:

Father: "The latest development at dinnertime is that I dish out the dinners. She's been getting much smaller helpings and seems to be taking them all right."

Mother: "And I've just sort of more or less washed my hands of Jean at dinnertime. We told her when we went home last Tuesday evening we had a discussion. Then my husband told her that she was going to have last week and this week with this treatment, if that didn't do we might try something else. So we have certainly been all right. She has been nattering, on the other hand, about getting such small helpings, but by the time she is finished her dinner she is satisfied . . . if she asks anything about her dinner at all, I just refer her to her Dad, and take nothing to do with it. I can't say that it is easy for me to sit there and see what goes on at times."

Therapist: "You find it hard to accept what is being done?"

Mother: "Yes . . . it may do, but I think it is wrong that it should have to be. I think that it's my duty, my place, to dish up the dinners. It seems I didn't make such a good job of it. I suppose the important thing is that the meal is more peaceful."

Thereafter, the interview shifted to a new theme. At the end of the session there was a recapitulation of how the resolution of the father-mother interaction had occurred. Said the father:

Father: "We're certainly a lot more conscious of the problem now. We seem to be more on top of it. We're not baffled as we were before, definitely not."

Mother: "My husband and I had a long discussion last Tuesday night, and we sort of came to the conclusion that we had let each other have their way rather to keep peace between ourselves rather than trip each other up . . . But we are not in the habit of rowing with each other. We have had discussions on the matter many times and never got very far. But I think maybe if we had been a little bit more concerned with the treatment of the children, rather than preserving peace between ourselves, that things might have been different today. But I think that now we realize that, it is half the battle."

The fact that some of the father-mother interaction may take place outside the conferences indicates that the therapist does not normally take an especially active role at this period in the treatment. His participation continues to be needed to provide a balance of opportunities for each parent to express himself. Mostly, however, his participation is for the purpose of clarifying the statements made. In some other cases, he has become involved in an exploration of the possible causes for attitudes, feelings, ideas, and actions of one or both of the parents. Often this has led to some analysis of the childhood experiences of the parents. The development of insight by the parents has been facilitated by various interpretations. Such analysis is frequently aided by drawing out the opinions of the other members of the family as to the reasons why a parent acts as he does. This is helpful during the latter part of the father-mother phase, after the suppressed hostility between the parents has been partially expunged and an atmosphere conducive to revising the role stereotypes has been created.

Jean and Sandy in Interaction

Discussion of sibling relationships arises during treatment under three sets of circumstances:

1. Early in therapy when the child is beginning to attempt a more open expression of feeling, especially hostility, he may direct his remarks to siblings rather more than to parents. Usually this appears to be as much feeling diverted from the parents as feeling originating in the sibling give-and-take. It has the effect, on occasion, of drawing the parents into the sibling crossfire.

2. Sibling ties enter the discussion through parental complaint about strife between the siblings. This usually occurs in the parent-child interaction and sometimes initiates more direct complaint about a single child.

3. Sibling interaction tends to be explored during the latter part of the father-mother interaction and thereafter as a separate stage in the treatment.

In the first two sets of circumstances, discussion of sibling relationships seldom leads to more than the removal of some of the specific irritants provoking contention. In the third instance, the content of discussion is less inflammatory and feeling runs less high than in earlier periods. A greater rationality is present, and there appears to be less use of the discussion to jockey for parental favor. In some families the attitudes between the siblings expressed at this stage have appeared comparable to those expressed toward schoolmates or friends.

The discussion of friendships is often carried on simultaneously with discussion of siblings. Whereas the mention of ties or conflicts with those outside the family served as a mode of resistance at the beginning of therapy, it does not now impede the developing of increasing openness in family intercourse. There appears to develop a mutual participation in feelings about associations maintained by the children outside the family.

With the McAndrews, sibling interaction began in the ninth interview. It was scarcely a discussion of the relationships between Jean and Sandy so much as of the contrast between them. The father commented on how Jean goes along holding on to her likes and wishes, whereas Sandy realizes what is unattainable and gets rid of his wishes quickly. Jean amplified this statement:

Jean: "I can't bear to have them [wishes] just at the back of my mind. I can't put them at the back of my mind without at least concentrating on it all the time. When I try to put it at the back it immediately comes to the front."

This led the mother to review the contrasts in development between Jean and Sandy. Sandy had started life as a "difficult" baby and then become the "placid type"; whereas Jean had developed in reverse: she had started life an "angelic child" and then become difficult. While the mother was talking and illustrating these contrasts, Jean sat masturbating.

The therapist advanced the interpretation that Jean seemed to feel badly because she was a little girl. He pointed out her resemblance in this regard to her mother, who had intimated that she was jealous of her brothers—the favorites in her family, she felt.

Jean openly admitted her jealousy and gave two interesting insights into her playing the misbehaving role. In the first place she told how being "good" was like going back to being a baby, which she would half like to do so her Mum wouldn't be disappointed in her, but which she implied she did not intend to do. Second:

Jean: "I always wished to be a boy. And I suppose unconsciously.

I'm just doing it [misbehaving] for the sake that boys are supposed to be braver."

She elaborated her meaning:

Jean: "It is just that I might have thought that boys were supposed to be brave—all boys brave, you know. Heroes are all wee boys who have done something great. Well I feel that this might be—I don't think it is—but it just might be that I feel I want to be brave, doing something when I know I am going to get a punishment for it. I don't think it is possible but it just might be that."

After it was pointed out how common these feelings of jealousy are, Jean began to talk about some of the advantages to being a girl. For example, if she were a boy she would persist in her "great love for dressing up" and that would be "sissy."

Jean: "You don't get such nice wearings when you're a boy."

The feelings between Jean and Sandy were discussed more thoroughly in the tenth interview. Jean told in an amusing fashion of a little episode that later had troubled her and made her cry herself to sleep for weeks. Now, though, she could laugh about it, and she just "drifts off, right to sleep."

Jean: "It still seems an awful thing for me to do, but I did not quite realize the fright he'd get (laughing). I better explain to you what it is—you might be getting mystified about what it is. Well, I went upstairs to bed that night, and I wanted to talk to Sandy—well I wanted to give him a surprise. So I hid under his bed and Sandy comes in—and it's him I should be sorry for, the fright he got. When he was at the bed, over at the desk I mean, not so far away from the bed, he must have thought somebody was moving under the bed. And he called through, 'Jean, come here I think that there's . . .' apparently wondering if somebody was in his room. So I popped up at the other side of the bed, 'Yes? what were you going to say?' He said, 'Awhoooooooooo,' and started crying like anything, and Mum and Dad came rushing up the stairs. Oh, dear! he must have had an awful fright—he thought somebody was in his room—and it turns out to be me popping out of the other side of the bed."

Sandy: "It was not very long after we had moved house and this is a far bigger house and it has a ghostly atmosphere (much laughter). To me I just felt it was a burglar or something—"

Jean: "Well, maybe that's who!"

Sandy: "—coming to get me."

Jean: "Oh dear, it was really Sandy who should have been crying—about the fright he must have got. For about a week after that I was always looking under my bed to make sure he wasn't there."

Therapist: "Because you thought he might come in and do the same to you."

Jean: "Yes, he'd do the same to me."

At this, Sandy exposed his resentment of Jean's demands on him to play:

Sandy: "Maybe I have been playing with her for the greater part of the time that I am at home, and I think to myself, 'Well I've played with her enough—I should let myself have a little enjoyment for part of the day.' So I say to her, 'Och, I think I'll go away and play with my stamps'—you know I collect foreign stamps. And she says, 'Aw, och, why not play with me?' and she goes into the sulks. And if I go away as soon as I've said that, she breaks down and starts yelling and making a noise—just because I've gone away."

Jean, for her part, told of her resentment at being bossed:

Jean: "I dislike immensely Sandy saying 'Don't do this! Don't do this!' or 'Don't do that! You shouldn't do that, Mum wouldn't like it!' This gets me in a huff. He very seldom does it, but at times it just gets me down."

Then followed a discussion of the ways in which Sandy and Jean handled their mutual resentment. Sandy revealed his identification with his father:

Sandy: "Well I just sort of play with her for a wee while, and then she starts getting angry, then gradually I sidle out the door and carry on with what I was going to do. About 5 minutes later, after she has been playing herself, she realizes that I have gone and just carries on."

Jean, however, is impelled to fly into a temper and have a "tantrum."

Other differences between Sandy and Jean emerged; for example, the father brought out how Jean,. especially, seemed to need company:

Father: "You see apart from reading Jean can't amuse herself. She must have company, whereas Sandy can amuse himself many ways on his own, away in his own room, and never need anyone."

Sandy: "I think that's where the discontentment with Jean lies. It's just that she needs some company, and when I don't give her it she gets angry, because, I mean, she's got nothing to do. And she feels all wrong inside. Well she has got to give vent to these feelings somehow. She just lashes out, and I just have to take it or leave it."

The mother suggested the problem seemed to be that neither Sandy nor Jean seemed well able to make friends while it was really inappropriate to ask that they be companions for one another.

Mother: "This is where the difficulty in making friends comes in, because she shouldn't have to be dependent on Sandy for company. But you see neither of them makes friends very easily."

And reference to her own problems in making friends followed:

Mother: "There is this to it, this seems to be hereditary . . . This is just all history repeating itself."

Jean amplified the story of her difficulties in making friends by telling of her problems in the play yard at school. Skipping ropes was the current game there.

Jean: "Well at school now I'm shouting out 'First, second, third at ropes!' I shout out, 'Third!' and eventually have to go to the end. They say, 'You get to the end!' They wouldn't let me in. Just every game I go into I have just got to be the last, or I'm not playing. 'You either take your end for always, you take your end first, you go to the end, or you don't play at all.' That's with me anyway. I don't understand this."

And then she requested her mother's help:

Jean: "Maybe as you've got so many friends now, you can tell me how you got to know friends, and that might help me."

Mother admitted, however, that she didn't know how to help Jean in this regard, that she herself seemed to make a bad first impression on people:

Mother: "I never made the grade at school, I'm afraid . . . I have the unhappy knack of getting off on the wrong foot."

It was striking to contrast the tone of voice the mother was now using with the way she had sounded at the beginning of the sessions. Earlier she had spoken dogmatically, in a strident and aggressive tone; now her voice was quite gentle, and warm.

The topic of the children's friendships was taken up again in the final interview. Sandy's problem about friends was described. With him the difficulty was in the neighborhood rather than at school where he had sports and the chess club. Father's suggestion was that he and his wife should "push them out every night," and they would have to go and meet friends.

Father: "Because once they're in the house they just won't go out. They read the same books over and over again and potter around the place. I think the best thing we could do would be to push them out. Like—Sandy says that his friends are scattered all over the town —well, he can go and meet them. I used to be roughly in the same predicament: the boys about were—they were a wild lot. I didn't go out with them much. The friends that I had always stayed far away, and we used to meet half roads and go from there."

Jean reported that things were better now at school. During the preceding week her mother had bought her skipping ropes. Part of the schoolyard problem had been a difficulty with a classmate:

Jean: "Oh, well this girl, Mary Isobel, she has ropes—they're great big long ropes—they take up half the room in the playground, nearly. And of course all the girls flock to Mary Isobel with her ropes. I go up to a girl and ask, 'Do you want to play a game of ropes with me?' I ask her like that, and she goes away and plays with Mary Isobel. I mean they sometimes let me play and they sometimes don't . . . It makes me feel rotten to see everybody being pushed away just to get this one big, great big, long rope out—it's about as long as this room, almost, if not longer . . . Maybe I am getting a bit jealous of her. I don't like saying it, but—she's quite a nice girl—but she —everybody flocks to the person with ropes. When I bring them, though, they all want Mary Isobel. When there's a choice of Mary Isobel or me, it's always Mary Isobel.

"They say, 'I'll be your partner for always,' Uh-huh? A few days later, yes, days, they go away with somebody else and say, 'I'll be *your* partner for always' and they stick. I have never really got any partner that's really my partner for always."

With her mother's help, however, Jean had worked through to new attitudes and new plans about how to make friendships:

Jean: "I must admit, after all this bother, I realize there isn't much of a problem in not being happy every minute of your life. Now

I've got the skipping ropes, anyway, it isn't much of a problem. I can play on my own, as Mum advised me. If anybody plays I can sometimes say 'yes' and sometimes say 'no.' But now I can just play on my own—double the ropes up—because they are rather long ropes, quite long ropes.

"I was thinking also, you, Mum, said it would help me to speak more freely, to be a bit happier when I'm with somebody. Maybe it's because I speak as if I had been rehearsing it all, maybe that's why. I speak more difficultly than other people do when they make friends. Maybe that's why they don't want to make friends. I was thinking that may be why. You, Mum, suggested that."

The interview time was drawing to a close. All Jean's difficulties had not disappeared, but the tensions that had prevented her family from working to help her had been reduced. The whole family had evolved a technique for dealing with difficulties and a spirit within which they could be faced which seemed to indicate that termination would not prevent the flourishing of the family and of its individual members. The McAndrew family differed from other families treated by this method in that a limited time (11 weeks only) was available to the therapist for working with them. Termination was forced by this fact. While under different circumstances, one or two interviews more might have been held with the family, the characteristics that are to be expected in the terminal stages of the treatment were in evidence in the final two interviews. The family was given the choice of continuing with another worker or trying to carry on by itself. They chose the latter course.

By the time sibling interaction reaches the center of family discussions, the therapist's part in the conferences has become less active. The conventions about listening to others, which he began by imposing on the family to maintain balanced opportunities for each to speak, are now generally observed voluntarily. There is a more active effort on the part of each family member to empathize with the others and to seek an understanding of the behavior of the others. Often the family virtually ignores the therapist. Whereas in the earlier sessions it was common for all remarks to be directed toward him, now discussion centers within the family group. Even in seating itself at the beginning of an interview, the family tends to order itself so as to form a compact circle within which each member faces the other members of the family rather than the therapist. This, of course, symbolizes a hoped-for consequence of the treatment.

Terminal Phase

Usually the terminal period has been marked by the following:

Disappearance of many of the referral symptoms. Not all the symptoms disappear, since some of them have been reinterpreted by the parents and thus have lost their disturbing effect.

The appearance of laughter in the conferences. Frequently this laughter grows out of the parents' laughing at themselves.

The reporting of occasions during the week when the whole family worked together to solve a problem or engaged pleasurably in some mutual activity.

Acceptance by the family of the independent activities of each member and provision within family living for each person to follow his own interests without interference or—an even clearer indication—with the support of the others.

The child's volunteering to take on necessary chores for the family.

The spontaneous expression of the feeling that family life is going so well the conferences are no longer necessary. They say, "I guess we can manage ourselves without you."

Termination is not usually suggested to the family; rather the family is allowed to take the initiative in indicating that termination would seem to be appropriate. If, in addition, most of the behavior listed above has been observed, it is usually suggested that at least one further session be held, partly to clear up any other difficulties that it might seem best to talk out within the treatment conferences. The scheduling of another session is also a precaution in case what has occurred is a premature appearance of the resolution of difficulties, such as occurred at the seventh interview with the McAndrews. If the next session continues to present the characteristics noted above and the family's wish to terminate also continues, the therapist begins to carry out his final task in treatment.

He seeks to accomplish two major purposes at this time. One is to recapitulate what has taken place by summarizing some of the features of the treatment. The other is to discuss future steps for the family.

What has been done in the treatment is reviewed primarily to support the family's conviction that it can now solve its problems independently of the therapist. Thus those aspects of the therapy method for which responsibility has been taken up by the family are stressed, sometimes in relation to the difficulties the family has overcome.

The family's own conception of what has happened in the therapy may be integrated with the therapist's review. With the McAndrews, for instance, the subject was introduced by the father. The therapist first talked about termination of the therapy in the tenth session. Mr. McAndrew opened the next session with the following comment on the treatment:

Father: "We were talking it over and we can't just put our fingers on anything, anything concrete, but there's a big difference, I mean, in our outlook and the way things are going.   I mean also the fact we've never had anything, any definite opinions from you yet, and yet there has been a great difference."

The therapist picked this up as support for the family's independence:

Therapist: "This is one of the things that encourages me that you can carry on on your own. Because it hasn't been that I have done this."

Mother: "No, we know that."

Father: "You wouldn't give us any advice, and we can't point to anything definite that was told us or suggested."

Therapist: "No, I have deliberately avoided making suggestions."

Father: "Yes, we saw that."

Therapist: "And giving advice, because the usual experience is that it is not very helpful. People try it out and usually it doesn't answer enough of the problem."

Father: "And when it doesn't, you lose faith."

Therapist: "Right. And you've worked this out yourselves, you see. You talked about it, you expressed views to one another, you've thought about the ways in which you can deal with the issues that you have brought up, you have searched your own hearts and minds. And whatever change has taken place is a change that the family has made."

Mother: "But I don't think we could have done it without a chairman (giggles)."

Therapist: "No, I think that's true. I think it is better to have somebody from the outside to start you thinking in terms of the family as being that which needs the help, and the solution as involving the whole family and everybody bringing in their ideas."

Mother: "It would certainly never have occurred to us to sit down for an hour each week and talk openly and frankly and try to analyze it all ourselves. And then, of course, you have been able to put, shall we say, questions that have led our thought into different channels, probably things we'd never have thought about ourselves. And I think that a big solution has been the dinner question."

Father: (later) "I think if we had attempted any roundtable conference without an impartial chairman it would just have developed into a sort of scoring points off each other. I think that's the root of the trouble."

This led naturally into discussion of steps the family could take after the treatment phase ended. The most common procedure is informal continuation of talking difficulties through as a whole family. The therapist said to the father, and to the family:

Therapist: "Yes, it's very hard to do it oneself, but it can be done, though, and it doesn't need necessarily to be done in a formal way by all sitting around a table. But this sometimes helps, because it serves as a kind of control over what you are doing when you set it up like that, like a committee meeting. But I know that in other families with whom I have worked they have gone on having sessions, maybe just brief sessions when things have come up that they think should be talked through in the whole family."

Back in the seventh interview, Jean had proposed meetings of the whole family, and had tried to solve the problem of a suitable meeting time. She now reminded the family that they had not met:

Jean: "Well, so far we haven't had one meeting, have we, Dad? I suppose you'd call it 'the committee meeting.' And, oh, well there were one or two things that I would have liked to bring up again—but I mean they're silly things when I come to think of it—any time we could have a meeting. As a matter of fact, there is hardly any time you can have such a meeting—either it's inconvenient, or it's not much use as you [therapist] are still here."

Mother: "Or Dad is filling up his coupons (laughter)."

Sandy: "We'll never get out of that one (more laughter). Mum's been nagging on at him about them."

A little later, Jean elaborated on a procedure that she thought might be used:

Jean: "What about the idea of carrying a slip of paper and a pencil about with you, wherever you go. And whenever you find something you're really not too keen on, some person, or something you would like someone to do and they flatly refuse to do it, you know, in the family or something, and you just write it down on a wee slip of paper. And bring it to the meeting if we're having one, and show it up, and read out all the things you've—maybe we'll have a head, maybe Dad or Mum. He decides what we're going to do about it, and then . . ."

In his final remarks to the family, it is always desirable for the therapist to mention the possibility that treatment may need to be resumed and the procedures to be followed in that event. In the case of the McAndrews, where termination of treatment was precipitated, more than mere mention of the subject was necessary. Accordingly, another worker at the clinic arranged to hold herself available for continuing family conferences with the McAndrews, as needed. With other families, return to work with the therapist has been feasible, but it has seldom been requested even though questions about the need for further help and offers of additional sessions have been presented in followup contacts.

The McAndrews did not choose to return to the clinic in the fall. Their problems had been worked through to the extent that they did not feel a need to resume treatment.

In the summer of 1955, the therapist's last sight of the McAndrews was as he watched them leave the clinic. Sandy and Jean raced ahead, laughing and chatting with one another. Father and Mother followed, her arm linked in his. She was wearing a white hat, newly purchased for the second conference, worn at the seventh, and reappearing for this, the final session.

Five years later the therapist had the privilege of inviting the family to come to the clinic for a followup interview. The members of the family had not visited the clinic during the intervening years, nor had they sought help elsewhere.

A number of changes in family circumstances had taken place in the interim. The father had left his previous employment and in partnership with another had set up a business which had improved the family's economic status. The mother continued to work but had found a more remunerative position as bookkeeper with a wholesale grocery firm. Sandy had graduated from the private high school which he was attending and, with some urging from his mother, had become attached to a firm of accountants. He was enrolled in night courses to help him prepare for examinations aimed at the profession of accounting. He was living at home, meanwhile, pursuing the hobbies of reading and making trinket boxes.

Jean was specializing in English literature and composition in an academic high school for girls, preparing for a career in journalism. Already at the age of 14 she had received payment for a story in one of the city's newspapers. The verbalism that had concerned the mother when she first came to the clinic was now manifested in writing rather than in speech, a transformation most acceptable to the mother and, apparently, to Jean also. Jean gave the impression of quietness, modesty, and hesitancy in speaking; occasionally, though, as the opportunity was given her, she spoke out with the eagerness, wit, and vividness of expression that had characterized her speech when she was 9.

The mother echoed some of her old complaints about Jean's irresponsibility, and generalized them to apply to all the other members of the family except herself. Nobody seemed especially distressed by the mother's critical remarks. The fact that Jean would not pick up her room and would forget an assignment when she was sent to do some job was dealt with as a foible that was annoying but also an opportunity for some joking and good humor.

While few details of the previous conferences remained in the memory of the family members, they recalled the overall changes in the tone of their family living that had taken place at the time of the therapy. Some of the changes had persisted, and all agreed the family was well able to cope with its present situation.

Task of the Therapist

At present, little is known of the meaning of the therapist to the family he treats. The pragmatic test of his work is change which the family considers advantageous, but this end result does not tell us how the family perceives the therapist, nor what specifically accomplishes the modifications that occur.

It is possible, however, for the therapist to describe aspects of his role and functions as he sees them. This chapter summarizes the procedures by which he engages the family in change and development.

STRUCTURE OF THE CONFERENCES

The therapist arranges the form of the conferences, their setting, the group composition, and the time. In detail, he shapes the conferences as follows:

First, he determines the setting where the conferences will take place. The room, the furnishings, especially the seats and table, seem to be important in establishing the tone for the discussions. A setting that is very informal seems to encourage spontaneity but also triviality; one that is too rigid seems to reduce the capacities for interaction.

I have preferred to have the family seated with me around a table (approximately 3 by 5 feet) and have always set out one chair more than is needed for all who are to be present. This has permitted family members some choice as to how they seat themselves and even the opportunity to move during a conference if they wish. The children change seats not infrequently, often providing important information about the family thereby. The 3-by-5-foot table puts some distance between the participants and yet is small enough to permit ease of communication.

This seating arrangement also helps reduce the authority of the therapist, who is not different in his relation to the table from any other member of the group. This seems to control somewhat the tendency of the family to look to the therapist for advice, directions, criticism, and pronouncements, which tend to be sought more frequently if the therapist is seated at a desk with the family around him.

Second, the therapist participates in deciding the composition of the group who will attend the conferences. This is a minor matter when the family consists of the parents and older children, with no other relatives or outsiders living in the home. When children under 9 years of age, or collateral relatives such as grandparents, aunts or uncles, or even nonrelated individuals such as a friend or housekeeper form part of the family unit, the therapist explores the nature of their relationship and the suitability of including them in the conference group. With younger children he may help in making plans for leaving them at home and possibly in explaining to them what the rest of the family is doing and why. When other individuals reside in the home, the nature of their participation in family life and the merits and liabilities of including them in family conferences need to be studied.

This analysis and structuring of the conference group is not necessarily completed by the time therapy begins. Enlargement of the group may be required as the treatment progresses, although adding individuals to the group is a delicate transaction and may disrupt the therapy for a long period or completely. Thus adding other participants after the group has met several times should only be undertaken when the need is imperative.

The maintenance of participation by all the family members originally scheduled for the conferences (except in those circumstances where an individual is no longer living at home with the family) must be directed by the therapist. Keeping the group together and preventing its splintering into subgroups is essential to therapeutic progress.

The therapist's part in planning when the conferences will be held and working through scheduling problems is discussed in some detail in the section on the first conference. Here we need only restate the importance to the central purpose and to the progress of treatment of the therapist's maintaining an attitude of pleasant but firm expectation that both parents will find the time to be present at conferences.

THE THERAPIST'S RELATIONSHIPS

The second major role assumed by the therapist is that of structuring his own participation and orienting the family to the ways he will and will not relate to it. He conveys this information in words and by his demeanor, both at the beginning and during the course of treatment. Summarizing from the earlier discussion of treatment technique, the therapist has certain basic functions to perform for the group.

He seeks to facilitate communication. He is interested and alert to what is said, verbally or nonvocally, and to the listening, understanding, and responding of those who hear. When he suspects a breakdown in communication, he assumes responsibility for attempting, with the family, to discover if this is true and, if so, why it has happened. [9]

He supports those who indicate, one way or another, that they are having difficulty in participating to the extent or in the fashion they wish. He helps them to explore their relationships, to express their thoughts and feelings, and to restructure their roles. Because this support is crucial in family therapy, I shall discuss techniques for providing it in a separate section to follow.

He remains outside the problem-solving and decision processes of the family for the most part. He does not give advice or impose particular solutions of problems. In essence, he keeps telling the family that control of its life outside the conference is its own business. He does not hesitate, however, to assert authority over the conduct of the conferences, for this is his domain—the aspect of treatment for which he is clearly responsible.

He permits the expression of ideas and feelings that have been restricted from direct utterance within the family group. This relates especially to hostile feelings that must be given voice. It is true, as well, that he may need to sanction the disclosure of feelings of love, protection, anxiety, fear, hope, and a broad range of fantasies and ideas in order to help the family free itself from communication restraints.

He helps to interpret what is being said in order to extend group understanding and the interrelationships in the family. The aim of interpretation is to build the family group as a group by facilitating group processes, not to build the relationships of individuals to the therapist, nor to assist the individual in understanding and resolving his own problems as an individual.

As in other forms of therapy, the therapist evaluates his own personal needs and problems in relation to his work in the sessions. He strives to keep the conferences oriented toward working on the family's difficulties rather than on his own, although he will notice many times that families are working on problems like his own in which he has a heightened personal involvement. His own human qualities and his own membership in a family may be problems, but they are also props. Again as in all therapy, some of his personal qualities will affect his relationship to the family and will determine those areas where he will be most (and least) likely to succeed in his work with them. The family may be curious about the therapist and may attempt to involve him in discussion he would not choose to initiate. He must decide in each case how he wishes to handle such efforts, which often come from the children, but in some instances are made by one member acting, recognizably, as spokesman for the whole family.

SUPPORT

The supporting position that the therapist adopts in relation to individuals (in the context of the group) and to the group as a whole deserves special attention. In essence, support is tendered as a means toward interlinking its members in a group where they are accessible to one another and, through mutual accessibility, able to act as a group choosing optimal directions for itself. Support is a central aspect of the therapist's manner of relating to the group from the very beginning. In his orientation of the parents he asserts he will undertake to help the family as a whole, and in his first approach to the children he upholds their position by turning attention to them and keeping the parents in the background.

Some of the tehniques for providing support are as follows:

The therapist creates openings, when they might not otherwise occur, for individuals to speak, to reply, to answer accusations, to present facts and interpretations of experiences from the individual's own perspective, to correct misinterpretations, and to enter the discussion.

He helps the individual to put ideas, wishes, decisions, and feelings into words. He may try to do this by rephrasing what has been said. He may direct the attention of an individual and the group to gesture, posture, and other subverbal expression. He may help translate subvocal into verbal expression by structuring an opportunity for an individual to speak, by drawing the attention of the rest of the group to individual behavior which they may be able to understand.

Special help to verbalize is required in the case of children who, at the beginning, insist on active motor response to the conference situation instead of showing the more common need to sit quietly, waiting to be drawn out. Some children are so active that conference procedure is impossible at the start. This problem must be dealt with, for there must be acceptance of the verbal nature of the conferences by all members of the family before the kinds of procedures used in the McAndrew case are appropriate. In the special approach that has worked best, the therapist:

Helps the parents to impose restrictions on the child's activity for the period of the conference;

Helps the parents to make the child understand that all are present for the purpose of talking about the family situation;

Prevents the parents from asserting their authority except in control of the child's motor activity during the session;

Refrains from imposing controls himself so that he will not seem to the family to be taking over a parental role;

Supports the child when he does verbalize in order to help reduce the child's anxiety about the consequences of talking.

It should not be assumed that it is easy to accomplish this series of maneuvers. It is so difficult, in fact, that beginners in family therapy probably should select cases involving inhibited children in preference to children who act out. Later, the family with an overactive child or with a child whose characteristic self-expression is motor rather than verbal will seem less complex and laborious.

The therapist seeks to counteract blockages in verbal communication. He watches for signs of withdrawal from active participation, for evidences of inhibition that prevent the individual from speaking in spite of internal or external pressures to do so, for seeming irrelevancies, distortions, circumstantiality, ellipsis, or for sudden redirection of the discussion.

Faced with evidences of blockage, the therapist can choose from a variety of supportive measures that help to overcome the difficulty. He may, for example, interrupt the discussion to suggest that it might be valuable to hear from an individual. He may initiate discussion of the blockage as a problem and help the individual and the group to handle the situation. He may reorient the group to the therapist's role as a supporter and assure individuals of the availability of his help. He may redefine the task of the family and, through stressing the importance of equal opportunity to speak, alter the tone of the conference. On some rare occasions he may encourage the circumstances that are building tension in an individual—for example, another family member's attack—so that the pressure to speak will build to the point of explosion.

In addition, the therapist provides support through several forms of interpretation. In general, his interpretation constitutes commentary on the interactions occurring during conferences. Depth interpretation of intra-psychic events, common in individual therapy, is rarely used. Useful modes of interpretation in family group therapy may be classed under four headings that are not mutually exclusive.

1. The reflective.   The therapist verbalizes his observations on the current state of family affairs and especially on the immediate occurrences in conferences. He engages in this interpretation to mirror the activities he sees, not expressly by way of criticism, although his comments take the form of judgments at times. More typically, he tells the family how what it is doing and its manner of doing it appear to him; in a sense he confronts it with aspects of its own functioning. Thus he intensifies and extends the awareness of itself as a functioning unit that is provided the family by the conference situation in general. Reflective interpretation is not required, then, except when it appears a desirable supplement.

2. The connective.[10]   The therapist makes statements which point out unrecognized links between acts, events, attitudes, and experiences. Such bonds may appear in the ways *sequences* of events

present themselves. Links may be observed in *reciprocal* behavior between members of the family—role matched with role, feeling touching feeling, conception meeting conception. Interrelations may be *causal,* and theories may be developed for the family about the intercommunication between causal and consequential actions, which are special cases of sequential relationships.

The particular function of interpretations making these invisible, inaudible connections conscious and public is to expand the information available to the family as a base for its operations. Through interpretation, the therapist supplements the other methods by which the family increases its knowledge and thereby its scope of action. He does not interpose connective interpretations except when the family shows that it has not recognized existing relationships, is unlikely to do so, and clearly needs such knowledge. [11]

3. The reconstructive. In this type of interpretation, the therapist recalls the history of the family, its relationships, and its peculiar ways of reacting. The reconstituted past provides a context for the present. Historical interpretation, especially of a speculative, theory-based nature, may produce new facts, memories, and ideas about the family. Reconstructive interpretation is therapeutically useful to the family primarily for its present and future reference —for its contribution to action now and later rather than its interest as an intellectual exercise. Thus the criteria for using and evaluating this technique must be related to immediate and potential goals for action rather than to historical and intellectual aims, important as the latter may be in research.

4. The normative. The therapist comments on parallel or contrasting relationships, or on behavior observable in other families. This is a form of interpretation to be used sparingly because such statements are usually received by the family as instructions or expectations for them. Interpretations of this type have been used in family therapy primarily to help overcome blocks. To illustrate, at the first conference where all the McAndrews were assembled, the therapist.implied common ground between Sandy and Jean and "most boys and girls that I've known before" in order to encourage the children to speak up. He was informing them that their participation would receive his sanction and support. Another use of norms, to relieve guilt and support an individual in speaking freely and emo-

tionally, occurred when the therapist commented to Jean on the relationship between girls and their mothers in "most families" (page 48).

The final method of support used by the therapist relates to the termination of the treatment. In response to expressed indications that the family is beginning to believe termination is possible and desirable, the therapist can assist in a number of ways:

Help the family evaluate its readiness for termination.

Interpret anxiety over termination.

Support the desire of an individual, or of the group, for termination.

Reassure the family about changes that have taken place by a review of the differences he has observed in the group since the conferences began.

Discuss the possible need for followup therapy and work out arrangements for it. He may suggest signs by which a family could recognize its need for additional treatment and even the arrangements that could be worked out for resumption of treatment.

These are the methods of support that have evolved so far from efforts to break down the isolation of individuals in the family and to facilitate group interrelationships. Probably many more technical approaches could be identified. As they become known and communicable, family group therapy will overcome much of its present dependence on trial and error and move toward control by efficient application of formulated rules.

Nature of the Therapy

The therapeutic processes occurring in family group therapy are sufficiently complex as to be capable of explanation in a variety of ways, but explanations can only be suggested as yet. While the ideas presented here have grown out of considerable thought about what takes place in the treatment, their statement is intentionally informal, and they have not been tested experimentally. That it has been possible both to develop technical procedures and to predict successfully the behavior manifested at various stages of therapy indicates the therapeutic process follows a certain order, however, and antici-pates a more accurate and detailed conceptualization of what occurs in family therapy.

It might have been possible to discuss the events occurring in family therapy within the reference framework of current psychotherapeutic theory. The psychoanalytic theory, for instance, which has been so fruitful for individual therapy, might have formed a useful starting point for the analysis. Inevitably the ideas of psychoanalysis have contributed to my understanding of what takes place in the treatment and, to an extent probably beyond my knowl-edge, have shaped my observations and interpretations of the per-sonalities in the families with which I have worked. And it could quite reasonably be assumed that since psychoanalysis has concerned itself so forcibly with parent-child relationships, its theory might be applied directly to family group therapy.

I tried applying psychoanalytic theory, but I found that its ideas and the interpretations to which they led lacked relevance for some of the behavior that was the special concern of family treatment. The unit of study here is different from that of individual therapy in other respects than the obvious one of focus on more than one person. In family group therapy the primary data to analyze relate to the interac-tions among the members of the family. In individual therapy one turns his attention more to the symbolic evidence of intrapsychic events. One might simultaneously analyze an individual's behavior from two points of view, of course, but what one would say of the behavior under these two modes of analysis might be quite different. But in family therapy we are not so much concerned with family members as individuals. By conscious intent we think of the family as an organic whole, individuals taking on their definition only as struc-tural parts of the family field.

Some of the consequences of this rule of thought comprise the theory of family therapy as I have developed it. Here I advance some of the products of my effort to analyze family processes, particularly those that occur in this therapy.

If the family is regarded as a unit, the status of the family might be regarded as the consequence of the balance of forces,[12] and the processes of change as the consequences of the redistribution of forces, within the group. We would take the point of view that the behavior of a child that disturbs his parents sufficiently to make them seek help is at the same time the product of pressure upon the child from the total family, of which the parents are significant parts. We may ask, of course, what pressures the child reacts to in his functioning as he does. But it is not inappropriate, also, to ask what purposes the disturbing behavior of the child is serving for the parents. We should be able to trace a complex interweaving of forces throughout the whole family, one consequence of which would be the disturbances in the child.

It should also be admissible to question the nature of the impact of the child's disturbing behavior upon the parents' functioning. If we regard the family as a unit, it is as justifiable to consider what the child does to the parents as it is to consider what the parents do to the child. Because psychoanalysis has emphasized the importance of early childhood and its genetic processes in personality formation, there has grown up a tendency to ask about the nature of the parent in relation to the child, to single out the more significant influences of the parent on the child that occur at particular stages of child development, and to evaluate the parents in terms of certain value systems that have been implicit in or the product of such conceptions as the oral and anal phases of development or the Oedipus complex. Thus the evaluation is made from the standpoint of the child, as though the interpreter were looking at the parents through the child's eyes.

In family group therapy it is not possible to empathize with a child to the extent of evaluating the parents only from his perspective. To do so would lead to thinking of the parent primarily in terms of his contribution to his child's pathology. It is not hard to see how parents would be offended at being reminded that the sins of the fathers are visited upon the children. In family therapy we have to think, also, that the sins of the children are visited on the parents.

Here again, however, we may have to challenge convention and cease to think of the family as dichotomized into parents and children. We need not think of opposing segments within a family, although we may in our minds see each individual in relation to the compact of forces from all the rest of the family. We may as readily visualize the family as a system of pushes and pulls as delicately balanced as the forces within the individual organism.

An illustration may clarify this point of view. A family consisting of a father, mother, 14-year-old girl, and 11-year-old boy came for treatment because of the destructive and antisocial behavior of the boy, who had been brought into juvenile court for vandalism at school. His offenses may be thought of as the acting out of his mother's deep resentment against the people in the New England village where they lived. The mother nursed an old wound: she assumed that the villagers would not accept her because everyone thought she profaned the memory of her minister father by not postponing her wedding when her father died a week before the scheduled date.

Because her boy was so troublesome in the community and at school, the mother took on the role of peacemaker and "fixer." Meanwhile, in unverbalized anger against her husband she took over more and more of the major responsibilities she had expected and really wanted him to perform. This drove the husband out of the home to bars and alcoholism, or when he was at home, to sullenness and almost too vigorous nonparticipation.

The only one who could rouse the father from his dullness was the daughter, who with an equal sullenness managed a kind of wordless communication with him. The mother raged toward the daughter, who in turn boiled with indignation at her brother for bringing disgrace on her in the eyes of all her school friends, an accusation that promoted rather than diminished his delinquencies.

The embeddedness of each member of the family in the life of each other was exposed by the way a seemingly minor incident that disturbed any member would reverberate through the whole family, producing mother's aggressive efforts toward rectitude or anger against her daughter, father's drunkenness, the girl's vituperation against her brother, and the boy's delinquency. It did not matter with whom it started, the family circle would spin out its violence.

But here we are concerned with problems rather than the processes in family life as a whole. By the same reasoning about the unity of the family, we can see that the processes leading to positive growth permeate the family in a similar way. This seems to explain why dramatic changes in the whole family can follow so brief an exercise in communication as a few group conferences. Within the family, phenomenal change like that characteristic of religious conversion can occur with great rapidity and with seemingly enduring results.

In the family cited above, within 2 months after family therapy was initiated, the father stopped drinking, took over the direction of the boy's schooling, began to talk to the rest of the family at supper, and in many ways gave evidence of having acquired a new status in the family and in the community. But equally rapid change was accomplished in all—the mother discovered with surprise that she was free from her obsessive preoccupation with the neighbors' attitudes to her. She began to get up to cook breakfast for the children for the first time in years, and she embarked on a plan for securing part-time work. The boy's destructiveness diminished; he brought home an acceptable report card for the first time in 3 years. The girl was sought out as a friend by a schoolmate, and she had her first date in a new dress her mother made for her. The conferences may be said to have freed the family from the circuit of its own malignancy and to have released the forces that could help support the efforts to grow of each individual and of the family as a whole.

How is such a change possible? If we regard the disturbed individual as one trapped in the necessity to repeat the stereotyped defensive maneuvers he learned in early childhood, it is hard to conceive how the changes that take place can be interpreted as other than the substitution of one symptom for another. Some might argue that this is so. It might provide a more apposite explanation to suggest that the developmental process in personality is of much greater complexity and of much longer duration than is implied in much current psychological theory; also, that the sensitivity of the person to his situation continues to determine his responses in a substantial way through much of life. The latter point should seem trite, since it accords so with our everyday experience, and yet in personality theory many have moved toward minimizing this point of view —toward speaking of internal structure rather than of situational responsivity. If we study what makes pathological symptoms and generalize therefrom to the whole of behavior, it is understandable that we may arrive at these narrower interpretations. If we study a fuller range of human behavior, seeking to understand the personally and socially valued accomplishments of man as well as his illnesses, we are directed toward greater awareness of his impressibility.

But, some may argue, is this not an unrealistically optimistic view? The evidence from family group therapy would argue that it is not. The treatment has appeared to be effective with a wide range of cases. I do not wish to appear overoptimistic about the value of this therapy. I would urge adequate experimentation to discover the limits of its suitability. On the other hand, the evidence that has already accumulated as to the feasibility, effectiveness, and range of the treatment is not to be underestimated. The point that I wish to stress most of all, however, is that in family treatment, the individual seems more keenly susceptible to influence and more capable of change than the person in individual therapy. This applies as much to the parents as to the children.

Next, how can we explain this greater capacity for change? For one thing the family is one of the most meaningful of all social groups for the majority of people; some would say it is the most meaningful. It provides the anchoring point for many extrafamilial events. It is so valued that what contributes to family welfare is especially prized; what destroys it, shunned. The motivation toward family stability and achievement is potent.

Evaluating events in terms of how they establish or perpetuate family well-being is a common and significant pattern of thought. To parents, at least, family therapy seems only an extension of their everyday efforts toward a well-recognized goal. Further, there is a conviction among parents that their goal is shared and their efforts supported by the therapist. Parents have commented spontaneously on how natural and sensible it appears to keep the family together in an attempt to solve its problems.

When the members of a family begin to communicate with each other about what troubles them in the family, the impetus to rectify the difficulties is already present. They are continuing a willingness to make strenuous efforts to change and to remove threats to the family. It would appear that family welfare is for many a stronger motivation than personal gain; at least the effort expended is less complicated by guilt. Thus family group therapy exploits a most forceful motivation.

Family group therapy also provides new ways of thinking about the members of the family and the relationships between them. The treatment depends on verbalization and should result in an extension of communication within the family in both the quantitative and the qualitative sense. The scope of family discussion can be enlarged; the meaning of habitual language can be clarified. Consequently, new ways of thinking about the family—and thence, we assume, new ways of acting—can follow. [13]

Some of the family's conceptions that may be revised in the process of treatment include:

The Nature of the Disturbance and Its Cause.   At the time of seeking professional help, parents have normally reached the limit of their private efforts to understand why their children are disturbed. They may actually have reached correct insights about their children, but failing to contrive a change in a child's disturbing behavior may have destroyed their confidence in their ability to understand. As parents and children talk over their problems, the children put into words their pictures of the disturbing behavior and its meaning, the parents express their ideas of it, and the mystery is reduced. In a way this behavior becomes an object placed between the parent and the child, a thing to be examined, puzzled about, discussed, and interpreted rather than a matter inducing vehemence and personal blame.

Responsibility for the Disturbance.   Blame that has been projected onto others meets blame thrown back on the projector in the give-and-take of family therapy. But rather than accentuating guilt, this has the effect of diminishing it, for guilt is given limits in the discussion and is shared. Especially is the parent's guilt reduced. Parents have been indoctrinated so thoroughly with the idea that they are the primary cause of all children's behavior problems that they feel they must blame themselves, outwardly, at least. But privately they may harbor an accusing attitude toward the children. Family therapy brings both the guilt and the accusations into the open where they can meet the test of reality. Parents discover, too, that the children are in a sense responsible for their own behavior, that children are aware of much that they do, are able to describe their motives, and are consciously willing a good deal of what causes their parents' disquiet.

Responsibility for Change.   At the beginning of family group conferences, the demand is almost universally made that others in the group change for the better. A parent wants his mate or the children to change; the children demand that the parents or the siblings behave differently. The responsibility to modify oneself is disregarded, or not even recognized. Later, change comes to be understood as a mutual responsibility: improvement becomes everybody's business —the business of the whole family.

Possibility for Change.   Many parents, and children too, begin treatment apparently hopeless about the chances for improvement. At least in the more serious cases, stereotyped attitudes of discouragement, resignation, or indignant disgust can become so fixed as to freeze the family in the status quo: change is impossible even to visualize. Frequently, in such cases, when the most minor shift in family status takes place in the course of the therapy, the family interprets it as a conspicuous sign that change may be possible after all, with the result that confidence and hope are restored.

Evaluation of the Family's Current Status.   Not only may the future be uncertain, but the present is often misjudged in the face of disorder. For example, there are often obstructions in the way of recognizing the positive aspects of the family's life, especially the positive side of the children's misbehavior. This is not the result, necessarily, of a simple inability to comprehend. There may be an emotional block to perceiving the whole condition of the family and of the role of each in the group, which is removed as feeling is discharged and events are talked into perspective.

Evaluation of Individual Status in the Group.   Where development takes place as rapidly as it does in childhood and adolescence, room has to be made for a constant revision of how the individual sees himself, how others see him, and how he sees others. These views are interdependent. A mother like Mrs. McAndrew, for instance, who described Jean at age 9 in almost the same terms that she had used to describe Jean at age 6, has lost touch with actuality and has imposed a rigid conception of the child on the child. Such a lack of flexibility is damaging to both mother and child.

We have little systematic knowledge of how stereotyping of roles affects family life, especially with adolescents, but we have seen many signs in family therapy that labeling takes place and is disturbing to the individuals to whom it is applied. To feel trapped in an unchanging role thwarts the initiative to change, especially when such roles appear to be generated by the need of others to impose them. Any person might say of his family that it does not understand him, but those who have developed symptomatic misbehavior have special cause for complaint: in addition to the lack of understanding, they must face also the failure of mechanisms that might lead to understanding. The growing directness of communication in family therapy leads to straighter thinking about oneself and others and to operations that can revise the concepts when change is necessary.

Goals, Values, and Procedures for Attaining Them. It has impressed me that perhaps one of the reasons why change takes place is as obvious a fact as that the members of the family make one another aware that change is desirable. Almost always the comment will be made somewhere along the way, "If I'd only known, we could have done that a long time ago." Or, "I didn't realize this was so important to you."

While there may be a deep resistance to changing some features of a family's life, about many there is no problem. The only barrier to change has been the failure to clarify goals and the procedures for attaining them. This seems to be true of many of the children's demands. It looks as though parents do not hear the requests, and the child, having been rebuffed, gives up asking. The seriousness of the child's wishes is probably more respected when he has the support of the therapist in expressing them. But the obverse is also true. Sometimes when children do not take the demands of their parents as seriously as the parents would like, the parents attribute to the child a resistance that is not necessarily there and go on to make more of an issue of their demand on the child than at first they had intended. Clarifying the nature and value of the demand and separating it from counter pressures against assumed resistance often lead the child to respond readily to the demand. At times the relations between the members of the family are needlessly complicated and may be simplified in the process of talking things through.

Having spoken of how family group therapy uses the impressibility of the person, the family's motivation for improvement, and the opportunity for clarification of ideas, we have not by any means explained more than a portion of what takes place in the treatment. Nor can we go further at this juncture. Little is known, for instance, about how various individuals in families perceive the therapist and what aspects of his role, his functions, and his personality affect them. This is why it is impossible to set forth the criteria by which a person might be judged suitable to conduct this form of treatment.

While reacting favorably to the idea, many professional workers in psychiatry, social work, and clinical psychology with whom this approach has been discussed have expressed anxiety at the thought of undertaking this form of treatment, even under supervision. Yet the technical skills would not seem more difficult to master than those required in other forms of treatment.

It may be that the thought of the emotional outbreaks that would take place within the family during the treatment promotes anxiety in the potential worker. There are occasions when the intensity of feeling within the family rises to flood proportions, but in all cases where this has happened the family itself has been able to control the feeling. The formal arrangements of the therapy conference, the sitting around the table, the balancing of opportunities to speak, the constant presence of an outsider, the time limits on the session—all aid in establishing the confidence that even though feeling is released it can be checked at the necessary time. Often it is a member of the family who reorders the direction of the session when excitement approaches hysteria, as when an 11-year-old boy casually commented in the thick of a raging contest with his mother, "But, Mummy, you know I love you!"

After all, here may be the secret of family group therapy: no matter how chaotic the family life, the treatment confirms that each of the parents and each of the children is an integral and meaningful part of the group at the center of life, the family.

Chapter III

An Array of Techniques[1]

Developing a Mind-Set

BEGINNING WHERE YOU ARE

How Do You Think of Family?   I had worked for many years in child guidance clinics, primarily from a psychoanalytic, personality theory approach. After my own analysis and from the long years of working in child guidance settings, my orientation was to the individual child and to the impact that parents had on him in the developmental process. When I thought of family in those days, I tended to think about an individual child, with a family in the background having an indirect or a direct influence. The individual was at the center and the other members of the family served as a kind of stage setting, an environment, for the individual in whom we were primarily interested. Further, I thought of the child as a product of the ways in which the parents had dealt with him and of the ways in which the rivalry of siblings twisted, turned, and oriented the child's development.

Fears and Perplexities. I started to work with families with some fear. In the back of my mind I was anxious because I had many uncertainties about what the effect might be, especially on the child. I thought, for example, that maybe exposing the child to things the parents might say or do would precipitate an emotional crisis that would disturb the child more than helping him. A number of questions, unanswerable at that time, presented themselves. Would fathers come to the sessions or not, because my experience in the child guidance setting had led me to expect that mothers would be involved, but to limited optimism about the possibility of involving fathers? Then I began to anticipate all the complications that might exist in the multiple transference situation where I would be trying to relate to the father, the mother and maybe a series of children. Then I became alarmed at possible counter-transference problems that might exist through my own emotional involvement with all these separate individuals. I found myself worrying especially about my possible relationships with fathers, whom I had not seen frequently in my work with children; what if they just sat there or in other ways created perplexity in me about what to do.

Would the discussion rock the boat as far as the family is concerned? Would the children be upset rather than relieved by these discussions of parental problems? Might I be precipitating some pathology in the children thereby? Could I handle the emotional stresses that might come up in dealing with the whole family? Might they get so hostile or so explosive that I could really be accused of disrupting the family processes?

Values in Mind. There were other complications as I approached the idea. I had committed myself in value-orientation toward work with children, to the position that independence from the family was a more important goal than integrating the child into the family. Thus, strengthening the child to be free of the family was more basic than helping to develop his harmonious relationships within the family. I was accustomed to thinking of parents as negative influences on the child, and that they created pathology. I found in myself a bias against the parents, on general principle, except when they chose to undergo individual psychotherapy themselves. Then, also, I found in myself some anxiety about the fact that maybe we could not change the parents very much. I believed that the basic patterns were set during the early years of the developmental process and that the older a person gets, the more rigid he becomes and the less responsive to influences that might change him. So, while we might be able to bring about some effective changes in a child, the outlook for the parents was not really favorable in any case—unless, of course, we could get them into the hands of a skilled therapist.

Venturing Forth.   These points of view, which represented my ideas about 1950, were so central to my thinking that I took them as given truths. I did not start out to challenge them. They were the basis on which I operated, and on which I started out to see the whole family together. To illustrate that I was primarily oriented toward the child, I can recall some early efforts in which I even confronted parents with what they were doing to the child.

In spite of the fact that there were many problems and difficulties that I ran into when I brought a whole family together, the task was not impossible to handle, fathers would come, children did not seem to be too greatly upset (in fact, they seemed to be calmed when there were storms in sessions). Even when the parents began to talk about problems they were having with one another, rather than become upset, the children seemed to relax and feel more comfortable. Parents turned out not to be entirely ogres. Sometimes I found that they were even fairly put upon by their children, and able to change and make modifications in the ways in which they responded to one another. I began to see that maybe I had been unfair and actually inaccurate in my conceptions of the family. There was no difficulty in persuading the fathers to take their place in the family group, nor in holding them in relationship to the treatment. Often mothers seemed less enthusiastic than fathers about this kind of approach. While I did have many moments when I was perplexed about what to do, when I was disturbed by my own lack of knowledge about how to deal with the situation, nevertheless, I could manage it. I was clumsy, awkward, and made many errors, as I later discovered. Yet, in spite of my own fears, and my own ineptness, I found family changes taking place.

I was in charge of a university psychological clinic. Partly for the purpose of instruction for our graduate students, the clinic was receiving referrals of troubled children and adolescents from different agencies within the community, as well as directly from parents. The treatment was sought because of disturbance in a child. The initial contacts with the family were for handling the referral; customary intake procedures followed from that point. The kinds of cases brought to the clinic ranged from the very withdrawn to the extremely hyperactive. We had an occasional physically handicapped child among the case load. Mostly the families were from the middle class, with a minority from the lower class.

Because those referred to the clinic were primarily children and adolescents, families brought in to family therapy included at least one child identified by parents as disturbed and their primary concern.

The First Effort.   My first experiment, in 1951, was with a 13-year-old adopted girl who was a severe behavior problem at school and with her family. She was on the point of being expelled because she constantly disrupted the classroom by jumping up, running around, shouting, shrieking, throwing objects, and because she was a menace on the playground. The latest escapade had been to tear the clothes off a little girl during recess. The principal agreed to keep her in school if the family would find help, which they sought from me. Not only was I interested in helping this girl and her family, but I was on my mettle to keep the student in the school. The fundamental problem in this particular case was the rivalry of this girl (remember, she was adopted) with her older brother who was 16, and who was the real son of the parents. Her problem and that of the family was complicated by alcoholism in the father and sticky over-sweetness on the part of the mother (to the point that in almost all her relations this mask for an intense underlying hostility wore thin).

Put yourself in my position when I started. I was acquainted with individual psychotherapy and had worked many years with children, college students, and adults. I was facing for the first time a family group consisting of a father, mother, a 16-year-old boy, and a 13-year-old girl who was the reason for the referral. I wished no escape, because I had said to myself, "Yes, I will try to work with a whole family." Now, what would I do? How would I help this family to deal with its problems?

Let me share with you some of the experiences I had with them. First of all, without knowing it, I had accepted the idea that the girl about whom the referral originated was *the* problem. I heard mother and father, particularly mother, who was one of those women, to quote Saki, who would have been "enormously improved by death," tell about the difficulties she and the family were having with this girl. The parents always spoke with firmness and often with rancor. Somewhat nonplussed by their attack, I would try to put myself in the place of the girl, to think about how it must feel to hear herself talked about in this way. I tried to see her father, mother, brother, and world through her eyes, to uncover the past so I could answer the question how she became the problem she is, and to engage her in a relationship through which I could understand and help her. I was full of good will. I had had individual patients like her before. I concluded that as a step toward the ultimate therapeutic goals I must help a transference relationship to develop, so I began to increase my concentration on her.

Theoretically this was fine. Practically it did not work. What had happened? The first sign it was not working came from the brother. He was restless; he began to protest that he could not see any point in coming, that he was not the problem, and besides he had many other things to do that he had given up to come to the conferences. Should I let him go or not? I scarcely knew then that whether I did or not, I would be lost. Now I know that if he went I would lose the chance to have an impact on him, and that if he stayed he would block me from continuing to work with the others in the family since he would only become more intransigent. He left, although he was persuaded to return many months later.

Secondly, I found the problem girl did not seem to welcome my help nearly as much as I thought she should. She seemed unconcerned about the things mother and father said about her. I thought she should have been unhappy and felt I would have been in her place. She was no more enthusiastic about coming than her brother. She seemed indifferent. Later I came to understand that she was showing that her parents were reciting an old familiar story against which she had long ago contrived effective ways to defend herself. In addition, however, elements of anxiety appeared that seemed primarily associated with her relation to me and that seemed to be impelling her to the safe course of running away from the conferences.

Later, I began to hear a detailed elaboration of the story of her difficulties from mother, father, and her—and I began to think I was getting to the foundation of the problem. But then little happened. She was not much different; her attitudes to her parents were relatively unchanged, and least of all was there any shift in the ways the parents were acting.

What to do? Where to turn? I was often reasoning that the transference problems were so great that I had better arrange an individual therapist for each of the family members. "Yes," I would say, "that would seem simpler, and then all the therapists could come together and compare notes—which would seem to be a good sound way to keep a family point of view."

At other times an alternative would appear more attractive. I now seemed to have such a good understanding of the family situation that if I were only to tell the family what I knew about them and give them some prescriptions or psychological sermonettes, they would surely be able to solve their problems. This indeed some families would do, although if the truth were known their solutions would probably be little related to my advice or even to the fact of their having come to me, there being in any family group strong pressures to work out the problems with one another. Giving advice was foreign to my usual therapeutic approach, however, so I was reluctant to use it, though others would later advocate it for family work.

Fortunately, even though I was usually unsure of myself and perplexed by what was happening, the family seemed to improve slowly. I met with them regularly for a year and a half, until they were content to rest on the progress they had made.

Learning from the Family.   From this first family, I learned many things, chief of which were that this way of handling a disturbed child was feasible, that it was possible to have the total family come together to talk about problems, and it seemed to help the family resolve their problems. In fact, the conferences worked well enough that I was persuaded to turn major research efforts toward testing out the approach in family group therapy.

THE COURSE OF TREATMENT

Referral

Let me tell you about how the treatment develops. At the first session, I insist on seeing both the father and mother together, if the family includes two parents. I base this insistence on the proposition that fathers and mothers each have to be a part of the process, and on the principle that on no occasion shall one parent have the opportunity to get ahead of the other in relations with the therapist. When a mother or father would call me on the phone, say there is a problem with a child, and request help, I would reply somewhat in this manner, "Well, in my experience such problems always involve the total family, and so my particular way of working is to see the whole family together. At the beginning, I would want to talk with both parents together, then with the whole family." If one parent asks to come to talk about the problem of the child, I indicate that I cannot see one parent alone, but that, if they come together, I will be glad to work out the arrangements to see them. Right from the beginning, this establishes a practice different from the usual procedures in child guidance clinics, where it was not uncommon to assume that fathers would not come. I now assume that fathers will come, and to my delight they seem often more motivated to take part than the mother. In fact, they seem to be showing a feeling that they resent being left out of family life.

If the parent talking would protest, I would reply, "Well, if it is not possible for your spouse to come, then I would suggest your going to the child guidance clinic or elsewhere. Working together happens to be my way to deal with problems." A protest is usually minimal and soon overcome. Sometimes the mother or father will check with the other parent, and sometimes make an appointment without even bothering to check. So both parents come together.

I am sure that before some parents come for the first session they have to work through negative attitudes in order to get there. When the therapist confronts them with the necessity to come together, then they are forced to proceed to work on group problems before actually coming, or to abandon the idea of family treatment. In some instances, there must have been controversies that demanded quite a bit of work for the parents to permit them to come. I allow that some will not fully commit themselves to the treatment. One of the ways in which I defuse the resistive feelings is to anticipate that they are present. I take a tentative approach, suggesting to the parents a trial to see how the treatment works. Mostly, though, families accept the idea that all members will be at the conferences together. And I know they would be anxious if they were not included.

I think one of the reasons why most fathers are willing to cooperate in the treatment is that they never have to start after the mothers in making a relation with the therapist. On the whole, I have found fathers eager to come and be included, and not as resistant as in most child guidance clinics. I even wonder if professional skepticism about willingness of fathers to come for treatment is communicated through the ways mothers and fathers are handled at intake, so that we create difficulties in including the father.

Families came to me at or near a point of crisis, whether they were self-referred or referred by an agency. There are occasions when the community or one of its agencies will force the family to seek change in its status. The family is pushed toward seeking help. Frequently, however, the push comes in relation to one individual, rather than the whole family, as, for instance, when a child is referred when a school is putting pressure on the parents to seek help. In that case, the agency usually works with the family to bring at least one parent to a state of readiness to seek help. The chances are against the family coming against their will. Of course you cannot work effectively with a family as a group until you have the parents involved and motivated to the extent that they are willing to do something about their problem. I do not believe you can move in on a family, and say "We think there is a problem that you have to take care of, and we are going to do this!"

Once the approach is explained to parents, they think it very natural. In fact, when they have not heard before about family therapy they often raise the question, "Why has nobody suggested this to us before?" It seems obvious to them that there is a problem with the whole family. They find a relief of personal responsibility and guilt for the problem, since it is being viewed as a family problem. There is a reduction of pressure on any one individual. The family is coming not because of the isolated guilt of any individual, but because all of the family members are participants in the problem and in the guilt. The fact that there is this kind of sharing of responsibility reduces the strain or anxiety of any individual.

We have noticed that families for the most part are eager to come. They think of this as a common sense way to work on their problems. It seems a logical extension of what happens at home. They feel it is a productive approach because they may work during the conference hour and may continue to work in the intervening periods between the conferences.

Also, I think in every family there are strengths and methods for supporting one another. I am sure that the family has an inner confidence that if they all come together, they have more strengths and resources available for solving their problems. The feelings of belongingness and unity in a family and of wanting to hold the whole family together are strong, even in the most disorganized family, though ideas of the unity and persistence of the family are frequently deeply buried under the problems.

Session Number One

A BEGINNING RELATIONSHIP

At the start when both parents come together, the time is first spent in hearing something of the problems of the child. The parents come with the expectation that they will talk about the child, and one cannot immediately confront them with a task that is outside their expectation. Securing information about the child's problems and the parents' efforts to cope with them is not particularly relevant to the therapy. Such information is interesting, and sometimes it is pertinent, but for the most part securing it is simply to begin building a relation, rather superficial at this stage, between the therapist and the parents. The relationship built up between the parents and the therapist is facilitated by the fact the parents are concerned about the child. They are motivated to secure help for him. It is necessary and possible, however, to shift them gradually from talking about the child as the problem to talking about the family as the problem. This is gradually brought about in the first session, and this is the aim that is in the back of the therapist's mind. He talks about how the disturbance of the child is a sign that the family is not right for the child, that there are problems in the family life which are somehow determining the disturbances seen in the child. He moves the center from the individual child over to talking and thinking about the family.

Parents often expect that the therapist will want to have a conference with their child about whom they are concerned. This is inconsistent with a family approach. It illustrates the popular assumption that problems are lodged in individuals. It demonstrates, further, the problem of making the transition from thinking in terms of individual personality theory, individual psychotherapy or casework, to thinking in terms of the family as a unit. When you are thinking of the family as a unit, as in this therapy, the usual diagnostic information about an individual and his problem is mostly irrelevant.

DIAGNOSIS IN ADVANCE?

I have given up trying to size up from individual observation if a person in the family has a strong ego or a weak ego, if he is dominant or submissive, aggressive or passive, dependent or one on whom everybody leans. I find these are superficial dimensions on one side of family relations; the other side is always underneath. Under the right circumstances, the underside comes out. So a person who looks strong, suddenly turns out to have all kinds of problems that evidence a "weak ego." Often ease in showing one's problems is what actually gives the impression of weakness, but the ease with which these problems may be expressed is a sign of strength. So it is very difficult, within the family situation, to tag people at different levels of strength, security, and so on. You find that they change in relations to each other, and show different facets depending on the particular relations that are in effect.

You need information on how persons are relating with others in the family, but we cannot learn this from conferences with individuals nor from tests now available. The only way we can now learn it is when we actually have the whole family in for the conferences.

Useful diagnostic understanding comes through actual exposure to the family, and cannot be gained before. It is not profitable to sit down with Johnny and say, "Johnny, what kind of a mother have you got? What kind of feelings do you have toward her? How do you talk with her? How do you get along with her? etc." Surely, that would be useful information if you were trying to make a study of Johnny. It is not sufficient to base predictions on self-other perceptions and concepts in the family. Such percepts and concepts are too remote from the action in the family. Though such measures might predict partially what we might expect in the interaction, they are not sufficient to provide predictions for family therapy purposes.

If you want to discover how Johnny actually relates to his mother, you will find his reports to be quite out of keeping with how he communicates and expresses feelings, when he is with her. It is what happens as they relate that is significant information for handling the therapeutic sessions. Once the family comes in front of you, diagnosis proceeds; you evaluate the state of the family at all times as you are going through the therapy with them. Diagnosis and therapy go along simultaneously, even up to the termination. Later, we may develop techniques for preliminary evaluation that will be predictive of what we might see at various stages during the therapy. These would have to be based on direct observations of the communication and interaction among the members of families. So the therapist deflects any suggestions of private conferences with the child. Instead, he shifts to orienting the parents about how the treatment will proceed.

Orientation

The orientation has several functions: to make clear what the role of the therapist will be, to make a statement about the obligations of the family, to anticipate with them what may happen during the therapy, and to negotiate the practical arrangements for the therapy conferences.

ROLE OF THERAPIST

In defining the role of the therapist, these points are made.

Manager. It is his responsibility to initiate and manage the treatment, to determine the kind of setting within which it will take place, and all the rest of the technical aspects.

Outside the Family. The therapist is an outsider as far as the family is concerned. He does not assume those kinds of authority that belong to the parents by rights, traditions of our society, law, and other sources of authority. The father has certain authority because he is the father; the mother has authority because she is the mother, and the therapist must not take over these authorities. The child also has authority, though we talk of child rights, rather than authority. Most typically, the child's authority is granted within the family; under certain circumstances, children seize authority. The therapist must not step in at any level to take over the authority of any family member. This means that he will not take on the role of any individual in the family, for example, a father to the child. The therapist will remain an outsider to maintain the group of the family. He will not become a person who will make decisions for the family; he will not give advice about how problems should be solved. Both these things would represent taking on a family (parental) role. He will not deal with a child in a different way from how he will deal with the mother or the father; he will hold to a comparable role in relation to each.

It is particularly dangerous for a male therapist to start acting like a father, and, without quite recognizing what he is doing, to assume father types of relations with family members. This drives the father into a cul-de-sac in relations with the rest of the family. Here is an illustration of how it can happen.

A mother turns to the therapist and says, "Now, Dr. Bell, don't you think things would be different if my husband would do this?" As a therapist I am on a spot. If I slip into answering the question, I am setting up a nice little relation with mother, who is saying in effect, "You would be a much better husband and father than my husband here, and I would like this." If I answer, I am not only fostering this cozy relation with mother, but I am also saying to father, "Look, I'm agreeing with mother that you're a louse, and you're not doing your job right." I can avoid this trap, however; and I did, by saying, "It seems you're trying to tell me something through this question, and also to tell your husband something at the same time. I'm not in a position to answer your question. Perhaps we should talk about what you're trying to say." By that stance I avoided a private relation with the mother and a hostile relation with the father.

There has to be an integration between what the therapist says and how he acts; insofar as possible speech and action must not be in conflict with one another. In many social roles, our actions develop loosely because the situations are ambiguous and another person may act in one, two, or several ways. We have to feel our way into relations in terms of various action and relational possibilities. The therapist, as any stranger, is perceived ambiguously by the members of the family. But the more clarity he brings to the relation, the less ambiguity in his behavior as seen by each family member, the more quickly the family can establish a relation to allow the therapy to get under way.

One of the major qualifications for conducting this therapy, then, is that an individual learn how it *feels* to be a therapist in family group therapy. I know of no other way to get that feeling than to try out the approach.

Concern about Communication.   Further, I orient them that I am concerned about the communication processes in the family: about how they talk with one another, and about how they listen. To a far greater extent than had been realized until recently, the language of family communication is nonverbal, although you probably know this through your own families. Much of the communication that takes place in the family is at a level that an outsider cannot understand. It is private communication, especially through action or gesture, and the language has private symbolic meanings, developed during living together and through studying the meanings of the little gestures, positions, and movements in which each family member engages.

Family group therapy depends on talking with words rather than with muscles. Whereas the therapist might get some meaning from the nonverbal speech, he will not be able to comprehend the richness of meaning in the gesture.

For instance, in a conference with the McAndrews, Jean was

telling us in a lively monologue, about some of the things that went on at home. At one point her mother raised her index finger ever so slightly, very quickly. Immediately, the content of what Jean was saying changed, and she continued, "I think Sandy better take over now." The whole discussion changed. To produce so radical a change in content and activity, as was accomplished by that simple little gesture, probably meant that much was being communicated. I knew that the mother wanted to change the nature of what Jean was saying, but what went through Jean's head I could not know. She and her mother were conversing about something that she was being told to hide; but I did not know what that skeleton was, nor why mother intruded. It may have been a threatening gesture designed to make Jean anxious, or maybe it was a shared joke, or maybe it was not important. I could have said to Mrs. McAndrew, "I noticed you lifted your finger, that you were trying to tell the family and Jean something that I couldn't know about." If I invited her to tell in words what her gesture meant, then I would have an opportunity to take part more actively in the communication, to understand the meaning involved in the gesture.

For the therapist to understand what is going on, the family has to interpret, help put private language into public words. The therapist advises that he will try to help the family verbalize things being said nonverbally, or things he cannot understand, so the meaning will become clear. This, of course, is not only for the sake of the therapist, but for the sake of the family as a whole, toward the aim of improving communication.

The parents are told that they have to work to facilitate communication, and particularly at the beginning to make it their obligation to allow the children to express themselves. This is to help to warm up the children so they can speak openly. They are urged, also, to make changes in routines and rules requested by the children, if possible, in order to encourage their participation. The parents are assured that they will have opportunity later to express what they want to say.

Family As Problem-Solvers. Further, the therapist defines that he is concerned with communication, not for its own sake, but, rather, for its use so the family will be better able to understand and solve their problems. The solutions that the family will work out must be their own. The value system that they will use in judging the suitability or unsuitability of problem solutions must be their own. I warn a family that I do not have the answers to their particular problems, because they must and can be solved in their ways, not in mine. I may have seen other families with similar problems, but their solutions would not necessarily be appropriate for this family here.

This has an important implication, that family therapy can be used with various levels in our society, lower, middle and upper class families, and is not contraindicated because we find different values in each of these segments of our society. Values emerging from a family's own cultural and community experience form standards against which a family evaluates the solutions they work out. It may be that a family needs to change its value system, but it is not the function of the therapist to promote this, unless by referral. Family therapy is not an educational method, except that the family learn, by their own efforts, techniques for solving their problems. It is not a counseling method, telling the family how to resolve its difficulties. It is a treatment approach. It is designed to improve the functioning of this group, so that it may deal more adequately with its own life situation.

ROLE OF FAMILY

Obligations.   At the same time, the family is told about its obligations. The first of these is that the family must attend; if one member of the family is unable to attend, the session is cancelled. In my experience, it is impossible to carry on this approach speedily and efficiently if one is meeting with only a part of the family on occasion. While it is true that one could work with part of the family now, and another part at a later time, this simply extends the duration of the therapy. The therapist always has to take time to help the whole family catch up when a part of the family has been absent. Also, the content that comes out is often, if not usually, prejudicial to persons who are absent. When they return, they may not be prepared to hear the content nor to continue the treatment. If the whole family is there all the time, everyone always knows what has happened. There is no development of paranoid thoughts: "They are talking about me"; "They are saying things behind my back that they wouldn't say to my face"; and so on. Such thinking is one of the problems of simultaneous treatment, where different therapists work separately with each of the individual family members. Then we have to cope with a family member's anxiety about what is happening in relations in which he is not participating. Since we do not meet this when the whole family is present, we put an injunction on the family that everyone must attend, and that there will be no contacts with the therapist apart from the relations with the whole family. Measures are taken to keep all the family in touch with what is going on and to instruct them that a group relation with the therapist, and not a personal relation, is the goal. One has to be on watch against persons lagging behind after a session to say a word or coming early so that they can gain an advantage over someone else. Tricks to isolate the therapist are used to resist the development of the family group process.

Facing Emotional Crises.   It is important to orient the family to expect emotional crises, since family members may not be prepared for the explosion of emotion that emerges in some of the sessions. One of the problems of communication in a family is the constant building up of hostility that cannot be drained off in the communication. It waits there, to burst out with a surge. This can frighten the parents. Preparing them through orientation sometimes makes it easier for them to face the severity of such a crisis. It is pointed out to them how a crisis of this sort is a preparatory step toward communication of the positive aspects of the family relations and positive resolution of problems. This puts the emotional crisis into perspective.

Practical Arrangements

Following the orientation, the practical details of the conferences are worked out—who shall attend, the schedule, the fee, if there is one, and the place.

WHO ARE THE FAMILY?

The therapist helps the parents to determine who will come to the family conferences. He rules out children younger than nine, usually, because they have difficulty verbalizing, and this is a technique that depends on verbal interchange. Normally their language development has not attained a level to permit them to fit easily into this highly verbal situation. Then, the level of their abstract thinking has not matured sufficiently that they are able to think in terms of an abstract concept such as "the family" or "problems of the family." They tend, rather, to think in terms of self-centered feelings and reactions and not to deal with the whole group at theoretic levels.

In general the therapist urges inclusion of all the family members, as defined by the parents themselves. Customarily this means all family members living together. Sometimes parents exclude a relative under the same roof, such as the sister of a father; she rented a room from the family, and was not in essential interaction with them. Relatives living outside the home are also included at times. In choosing the group to treat, it is helpful to remember that each potential member who is excluded will be a force working against changes in the family; or he will be driven away from the rest of the family, since the distance between him and those in the group will be accentuated as cohesive processes bind the family into a group organized in new ways.

TIME SCHEDULE

Reflecting a schedule I had carried over from individual therapy and found workable with most families, it is planned that a family will get together with the therapist once a week for an hour. But there is no magic in this. In my experience children tend, if they are young, to become exhausted if the conferences last longer than an hour.

Often it is the fathers rather than the mothers who take the lead in scheduling the times for the family conferences. There are many instances where mothers, rather than fathers, have put blocks in the way of finding time for the conferences. For instance a mother would say, "Oh, we couldn't possibly come at that time, I have to get supper." Or, "I couldn't come then because my cleaning woman is there at the time, and I have to be around when she is cleaning the house." Or, "My boss would never give me time off." Or, "I have to do the shopping at that time, and I couldn't possibly come." The matter of giving time is the same as the matter of paying a fee; this is something a person contributes to the therapy. It is a certain price that the family pays for the help that is secured; and the expectation of being released from this cost is one of the incentives toward termination.

I found that it is very hard for the number of individuals in the family of this day and age to find an hour when they can all come together. The life of the children seems full of commitments, and the parents' lives are normally so busy that it is difficult to find a single hour when all members of the family are free from conflicting engagements. It may be that in some families it would be possible to find time for conferences more frequently than once-a-week, but I would not be certain that this would hasten the therapy; in fact, I would fear that too frequent conferences might lead the family to infer that their own resources for problem-solving were deficient, and only dependence on the therapist could rescue them.

I make it a rule in my work, partly because I think it a good principle and partly for personal reasons, that the family come during the day. No special arrangements are made to accommodate the fact that a father or mother is working. It is frequent that fathers are able to work at other hours to make up for family conference time, even though they may be reluctant to ask for the opportunity, for such a matter as therapy. In fact, I have come to look on a father's giving time, and his working out the plans as signs of his motivation for getting help for the family. Usually the motivation is high when it is put to the test. This has greatly eased the problem of working with the total family. I am a morning person, and if I had to work in the evening this would be hard on me. More importantly, it would be a problem for the children. It is true that I opened late afternoon hours to meet the convenience of families, up to six o'clock, but I have never extended my work into the evening.

STRUCTURING THE ENVIRONMENT

It is the therapist's responsibility to structure the environment for the conferences. He selects the room and seating arrangement —often without thought, since a pattern develops. For me, by choice, the room is simple, with a table in the center around which a number of chairs are placed, usually at least one more than needed by the family and me. This allows the family some choice in placing themselves, and some room for movement during sessions.

One little note: when I bring the family into the interview room, to begin a session, I normally do not sit down until after the family has arranged itself around the table. Some always go for exactly the same chair each conference, and keep their position around the table the same. Week after week, they keep to a rigid spatial relation to one another. Others are very flexible about how they arrange themselves; they show you something of what is happening in their interrelations by the way in which they seat themselves. Then, after the family is seated, I take a vacant chair.

Some therapists use a circle of chairs for their work. My experience is that this results in less formality and more digressions. It seems to lead to segmenting the family into pairs, who chat, tease, or joke with one another on the side. The table, in contrast, seems to accent the family's unity and the importance of their work toward solving the family's problems.

The Family Together

The whole family comes at the next session. To have the parents come first, and then bring in the children, even though that may be handicapping them, is a deliberate part of the technique. It was worked out after efforts to start with the child alone, or to start with the whole family first. It was found that orienting the parents and later orienting the children in the presence of the parents accomplished the introduction to therapy in what seemed to be the best way. For one thing, it prevented the parents from aggressive attacks on the children at the beginning. In a sense, the parents are playing therapeutic as well as parental roles with the children. They become co-therapists along with the therapist in helping the children to loosen up. As the parents give their attention to the therapeutic role they are diverted from exposing their own annoyance, resentment, and other feelings to the children. The children have a great deal of attention placed on them at the first interview they attend, and they are actually given a chance to catch up in the relations. Children do not come with the expectation to participate fully in what parents do anyway, so they seem not to be disturbed about what might have gone on before they arrive.

REPEATING THE ORIENTATION

An orientation after this manner is also presented when the whole family comes for the next appointment: we are getting together because there are problems in the family; the parents have reported that things are not going as well as they should; we will talk about the family, to see what must be done to help the family work out better ways of living; we are going to meet once a week; no one is going to be placed under any pressure to talk, but I will have the function of trying to help everybody gain an opportunity to speak. I help the family to understand that some of the members of the family will be more reluctant to speak up than others. At the beginning, it is especially necessary that I help those who have more difficulty in talking, and usually I address myself to the children in making this comment. I have learned that in most families, but by no means all, the children have problems in freely communicating their feelings about the family. I use the word "feelings" frequently; family members typically place an especial importance on verbalizing about feelings.

The Therapist.   I point out to the family that I am not going to become another father or mother; I will not give any advice, or make any decisions about how the family should be run. The family will remain on its own because no outsider can come in and tell the family how it should function. I describe myself as the family umpire or referee to see that each person has a chance to communicate with the family members. Especially in talking with the parents, I suggest that feelings may come out which have been held back in the past. Feelings of guilt may be aroused about what is said and people may be made angry. Nevertheless, as far as possible, the family will try to talk about the kinds of feelings that they have, and the ways in which what other people say touches them as they hear it.

Avoiding Private Conferences.   I warn the family that I shall resist in every way any efforts for a member of the family to communicate with me alone, that I will talk only with the total family. I say this since to try to work out a private arrangement with the therapist is the most common way to disrupt the therapy. I start at the beginning to prevent efforts of individuals to get me off to the side and deal with me privately. Once the whole family has met together, working with only a part of the family sets the therapy back.

I recall one mother who attempted to set up a private interview with me after a couple of sessions. I refused, mentioning, however, that there might be reasons why she should talk with someone privately and, if so, I could work it out with another therapist. After this, she took time to telephone me. Finally, I had to instruct my secretary how to deflect these calls. So the mother took to writing letters. After receiving three letters in one week, and being curious enough to read them, I knew I was caught. If I did not make my action with the letters known to the mother, she could assume that she had won my ear privately. So at the next session I brought in the three letters, sat down at the conference, and read them. The mother went into a rage, but this was the end of her efforts to communicate with me privately.

In another instance a very domineering mother came one afternoon with her daughter and husband, and left two boys at home. She came in and said, "I just decided that we really had things to talk about with reference to Ruth, so I wanted to have her alone here without the boys." I had to say, "I'm sorry, unless Lennie and Jim are here, we can't proceed with the conference. I'm sorry, we can't continue this afternoon." So I walked out. The mother, of course, did not like this. At that particular point she was trying to assert herself in a role which she thought was being undermined by the way in which her family were dealing with her. If I had given in to her maneuver, I would have prejudiced my chances to continue working with the individuals left out. In all families I have to hold the line against the efforts of individuals to break up my communication with the total family, and center it in a therapist-individual relation.

Another side of the efforts to develop private relationships and to segment the family into smaller units concerns the therapist himself. Because he is human and has lived in a family, he cannot escape at times becoming overidentified with one or more members of the family, preoccupied with what is happening inside an individual, or negative toward some persons in a family. When this empathy or antipathy occurs, it is always followed by a difficulty in handling the session—sometimes immediately. You lose contact with the other members of the family. Soon the family reminds you that you are obsessed with one person and not paying attention to the rest of the family. You have perhaps lost sight of the fact that the family unit has the problem and that the family is the unit of treatment. It is easy to revert to the common pattern of thinking about individuals as problems or centers of function. If this happens, you become acutely conscious of it because it manifests itself so immediately in management problems in the treatment.

Hostilities toward you develop from other members of the family, or the interaction breaks down. Suddenly there may be a silence that nobody wants to break. You can try to sit out the silence, but it does not seem to respond to this common approach. Often as you trace steps back to what precipitated the silence, you find that you were overidentified with one of the adults or a child. So there is a corrective device built in to alert you that you have moved too actively into identification with individuals. By focusing on the relations among the family members, you learn to avoid empathy with individuals, so valuable in individual therapy.

The therapy proceeds by these steps. At the beginning I concentrate my attention mostly on the children to warm them up, to help them feel secure in the situation and talk freely, and gain confidence in the therapy process. Sometimes it takes two, three, or four sessions before they feel sufficiently confident that they can begin to express their wishes, ideas, and feelings. I attempt to keep the parents somewhat in the background, because if they are given full rein at the beginning they normally assert their authority, and express many complaints that discourage the children. The complaints are repetitions of old reproaches kept in the fore at home. These steps are not inconsistent with avoiding attention to individuals, as mentioned above, because the parents have been alerted that I will attend to the children at this time.

BUILDING RELATIONS

There are certain activities in which I engage to build relations. First, I use my posture and gaze to center my relations on the children. Even so, I work to keep the conferences centered on the family as a whole. Even while I am facing the child to help him feel secure, I am talking about the family. I address myself to the child, for example, in these terms: "Last week when your mother and father were in, they were telling me that things are not going along too well in the family. We're here to talk about the family and to study why it is that the family isn't working as well as it should, and what can be done to solve its problems, and to work better." The verbal emphasis is on family and directed away from individuals. I do not talk about the fact that a child is enuretic, delinquent, a school problem, or such; I do not introduce discussion of these kinds of symptoms. I talk about family problems. If the parents turn toward discussion of individual symptoms at the beginning, then I say, "Yes, these are problems, but we're here not to talk about these difficulties, but about the family."

The emphasis is work-oriented. I do not stress the relation of the therapist with any member of the family, nor with the whole family as a group, for the sake of the relationship alone. The family task is always in the forefront. That task is to learn techniques of communication toward the ends of the family analyzing problems, making decisions, and acting more effectively according to their own value system.

When the children are asked to discuss the problems of the family and how they would see problems resolved, one of the ways in which they test out their freedom in the situation is to request specific changes. These changes are normally minor, and never very important in terms of the total social economy of the family. For later, they reserve the things that are important matters far beyond these minor difficulties in participating in the family.

The Withdrawn Child. An inhibited child is usually just waiting for the chance to talk. It is amazing how quickly withdrawn children will break through their inhibitions. Of course, there is an advantage for the withdrawn child in this situation, because he is working with his family, who know he is not completely inhibited. The family will come in on occasion to support the child. "It's alright, we want to hear what you have to say." I have seen the parents be very helpful during these initial stages, and really back up the child. If a withdrawn child is with an individual therapist, he has no security in that relation until it is built; but when he is with his family, there is already some security for him in ongoing family relations. This is a basis on which he can begin to express himself.

The Acting-Out Child.   The situation is quite different with acting-out children. One pulled his cap down over his eyes; another dropped under the table and refused to budge; another ran in and out of the therapy room; another made faces, and another rapped his fist on the table rhythmically and said "damn" each time. When there are problems in a child and he is expressing himself through his muscles, we are probably justified in assuming that the action is an effort to communicate to his parents. We may assume, also, that he would prefer to communicate more directly if the opportunity and a verbal way of expressing himself were available to him. Then he would give up motoric expression of his ideas, feelings, needs and so on.

But the primary problem is to convince him that it is safe to talk in the therapy. He has to learn two truths: first, that he cannot use acting-out behavior as his primary way to communicate here, and, second, that it is safe to talk. The first requires control; the second, security.

Here is a tough problem for the therapist. If he controls the acting-out, he is taking over the role of a disciplinarian. In so doing he may alienate and inhibit the child, but also the parents, whose inability to control is painfully evident, and for whom the therapist's action becomes a rebuke. If he becomes the disciplinarian, he also loses the opportunity to support the child in expressing himself verbally.

My solution for this problem has been to work through the parents. The aim here is to place the parents in control of the immediate acting in the conference session, but not to permit them to go beyond this at this point. The goal is to help the family members themselves see that talking is the mode of communication, to help them to control the youngster when he wants to express himself through his muscles, and to support him as he tries to speak in words. I encourage the parents to become the ones who say—often in various ways—"Here we talk. Here, we don't play." They are to assert that point of view over and over again. If necessary, I am now free to add, "And when you are ready, we want to hear what you have to say." I would say, too, "We want you to express your worries, feelings, anger, and so on, that you have about the family. And when you are ready, then we will be ready to listen to what you have to say. There is no hurry." I always stress the fact that nobody is putting a great amount of pressure on anybody to speak, although this situation does press each individual to talk.

If I were to find the parents saying, "Now you are doing just what you do at home," and beginning to extend criticism beyond the fact that the child is acting out and not talking at the moment, I would say, "I'm here to protect Jimmy when you become overcritical. We want to hear from everybody, and if we don't get a chance to hear what Jimmy has to say because you criticize him too much at this time, then we will not be able to make any progress." So I would block the parents immediately, perhaps telling them that when we are sure that Jimmy is not frightened here, then they will have their chance to talk. Sometimes the parents are not easily blocked; they will come back time and time again to criticize; and you have to block them over and over. But this is a part of the therapist's structuring of the situation. He is there to see that conditions are established so that everybody may feel an equal opportunity to talk. That is his job. If he does not do it, he is letting the family down.

Knowing the problems you can sense the amount of speed you can make. You have to wait until the family is willing to talk, and in particular, the acting-out youngster. Over and over again at the beginning you may have to state a basic rule, that here we advance the process of solving problems through talking rather than through showing one another what we think and feel by how we move and by how we express ourselves facially.

Once the youngster makes the transition and agrees to conform with the rules by talking, the therapist can proceed just as with a child who is inhibited. Sometimes it takes one or two conferences before a child participates on a verbal, rather than a motor, level.

In children who have behavior problems we can count usually on motivation to participate in communication in the family.[2] Given the opportunity, protected from the threat of punishment, given support, children begin to expose their inner life to the family.

THE CHILD TESTS THE THERAPY

Children evaluate the therapy situation by talking in a tentative way about aspects of the family life that annoy them. These are not important issues, at least not so important that the child is going to stake his own relations with the family on whether or not these issues get resolved. For example, one boy wanted to stay up a half-hour later to watch "Dragnet" on Thursday nights. Another boy complained because his father awakened him at quarter of seven instead of seven o'clock, when the later hour would give him plenty of time to get to school. A girl complained about the fact that she had to eat cereal in the morning when her mother knew she did not care for it. Minor irritations ongoing as part of the family life are brought forth, and testing is made of the way the rest of the family listens and expresses willingness to do something about it. Children do not run the risk of saying really important things they want to express. They test out the situation on irrelevant or minor issues. They exhaust these issues quickly because they are really of minor importance to them, except for evaluating what will happen if they speak. They seek to learn whether or not the therapist will really support them when they say things the parents may not like, whether the parents are really going to listen, and whether changes are actually going to occur. If the family can go along with making little adjustments, even if they are regarded as temporary, soon the child exhausts his demands. I do not recall that more than three or four conferences were spent in talking about these kinds of minor issues; a child seldom introduces more than half a dozen such topics.

When the child has grown sufficiently confident that he will be heard and that changes can happen in the family as a result of his speaking, then he interjects some positive reaction to the family, for instance a statement about the state of family affairs, such as, "Well, things are going so well now that I have no more problems." This is a clue that the primary testing period has been concluded. At this point, I give the nod to the parents, encouraging them to talk openly and freely in the conferences.

The Parent-Child Phase

Immediately, then, the direction of the therapy shifts. We move into what I call the "parent-child" phase of the treatment.

HOSTILITY

During this stage initially there is exposure of a great deal of
hostility between children and their parents. Sometimes it is one
child and one parent, sometimes it is the child and both the parents,
or sometimes it is a whole group of children against their parents.
The problems vary, but the interaction moves in the parent-child
dimension of the family life. Much previously unverbalized hostile
feeling is brought out on both sides.

BALANCING THE FAMILY

It is the therapist's function to keep a balance, so that when the
parent induces anxiety in the child, the child is not driven out of the
situation; or when the child induces negative feelings, the parents do
not withdraw. Sometimes it is extremely difficult to maintain the
balance during this particular phase of the treatment. If it is not
sustained, the family members will compete in rivalry for the attention of the therapist; one or more of the members of the family will
make efforts to see you privately, or to terminate the treatment;
adults or children will retreat into acting out instead of speaking;
someone will begin to talk about people and activities outside the
family; or, on occasion, someone will court favor with the therapist
and set a seductive trap by saying something positive, such as "Dr.
Bell, you are doing such a good job with us. You are very helpful,"
while looking straight at one of the family members. Also, families
are often curious about the therapist as a person, and I decide the
extent to which I will or will not identify myself to the members of
the family. Often the children are especially curious about me and
will ask questions. Sometimes the easiest way to take care of these
questions is to answer them briefly and get back to the business at
hand.

Sometimes I see myself as a neutral figure at whom each person
can direct his remarks, a sort of impersonal target in communication.
But, mostly, remarks directed to me have the meaning that communication has broken down in the family; so I have to shift attention
back to the family. This may be done by commenting that it seems at

this point an individual wants to talk to me, rather than to all the members of the family. I may draw attention to some observable problems in communication, the ways a person is grasping or shifting in the chair, or the ways in which he relates himself to the therapist gesturally. These are translated for the individual on occasion. I make interpretations based on an assumption that there is intent behind gestural language. I do not try, in fact, to phrase the meaning of it, because the actual verbalization has to be left to the individual who is gesturing.

TRANSFERENCE AND COUNTERTRANSFERENCE

It does not seem helpful to think of the relations in family therapy as analogous to those in individual therapy, and to apply such terms as transference or countertransference. Transference relates to the displacement on to the therapist of the feelings, attitudes and relations that have developed with significant individuals outside the therapy situation, and, further, to working through in relations with the therapist such problems as exist in extra-therapy relations. Displacement from extra-therapy relations into the therapy situation does not take place in family therapy in the same sense as in individual therapy. Family relations are most commonly transferred in individual therapy. When a child is sitting with the parents, as in family therapy, he can express directly to them the feelings, attitudes, problems, ideas, and so on, that trouble him. So, in this therapy, he does not need to express them primarily to the therapist. The therapist is not involved emotionally to the same extent as he would be in individual therapy.

I do not mean that there are not emotional relations that build between individuals in the family and the therapist. But these relations are not transference phenomena as we know them in individual therapy, where displacement on to the therapist of feelings generated primarily within previous family relations is to be expected. A different kind of relation takes place when the family members are present. Feelings are likely to be expressed directly to other family members; or if the expression of the feelings is inhibited, the presence of the family members makes it unlikely that the feelings will be displaced on to the therapist.

Also, the formal ways in which the therapeutic conferences are conducted restrict the intensity of this feeling. Certainly they block the family from lifting feelings out of the family and transferring them on to the therapist. In the conference session when all sit around a table in an office, the family becomes task-oriented in a rather formal way. This reduces the emotional involvement of the family with the therapist.

With one family I went to the home for several sessions. The boy in the family developed rheumatic fever, and was bedridden; so I saw the father, mother and boy around the bed. This would seem to be a controlled situation, but it was not with this family. The doorbell chimed; the telephone rang; someone would come to the house with a package. One minute mother would be with us and the next minute she would be off to turn down a burner on the stove. After efforts to make the therapy work here, I gave up and waited to resume the therapy until the boy was ambulatory. I felt I had to respond too much to the total life of the family, including the objects in their living space. The kind of relationship needed for the therapy seemed to deteriorate under these circumstances.

CHILDREN UNDER FIRE

For the most part, children are only temporarily upset by parents' outpouring of anger. For one thing, much of what appears to be highly charged to the therapist has often been heard from the parents. Bitter attacks that parents make on a child are usually old stories, so that what seems to be coming out from the parents with a tremendous hostile push is not necessarily something for which the child does not have defenses. Normally, the parent would not bring out material that he would sense is going to be beyond the ability of the child to integrate. The parent retains his concern about the child; even the most distant, rejecting, and hostile parents have revealed, when given the opportunity, that they have positive concern, and real eagerness to fulfill their roles as good parents. Occasionally, this part of their motivation is so deeply hidden that we cannot see it. But it comes in to protect the child.

Out of my recollections, I can hear one mother making a certain kind of statement at which the boy shut off his ears and did not listen. At the next conference, mother made this same statement and the same kind of reaction occurred. Under these circumstances, I pointed out how I had observed last session that when mother said what she was just repeating that her boy did not seem to listen, and how there appeared to be some kind of block that the boy threw up against hearing and reacting to these statements. This was helpful in directing the family to examine what was going on in the communication.

I have found that around the problems for which a child is referred, parents may keep up a constant hammering against the child. The child seems unresponsive. It is almost as though he is saying to the family, "Go on with this. This is fine. This is all right with me. It is not going to change me. It is not going to trouble me." Yet I know by the intensity with which the parents are making comments about the child and to him, that they would really want to see things different. At the same time, however, it looks as though they do not want to see change enough to venture into new ways of relating to the child.

For example, one hysterical mother kept complaining session after session about her insufferable little boy who did all manner of terrible things to annoy her. It was very obvious to me that she was gaining much personal satisfaction out of his behavior, and reporting it with glee. So at one point, since we did not seem to be making any progress, I said to her, "Well, even though I know you hate what Jimmy is doing, it really troubles you a lot, and you want to see it change, the interesting thing to me is that no real effort is being made to bring about a change. This goes on year after year. Nobody really controls Jimmy and nobody does anything to stop what he does. It almost appears to me as though there is something about what Jimmy does that you want to have continue."

Pointing out a kind of connection between one session and another session, or between an interaction at one point in an interview and one that takes place later, helps the family to face the connections between things that they do.

PROTECTIVE FAMILY DEFENCES

Sometimes you wonder if a family can actually reconstitute itself after intense outpouring of feeling—when, for instance, you observe a mother dissolving in tears, a child screaming, and a father incapacitated and silent. The hostility is so provocative that it seems it may precipitate a psychotic episode. Frequently a mother will become hysterical. It is a very tense, difficult period, that is inevitable if treatment is progressing properly. You ask during an hour like this if a family can return home to live together. Even though I was frightened, I learned early that, as in individual therapy, protection is built in. The family normally does not exceed the limits beyond which it cannot recuperate. Almost inevitably—in fact, I cannot think of an exception—the family makes an effort, even before the end of the session, to seal off the explosion, to pull itself together, and to provide a basis for its continuing during the next week. The hostility may recur, even in an expanded way at succeeding sessions, but commonly at the end of the session when mother has dissolved in tears, father has been helplessly looking this way and that, the youngster has been railing at them both, and the therapist has been wondering if they will be able to go home and live together during the week, there will be some movement, some gesture, some gentleness introduced to bring them together and to open the way for their resuming their family life at home.

This happens typically after distressing hostile crises. There are, of course, occasions when one person might say, "Well, I don't know if I really want to come anymore." So you have to help the family to discuss this protest, and always deal with it in terms of his being a member of the family group—which would be incomplete and would not hear his point of view if he left. Then, just at the end, the family will usually pull itself together, show some way of keeping a relationship, go out, and be able to get along until the next conference.

Mike, a boy about eleven years of age, for three or four sessions had been threatening, with great intensity of anger against his parents, to run away from home. As he continued to say this, his mother became increasingly hostile. Then the father came into the act and we had a very tense conference. Just at the end, Mike turned to his mother and said, "But, Mummie, you know I'm not going to run away. I love you too much." Of course his mother dissolved into tears. It took her a few moments to regain her composure, and then in spite of all the hostile things Mike had been saying, the family walked out of the conference session ready to continue its life, buoyed up by the statement of this child's feeling of love for the family.

There were instances when I could see that the parents were likely to take out on a youngster the things that they were feeling in response to what he had said. I have said to a family, "I think there shouldn't be any discussion about this problem at home this week." I do not use this very frequently, but have done so when I felt that the parents or the children were demonstrating to me how the family life in between the sessions was operating to destroy gains in the therapy. More frequently, I have found, though, that the things that are brought up in therapy, even though disturbing and damaging to the parents' self-respect, are not made the subject of recrimination when the child gets home, since they were brought out to the full knowledge of the therapist. I think this is partly because the parents know that if they punish the child, it is very likely that at the next conference, the child will report to the therapist. And, indeed, he does on occasion.

Sometimes the parents become upset, being reminded of their own childhoods, painful relations with their own parents, and traumatic experiences they suffered. They may have problems in handling some of these recollections. Sometimes they talk about this to the rest of the family. On other occasions, I know, they worry through these things at home in discussions with their mates, or on their own. They reveal these recollections in different ways in the therapy. Normally the therapist does not seek to bring out and integrate this material from childhood into the discussions. He accepts it in the context of asking what the meaning is to the family of this being talked about at the moment.

You start with the here and now of the family, and work in the direction of providing an environment in which they can move into the future. Of course, in the process, you are disturbing the present relations among the family members. As a result, you may see behavior emerging in individuals or the group that we would think of as being less mature, apparently from earlier stages in development. But we do not work toward regression of individuals, toward more infantile ways of acting. We work to facilitate the changes in interaction required in order to help a family move toward the status it is seeking for itself. We certainly do not attempt to uncover the past as a content in the discussions. That will come out, but we do not seek it.

A Therapy Failure.   In the uncommon situation where a family member is driven away at this time, the treatment has to be discontinued. One case stands out in my memory. After the third session, when hostility began to emerge, father refused to return. In his particular instance from the beginning he had said strongly that there were no problems with either of his children. The mother was equally certain that their eight year old boy had a severe problem, and in my judgment, looking at him clinically, the mother was corect. But the father kept saying that his boy was just like him when he had been eight; he implied that it was obvious there could have been no real problem with himself. I realized I could not keep the father integrated into the conferences. I recommended that the mother and boy go to the local child guidance clinic, which they did.

I could describe this father as extremely rigid, inflexible, and compulsive. Practically his total life was devoted to business. As long as he did not move out of that very familiar role, he could function comfortably. The whole situation of family therapy seemed threatening because it was requiring him to be flexible. I do not think the therapy could have worked. Some might say he was a very sick individual. I think the boy was ill. The mother seemed in better control of the situation than any of the other members of the family. You can make these kinds of judgments on the basis of individual theory and diagnostic techniques at the beginning of treatment, but you find that your judgments have to be revised for individuals seen in the context of the family. There, everybody is playing a role, acting, ill, healthy. When you are looking at the family unit, labeling the individuals does not matter.

Such a case illustrates also that family therapy cannot succeed with every family, and that a therapist will meet failure occasionally. I try to learn from these failures. I do not trust that the problems occasioned by the father above were sufficient to explain fully his withdrawal. The explanation should depend on analysis of the whole family, and particularly of my relations with each individual and with the family as a whole. In all probability such analyses would uncover ineffectiveness of some methods I used to build a working relation with each person and with the group.

EQUALIZING SUPPORT

In general, I seek at all times to support interrelations among the family members, and implicitly, to support each individual in the family. Of course, there are times when one person will not need as much support as others, to keep them all on an equivalent level in intercommunication. It is the therapist's function to determine when individuals need to be supported, what kind of support will be effective, and how intense the support should be. This issue of keeping a balance of support among all the members of the family is an important element of the technique. Direct support is needed when we find that an individual is blocked in communication; if for some reason or other, he cannot go on, cannot introduce a theme which one senses he is ready to introduce, or appears blocked in some other way. For instance, here, as in individual therapy, we find that there may be sudden shifts in content. When such a shift happens and an individual comes abruptly to a point where he can no longer continue on a theme, he provides us a clue that communication is now a problem for him. Then the therapist has to open opportunities for him to overcome the blockage.

As an illustration, fathers do not normally speak much in early sessions with me, but become vocal later on. After remaining silent for several sessions, one father came in with a great tirade against his son, daughter and wife. I noticed how each individual in his own way, within a few minutes, was withdrawing from the conference. Then I said, "Now I think we should hear what Jim has to say about this, and Nancy should have her say, and perhaps we should also hear what your wife feels about it." This restored total family participation without closing out the father.

Techniques grow and are modified. I would now say to this family, "I notice as you are speaking that Jim is looking out the window, Nancy is tying her shoe, and your wife is sitting with her head down." The direct approach suggested above, and used at earlier times, has been replaced by a more subtle intervention, designed to draw the family's attention to the mode of communication in the family at the moment. I would now say this is the therapist's job, to help the *family* open opportunities to speak. In their speaking at this time, the content will probably be hostile.

MAKING ROOM FOR
POSITIVE FEELINGS

The exposure of hostility is a prelude to a deeper understanding on the part of parents and children about the feelings they are carrying around inside themselves, not communicating directly with one another. Wherever there is a disturbance in family relations, particularly where the family members have settled into an unsatisfactory rut, and whenever there is insufficient flexibility for change through the family's own effort, then you have the germination of latent hostility between the family members. To move into the position to act constructively in changing their perceptions of one another, and the ways in which they wish to relate, the family must first rid the group of the accumulation of hostility from the past. This bursting out of feeling unleashes the pent-up hostility that has filled up the reservoir of feelings in the family. It is expunged, and then there is room for the positive feeling that has been there all the time.

There emerges then an exploration of why these feelings have been present, why they have been held in, and not expressed before. We have a shift from *expression* of feelings to *analysis* of the nature of the feelings and their causes. This shift is the first step toward deepening the understanding that exists among the family members. But this seldom changes the symptoms.

FAMILY ISSUES FROM
THE CHILD'S PERSPECTIVE

Gradually, as hostility is released, there is a turning to particular issues in the family that annoy the family members. Complaints emerge and discussion moves back and forth about how the issue looks to the person or persons against whom the complaint is directed, as against how it looks to the person complaining. Normally a specific problem, any one of thousands, becomes a focus of the family discussion. There may be a great deal of discussion of the symptomatic behavior in the children that brought the family for treatment, and I now encourage the parents in this discussion, while making sure that the children are protected enough that they may still speak. Occasionally, however, this topic is avoided throughout the whole course of treatment.

The parents and even the therapist are often surprised by the ease with which a youngster recalls events that have gone into the development of his symptoms. Sometimes the statements are too patent, and you have to go beyond the child's superficiality about why he engages in the behavior. Sometimes, however, the recollections are on the surface and the child can expose for everybody's understanding the kinds of reasons for the ways he acts.

For example, a boy of eleven, who was brought to therapy by his parents because he appeared withdrawn from social groups in his school and neighborhood, told us that part of the reason for his withdrawal was that his mother had stopped him from going out to play when he was a little boy; the circumstances behind her stopping him kept sticking in his mind. Now, when he went into social groups outside the home he was ambivalent about doing so; he did not say "ambivalent," but indicated that he was torn between alternatives of working on projects in his room or joining others outside.

It can be a frightening experience for parents to hear how close to the surface are sensible explanations of symptomatic behavior that show the parents their deficiencies in understanding. The fact that the child can not only give explanations that make psychological sense, but can even from his point of view justify the behavior, modifies the parents' attitudes toward him. Bringing out the reasons to account for why he responds as he does, seems to increase the readiness of the other members of the family to look for ways to help him overcome the consequences of unfortunate previous circumstances. But this does not produce the kind of changes that the family is really working toward. It becomes obvious that while some symptomatic behavior can be seen in a new light, the general tone of the family life does not brighten sufficiently to provide the satisfaction that everybody wants.

Mother-Father Problems

Soon you see a shift in the emphasis of the conferences toward discussion of the problems between the mother and father. Sometimes the greater part of this discussion takes place outside the family conferences, sometimes right in the sessions, occasionally through heated arguments. Often it is surprising to parents how many problems they can talk over in front of the children without distressing them. In fact, they are amazed to find that children may be relieved when the parents begin to talk about their difficulties. This confirms my impression that children really know in great detail the kinds of problems that exist between parents, and are made anxious by the fact that the problems are not topics in open communication. As a result, children are left to ruminate about the problems, rather than being part of a direct discussion about them. The children seem reassured by the fact that mother and father are now willing to talk about problems between them, instead of acting them out in front of them. Often at this point referral symptoms disappear, and there is a dramatic change in the whole tenor of family life.

HOW PROBLEMS COME UP

Insofar as individuals in the family wish to introduce content, it becomes a matter of discussion. There is no probing by the therapist. He may on occasion make such comments as: "It seems to me that there must be reasons behind what you are doing that would help us to understand this." Or, "You must have other thoughts that you are not really bringing out here because somehow your meaning is not getting across to other members in the family." Such comments as this may open the way for additional content to come out, but one does not specifically say, "I want to know more about this area of the family life." Or, "What happened when you did such and such?" Such direct questions seem to be redundant, since the content necessary for the resolution of family problems will be brought out when the family needs it and is ready to assimilate it within their relations.

Also, the words used in achieving new ways of interacting are of less fundamental importance than the realization of the new patterns for relating. One content can be interchanged with another, and the basic problems can still be solved. This is why there are certain topics that are not talked about directly in most families; one, as you might expect, concerns the sexual relations between the parents. They do not normally talk about their sexual problems in direct physical terms. We have references, however, to the physical relations between the parents expressed mostly in symbolic terms. in discussions of the emotional qualities of their relations with one another, of dominance and submission, of resisting or yielding, or of taking roles as active or passive members of the marriage partnership. I am sure that the children understand to a major extent that these qualities extend into the physical relations between the parents.

For example, in a family that I worked with recently, the father at one point said to his wife, "You know, never in our marriage have I been able to get on top of you." He was talking about how she somehow always won the family arguments, made the decisions for the family, and so on. But it was perfectly obvious, and I am sure to their son as well, that he was talking about his physical relations with his wife. But he did not talk about what happened in coitus, he talked about other interactions that symbolized many of his relations with his wife.

Sometimes we see symbolic expression of concern about the sexual area in what people do with ther hands, or the ways in which they display or hide the body, or touch other persons. Since the references to sex are not always spoken, some sexual content seems excluded, but may actually be expressed.

There was one case where a 15-year old girl was referred, in part because of severe problems of a sexual nature. Here the parents openly discussed their physical relations, and seemingly it was quite appropriate to do so.

A FOCUS ON INVOLVEMENT

The therapist commonly intervenes to assure the involvement of the whole family in the discussion of the parents' problems. It may be no more than reflecting what he sees happening among them, especially about the effects on an individual as another is talking. He directs attention to the interactions of the moment, and only occasionally makes references to other times in the therapy. The therapist's comments, or interpretations if you wish, are for building the family as a group, not for relations with individuals. He is not concerned with helping an individual understand his own inner life per se, his own situation as an individual, but with helping the family to understand the participation of the individual in the family group.

The therapist's attention must be kept consistently on what is happening between individuals, among the family members, not what is happening inside them. Although information about what is going on inside will be thrown into the communication, the central information is how members are communicating with one another, the responses going back and forth, the decisions they are making as a group, the ways in which they move in relation to one another, or other interactions. The therapist focuses his attention here. This is a different focus than in individual psychotherapy; we have to break the habit developed in individual casework and psychotherapy, of being concerned about intrapsychic events. We have to force ourselves deliberately to look at what is happening out in the center among the members.

THE CHILDREN SOLVE PROBLEMS

Parents are pleased by the ways in which a child can occasionally take a central part in solving problems. The child sees the parents somewhat from the standpoint of an outsider, and can bring perspective, information, and insights to the parents to help them in resolving their difficulties.

I recall a boy, Skippy, about 11 or 12, whose father was a lumber salesman for a wholesale firm. He felt the only problem in his position was that he had great difficulty getting warmed up on Monday. He called the problem his "Monday neurosis." During six years of work for this particular company, no Monday had, in any way, come up to the level of the other days of the week. He brought in the problem for family discussion. Skippy said that he knew what to do. He proposed that, on the next Monday morning, he and his father would start the day with a game in which Skippy would be the first customer. Though he did not know anything about psychodrama, he suggested just such a drama in the family. The next Monday morning, he and his father played this game. The father was greatly amused; he had a hilarious time with Skippy, got a lot of whimsical enjoyment out of it, and to his delight that day was superior to any Monday he could remember. The back of his Monday problem was broken. The father was simply astounded at Skippy's wisdom in suggesting this solution for his difficulty.

CENTERING PROBLEM
SOLVING IN THE FAMILY

Sometimes parents will ask the therapist how to solve their problems. When they ask me, I say, in a simple way, "I could answer this question (assuming I could), but this is not my job. My job is not to provide information or give advice; my job is to help you arrive at your own answers for your own family. If you need information, I can refer you to someone who can give it to you. If you want advice on what you should do, then I can't help you, because I believe it is the family's job and opportunity to discover its own answers, and arrive at its own decisions about how it is going to handle itself."

The therapists's action is that which will help the family itself work out the problem. It may be through helping a child to express his anger, his desires, his needs, and his resistance to the dominance of a parent; or through helping the parent to expose the reasons for his point of view. The therapist comes in to help the communication that might eventually lead the parent and youngster to work through this problem on their own.

The course of problem solving is not always even. Digressions are common. Some problems outside the family may be introduced because they are pressing on the family and seem to have urgency. If the family members find the communication is too tough within the family group, in addition to trying to develop private relations with the therapist, they may use the ploy of talking about people and activities outside the family. At the start, I did not know that to talk about people outside the family is simply marking time, spinning wheels. But I learned gradually that such talk is not productive. It is simply allowing the family to evade the necessity of looking at itself and working out its problems. So the therapist must control the content. If it involves relations beyond those which exist within the immediate family, such as with a business partner, school teacher, neighbor, or relative, I bring the family back to the discussion of the interchanges within it. In effect I am saying, "The problem is here, your job is to solve this problem. You, within this circle, are the only ones who are able to solve it. You will never solve it if you allow yourselves to move out of your family circle to have private talks with me, or to talk about other people and problems outside. By my efforts as a helper, working to confine the discussion to your interrelations and to the problems in your family, you can work through to a change there."

Quite frequently a grandparent has been a problem about whom the family has begun to talk. When the content is about a person outside the immediately present family, I call the family to attention and say, "We're here to talk about what is happening in your family here. I realize that your grandparent is a problem; I know you are having difficulties. But unfortunately, though you are involved, your grandparent is not here. So we have to talk about those of you who are sitting right here now." This does not mean that there can be no resolution of problems with an outsider; problems beyond the family group are worked out. Sometimes at the last session content about the extra-family life comes in, normally in the reporting of some success there, but sometimes as a way of involving the total family in helping to deal with problems there. Discussion of persons outside the present family is never encouraged, however, and early in the therapy I would discourage discussion of extra-family problems.

PARENTS CHANGE

After the parents' difficulties are worked through, you often see a major shift in the way they handle their children. A very aggressive and domineering mother may turn over much of the responsibility for discipline to the father. A man who appears on the surface to be a rather passive father begins to exert real assertiveness in the family life; or it can shift the other way. It seems that each family wants for itself the privilege of determining the kinds of interrelations that they will work to achieve.

Change is a matter of timing. In some instances, I can think of families where they have gone on week after week talking about the same problem, in a context of other discussion. Sometimes these problems are introduced as an ongoing point of reference, a focal point for the total discussion. They provide continuity from week to week. Gradually enough of the emotional climate around the problem has been expressed, and enough of the peripheral aspects of the problem have been worked out, that there can be a sudden and dramatic change in the way a family tackles the problem. In fact, one of the things that surprised me at first was the speed with which changes take place. One week you have the problem, and the next week you don't. But I now understand that there is a lot of building up to the stage where there is this rapid shift, sometimes happening after what seems a minute shift in the position of one of the family members.

SIBLING INTERACTION

Just before the family is ready to terminate the conferences, attention turns to interaction among siblings. During earlier sessions mention may be made of relations between the siblings, but it is surprising that little emphasis is placed on analysis of sibling problems until late stages of the treatment. I think there are theoretical reasons why this is so, one being that in most families there is openness of communication between siblings. Also I think that what we often see behaviorally as disturbances within the sibling relations, represent displacements from disturbances elsewhere in the family, particularly between the parents.

We often talk about sibling rivalry, such as jealousy of an older brother, or jealousy of a baby, as central causes of disturbance in a disturbed child. I have come to doubt its centrality. As a result of observing the small amount of effort that the family puts into solving sibling problems, I have come to believe that they are primarily expression of problems in other family dimensions. Problems between siblings may be ways in which the child or children deal with their personal problems with the parents, or in relation to problems between the parents. When problems at the adult level are being tackled directly, there is no push to confront them as though they existed on the level of sibling interaction. Problems do originate between siblings, however, and these are discussed.

FALSE RECOVERY

Sometimes a false plateau is reached where the family appears ready to terminate but, unfortunately, is actually covering over new difficulties. This happens when it comes up against a problem that for the moment is too difficult to resolve. One should take with seriousness a family's statement that it is ready to leave. But readiness must be determined by evaluating if there are enough positive signs. Usually it becomes apparent, if the family is moving toward a state of "wellness" which is pseudo-improvement. There are indications that they are not convinced that everything is all right—often evidence that the referral problem remains a sore issue. If the family says, "We think we have come to the point where we should stop," I often suggest one extra session to consolidate the gains made. If the family is only on a plateau, and not really recovered, usually the next session brings out a whole new range of problems.

Termination

In the concluding family conferences, the family puts the finishing touches on its work. Struggling through multiple problems of interrelations, they achieve patterns of new complexity and variability. Changes, readjustments, reassignments of roles, re-evaluations, new kinds of communication, and so on, appear. Their modes of interaction may be very diverse from those of other families. It seems that they have caught from the therapist sanction for living by their own value systems and within their own ways of interrelating.

SIGNS OF READINESS

Termination comes when certain signs of readiness are produced. The family is likely to request termination, or to announce that they have decided not to return. For the most part, there is unmistakable evidence that termination is appropriate from the way in which a family is able to operate.

Coping with Symptoms. Usually the symptoms of the referred child will have disappeared, or will have been reinterpreted and incorporated acceptably into the family life. Some symptoms, of course, we cannot change, those stemming from physical handicaps, genetic problems, difficulties in employment stemming from economic recession, and so on.

Cooperation. The family will speak about how they have been more cooperative in their mutual activities, tell stories about activities together, decisions made together, or projects they are embarking on as a group.

Independence.   They also begin to bring in more information about how individuals are going out from the family to engage more freely in independent activities; how, for example, a daughter who has been wanting to go to high school dances is now getting permission to go, or a mother who had wanted to take a course, join a club, or whatever, has actually been able to do that with the encouragement and support of the family. An illustration will perhaps clarify this. There were two adopted girls, one 14 years and the other 11 years, in one family with whom I worked. Judy, the 14-year-old, wanted to go with friends in her school class to basketball games in the high school league. This meant getting into a bus and traveling to schools quite a distance away. Her family were reluctant to have her do this, even though she kept bringing up the issue. "Why won't you let me go to the basketball games, when everybody else in my class has the chance to go?" Mother said, "It means you won't get home until midnight, and this is bad for your health." She had all sorts of other reasons, too, for not letting Judy go. They talked this through, and toward the end, decided that Judy should have the chance. This illustrates an independent action of a family member outside family life, undertaken with the support of the family.

The same thing happens with mothers and fathers; they gain new opportunities for private, independent activity, sanctioned by the family. Where formerly the family used to set blocks in the way of such independent activities, now the family decides in favor of them and for removal of barriers to them. For years, one mother had wanted to take a course in hairdressing to prepare herself for some part-time work. Her children were now in school, and she felt that the meager family income could be supplemented if she could secure training for work at the local beauty parlor. Father and the youngsters had always protested when she brought up this idea. One of the outcomes of the treatment was that the family decided that it would be good for mother to take this course. She enrolled, and they worked out the plans for getting meals and doing other household chores. They moved from criticism and negative feeling about it, into support.

Humor.   The family further indicate their readiness to terminate by toning up their communications. Banter enters; they have jokes; they laugh frequently, and the whole interrelations lighten.

Instead of serious business with one another, they share some of the family lore which is the basis for kidding, and tease one another. Sources of irritation in the earlier part of the treatment are often transformed into topics for teasing and humor in the final sessions. One reason may be that problems have been shown to be flexible matters that could be talked about and changed. Now they are able to laugh, even though the problems continue, because change could be accomplished if there were urgency to do so. The strain is gone and the behavior which was previously a retreat from the family is now incorporated into the family. Perhaps this is one factor in humor, that a feeling is released about a situation that is not vital and unchangeable, so that the exposure of the feeling or problems can still lead to some sort of modification if necessary.

Free Interaction.   There is a loosening of the communication as the therapy progresses to a point where instead of taking turns, as at the beginning, all members seem to be interacting freely, with much flexibility. There are changes too in the content of things talked about. There is more in the way of expression of both negative and positive emotions at the end of the treatment than at any previous stage, where the emotional tone is more characteristically negative.

Individual Growth.   Change can also be evaluated by what happens to individuals, although these are secondary results. In almost every instance, you would say that there is either a greater security about previous roles, or greater flexibility to shift into new roles. Some old roles, even those regarded as troublesome, are kept , but now with the support of the family. The behavior has not changed; the child or other family member is doing exactly the same thing; he looks upon himself in exactly the same way, but the others see him differently. So these changes are commonly measurable by what happens in the group.

In contrast, a regular tyrant of a mother may suddenly show other sides of her personality, her underlying warmth and sweetness, when a passive father becomes more active and aggressive in his family role. From one week to the next, a voice changes, appearance alters, ways of relating to members of the family are adjusted. An aggressive, dominating person can suddenly become passive, submissive; and vice versa. Family A may decide that at this period the most wholesome way to work out their destiny and accomplish required interactions is for mother to take the responsibility as the dominant one—not completely dominant, because dominance and submission are always relative positions. In some families this was the outcome. In Family B, the whole family may work toward father assuming greater responsibility for being a dominant person in the family constellation.

Unique Family Values. It is encouraging to see that in this therapy each family emerges with its own patterns of interrelations, unlike those of other families. It would be a sad thing for society, families, and individuals, if all families had to be the same, if they always had to work out solutions for their difficulties according to a common formula. The family members come to ways of resolving their problems in accordance with the goals that they have as individuals, partners, and a family. The end is in accord with the values that dictate their goals. Sometimes we find that the solutions to the family problems that one family will establish are diametrically opposed to the solutions that another family will achieve for itself. This we expect and feel is appropriate and probably the best indication that the therapist has not imposed upon the family his value systems and solutions for the family's problems.

The therapist has no solutions to propose to a family; he has no value system to give to the family to follow as its own. He does not give advice; he does not direct the family how to function outside the therapy session. He uses the value system of each family; he uses the organization of the family as it is composed, and he does not enjoin the family to follow his way. At least, if this happens we can say that it does so only to a limited extent. Insofar as he believes that communication and group decision are important processes toward a family's reaching the objectives determined by their own value system, he may direct them. But what the group communicate among themselves, and what they decide, must be determined by the family. The therapist wards off governing the family in its whole life; he does not instruct parents how they should raise their children; he does not promote middle-class, or any other class, values and processes; and he prevents efforts of the family to push him into advice-giving. He engineers a situation for a family to explore itself.

I can conceive the situation where the family might decide that the best thing for all its members would be that they go separate ways. My experience would suggest this is not likely to happen frequently. If the therapy is handled well, the more likely result will be that the group will have attained means of communicating and of group decision-making that will facilitate their handling crises. Actually I think there is far greater protection for an individual impelled into a crisis within family therapy than there would be for him in individual therapy. The chances are less that his crisis will ripple out through the family to such extremes as hysteria, an anxiety attack, or a suicide attempt—all effects that I have observed in family members as a result of individual therapy.

I would not wish to leave an impression that I believe a democratic solution of problems is the solution of choice. The communication about problems must involve every individual, but this does not necessarily mean that the way in which the family will decide its choices among solutions will be by a group vote. Frequently, the family may decide that father is the boss in this family and so father is going to make the decisions. They perpetuate an authoritarian, patriarchal role, appropriate for them if they choose it. Elsewhere, a family may say, "Mother seems to know what this family needs, so we will get her to tell us what we should do." Other families will be democratic in the ways in which they will solve their problems, but this represents their system of values, one of diverse ways of living satisfyingly. The families work out their destinies and mutually reach the best possible solutions in their terms. I do not have the privilege, as a therapist, of saying that the ordering of a child's or a family's goals is right or wrong. In fact, I would say that it is the family's responsibility to determine for the whole family, and for the individuals in the family, the goals for which they will reach, and the methods by which they get there.

In evaluation, the families express such statements as, "You know, we really didn't know what was going on in our family, until we sat down and really looked at ourselves." Or, "I wish we had started this years ago when we would have been able to prevent all the distress we've been through in the last few years." They are commonly very positive in response to what is taking place. Sometimes it is in terms of understanding individuals better, but more often in terms of reactions to the change taking place in the total family.

To find adults changing, as well as children, has been an eye-opener to me. I had been strongly indoctrinated in personality theories that emphasized that the period of life when you expect change is during early childhood. Afterward, according to the theories, patterns progressively rigidify, with the repetition compulsion becoming far more important than impulses to new ways of response, especially after you reach adulthood. But adults can change, and a great deal more than I think our individual theories have allowed. I believe the reason why we have underestimated the amount of change possible in adulthood is that we have based our observations and deductions about adulthood on pathology. We have not looked so much at the healthy side of people, where change can be expected. In the family therapy process, where you are exposed to healthy adults, as well as those who are disturbed, we can observe dramatic and rapid changes in adults.

Developed Methods for Problem Solving.   When change is produced in the presence of the whole family, when everyone participates in the change, then we carry all individuals along simultaneously in working out a solution to a problem. At the same time, we are helping the family to achieve mechanisms by which independently they may continue to tackle their problems. In effect, we are demonstrating to the family that through their own efforts, through their own values, and through their own communications, they have processes at hand for taking care of problems as they come up in the future. We are setting forth ways for them to interact that can allow them movement when they come up against a need for change or a need to take care of a problem. As an example, if a family may decide at this moment that mother should take a more dominant role, maybe ten months or five years from now they will find her dominance no longer productive for the ongoing life of the family. They may then use the previous change processes as a pattern for again modifying the mother's role, and the corresponding interactions throughout the whole family.

PRACTICAL CONSIDERATIONS

Number of Conferences.   The number of therapy sessions may range anywhere from eight, which has been the least for me, to three and one-half years of weekly conferences. In the latter case, I would not need that much time, now; this was one of the very early cases, the second as a matter of fact. For various reasons the time was prolonged beyond that actually needed. Eight to 20 sessions would be within my normal expectation.

Prediction about how many sessions a particular family will require cannot be made easily. The number would depend partly on the extent of the disturbance of the family, partly on the ease with which its members can communicate verbally, partly on the clarity of their value systems, partly on the ways in which the family members are handled by the therapist. On the whole the treatment is relatively brief, especially when you consider that it is a multiple therapy where several people are being treated at the same time.

Follow-up.   Families may set up continuation conferences among themselves at home; they set aside a time of the week, sit down together, and confer. Others use informal occasions when the family is together to talk about the family's status. Some families would be hard put to it to say that there is any particular occasion when they talk about the family. The pattern varies with age, concerns, intelligence, and opportunities for their getting together.

Only two families came back for treatment later, after they had terminated. One came back saying that the family wanted to start up again. The family came for one session, and then said they could carry on by themselves. The second telephoned about a year after the initial set of conferences, said they wanted to come back, but the thought of returning was enough apparently to start new communication, and they did not actually return.

Age.   The youngest children brought into the total course of therapy were eight years of age, and average in intelligence. I think my original assumption that nine years of age was probably a lower limit has been confirmed by my own experience; but if the child were gifted, or at least well above average, this assumption would have to be tested by a trial with the family. If the child who was the identified problem were too young to include, a different theoretical and technical approach would be necessary for working with the family.

Young children who are left at home while the rest of the family is in therapy do not seem to feel rejected if care is taken about how they are looked after when the rest of the family is away, if they are in the hands of persons whom they know and who try to keep them happy. The talk in the sessions is at a different level than they are able to manage. A child younger than eight or nine years of age, has primarily a trend toward his own particular and concrete needs. He cannot make much sense out of talk about the family or about the family as a problem. Even though parents or other children try to tell the little child about what is going on, they seem to regard the content as irrelevant or unimportant; they seem to catch and react to the mood.

Those who treat young children in therapy through the use of play materials have found that the level of interaction is different from that possible when working with an older child. When you have the parents present and use play materials for the child's communications, you are dealing primarily with the child and his problems. The parents are involved in the activity so they can understand the child and learn from him how better to deal with him. Here there is not a reciprocal concern of the child about the parents' adjustments, how he can help the parents to work out their problems, and how the mutual relations can be made more effective. Since the focus is on the child, this means that we are not then engaged in family group therapy; we are conducting individual therapy for the child in the presence of the whole family, and with the help of all the adults.

Who Participates?   By definition, by selection, I have mostly restricted the participants in my own work to the father, mother and children—in some instances a step-parent or a child by adoption. A recent family consisted of a mother, her 14-year old son, and her husband, who has been the stepfather for 9 years. There were some problems because this boy had resented the stepfather from the beginning. The family therapy provided an avenue for talking through and solving some of these problems. I have always considered the possibility of including grandparents, aunts, uncles, and any others who might be living in the home, but in my own work I excluded these partly to simplify the research problem I had set myself to tackle. Other therapists, however, have included relatives beyond those in the nuclear family group. In one instance I was sorely tempted to include a housekeeper. She had been with the family for 17 years and had been the nurse for the children; she was the center of the family. Everything pivoted around Meg. When they could not communicate directly with one another, they communicated through her. It seemed as though she was so important to the family that she should be included. The family chose, however, to exclude her. As a consequence of the therapy, the family decided that life would be better without Meg, and since she was 73, they arranged for her retirement.

There is no restriction on the size of the family that may be treated. The largest nuclear family in therapy I have heard about was in Hawaii, a Japanese family with seven children, mother, and father. Large families can be dealt with. Families develop a kind of order in participating; they come in and say, for example that it will be Michael's or Judy's day to talk, and they give precedence to that individual. If that person finishes what he has to say, then another person starts a new communication theme.

I have seen only children in the therapy; the largest family I have handled included parents and three out of four children; Peter, a five year old boy, who was not referred to as a problem, was left at home, except for a brief time when we tried unsuccessfully to include him by providing a sand-tray and World Test materials. Part of the problem may have been my own incapacity to handle the sessions when he was there. We were all getting sand in our hair; the family were concentrating on the small child and on the behavior going on at the sand table; they were forgetting the basic responsibilities for which they were there, to the point of using the disruption as an opportunity to go to the bathroom, wander out of the room, absent themselves from the group and absorb themselves in their own preoccupations. I knew I did not have the resources for controlling the boy and his family. Maybe somebody else could have worked out a way to deal with them. I have tried to be experimental and not set rigid limits on what should and should not be done. Having the five year old boy in the group was an experiment on my part, to see if I could manage it; I could not. Maybe someone else, however, could develop the necessary techniques.

Presenting Problems.   In the families I have seen there have been problems of a wide range, though I have not worked with any young persons who were schizophrenic. One adolescent boy was on the borderline of being psychotic. Some youngsters were sufficiently on the withdrawn side to be thought schizoid; others on the acting-out side were near to being violent. Experience now with family therapy is widespread, although it is my impression that practice with this treatment method has typically favored those who are better educated, more affluent, and more urbanized.

The first effort to use family therapy with a mental hospital patient, to my knowledge, was in the Veterans Administration Hospital in Brockton, Massachusetts. One of my students, Herbert Lipton, and a hospital social worker, Rebecca Glasmann, took on a family that involved a hospitalized schizophrenic. On visiting days the whole family met with the patient and the therapists. After two months, the patient was discharged, and the whole family came back to the hospital weekly to continue the treament. This was reported at meetings of the American Orthopsychiatric Association and later published (Glasmann *et al.*, 1959). I did not learn the status of the patient and the family after the treatment terminated.

There have been quite a few other attempts to work with schizophrenics. Early, the persons who have tried family therapy most extensively with them were Don Jackson (1959) and his colleagues in Palo Alto, and Murray Bowen (1960; 1961; *et al.*, 1959) who used to be at the Clinical Center of the National Institute of Mental Health, and who is now in private practice in Washington, D.C. In Jackson's case, he worked mainly with ambulatory schizophrenic patients in an outpatient setting—people who may have been hospitalized, were still demonstrably schizophrenic, and were not at the moment in a hospital.

Dr. Bowen worked with hospitalized patients. He brought the whole family into the hospital, to live there. This was an intriguing experiment. Some startling observations were possible when the whole family was present. He found that the family could push the staff quickly into taking the roles necessary for perpetuating the ways in which the family members were interacting and responding. They could force the nurse, attendant, physician, and others into supporting the schizophrenia in the patient instead of coming to grips with it as a family problem. The staff learned much about how to have families in charge, and we have much to learn from them about this.

I am sure what we do with families when they come to hospitals on visiting days to see a schizophrenic family member is often destructive of the welfare of the patient and of the family members themselves. In 1963 I proposed a program of study on the ways in which we could move helpfully with families while a patient is institutionalized for various kinds of illness. Of course, this did not look after many patients in hospitals who are single, who are completely alienated, often geographically too, from their families. We would have to work in new ways if we are going to use natural groups to help those patients. A large percentage of our patients have families, and so far we have not maximized use of the constructive forces they have for helping patients and themselves.

Referral of Adult. Others are working with cases where an adult is the referral problem. For instance, work has increased with families where the problem has been alcoholism in one of the parents. It seems that this method is especially well suited to dealing with this type of problem, where in so many cases individual psychotherapy has been shown to be inadequate. Family therapy seems to enlist the kinds of support from the family that make it possible for the alcoholic to consolidate progress as he steps ahead.

Mixing Individual and Family Treatment. I have worked with families where members have been formerly in individual treatment, but not where they were simultaneously in individual treatment with someone else and in family treatment with me. This would be a possibility, and, in fact, one of the things that some family members will ask for during the treatment is to have individual sessions with the therapist. I resist this, but at the same time say, "If it is important to have such sessions, we can set them up with another therapist." The interesting thing is that no patient has ever sought this. This has convinced me that the request for individual care is most likely a resistance to the family group treatment, rather than a fundamental demand for a more private relationship.

I have found that it is not advisable for me to conduct family group therapy and engage in individual therapy with members of the family at the same time. There are often requests on the part of family members that I see them alone, to talk over private problems. I prefer not to lose my ability to relate on an equivalent basis to each member of the family.

However, others have conducted simultaneous family group therapy and individual therapy. One psychiatrist told me that in his group practice, one therapist will take the family, and if there is an individual, such as an alcoholic or a drug addict, who needs extra individual attention, another therapist will treat this individual at the same time. I would think this might be a very desirable method for helping individuals who are seriously disturbed, or who are wanting help with problems that are individual concerns and outside the family problems. For example, the father in one of the earliest families with whom I worked, had severe business problems. A partner had absconded with the firm's funds, and the father was facing bankruptcy. This was intruding, of course, on the family life. But it was not suitable to take up all the details of the business problem in the context of the family discussions. Here it would have been desirable to have another therapist, a consultant, or a counselor, advising and helping to solve these business problems. Other persons than individual therapists could easily be helpful in work with members of the family—welfare workers, vocational counselors, or probation officers, for example.

The Retarded Person.   Naturally, the extent of participation of a retarded person would be reduced, if not impossible. I think that this may be a contraindication to attempting to work with a family that involves the intellectually handicapped. I have avoided experience with such a family. I think many of the problems would be comparable to those encountered in therapy with schizophrenics, where, at the beginning, you have to make a special effort to keep communications on a patient-centered channel. I would like to see many experiments with families where there are persons who are physically handicapped, mentally retarded, or with other difficulties. In general, it is perhaps relevant to remember that every individual is limited in some respects, and the therapy has to work within the limits imposed by basic handicaps.

Children in Institutions.   It is especially important in the institutionalizing of children to continue contact with the total family—painful though this may be for the staff. Family group therapy provides one liaison method, and earlier I thought that our child institutions should routinely invite the family to come to the institution for family conferences. This suggestion did not prove adequate to facilitating the transition of children out of institutions back to their homes and communities.

Foster Families.   Others report that family therapy is not contraindicated though the child is placed in a foster home. You can use this approach with foster parents and the children who are living with them, but, of course, you are meeting with a group that is markedly different from a natural family. There is not the long background of life together, and often the child has brought a role of pathology to the foster family, rather than developing it within the foster group.

Range of Problem Cases.   I think the range of cases that can be handled this way is wide. I know that the acting-out children are more difficult to initiate into family treatment, but not impossible. It is easier to help the withdrawn child to express himself in family therapy than to help the acting-out youngster to verbalize.

We do not know enough yet to say definitively what kinds of families are contraindicated for this kind of therapy. I think this is a matter for clarification by experimentation. I would hope that those who are working with this method would keep an open mind about the possibility of taking on any family, so that we do not codify too quickly judgments about where the therapy would work and where it would not. We know that the extent of motivation for change is an important factor in the success of the work. If the family comes with a strong desire to see change accomplished for the youngsters and for the family, we have a more hopeful situation for bringing about treatment success.

Social Class.   Most of my experiences have been with middle class families, although I have worked with some lower class families. In one of the latter, definitely lower class in terms of income, ways of communicating, language, education, and so on, each of the individuals was very gifted. Here the method was very effective. In another instance, the family of a laborer in a construction firm, the process worked just as well. It was a little more difficult to help the family begin to talk; there were some problems about easy communication. But even families that do not base their relations primarily on verbalizing are not so unique, so different, from middle-class families. I have been struck by how much of the communication in all families is nonverbal. There should be no major problem in handling such families in the conference session, because they still communicate with one another, they still have some sort of group organization, some sort of identity as a family, and some strong motivation to hold themselves together as a family. It may be a different kind of family than normally seen in a clinic, but one of the things that should happen from this approach is that we sponsor differences among families and not mold all families into a similar pattern, either in the family conferences or in their own homes.

Sex of Therapist.   As far as the sex of the therapist is concerned, I have found that at the beginning a male therapist has to be especially cautious not to threaten the father and his role; whereas, a female therapist seems to make it easier for the father to participate quickly in the discussion. With a male therapist, fathers tend to be the last to take part actively. They sit back and size up the situation. When they decide they can speak and make an effective impact, then they speak. They begin more quickly if the therapist does not threaten the father's position as a father. A female therapist may run into all sorts of complications with mothers.

Co-Therapists.   Co-therapists might be suitable, but I would warn that if you work this way there is risk of the family pushing the therapists into parental roles. This is especially true if one of the therapists is female and the other is male. The children are likely to set the therapists up as substitute parents; a great deal of effort has to be directed toward preventing the children from seeing them as mother and father.

FAMILY THERAPY IN A SOCIAL AGENCY

As I have talked with many agency people about family therapy, there has always been a concern about how easily this kind of treatment might be fitted into an agency other than a child guidance clinic. This is a problem. Agency policies may limit the kinds of work done; these may vary a great deal from agency to agency. It may be, for example, that in a particular school, it would be proper for a school social worker or psychologist to have as many as eight conferences with a family. Elsewhere there might be regulations that would permit no more than one or two conferences, and if more were necessary, one would have to refer the persons to a clinic or other agency. If there are such limitations, there is very little point in initiating family therapy. The processes with a family cannot take place as rapidly as in one or two sessions.

Administrative patterns in agencies bind professional persons into set procedures. Another limit is that the programs of agencies tend to become defined by client demand, and there is little time, inclination, or energy left for trying new things. But I think a major barrier to initiating family therapy in many agencies may be the anxiety of the staff about undertaking this approach. That anxiety may be partially related to what the approach does to the roles of professional persons in the agency.

Changes in Intake. Within changes in intake procedures we may find a good illustration of how roles may have to be modified to initiate family therapy.

Take the position of the psychologist, for example. If he is now devoting considerable effort to the diagnosis of individuals, using various kinds of tests and interview procedures, and arriving at deductions about the status of individuals, he may find himself displaced if a family emphasis is begun. His customary techniques and tests used in individual personality and intellectual diagnosis are not designed to gain much family information. He may have to learn about ways to measure communication patterns in the family, how decisions are made there, the activities in which family members engage together, and the problems they see in their interactions.

Or, take the situation for the social worker. If an agency arranges that one member of a family come to the agency to provide a history and to work out the practical arrangements for the course of casework or treatment, an intake social worker may find herself redundant. In family therapy it is important that the therapist or worker not build a relation with one member of a family. From the beginning, the idea of meeting with the whole family should be in the forefront of the worker's thinking. If an intake worker is to follow the customary pattern of an intake interview, secure the history, study the problems, and so on, this reduces the possibility for the intake worker to participate in family treatment. Even one interview, or a few telephone calls, is enough to build a relation with a family member to the point where other members of the family may feel that they cannot catch up.

I can think of another situation which has some parallel: if a social worker has had one of the family members for individual casework, then it is contraindicated for that therapist to take on the whole family. Her relations with the individual will disrupt her relations with the total family group. In this instance, the whole family should be transferred to another worker. There then might have to be exchanges of cases back and forth between members of staff, often a complication.

Or take the psychiatric interview. It is important that we know the physical status of the members of the family. Family therapy is not directed toward coming to grips with physical illness, and many symptoms we might identify as psychological or social may in actuality have an organic base. Family group therapy is a treatment for the social interaction in the family, not the physical medical problems. The psychiatrist will find himself of use to the family therapist in ruling out neurological or other organic factors in any family members; but the characteristic psychiatric interview in which psychological data are sought may not be of particular use to the family group therapist. The kinds of questions that the psychiatrist asks in learning a patients's history of illness and current status are not very relevant to the processes of interaction in the family.

So the intake procedures in agencies have to be modified in order to fit in family group therapy. This can be unsettling. It can produce concern about where the limits of change might be and how professionals can accommodate themselves to them.

Of course, it is possible for part of the staff in an agency to use family therapy while others are using individual methods. This has been done on a selective basis in family agencies with which I am acquainted. Fortunately for the workers, a good support for this idea was given by the administrators of the agencies. They have not been using family therapy exclusively; some reported that it is a rather exhausting kind of treatment to use. This is one reason why they charge larger fees for family than for individual sessions. I must confess that there are occasions when family interviews are very exhausting, but for the most part it has not been my observation that they are more exhausting and trying than individual treatment. My own fee practice was always to charge the same fee for individual as family sessions, on the principle that one was paying for the therapist's time rather than charging for the number of patients dealt with. But I am sure there will be different practices about fees.

BRIEF SUMMARY AND OVERVIEW

Family group therapy, as I conceive it, and try to practice it is treatment for the problems of the social group of the family. It is one of many family therapies, but is specific in its effort to ameliorate the social difficulties in the family group.

Family group treatment is distinct from individual treatment even where collaboration of the family is sought for the patient's welfare. It is different from family casework which is mostly carried on with one or two family members and the content may be on family problems of a much broader range than those dealt with in family group therapy: one illustration—in family casework the social worker might help the mother to develop a budget; in family group therapy, probably never.

Family group treatment is differentiated from simultaneous individual treatment of each of the members of a family, whether the treatment is conducted by a number of therapists each working independently with a single family member, by one therapist who sees each of the family members at a different hour, or by one therapist who sees them all together but by the direction of his approach concentrates his attention on family members in turn. Family group treatment deals with problems in the interpersonal action in the family group; it aims to help the family solve the problems in their living *together*.

If the intention of the therapist is to amend malfunctioning within the family group, and to concentrate his attention on family group processes, these are some general observations about what he needs to do.

At the beginning he becomes a member of a group whose immediate objective is to reduce the anxiety in the new situation. Added to the anxieties created by the problems which initiate the referral are those developed by the newness of the therapy. An early aim for the therapist in addition to handling his own anxiety is to reduce anxiety in the family's relationships with him in order to permit the family to work then on anxiety within its own group. In other words, the therapist seeks that moment when the family will identify its problems as within itself rather than in how to get along with the therapist. Six quick points on how he does this:

1. He *orients the group.* He sets forth his expectations about the ways in which the family members will conduct themselves. He establishes the rules by which the therapy will proceed; he specifies the work to be done; and he details the methods by which it will be performed.

2. He *structures his own role.* Being human, the therapist cannot engineer perfectly his impact on the group. He can, however, if he chooses, discipline himself to the extent of adopting certain forms of conduct and avoiding others. To the extent that he can make his behavior become predictable to the family members, each of them can move in relation to him with increased self-assurance and reduced tension.

3. He *delimits the content of the discussion.* He begins family group therapy with the assumption that it can be effective with only certain types of problems. Therefore, the content discussed should be contained within the boundaries of what may be productive for understanding solvable problems and for developing the ways of solving them. In general, the content is restricted to what grows out of or pertains to the action within the family. The line that divides what may and what may not be discussed is not sharp but some rules help me to decide the allowable content:

Direct family discussion about how its members are getting along with another is supported.

Discussion of relationships with individuals outside the family group is blocked, or attention is directed to the family implications of talking about outsiders.

Reporting of preoccupations of an individual family member with his own inner life and problems is encouraged only as one side of an interpersonal process which is the central point of examination. In family group therapy, we receive content about a person similar to that presented in individual therapy but we do not pursue its history, form, and personal implications. We follow, rather, the consequences *in the group* that ensue from an individual reporting personal content.

Such rules for limiting the content help to define the task for the family.

4. *He depends on the family's capacity to develop insight.* The family group therapist does not need to be an instructor. Evaluation and insight emerge out of the action that takes place among family members. If the interaction among them changes, the understanding of their interrelations is changed. Increasingly I have learned that insight about interpersonal relationships comes not from an outsider talking about them, that is from the therapist making observations based on theory (interpretations), but from evaluation within relations as one tries to deal with others, to accept, fight against, support, hate, love, join, oppose, pacify, agitate, or whatever. It is the everyday tussle of living with others that defines ourselves, our insights, our self-understanding, sharpens our perceptions of others and firms up our intentions in relating to them. Depending on this, the family group therapist has only to promote the interaction among family members, to use his impact as an outsider, to produce change in interrelations, for new insights to be generated.

5. *He endorses the family's right to work out its problems within its own value system.* He seeks to avoid deliberate promotion of his own values and problem solutions among the family. He seeks to reduce the extent to which he may inadvertently transmit his own values. He consciously and by design adopts the position that there are other agents in the community, teachers, clergy, neighbors, legislators, courts, among whose functions are the promotion of value systems, and that he as a therapist is to help the family live more adequately according to the values it wishes to use.

6. Finally, *he accepts the limits of what is possible by his methodology.* Broadly speaking, he can affect the interpersonal action in a family that has been the cause of problems or that has been derived from problems. But there are many other problems that the family members know or that disturb outsiders engaged with these

family members. Family group therapy is not able to affect directly all problems associated with the family members as individuals, as participants in the family group and as citizens in the community. The extent of the therapist's concern about the family members will probably exceed that which he can affect by family group therapy. He has to learn then that trying the impossible is well and good, but that his more important obligation is to learn to do efficiently but humanely that which is possible.

Part Two

REFINEMENTS AND REFLECTIONS

Chapter IV

Advances in Theory
of Family Group
Therapy

Early efforts to understand family processes, and especially the family's impact in causing pathology in children, started primarily from assumptions that families could somehow be classed by pathology-inducing features of individual members. This would be in contrast to others whose behavior would be health-developing and sustaining. If such classification of families were supportable, a nosology of pathological families based on identifiable characteristics of individuals should be possible, just as nosologies of individual pathology permitted classification of persons according to syndromes of symptoms. For example, Brodey (1957), a spokesman for a group working with Bowen who had experimented with hospitalization of total families of which one member was schizophrenic, detailed how the narcissism of parents led to their dealing with their schizophrenic child as an externalized projection of their own ungratified needs, preventing them from facing realistically and helpfully the child's own unmet needs. As a consequence the child reacted with schizophrenic responses.

A Criticism

Theories such as this, extending systems developed to explain pathological processes within individuals, may prove less efficient for understanding family processes than those which start from a social psychological orientation. We have to ask whether or not the narcissism of the parent of schizophrenic or of any disturbed child is different in quantity or quality from that of the normal parent. If so, there should be some method of defining the distinctions and determining the extent of the narcissism. It is doubtful, however, that this can be accomplished. Social group theory would suggest that we are dealing here with a phenomenon that is virtually universal rather than distinctive for these types of family.

One might propose that all individuals in their social relations, whether parents, children, friends, are constantly engaged in a balancing act, juggling the self-wishes against the imposed demands from other individuals. Out of this elemental action in the social group emerges the variety of roles possible within the group. As a consequence, the child and parents will function in certain ways, which will differ from parent to parent and from child to child. Each will attempt to induce the others to accomplish what he is unable to accomplish himself. Each will interpret the needs of others in the light of his own ungratified needs. These simply represent two among the many mechanisms through which social interaction is accomplished, and which are not necessarily pathological.

An Extended Perspective

The point of view on family process to be developed here has been anticipated in the publications of Spiegel (1954, 1956, 1957 [2]; with Bell, 1959; with Kluckhohn, 1954). They follow the philosophic position of Dewey (1925), and approach the family from a transactional point of view. They postulate that the events involving the family occur within a total system of interdependent subsystems, any one of which—for example, the individual, the family, the community, the value system—may become temporarily a focus of observation. The "world" being observed must include the observer and his observing. Within the field encompassing the interconnected subsystems, a component system such as the individual can be isolated and studied as an entity. But this is an heuristic device that will involve some distortion or sacrifice of precision and predictability.

With others, they composed a multi-disciplinary team to develop the relationships among three levels of systematic concept formation, namely, the intrapsychic, the interpersonal relations in the family, and the culture. In the first, they used the theory of psychodynamics from psychoanalysis; in the second, the concepts of social role and role-conflict resolution; in the third, culture-value orientations.

They especially emphasized the cultural and social role aspects of family differences, in marked contrast to the individual-orientated perspective mentioned above. They dealt with such phenomena as the presence of an emotionally disturbed child in families from Irish, Italian, or early American families. In such families they reported acceleration of attempts to assimilate new cultural values. Undue rapidity of these efforts resulted in intrapsychic conflict in the parents, which intruded into the social relations between the parents and the children, leading to selection of a child as a scapegoat to accomplish a pathological stabilization of the parents' role-conflicts. Here is a demonstration of differences of explanation that emerge from different foci of observation. The definition of "family" determines the theory that will eventuate.

Four Definitions of Family

Basically four definitions of the family have been reflected in theory and practice:

1. The first is based on the family as seen through the eyes of a child, or as reconstructed by an adult patient. I call this definition idio-centric, centered on an individual. This is the most common

definition found in psychiatric settings. There we learn about the family through reports from individual patients about their ideas, feelings, fantasies and other intrapsychic reactions to father, mother and siblings. The family appears as a beneficent or a malicious influence and context, determining alternately the growth of healthy and pathological personality reactions. In the major writings, on which our clinical practice of psychotherapy with both children and adults was founded, the basic idea of the family turned around an individual seen generically in polar relationship with other family members, particularly the parents. To the observer, the members of the family interacting with the individual were given form primarily by the manner in which they appeared to this individual, and how he conceptualized them. Any amplification of the picture provided by therapeutic interviews with a mother, or occasionally a father, or a home visit, still did not modify the orientation toward the child, but simply expanded the information available for understanding him and his reports and fantasies about his family.

Ackerman has said that not only is it important for a therapist to see one individual in the family to get information, but to see each member in the family. He recommended that we bring in the father, interview him, give him diagnostic tests, find out what his experiences of the family have been, and what are his resultant ideas and feelings. Then he suggested bringing in the mother, and each of the siblings. Out of such data, analysis can be made of experiences set up against each other, to see what sense comes out, in what ways these ideas and feelings correspond or are different, and what meaning can be found in the complex patterns of reciprocal ideas and feelings. This approach does not represent a radical departure from individual personality theory.

This method of interrelating data corresponds with a common approach in research on the family, where family relations are examined as they exist between two persons, a diad. Family literature contains many discussions of self-other perceptions within the family. Here we are concerned with reciprocal aspects among experiential relations in diads in the family. We may extend our thinking and study to include all individuals in the family, yet we are looking at an individual's experiences of others and their counter-experiences of him. As an example, Leary's *Interpersonal Diagnosis of Personality* (1957), applied to the family would be based on a definition of the family where we look reciprocally at the experiences that the respective individuals have with each other member of the family. Such psychological studies may restrict data to those coming from observations of specific two-person relations, such as mother-child, husband-wife, or between siblings, while classifying the research as in the field of the family. To the extent that diadic relations are seen as between opposing individuals, we may qualify the relations by referring to them as polar.

2. The second definition uses a cultural approach, emphasizing the family as an institution in both its nuclear and extended aspects. Here we are not speaking about a specific family, but speaking in the abstract about the family as an institutional form. Much of the theory that comes to us from sociology and social psychology deals with this kind of definition. Some specific types of institutional definitions are also used. For example, Pollak (1956) and others have talked about the *family of orientation,* an institutional definition marking the family to which the individuals are immediately responding, who live together whether related by blood or not. This contrasts with the *family of origin,* from which an individual has sprung. Obviously these are important ways to talk about the family.

A somewhat similar definition is that which emerges from statistics. Each decade the Census Bureau gathers family information, and produces descriptions of *statistical* families—the "normal," the "lower class," the "Black" families—as revealed from counting the data on Census forms. The Census reports present the composite family put together from the measures secured from household to household. These reports generalize to the point where the statements about the family provide only a normative standard against which comparisons with individual families are possible.

Associated with the statistical definition, also, is the family literature that comes from anthropology. Here workers are concerned with the family as a statistic too, but more often a variety of methods of arriving at generalizations is used. The anthropologist may describe a single family in a society and the patterns that emerge from observing it, but he describes it for the light that it throws on the family in the whole culture. Or, he may observe many families and generalize from them. Or, he may observe the society in general and infer the kinds of family life that may be found and that would support the culture.

Anthropological, normative, or sociological orientations to the family contrast sharply with an idio-centric orientation. The aim is to describe the family generically. We hear such deductions as "The lower class family is for the most part patriarchal in function." "The suburban family is primarily matriarchal," and "The role and concept of the father is changing in this direction today." These theories commonly identify the culture and the community as a source of values, norms, standards of behavior, roles, generalizations about fathers, mothers, children, the style of the family, and sociocultural factors in the emergence of pathological conditions.

3. The third definition I call *corporate,* signifying a body. This is where the family is conceived as a unit. For my part I am thinking of this primarily as a social unit. Here we are dealing with the family as a small group, and defining it from social-psychological theory on the behavior of small groups. We are not thinking of the family as a series of individuals contiguous to one another. This approach leads to theories concerning communication in the family, group attitudes and ideals, family group decisions, and family group activities. This point of view deemphasizes the individual and focuses on the interactive aspects of the family; this is the direction of some theories relating to family group therapy and will be explored in detail later.

4. The fourth unit is that group which is bounded by community pressure and identified publicly (and legally) as a family. The legal family is formed, exists, and can only be dissolved by the application of laws, either those arrived at by common understanding or those found in written statute. But even beyond law, the family is forced in certain directions and governed by many pressures, overt and hidden. Thus the composition and interactions of the family coming for family therapy are affected externally as well as within the family group.

These four modes of defining the family are not necessarily compatible in the present stage of theoretical development. Eventually we may be able to arrive at a single theory that will deal simultaneously with the phenomena of family behavior as seen from these four perspectives. For the moment it may be more productive to isolate the relationships within these four modes of observation and to organize our theories accordingly.

Family Group Theory

Family group theory represents an application of small group theory from social psychology to the natural group of the family. The therapy which led to the development of the theory and which is also, in its later stages, an outgrowth of theory, is an effort to apply knowledge of the operation of small groups to the production of change in the family unit. The aim of the effort to theorize about the family group, and about the therapy process, is to answer, as far as we can, a series of questions.

THE FAMILY AS A GROUP

The first question concerns the nature of the family as a group. To understand the processes in family therapy, it is necessary to attend to four social units:

1. The first is the single collective unit composed of the parents and children. This unit is founded on and developed from the organic base of a biological relationship. This is a given. Even an artificial or an adoptive family is modelled on the biological family. This unit is commonly referred to as the nuclear family. Family group therapy consists normally of treatment of this collective group as a unit.

2. Second, we must recognize that within the single collective unit of the family, there are a series of subgroups, not static in composition, but forming, expanding, contracting, dissolving. These subgroupings help to explain the dynamic processes in family life. Whereas the collective unit of the family has identity as a concept and as a structured entity, the subgroups within it are characterized more by their functional aims and action than by any defined structure as social units. These subgroups may be discerned when we observe two individuals in a family teaming up together for some mutual purpose that excludes the rest of the family members. Such teams are constantly being formed, dissolved, or expanded, as when a

team opens its group to include one or more additional members. In reverse, a larger subgroup may shove a member out and close ranks against him. The process of family life may be described, then, as a sequence of emerging subgroupings within the collective unitary nuclear group. The unitary group may be regarded as an assumed system of subgroups which may be separately identified at any time. In point of fact, despite the physical contiguity of its members, the family may seldom appear as a single group, particulary when observed over a span of time. While not forgetting that the overall family is a group with recognizable boundaries, one is usually made aware of the subunits.

3. Third, we will need to keep in mind that family members interact with the members of the extended family; and other persons with whom the family or its individual members are in touch during daily living influence family members and the family as a whole. Such extra-family persons determine the family status and its future, in part. The therapist is one of these outside persons, but his influence is different from that of many outsiders, especially because he is available to all family members, and not to individuals alone.

These external relations offer gratifications that overcome limitations of the family, and compensate for problems there. They motivate individuals to bring pressures on the family to allow and provide the same gratifications. These relations outside also allow fantasy escape from the family relations. Such fantasies, sometimes in the form of rationalizations for behavior criticized by family, are presented by family members in evading immediate stresses within the family. Thus such content appears in family group therapy.

The family members react also to community pressures. They complicate interpersonal relations in the family and keep forcing them toward holding members in relations with one another. They cannot just go their own separate ways casually. They have to work out some modes of interaction. They may choose goals, action, and gratifications in relations outside the family, and save only a little bit of action for the family itself. But no matter how much the family may disperse, there is still, because of the pressure of the community, some degree of relationship, no matter how minimal. This differentiates family interaction from more casual types of interaction.

There is a boundary around the family that keeps it together, and forces the necessity of some interaction.

4. Fourth, as will be amplified later, it seems valuable to acknowledge that the group therapy situation involves a fourth group, composed of the family members plus the therapist. In regarding the family as a collective unit, we consider it in isolation from the observer. Similarly, when we identify sub-groupings within the unit, we deduce structure and describe behavior as though they existed apart from the social process of observation. The resultant oversimplifications are partially corrected through focusing on the total social group in the therapy situation, which, of course, in its dynamic progress involves subgroupings comparable to those in 2 above. In contrast to the first two natural groupings, the total therapy group is constructed, encouraging us to apply extensive published findings about such groups (compare Hearn [1957]).

PROCESSES OF GROUP FORMATION

Having identified the above four social units, we encounter a second question: how may we define the processes of group formation in the family? As with all human relationships we may think of those in the family as beginning when the aims of an individual confront those of others in his situation. "Aims" is used here as a general term encompassing the meanings of the words "instinct," "drive," "motive," and "goal." Two consequences may follow:

1. First, when the individual's aims are complementary to those of others, he receives their support for his goal-seeking activity. Action then ensues.

2. Second, when the individual's aims are noncongruent with those of others, an ambiguous situation is created which the respective individuals, singly or in small groups, seek appropriate ways of resolving. There is an oscillation of action and reaction, moving individuals together and apart. These actions I have called *transitive actions,* for want of a better overall term to cover all the specific transitive verbs such as "love" and "hate" that describe the process. I have avoided terminology sometimes used for this purpose, such as "interaction," "interrelationships," because it carries too much em-

phasis on the subject and the object and too little on the process between them. Under conditions which we cannot fully specify, these processes eventuate in the resolution of the conflict by the use of either new or habitual patterns of behavior.

Applied specifically to the family, we may define the processes of group formation as *action processes leading to the accommodation of complementary or conflicting demands of individuals who are contiguous by reasons of specific biological relationships or of selection after the pattern of these relationships.*

Such action processes are observed within the manifold relationships possible in the various combinations of family members. The processes may be further specified in terms of their *purposes*, that is in terms of their motivational origins; the *media* in which they are couched, whether verbal or nonverbal, i.e., as processses of communication; and the *mechanisms* observed as the family members maneuver in the attempt to reconcile their conflicting aims through such action processes as decision, evaluation, and revision. They may be further described by the *form* of the structure of interrelationships observed at any point of time, especially by specification of such polarities as dominance-submission, independence-dependence, leading-following, or through such mutual correspondences as loving, hating, and fearing.

Some commonsense observations about the family permit us to elaborate our understanding of these action processes. Normally the family goes through a longer and more varied history of group action that any other small group in our society. It is distinguished from other groups by some particular characteristics of its relational possibilities.

At the beginning, many interrelations are situation-specific, *ad hoc*, and purposive. But the interrelations become ends in themselves, sometimes consciously because the family chooses to keep doing things in the same old way; sometimes unintentionally, because the patterns have become familiar ways of doing and relating. Often the use of such patterns spreads, because they become automatic ways of dealing with family situations.

Consider, for instance, the ways in which a mode of communication becomes patterned in a family. Initially a communication may start with an effort to adapt to the specific level of understanding of a particular family member. To illustrate, one cannot talk to a newborn infant in the type of sentences I am using, and expect a specific reaction. One has to talk primarily in the way one handles the child—through motor communication, touching, holding, rocking, cuddling, and so on. The amount of language that the infant has for communications of a vocal nature is really very restricted. A cry or a coo takes on meanings that parents come to identify, but the basic vocal symbols that the infant has to work with are limited. He cannot communicate in words, phrases, sentences or paragraphs. So the interaction among the parents and the child takes into account expectation about the extent of comprehension possible in each member.

Many of the ways in which parents learn to communicate in early days during a child's infancy are clung to as the children and the parents mature. So we find later, where we may now be dealing with older children and adolescents, that the family still communicates on the same level. We now see it primarily in the subverbal language —through family-syncratic facial expressions, gestures, postures, movements—rather than through words. This is private communication within the family, derivative of a time when words were not available for communication. These nonverbal modes of speech were functional, and continue to be so as they accumulate added significance by repeated use within the family.

For another thing, the family usually consists of both adults and children. The family is composed of individuals at different age levels, developing at different maturational rates, and with disparate age valuations. People are at different stages of physical and psychological maturity. The psychological characteristics of particular ages produce dissimilar requirements for change and possibilities for action. Responsibilities have to shift according to levels of development in individuals. The kinds of problems with which the family has to cope keep changing.

At particular periods, new processes of interaction are demanded with great speed. For instance, parents of a first-born child are often amazed at the rapidity with which they have to revise their ways of handling him in view of the sudden and dramatic shifts in behavior that take place overnight. A pattern is no sooner established than the child's maturation requires a new schedule or a new method of handling.

I remember when our boy was an infant, my wife and I were astounded at the rapidity with which we had to change our life styles. We would just get used to feeding him at two o'clock in the morning, when he would decide that he would sleep until three. We shifted our schedule to oblige him and work out all the things in our lives that hung on that schedule; then he would shift again. We were constantly going through a sequence of being confronted with a demand on his part, gradually getting adjusted to the change, then meeting another demand and having to incorporate that by another shift. The duration of these periods of revision and consolidation when you are dealing with a young infant is shorter than when you are dealing with older children. Later the patterns of restricted interaction seem to be retained for relatively long periods. But a child's growth leads inevitably to new family demands. So, also community demands on a child, such as at school entrance, the first date, the time of career choice, all precipitate intense pressures to complicate family ways of interacting. The demand for working out new forms of family patterns keeps producing crises. This, it seems to me, is part of what is implied in the statement that "children keep you young." Their maturation requires flexible reactions from their parents.

No maturational process is more telling in its effects than the growth of language. As the development of language progresses from communication with the simple signs available to the young child to the complicated symbolic language of the adult, new possibilities for action and demands for changes in family relations continually emerge. We shall see how inability or failure to accommodate to such demands may be related to the breakdown of the family and the precipitation of psychopathological behavior.

Other agents (of a dynamic and changing nature) which help to define the action potentialities of the family group are found in the biological or genetic make-up of the individuals; yet others are found in the community and cultural pressures on the individuals and the group. We are not overlooking the importance of these when we concentrate on the family as a social group, but rather simplifying our own analysis of the nature of the family. We acknowledge the need to revise our points of view to take into account these other components of family interaction.

As stated in our definition, the action process of the family leads to mutual accommodation, which consolidates complementary aims and reconciles the conflicting demands of individuals, thus leading to the structuring of the formerly ambiguous and inchoate operational field (forming of groups). This process includes action within the whole unit or between subgroups of the larger unit. The group units are being revised constantly as other action steps are needed. Thus we describe the forming, remaking and dissolving of the family group(s).

In developing their respective roles in relation to one another in the family, the members tend to seek some of their gratifications in the family alone; some may be found in either the family or outside; others may be secured only outside the family group. We may observe an individual using a broader repertoire of ways of interacting with people in the community than he is allowed within his own family. To reconcile all the complex interrelations that exist with the family, it appears that there has to be a progressive reduction of the ways in which family members interact. One indication may be the way in which the family develops labels for its various family members. Another indication may be the ways in which the themes in communication are reduced. Certain themes talked about in everyday life outside in the community are not presented or discussed in the family, even though intellectually and physically one could talk about these matters at home. Certain kinds of decisions are not confronted within the family.

It appears that the simplifications in family interaction are not entirely stable. Factors enter that interrupt simplified patterns. The interactions keep being reviewed and revised. Thus, the family alternates between periods when interactions have been simplified within narrow ranges, and periods when the family struggles to broaden the range. Family life goes from periods of restricted interaction to periods when there is heightened potential for interaction. The transition points where simplified modes of action are no longer usable appear as family crises. A crisis persists until the family has expanded roles and interactions permitted in the family. Thereafter follows a progressive reduction and simplification of them. There is a continuing periodicity about expansion and contraction throughout family life.

HEALTH AND PATHOLOGY IN THE FAMILY

Next we must consider the question of health and pathology in the family. We are speaking here of social health and illness, especially the latter, which may subsume a broad range of social problems shown in one or more family members. We recognize that health and pathology are value judgments applied to the behavior of the family group or individual members by those inside or outside the family. In dynamic terms, the judgment that behavior is pathological is a demand for change in present behavior, whether or not this is possible. Health, in similar terms, represents behavior which is socially supportable and sanctioned within the family group, outside it, or both. Behavior may be called healthy or pathological as though it were clearly one or the other, which is never actually the case, since the judgment is always related to the personal standards of the judge, none of which occur universally.

To speak of the healthy and efficient family implies, then, some broad concurrence on the characteristics of such a family. Among those that might secure such broad agreement are the following:

It shows, by the mutual satisfaction of its members and by action in concert, that complementary aims exist and are supporting the functions and structure of the group as a group.

It has available multiple methods for accommodating the mutually incompatible demands of its individual members. It demonstrates from day to day a variety of patterns by which it faces and handles the conflicts between individuals and factions within it.

It has means of repeatedly evaluating the consequences of its achievements of accommodation.

It chooses to operate flexibly, so that new methods of accommodation may be discovered and taken up when radical shifts are required.

In contrast, we believe that the family that produces a disturbed individual has not been able yet to achieve the above action patterns.

Pathology and Change

We are learning more and more how complex disturbance is, and how important it is not to over-simplify explanations of why people become disturbed. It is probably important for us not to look for single causes, but to look for the multiplicity of factors that produce a disturbance.

We have deluded ourselves into thinking that the major causes of disturbances can be explained by knowing what is happening inside an individual. Emphasis on the social situation of the persons—his position in the family—is a necessary expansion of our understanding of disturbance. Most of the pathology that we speak about in psychotherapy, or case work, is pathology that is regarded as happening intrapsychically, within an individual, to disturb him, and to make him act in a symptomatic fashion. Using the individual as an orientation unit, it is perfectly appropriate that we produce a theory that relates to what is happening within an individual. Yet our theories of pathology and of health are inefficient when they are based on the attempt to understand what is happening in an individual.

I am not saying that every evidence of emotional disturbance in an individual is a product of disrupted family interrelations, and that we can always carry the responsibility back to the family. We know that there are people whose pathology is better explained in terms of physical and organic problems. We know that there are other individuals whose problems are accounted for better in terms of neighborhood, community, or larger social groups within which they are living. Often the only way in which a family seem able to handle the complex pressures that come from outside the family is for them to work out ways to cope with the resulting tension as though it had its source in family interaction.

But insofar as it is suitable to say that an individual's difficulties are created by or the product of his family life, it is probably just as appropriate to say that the family is disturbed. So I have begun to shift explanations of pathology away from the type of interpretation where we see it as a product of what families have done to an individual, toward seeing it as behavior of a person embedded in the family, a very strategic social group. The ways in which an individual is caught up in a family which, in itself, is not functioning adequately, may be used to account for this disturbance. This is to supplement, not to supplant individual-oriented theories of psychopathology.

Also, we have to go further and look at the broad aspects of the culture in which we live and work. Moving the other way, we must look even more intensely than we have so far, to the biochemical, physiological and other factors associated with the body as an organism, and attempt eventually to make theories which will incorporate the ideas and explanations from the perspective of all these various vantage points. At this time, however, we do not have the facts available, nor the background ideas, to integrate physiological and other physical theories with psychological, based on individual personality, sociological, based on the analysis of groups, and cultural theories. I think it is probably to our advantage to deal with each of these thought systems separately, and to look forward only eventually to a time of comprehensive, integrating theories.

When you move over to seeing the family as a group, one of the first things to be noticed is that the individual members project blame onto others. Systematically father, mother, or both say, "Well, you know we wouldn't have any problems in our family if it weren't for the way the kid acts." Or, we'll get a youngster saying, "I wouldn't have any difficulties if my mom and dad would be different." Or, "If my brother didn't fight all the time, it wouldn't be any problem getting along at home." Or, if they are feeling particularly insecure, they may place the blame on some who are not even present—other relatives, neighbors, teachers, a boss or fellow workman, or even less personally, on circumstances. Some other person or thing is given the responsibility or the blame for a condition that exists.

When you have the whole family in front of you, and they evidence projection all the way around the family circle, it begins to raise questions as to who is really to blame. You find you cannot pinpoint the individual who bears the ultimate blame, nor one whom it is necessarily more advisable to trust than any other. You begin to see, rather, that making a person a patient is probably an outgrowth of the blaming process, and that it might be appropriate to ask if the whole family relations are not disturbed and needing change more than any individual who belongs within them. You begin to wonder if it is fitting to treat a person privately, since these other family members will not stay in the background and will not stop having an impact on him. Your attention shifts to studying the meaning of each individual to the family group as a whole.

Take, for example, the instance when a family comes to a clinic, because a father and mother want help with their child. If we are thinking of the family as a group, we ask, "What is the meaning *to the family* that they are coming for help for this disturbed child?" We are immediately led to assume that, for some reasons, the request for help with the child means that there is disturbance in the group of which he is a member. This must mean that there is some disturbance within this family group manifesting itself in the pathology of the individual child. In a sense, the child's pathological behavior is revealing the pathology of the family.

The next stage is to see that the family group process has forced the child into a pathological role. So, you begin to analyze how the group is responsible for the production of pathology in this individual. Even further than that, you question how the perpetuation of this pathology is meaningful and necessary for the continuing operation of the group in the fashion in which it has been organized. If one treats this individual in isolation, the whole family will confront his changes, and be forced to adjust to them, or to mobilize counter efforts to restore the pre-treatment behavior of the individual. Or we will find, if a child is no longer carrying the role of being the sick one, it would happen that someone else will be forced to take it on, and pathology will be produced somewhere else in the family. We see the family shifting the focus of blame and responsibility onto another. We see in another disturbances and pathology that we had not suspected, because, in fact, they have been newly imposed by the family. Often we find this in clinical experience, that as one person gets better, somebody else in the family gets worse.

A very good illustration of this was found in the McAndrew case in Edinburgh. The mother, son, and daughter had all been in individual and some group treatment over a three-year period at the clinic. The father had been seen at the intake interview, but had never been seen since. Whenever there would be the slightest bit of improvement on the part of an individual—mother, boy, or girl —there would be some outbreak of pathology elsewhere in the family.

It was only after I had the whole family come together, that the clinic staff were able finally to understand that every time the mother, boy or girl would progress, in their view, the father would begin to push to restore the former kind of equilibrium in the family. The push, perhaps unconscious, was mostly in the direction of perpetuating the difficulties of the little girl, who was the primary referral problem. But, if the push did not show itself in the daughter, then it was evidenced in the mother. So over a three-year period, the clinic found no major family or individual change, no major remission in the difficulties. It was only after the family, including the father, came to the clinic, and everyone involved in generating pathology was present, that the family's problems were resolved.

In family group theory, we are dealing with pathology not as an intrapsychic event, but as an occurrence in family interaction. On the basis of my experiences, the characteristics of the family that is pathological, that has broken down, that is not functioning well, seem to be of this sort. Where you have an individual, let us say a child, showing behavior disturbances, you usually find that the family structure, the interaction among the members of the family, has rigidified, tightened up. Specific roles have been imposed, and there is little opportunity to turn away from these roles to take up other roles. The number of ways in which a child can relate in the family has been reduced to the point where there is virtually no scope for interaction except in a narrow stereotyped channel of operation, within the confining rigidity of a limited pattern of interrelations and of labels. This is the sort of rigidity we find in a family where an individual is showing pathological behavior. The number of roles that are available to the individual is reduced to the point where he is unable to escape from those he is allowed to use.

A manifestation of this rigidity is the reduction in communication, the possible things that an individual can say to others in the family. Behavior that is disturbing to others is intensified, becomes a problem in the community, school, and family, because there are few ways an individual has to communicate about things happening inside the family group and few ways to act.

Another characteristic of the pathological family is that one individual often carries the pathology for the system. It is a distillation out of the particular interactions among the various members of the unit. An individual is referred because he has problems, but he carries the pathology for the whole family. This does not necessarily mean that this scapegoated individual is more incompetent, inadequate, or ill, than other members of the family. It means, simply, that a person has been cast visibly into the role of being the bearer of the family problems.

Thinking in these terms, then, we have to reassess the status of the mother and father, and other individuals in the family. Acting in a disturbed way is a role, just as being a "model child," "the baby," "the black sheep," and so on, are roles. Such roles are imposed on a particular individual because the family has discovered that this structuring seems to be the best way to handle the complex interrelations that exist within the family. As soon as the communications between the members of the family are opened up, one finds that in individual personality terms, each of the individuals in the family is disturbed. But the disturbance of each is not internal but rather external, imposed on a person as part of the role that the family will permit him to play. When such roles, labeled "pathological," become established, the basis for chronic behavioral disturbance is set down.

It follows that in every instance where we have a disturbed child we have the family motivated to preserve that disturbance, seeking to perpetuate the pathology of the individual. This is not to be followed as an absolute truth. Youngsters will go on year after year showing the same symptoms. You bring them to individual therapy and think they have changed; but the same behavior will recur because the family is motivated toward reinstituting the disturbance. One reason why it is important then to deal with the total family as a therapeutic unit is that you can change the complex out of which disturbance in this one person emerges. To deal with the family together is a more efficient way of changing circumstances than to deal with each of the individuals in separate individual therapy. You do not have any problem from hidden family communications. You are working directly on the interactions that produce the disturbed role for the individual.

Acute Symptoms

We have found it necessary to differentiate the conditions within which acute symptoms are developed and those within which chronicity is produced. Where we have an acute crisis in a family, when an individual is first showing disturbing behavior, when symptoms suddenly break out or seem to, or when his behavior has newly become a cause for family anxiety, we are probably facing some demand on the part of the individual for change in the family constellation. The acute symptoms may be regarded as signs about a person's needs, his desires and anticipations for the others, and his resulting goals. Thus, among other concepts the symptom may be thought of as an attempted communication expressed in such a manner and intensity as to effect disturbance in the group.

Frequently these demands for change in the organization of the family occur because of developmental changes taking place in the child as he matures. When these demands come along in the healthy family, they are communicated directly. If the family interprets, understands and works out an adjustment to this communication, then the symptoms will disappear, the family will restructure itself, and move on to new family group activity.

If, for some reason, however, certain changes are required and the communication of the need for these changes is blocked, if the family does not understand, or the parents do not want to give in to the demands, or the whole idea of change is an uncomfortable one, then the youngster has to develop ways to communicate to the family that things are not right, that change has to take place.

One tendency of the person whose demands for change are not being met, is for him to use increasingly primitive language when the mature language available to him is not functional. Commonly, we have the bursting out of various kinds of action language, shown in bodily changes or acting-out symptoms, in order to communicate to the family group that change is required.

Often signs learned in early life are used because of their simplicity, even though they may have lost their historical sign-value and be now less efficient in most situations than more complicated symbolic language. The use of a more primitive sign language suggests the breakdown of more complex communication, and ineffectiveness in more mature language. This inadequacy may be the result of defects in the symbols formerly available, as when the symbols are too ambiguous, when their meaning to speaker and listener is not equivalent, when the intended recipient is not attending, when, having heard, he fails to respond or mobilizes powerful countercommunications in protest against what he hears.

In practice, the acute symptom is commonly expressive and/or motoric rather than verbal, in accordance with the observation that nonverbal communication generally takes precedence over verbal communication in the family. In a group with such a long history of development, where the earlier nonverbal language was a required form of communication, a brief gesture often speaks a whole paragraph. Analysis of the communication system in the family leads to the following observations:

1. Frequently the nonverbal is the preferred language, especially when there are young children, but also with older children and adults.

2. For the most part, the verbal and nonverbal are interchangeable as modes of communication; this is a basis for family group therapy, where the non-verbal must for a great part be translated into the verbal.

3. Sometimes the nonverbal represents a breakdown of the verbal method of communication. The latter may then be restored only when there is especial support and sanction for expressing content verbally.

4. Sometimes the nonverbal represents that which has not attained consciousness and cannot therefore be expressed verbally. Support may lead to the development of new interaction, which, as experienced, produces insight, awareness of the meaning of the behavior, and the ability ultimately to verbalize; but expression cannot be attained until insight is present.

5. Sometimes the nonverbal and the verbal are mutually contradictory or inconsistent.

6. Sometimes nonverbal language tends to be used for private communication within the family group in preference to the more public verbal communication. Particular words and verbal expressions may also develop a private symbolic value within the family and be used in intimate ways, even though the outward form is public.

Returning to consideration of the acute symptom, some have

thought that the implication of the reversion to primitive communication is that a therapist should try to explore what the meaning of the behavior was at the time it originally appeared and was used—an historical approach. Family group therapy would suggest that the appropriate exploration is into the communicative intent and meaning of the symptom within present interrelations.

Concomitants of Chronicity

If the crisis represented in acute symptoms is not resolved, then the symptom processes are incorporated into the patterns of family action, and groups are formed on the basis of the existence of the symptom action; such groups may include or exclude the individual with the symptom. The symptom then is perpetuated as a role, partly developed, partly assigned. Such a role may retain to a certain extent some of its communicative purpose, but it tends to lose this aim as it is reinforced by the pressures of the family group and thus becomes habitual. Here we have, then, the development of chronicity.

The chronic symptom becomes a way of interrelating—a mode of action—and attains the usefulness of the familiar as the family works out its purposes. It is perpetuated because it has become integrated into an established web of family interactions and its persistence is functional and necessary to the continuation of this structure. Within this pattern the value of the symptom to the respective family members may vary; it would not serve the same purposes for the patient who carried the symptom as for any other. Though each may use it in his own way, the family significance is primarily its functional necessity to a stabilized mode of interaction. No one may consciously wish it to persist, although an unconscious need for the pathology may be demonstrated by the emergence of symptomatic behavior in one or more other family members when the patient begins to improve. The symptomatic mode of action seems to be forced on another family member in order to preserve the overall pattern of the family process.

When chronic symptomatology is deeply entrenched in the behavior patterns of an individual, we may often observe one or more associated conditions or situations in the family.

1. There may be a limitation or reduction in the range of methods

of accommodation to conflicts between the family members, for instance, progressive limiting of the action patterns permitted in the family. Patterns of behavior become stereotyped; the manners of relating become fixed and unresponsive to modifying influences. The stereotypes may be represented in the rigid structuring of subgroups within the family; in the constriction of the exposed goals toward which individuals, subgroups, and the family as a whole direct themselves; and in the inflexibility of their choice of action patterns.

2. There is a diminution of symbolic communication and an increase in the use of simple signs. Thus the messages which can be transmitted are impoverished quantitatively and qualitatively. There is also reduced reception of messages through failures in listening, hearing, and in the visual perception of gestures and facial expressions.

3. There is a breakdown in the evaluation process through which individuals attain and revise their perceptions of others, their awareness of their own methods of responding to others, and their aims, both personal and mutual. Consequently, they act in such a way as to perpetuate the pathological behavior and as though it were impossible to revise. Verbally they may protest their distress at the behavior of the sick family member, while at the same time perpetuating, without insight, the conditions that result in the pathology.

4. The family values "change" insufficiently or excessively. Change is an aim of families in varying degrees. This difference is reflected in the extent of the development of family lore which provides traditional patterns of interaction. For a family to be effective as a group, a balance seems to be necessary between the aim of preserving tradition and achievement of change. If the clinging to old ways is too strong, as in immigrant groups, the family will face disruption, both because of the conflict in values with the culture and the internal rigidity of the family; if, on the other hand, change is overvalued, advantage cannot be taken of the economy of stable patterns.

Family Therapy as a Mechanism for Change

Let us now consider some points of view about how family group therapy produces change in face of such pathology. We do not know if the processes are fundamentally different when the symptoms are acute and have produced a crisis in the family, or when they are chronic and integrated into the family interaction. We suggest that, in the latter case, some crisis must be precipitated, perhaps by the pressure of community reaction, or perhaps by some change in the state of the person who has been carrying a pathological role in the family.

The initiation of change through family therapy begins with the referral, which is itself a request for change, but characteristically for change in an *individual*. The first problem in family therapy is to translate this request for change in the individual into one for change in the *family* where it may be assumed change is needed. Such an assumption would not be foreign to the thinking of family members in most instances. In a sense, the therapist is dealing with the family in many ways as a therapist deals with an individual in individual therapy. But, he sees the family as the patient rather than an individual. The therapist supports this point of view when he insists on seeing the family as a group rather than as a series of individuals in isolation. He remembers that the family is already constructed as a group. That began as a natural process many years ago. The group existed before the therapy, it continues through the therapy, and, most important of all, it will move into the future as a group. It is not only an instrument of the therapy, it is an end in itself. We are to promote its well-being.

Beyond this, in family group therapy the group life persists throughout the whole week. Whereas in group therapy a group comes together for the therapy hour and then disperses, with the family, the group is together in one way or another all the time. The therapy hour is a continuation of family life. Thus change that is initiated in a therapy hour is likely to have a direct and immediate transfer into the continuing work of the family. Immediate support or reinforcement for changes can be available on a 24-hour-a-day basis.

When the motivation for family change is established, the therapist forms a group with the family in which he attempts to play a planned, controlled, and communicated role. Such a group has been newly constructed in the therapy room. The nature of this constructed group around a conference table is important for producing and understanding the therapeutic results. It is not enough to restrict our efforts to trying to figure out what happens within the family group. One has to see that between the therapist and individuals, between him and subgroups of the family, and between him and the family as a whole, interactions are taking place which modify the interrelational functions of these individuals and produce circumstances within which change can be effected.

One could say to a family coming to a clinic, "Well, now you go home and sit down for an hour every week together, and talk about yourselves, and you will see the therapeutic results." For some families, this might be sufficient. In fact, the majority of families have this kind of interactive discussion as a regular part of their family life—around the dinner table, and when engaged in other mutual activities. This is a part of family life. It probably is a lesser part in families where we see sick children, and in most families that come with a disturbed child to a clinic. It would not be sufficient to suggest their conferring among themselves.

The therapist is using a conscious and disciplined technique to assist family members to accomplish the job of solving their own family problems. The difference between a family's own efforts or casual attempts of friends, neighbors, and so on to help a family, and a therapist's attempts, is that the latter is following a technique: he is in control of himself in some predetermined ways in realizing the job he has to perform. He uses himself as an instrument in helping to accomplish that. He develops particular ways of relating to the family that bring about certain therapeutic consequences; he can facilitate the changes, and speed up the change process, when his technical competence is such that he can handle the treatment.

Something about the nature of the group that includes the therapist produces change. We are gaining now some partial understanding of what is involved when the family and the therapist are together. The group in family group therapy consists of the therapist *plus* the family. In this group we have set up a situation within which the therapist can be brought into communication. He comes into contact with the private ways the family has for moving together in action toward mutual goals, for reducing the tension when their goals are incompatible with one another, and for extricating themselves or pushing another out of the group when a member can no longer find gratification there. The therapist learns the private ways that have become systematized within the family by which individuals deal with goals which are incongruent and conflict with one another.

Within the group the therapist has constructed with the family, he establishes with each individual a subgroup in the presence of the whole family. Each subgroup involves individuals interacting with the therapist as a non-family outsider. He calls into play actions embodying patterns that the individual uses in his public life beyond the family, beyond what is typical within the family. When family members go out into the community, they may use ways of responding that remain only potential to them when they are in the family. When a child goes to school, he will behave in ways other than those in which he responds to mother or father. He will show different kinds of patterns than those he shows in the home. When father goes to work, he will use different social skills than those he shows in home relations. When any of us play or take part in social groups, we show a range of behavior beyond that which we use within the family. This is not a sign of perversity, but of habits of interacting and of the cohesiveness of the family group.

When the therapist joins with the family to establish the therapy group, he is able to draw out from each individual ways of responding that the other family members do not usually see, beyond those normally used in the family group. This introduces new perspectives for the family members. Each comes to see the behavior of the various individuals of the family in new ways, see new potentialities for responding, new ways to work out interactions with others, new ways to team up in the family, and new interests that can be built up into aims for the total family.

In order to promote participation, the therapist must develop and maintain the clearest possible definition and presentation of his own functions. As with all groups that are constructed, there is an initial stage of common exploration of the respective roles of individuals and the sanctioned modes of communication. Our most difficult relations are where we are perplexed about what to expect from other people, where we have to go through elaborate processes of testing what the other person is like, what he is likely to do, and how he is likely to respond to us. The greater the consistency that the therapist can bring in his own ways of acting and responding, the clearer the family's conception of how this therapist is going to act, the more rapidly the treatment will progress. This is why it is so important at the beginning for the therapist to orient the family about what he is going to do and how he will respond. He needs to make clear for them:

1. the therapist's clear awareness of the formal responsibilities he will undertake;

2. his defining of the manner in which he will accomplish them; the limits of what he will be and do, and what he will expect from the family;

3. the relationship between what he says and what he communicates non-verbally; this determines the extent to which he can make his role explicit. Inevitably the family will test out the truth of what he says, whether the ways in which he talks about himself are actually consistent with the ways in which he relates. But the more his behavior becomes predictable, the more rapidly the testing will be completed, and the group will structure itself into a functioning conference.

When the therapist has established working relationships with each individual participant in the family, the members begin to perceive the new possibilities of action which are being revealed to them and to incorporate them experimentally into their joint action. For example, a father will use responses to the therapist beyond those that he uses with mother and his children. From the community he brings, as it were, some of the ways of acting which he does not normally show in the family. Mother and the children see him in a new light. The father functions, then, in an expanded way, with public behavior that family members can evaluate in its potentialities for responding at home.

The same thing happens for mother. She may have been going along in a rut day after day. When she comes into the therapy, and has to react to the therapist who, as an outsider, deals with her in ways different from members of the family, she responds differently than she would at home. Her husband and children see her differently. The same thing happens with the children. A child who goes to school may actually respond to the therapist with many of the techniques he uses for responding to the school teacher, techniques that make it possible for him to get along in the school setting but beyond those used in the home. Mother and father see the child differently.

Some of the observed behavior family members may not like; then they will work hard within the family to keep such behavior from taking place at home. On the other hand some behavior may be adopted, constructively for the family. Within the family, they may decide to incorporate, use, and support these ways of acting. Normally this begins in two-person subgroups in the family (parent-child, husband-wife, etc.). These two-person subgroups are consequently enlarged, combined, grouped, and regrouped toward inclusion of as many family members as is optimal for the action to be accomplished.

The therapist's overall activity may be described, then, as an effort to promote social interaction through communication within the family unit, permitting it thereby to experience, appraise, define, and reorder its relational processes. The therapist builds social action on the basis of his own methods of participation. He conducts relationships—now with one, now with two, now with all—in the presence of the others. He disrupts unsatisfactory patterns of relationship as he permits individuals to reaffirm old intentions that have been frustrated. He calls up new intentions. He encourages the family to clarify its goals, to choose more appropriate group goals for the whole family and more suitable personal goals for use in life outside the family's direct involvement. He demonstrates, through the ways individuals relate to him, that within the family there may be: increased fluidity in communication; greater flexibility in roles and functions; and greater discipline in the choice and forms of relationships.

He promotes thereby new evaluations within the family of the potentialities and skills of the individual members. He encourages reassessments of the past, of the responsibility for earlier difficulties, of the meaning of symptomatic behavior, and of the family climate within which it grew. He prevents any family members from evading the implications of their relationships with him and others. He demonstrates forms of relationship that can be transferred to other interactions in the family. This leads the family to the conviction that change is possible and desirable and may bring about a greater measure of behavior that the family would interpret as positive. Thus, the content of the sessions is about their interactions with one another, what they are like as people, the kinds of feelings produced as they talk to one another, the ways they would like one another to act, the things they want to accomplish with each other, and what is necessary from each one in order to accomplish these things.

I have set forth, then, a thesis about how the therapist effects change in the family group. Recapitulating, it may be stated in five propositions:

1. *In all social groups, and particularly the family, the communication and interaction is structured within certain operational limits that produce stereotyped patterns of reactions among family members and a restriction on the permissible ranges of individual behavior.* These are normal consequences of belonging to the family. They often result in mutual depreciation of the potentialities of the other, a kind of cynicism about what can be expected of him, and an unrealistic appraisal of what he might accomplish. Such limits are an obvious consequence of any group membership, are consistently evident in the family, and are necessary to establishing and maintaining the group operations of the family.

2. *Most older children and their parents have available to them potential patterns of behavior beyond those they use in the family.* These are revealed in the community in relation to persons outside the family. I refer to these as public patterns, as separate from familial patterns.

3. *The therapist is a community figure in relation to whom the individual family member may show behavior that extends beyond what he normally reveals in the family.* He may react in these ways toward the therapist without engendering the intense anxiety that would follow venturing these new behaviors alone in the family. The therapist seeks such public behavior from each of the family members. For the family this introduces change.

4. *In response to the new patterns revealed, the rest of the family members must revise their stereotypes about the family member, must re-evaluate him, must respond to him with new attitudes, and new accommodations of their own behavior.* Together they test out, thereby, potentialities for relations incorporating changes that prove useful, and rejecting those that fail.

5. *Having developed new modes of interacting, supported by mutual commitment that they are better and should be continued,*

the family consolidates these new patterns. They work in common to inhibit or eradicate the old outworn patterns, and to strengthen the new. A whole field of research in learning could be spread out before us through study of the methods by which the family members act upon one another to reinforce the patterns they have newly achieved.

The Nature of Family Changes

How do we describe the changes that take place as a result of the therapy? First of all, we see an increased fluency in the conversation, an increased participation of everybody in communicating and an increased range of content about which communication takes place. Especially we see an increase in listening, appropriate since communication involves more than just expressing one's self. It involves hearing, feeling, taking in what the other person is trying to communicate, and attempting to try to analyze its meanings. As a result of a change in listening, and total communication patterns, other changes seem to follow.

Second, an increased understanding takes place about the roles that are required or permitted in the family. The range of roles is increased, and sanctions for new roles become apparent. Greater flexibility is allowed an individual to choose the roles he will play in the total group. He can begin to talk openly about what he wants to be for the family; what the family wants him to be; and what the effects of taking on these roles might be. For example, a child who has been babied all his life may begin to want to assert himself so he will not be dealt with like a little fellow, but like a grownup. Communication about his wishes leads to understanding, exploration of the possible consequences of such a role, and eventually to increasing the range of roles he may assume in the family.

A good illustration of this occurred with Alex, a 14-year-old boy, who kept saying to his mother. "You are always treating me as though I were eleven." Why he chose 11 I never did find out, but he said he felt inside himself that his mother had defined his role as being that of an 11-year-old. One of the issues in the family was whether he could choose from the store his own jeans, the kind he wanted to wear, or whether he had to take the kind his mother wanted to buy for him; whether he should have Levi's or Lee's. Levi's apparently shrink, and mother did not like them; but this was the brand the other kids were wearing at school, so Alex wanted them. There was a tremendous discussion about the meaning of Levi's, the need of appearing to be 14 years of age. Through this discussion and exposure of the feeling all around the family, functioning like a 14-year-old became a role that this boy could assume. Finally, mother and father agreed to his having Levi's. There was an increased tolerance and support for his individual freedom. But also the relations between him and his parents became formed and chosen rather than unformed and imposed. That is, the relations chosen by everybody in the family were redeveloped within a disciplined framework.

Another way of describing the changes is to point out that symptomatic behavior, the topic of so much discussion, recrimination and distress in the family, begins to make psychological sense. The family comes to understand that it is important and has a meaning.

Take, for example, the case of Emma, a girl of eight years of age, below the age I normally regard as suitable for family therapy. She was, however, a very gifted little girl, able to verbalize fluently, and able to conceptualize on a high enough level to participate readily in the therapy.

Emma would take her little brother, one and a half years old, put him under the table, and pull the tablecloth so all the dishes would fall on him and hurt him; or she would dump him out of his carriage; or she would make sure that he would fall off the bed, or bump his head on the bathtub, and so on. The parents could not understand why she was so malicious and aggressive in wanting to hurt her brother.

When she began to explain what was behind her feelings toward him, it all made sense, however; it fitted into a comprehensible pattern. Emma was the child of a war marriage. Her father had been killed overseas and her mother had remarried. The little boy, aged one-and-a-half, was the son of the stepfather and the mother, who had come to an agreement when they married that he would not discipline Emma.

Shortly after the new baby was born, Emma turned into a little hellion; among the worst problems were her attacks on her brother. In the family conferences Emma began to say, "Daddy, you never arc a real daddy to me. You toss Joey around when he is bad, but you never punish me. You don't love me or you would punish me." The father took the cue. He realized that he was relating in a noticeably different way to Emma and to her brother. He began to treat both of the children more nearly alike, especially as he began to punish Emma. Her aggression, her acting out behavior, was strikingly reduced. There followed a major change in her ways of reacting to her little brother and in school. Centrally important was the fact that her parents now understood the reasons for her misbehavior.

Still further, changes may be defined as reevaluations of who is responsible for problems existing in the family. When a child is referred because he has problems, the assumption of the family members may be that he is the one who is responsible. If only he were different, then everything would be fine. Of course, the youngster may be feeling exactly the same way about mother, father, and the rest of the members of the family. A natural tendency is to place the responsibility, the blame, for problems on other people. This happens in almost every family. But when family members become more open in their communication, they begin to discuss what is behind the problem behaviors; they begin to accept that everybody is to blame, everybody is a part of the problem, and that their difficulties have arisen out of the unitary family interaction. Then you find parents beginning to say such things as, "Well, I can see now that if we had acted differently, we would never have gotten into this." Or you find children saying, "If I had known that my brother was feeling this way about the situation, I never would have beat up on him."

In the course of interactional discussion, the family finds out what changes are needed, who must make the changes, and, through the efforts of some members of the family, demonstrates that changes are possible. Often it takes a very modest modification of the interaction to precipitate a whole reshuffling of the organization and interrelations of the family. Seemingly minor things, showing that change is possible, precipitate consequent major changes. Change multiplies, and supports the idea of change. Often there is available the support of the whole family behind an individual as he decides to make a change, especially if there has been open communication about the need to change. Change may not be easy, but if the whole family stands behind him, he is held more readily to a decision and to effecting the changes desired. In other words, reinforcement is available for new roles that the individual is attempting to assume.

A further way of defining the changes is to note that new communication is demonstrating the extent of the love and respect in the family. Therapy begins with talk about the negative and pathologically hostile aspects of family interrelations. But even in the sternest family, in the most pathological situation, there is an intense bond of relationship, of love and mutual respect. Why is it that our most severely disturbed juvenile delinquents, when they are asked, "Where do you want to go—home or to an institution?" almost invariably say "Home!" You know this home is a disorganized, sick, hurting, frustrating place, but they want to go back to it. Why is it that a mother who appears completely rejecting, when she has a chance begins to expose a tremendous longing to be a good mother, to hold a family together, and to take her full part in it. This is not only true of the person who is neurotic, anxious, mildly disturbed, but also true of the psychotic, so far out of touch with reality that you wonder if there can be any longing to relate to anybody. Some of my friends who have worked with the families of schizophrenics, report that withdrawn and seemingly unrelated individuals experience the intensity of love and respect we see in the families of normal or neurotic people. This bond is not only of a biological nature; it is based on the long history of group process, even though the group is disturbed. The group has a meaning, a kind of appropriateness in the individual's mind, that makes him want to continue his membership in it. After the unpleasant truths come out, love and respect show themselves. If the unpleasantness is not expressed, then the love is hidden too. Revealing the intensity of disruptive forces in the family seems a necessary step toward discovering the strength of the bonds that tie the family together.

A special aspect of the family's awareness of its bonds emerges as family group therapy overcomes the disintegrating of the family into divisive segments. Very often, as a part of the rigidifying of the family a pair of the individuals relate primarily to one another, a father and daughter for example, excluding others. These segmented relations exist with a special intensity and persistence, so strong that the other individuals in the family cannot break through them. In the instance of pathology in a family not only is an individual caught in a structure that is rigidified, but also segmental relationships in the family are rigid. Change has taken place when there is a reduction in this kind of segmentation, through opening up of the communication so that the whole family again operates as a unit. Change occurs when the hostility about this kind of segmentation is expressed, and when the family discusses together what should be done about the special kinds of feelings represented in these segmental bonds.

As I examine this variety in the ways by which changes may be identified, I am impressed that they are not superficial or unimportant. I am reminded that such changes could not have been confidently expected to occur spontaneously in many of the families wherein they were observed. The therapy process, at least, speeded change, and the presence and control of the therapist was required. To gain such ends the therapist uses his own personal and social skills to help the family attain what it has shown itself unable to reach before, the ability to live for its own total welfare, for the welfare of each of its family members, and ultimately for the betterment of the community.

Summary

The history of the development of family group therapy and of other recent studies of the family has been reviewed briefly. Various definitions of *family* were discovered, and a proposal was advanced to define family in terms of social psychological theories of small group behavior. From the perspective of such a definition, formulations were attempted relative to the development of the family group, its stability, its action processes, its health, and its pathology. In light of these conceptions, a brief analysis was undertaken of the processes involved in family group therapy as a mechanism for the promotion of change.

Chapter V

Promoting Action
through New Insights:
Some Theoretical
Revisions from
Family Group Therapy

Every significant theory of psychopathology has pointed to the family as a basic social force in the production of emotional disturbance, or, conversely, in the promotion of mental health. Likewise, every effort toward restoration of emotional health aims not only at the alleviation of an individual's problem but also the modification of the person's family status. It was inevitable, then, that treatment methods specifically designed for the primary goal of helping the family, such as family group therapy, should emerge.

Family group treatment takes the family, and by professional action tries to help it transform itself into a more nearly perfect, functioning group. The contract with the family specifies this end. Family group treatment is a consulting sociological or socio-psychological technique, and as such is unlike psychological treatment methods that aim for the welfare of the individual. Let it be recognized, however, that although family group treatment seeks the well-being of the family, secondarily it has important consequences for the status of the individuals who make up the family.

A New Angle of Vision. This reminds us of the arbitrariness in our distinctions between the family group and individual members of the family. Both the group and the individual are correlated open systems. To look at one or the other as independent is only a professional choice which later requires us to allow for the limitations imposed by our selective starting position. It is easy to see this in electing to work with the family. What now has become more apparent is that a similar choice process has been in operation in our work with individuals. Culturally we are so biased in favor of the individual that we have tended to ignore the fact that the choice to deal with him could be arbitrary, and that we were prejudiced in favor of seeing him as a closed system. Carelessly we ignored that we had adopted a posture for thinking. We believed that there was some positive objective validity to the individual, and that as a consequence it was our primary obligation in treatment to concern ourselves with his personal progress.

When we shift consciously from an individual orientation to a social orientation, many old psychological problems have to be reexamined or reformulated to adjust to the new perspective. In part we add a correction factor to older formulas—not throwing out the old, but adjusting them to new observations. Sometimes whole theories need recasting or new theories emerge so incompatible with the old that they seem irreconcilable. I have chosen to give an illustration of the latter.

THE VEXING THEORY OF INSIGHT

The problem with which I shall deal is a fundamental and historical therapy issue: How does intellectual insight become a force in producing action?

In psychotherapeutic theory one solution to this problem poses an intermediate step between intellectual insight and action. Proponents state that intellectual insight is advantageous but it is not enough; the patient must gain emotional insight. Exploring what is meant by this term, we find that it is described as having four elements:

1. An intellectual formulation about one's behavior—that is, it includes intellectual insight.
2. An emotional acceptance of the formulation, evidenced by a positive feeling toward it, confidence that it is true, a rejection of other actual or potential alternative formulations.
3. A choice of action possibilities in terms of the formulation.
4. An operation in behavior which indicates that the insight has been effective.

Of course, when we set it out this way, we find that the whole definition of emotional insight deals essentially with description of its behavioral evidences, and does not explain the links through which one form of behavior leads into another. Nevertheless, psychotherapists assert that a person can take an interpretation (the therapist's intellectual insight) and, even though disbelieving at first, by some process transform this into emotional insight, and thence to action. Many in clinical psychology report to have seen this happen—and educators acknowledge a similar process—but how to explain it?

INTERPRETATION IN FAMILY THERAPY

From my experience in family group therapy I shall report new observations to take into account; and perhaps I can even lead you into some new ideas about the matter. Maybe also I can help you to move a little closer to being able to account simultaneously for those instances where interpretations succeed and where they fail. If I can do this you will be able to make more sound prejudgments of the effect of interpretations and of the appropriateness of their timing or understand why you are unable to do so.

Let me describe some actual situations where I used interpretations in family group treatment and the consequences I observed.

When I first began in 1951, I used interpretations freely. Relying on my knowledge of personality theory and my direct observations of family interactions, I would make such statements as: "When you say that, it appears to me that you are wanting to dominate," that is, an interpretation of *motivation;* or, "When you scowl, it seems to show that you are angry," an interpretation of *feeling;* or, "It appears to me that your anger goes back to your early experience of being rejected," an interpretation of *causation.*

Additionally, I used many other types of interpretations, such as those which linked up ideas, feelings, and problems with persons with whom one may have identified, or rejected as an identification figure, or with family, societal or cultural roles, or with various inferred psychological mechanisms such as projections, displacement, and denial.

When you have the whole group of the family in front of you, reactions to such interpretations are multiple. This accentuates your awareness of the impact of what you have said and complicates the problems of predicting the effects. It also dramatizes certain reactions which may be observable in individual treatment but which can be more readily overlooked there. The impact of continual exposure to multi-person reactions is heightened by the fact that interpretations lead individuals to respond and also involve changes in the ways the family members interact. Four common results were observed:

All, together, ignored the interpretation—there would be a pause and then the family would pick up again exactly where they left off.

They would unanimously deny that it was true.

One side of the family would agree with the therapist's interpretation against another side that negated it, putting the therapist in the middle, and requiring him to act by evading the conflict, openly supporting one side, or openly attacking the other—none of which he might welcome as consistent with his therapeutic aims or techniques.

The family incorporated the interpretation into the family argument as new content to discuss, but other than perhaps intensifying the argument it did not modify the relative positions of the family members as observed before the interpretation was made.

These kinds of responses occurred so repeatedly that I came re-

luctantly to the conclusion that interpretations based on my infer-
ences about intrapsychic conditions were singularly unproductive of
desirable behavioral changes.

As a next step I increased use of the supportive assertion, "You
must have good reasons for doing what you do," initiating the opportunity for an individual to tell about significant internal experience
that seemed to justify his behavior from his own perspective. In many
instances this seemed valuable, instructive, and therapeutic. On the
other hand, it was not sufficiently predictable for indiscriminate use.
It frequently had undesirable consequences similar to those produced
by my interpretations of intrapsychic events. There developed no
reliable basis for differentiation between those times when it would
be effective and those when it would fail.

Finally a simple technique suggested itself. It seemed to produce
constructive consequences, to protect the therapist from partiality
toward any individual or segment of the family, and to promote
desired family interaction and change. I began to report in an uncomplicated way on the sequences of behavior as I observed them at a
moment in the family; making statements that sounded like this: "I
noticed when you were saying this, Mr. Jones, that Mrs. Jones was
opening and shutting her lips, and Jimmy was flicking his finger at a
spot on the table." I would not intrude such a statement at a time
when Mr. and Mrs. Jones and Jimmy were busily engaged in talking
intensely with one another. But when their verbal participation
would be reduced, especially when one person was holding the floor
and tending to repeat the same content over and over, and I sensed
that others were seeking to take part more actively, then I would use
these uncomplicated observations to move the interchange ahead. In
particular these are not interpretations of intrapsychic events, but
rather statements mirroring observable behavior.

Some consequences of this kind of intervention by the therapist
are worth noting:

It did not seem to engage him in one to one relationships with
family members.

It seemed to keep the center of action in the family group.

It led family members to verbalize content relative to their interaction.

And, most importantly for our problem, the content was frequently interpretative, expressing precise formulations about intrapsychic life—feelings, experiences, ideas, images, memories, causes,—the kinds of statements that the therapist might have interjected as interpretations, and which he would lable "insights."

Preferred Theories

As a consequence of this technique and the reactions that occur, I have revised my theories about the relationship of insight to action. I have concluded that in part we have seen the sequence entirely the wrong way about. Whereas formerly we assumed that insight ultimately led to action by some unknown process, I have now concluded that action may be seen more fruitfully as coming before insight. Action has the primacy rather than insight. That is, insight and action do not take place in some parallel psychological processes, but insight is within the mainstream of action.

What is even more important, I have concluded that the action that leads to insight takes place with, for and because of others—that it is a process in and of a social group rather than of and especially within an isolated individual. Insight has the appearance of identity with an individual because it is abstracted from the social action, and, as all thinking, is seen from the point of view of a person who is acting. Thus, to call it intellectual insight is indeed appropriate. But we have traditionally overlooked the social matrix within which this occurs, forgetting that the individual is never independent, a fact which becomes especially obvious when the whole family group is before us. You may wish to pursue privately the implications this has for making interpretations. But returning to our main problem, if we look at insight as emerging from action in a social sense we have increased illumination on the problem of why intellectual insight does not lead consistently to changes in action. Being derived from action it is always past in its time reference. It has reference to action already completed, rather than to actions anticipated. It is understandable, then, that we have seen the need for another term, emotional insight, with its connotation of something more than an idea.

Continuing, we must still inquire if such ideas do not shape our future action. Our experience would seem to indicate that they do. Can we further illuminate the process that exists between insight and how we shall act later? I have found it helpful to note that insight, or the evaluation of past action, participates in the construction of our intentions for the future. As an internal and intellectual process, the developing of intentions based on insights does not confront us with the theoretical conundrums we face in explaining how action follows insight. So perhaps if we concentrate on how intent leads to action we shall make more useful theories. And we are not removing ourselves from the problem with which we started, for you will recall that we identified "the choice of action possibilities," or intentions, with emotional insight.

Let us change our inquiry then to how intentions lead to action. Where we have encountered problems in the past in dealing with this issue we have removed intent, motivation, or decision from its social nature and purpose. As soon as we restore it rightfully to its social matrix, where action is constantly in progress, we recognize that we have been asking too general a question. Our inquiry now turns out to be not, "How does an intention lead to action?" but, "How does an intention change the action in progress?" Even more specifically, we are asking how an intention changes the action in a preselected way. When we look at an intention within the social action of which it is a part we see how it is a communication, an advice to another, a direction to him, expressed either verbally, or, as frequently occurs in the family, nonverbally. Then it becomes clear that the intent leads to changes in the action, but may not lead to specific changes. It cannot be operative in producing desired changes in action if the other does not cooperate, and before the cooperation, the intention must be communicated. The message sent may be deficient; the medium of communication may be inappropriate—for example, a foreign language; the other may not hear, or understand; the other may resist the intent because it clashes with his own or he may try to reshape the intent towards some modified aim. Desired action changes ensue when the other yields according to my intent, that is, when his intentions are compatible with my own, so together we promote new action. Thus we may say the intention leads to new action through directing the other, through dissolving or reducing resistance formerly pressing from the other, or through mobilizing another's support. Here we see why it is so important to recognize action as social behavior, rather than as behavior of an individual.

Now our capacity to explain the steps that follow an insight is expanded, and ultimately we should find our capacities for prediction enlarged. We have identified that:

We are always in action, which is a social process.
Out of action emerges evaluative insights.
Insights shape our intentions.
Our intentions as communications change the action.
Our intentions result in specific, preplanned changes if their communication leads others to sanction and join in a specific act.

Jointly we continue to act, but in changed directions, either as preplanned by the agent or otherwise.

Perhaps the effectiveness of mirroring interrelational behavior in family group sessions can now be more clearly understood.

It begins where people who are vital to one another are in action.
By his communication the therapist intends a change in the action.
The communication redirects the action and imposes the command and conditions for evaluation of the self.
It focuses attention on how and what others have been communicating and requires evaluation of their intent.
It leads a family member then, to revise his own intent in the light of further self-knowledge derived from meaningful action and further knowledge of the other.
It promotes communication of his intent and thus sanctions for changes in the action.
Action continues within the group, but in new directions, perhaps according to the intent.

Social processes are at work in individual therapy, too, and we are not talking about a sequence from intention to specific changes in action exclusive to family group therapy. But in psychotherapy or any individual counseling, the action is between two persons, the counselor and his counselee. It is impossible for a mirroring statement to be made here because the counselor cannot be a mirror to himself —he has to be a different kind of participant in action. He cannot abstract himself from the action in the same ways the therapist can from family action in family group therapy, where he can reflect as a mirror the social behavior he sees. Let it be acknowledged that there is another kind of action in family group therapy in which the therapist is the kind of agent he is in individual psychotherapy and where he cannot mirror what is happening. But insofar as he can attend to the action taking place among the family members, he is able to describe action processes at work. Though the action in progress in family group therapy differs from that in individual therapy, the ideas about insight, intention, and action pertain there too, for they are general ideas, developed in family treatment but applicable to all action.

A DERIVATION FOR INDIVIDUAL THERAPY

As a kind of summary let me apply these conclusions to the individual treatment situation, then, and from there your imagination, analysis, and conceptualization can take over. We would say about individual therapy:

The therapist and the patient are in action, a continuing process.

As a part of the action both the therapist and the patient develop evaluative ideas or *insights*, following specific acts.

As a consequence the therapist and the patient shape new intentions which are directed toward changing the action in specific ways. The therapist's interpretations are direct or indirect statements of intentions for the action that includes the patient.

Intentions as communications from the therapist to the patient, and vice versa, direct the other to change the ongoing course of action in specific ways.

When in the interplay the patient and the therapist jointly sanction the change intended, specific action follows.

Action continues.

Consequently our job in predicting the likelihood that an interpretation will produce a specific action change requires us to take into account many variables we have not studied before in this regard. I think particularly of the intentions of the therapist and of members of significant natural groups to which the patient belongs. But also involved is the evaluation of the ongoing action in the therapy by the patient, the communication patterns, verbal and nonverbal, and the ways in which therapist and patient permit one another to carry their intentions into action.

Chapter VI

The Family Group
Therapist:
An Agent of Change

As an advocate of family group therapy, I should like to discuss what it means to be a family group therapist.[1] I see him as an agent in changing the family. And since, derived from the changes that he initiates and helps the family to accomplish, there are secondary changes in the individuals who make up the family, he is also an agent of individual changes.

The family therapist as an agent of change starts with a deliberate posture. He sees the whole family because he intends to see it. The key word here is "intends." He proposes and initiates treatment of the whole family because he decides to do so. Since family group therapy is a new method, the therapist is likely to recognize that he has made this choice and that he has rejected other possibilities, such as individual psychotherapy, group psychotherapy, or no therapy. Perhaps the first reason for the effectiveness of family group therapy is that the therapist has acknowledged his role as an agent by his decision to act. There are risks in attributing too much to such a decision, however. To the extent that the choice is less than rational, we are on the way to promoting therapy primarily for uncommunicated and often unconscious reasons. Others may join us out of their own private needs, and soon we are operating a cult. Although the members may propound rationales for their work, these may become dogmas, revealed to be so by an absence of public and systematic evaluation. Family group therapy is in very great danger of such cultism.

On the other hand, to the extent that we choose a method of treatment for conscious reasons advanced publicly, we open our choice to judgment and revision by others. Consequently, our intention is capable of more and more detailed formulation. It can be limited increasingly tò starting those acts the outcome of which may be predicted confidently. Science can move in to discipline the therapist's intent and to determine its consequences. As an agent who chooses family group therapy, I feel an obligation to define my choice, to state my reasons, and to put them forth for your examination.

The Therapist's Intent

The elements of the family group therapist's intent, as I know it, are threefold:

WORKING WITH A FAMILY

In the first place the therapist intends to work *with a family.* Until I began to be involved in the treatment of families, I thought I knew clearly what a family is. Now I am sure there is no simple and absolute definition.

At one time I was a member of a committee of the National Institute of Mental Health Biometrics Branch to formulate a program for the national reporting of family work in clinics. When we examined what some clinics were doing with families, we found much inconsistency at the basic level of their definitions of who is a family. If you see a disturbed child and his mother, is this a family? Some say "yes," some, "no." If you work with an alcoholic man and his wife, is this a family? If you see the parents and a single child, leaving out the other children, have you a family? What about grandparents or other relatives who live in or out of the home? What is the family when the parents have been separated or divorced and one parent has custody of the children? Does the Census Bureau's use of *household* offer us a way to describe family? If you compose a therapy group of a series of mothers, are you working with families? There are more possibilities, but these are enough to show the difficulties. How then can I say I decide to work with the family? Only when I provide a definition.

In my early work I limited myself to meeting with the basic biological unit of the parents and their children. Now I relate myself more and more to family units put together in a variety of ways. Several considerations guide me in my decision about who is to compose the family:

1. I concern myself with the ways in which those who might qualify as family members answer the question: "Who makes up your family?" Who is to be included depends partly on their answers. As in that perennial French film, *The Baker's Wife,* it is reasonable on occasion to include the family cat.

2. I am interested in the feasibility of collecting the family members together for the therapy. The son or daughter who is 1,000 miles away in college has to be excluded because of geography; the grandmother who lives with the group but is bedridden is left out for obvious reasons; a divorced parent may be omitted for legal or other causes.

3. I recall what I have observed: that no individual is necessarily more significant in the family than another; judgments of the significance or lack of significance deny the essential interrelatedness of all family members. Each is part of the other and none would be as he is if anyone was removed from the group. When we shift to a family group emphasis, the question of the significance of an individual to another is irrelevant. All are significant.

4. I have learned that there are limitations on who may be in-

cluded because of the very nature of the therapy as I conduct it. In general the maximum level of communication with which I may work is that of the least-developed member of the group. Obviously the child who talks primarily with his hands and who cannot use complex verbal expressions must work within the limits imposed by his stage of maturity. If the therapy process can accommodate itself to this level, then he can be included, but my way of working would rule him out since I have to work with talkers. Likewise if the conceptual thinking required in the treatment is beyond the intellectual scope of an individual, whether by reason of age or of retardation, he is excluded. This criterion is related to how I conduct the therapy process, though. My approach requires that the participants have developed a concept of themselves and of others as differentiated individuals, and also have attained a concept of the family as a whole. In the development of the average child this seems to be reached by about nine years of age.

5. Finally, I remember that everyone who is left out of the group is potentially an enemy of treatment. He may work against changes in the group; they will seem undesirable to him because he is not a party to them.

I select the family, then, on the basis of the functional relationships among a group of individuals and on the basis of certain predictions about their adaptability in the treatment situation. I aim to include the largest possible number of members. Not infrequently, suitability for inclusion is tested by bringing in those about whom I may have reservations at the beginning and making all members partners in the experiment to see if they can meet the requirements of the treatment. Having selected the family by the criteria that I choose to apply, the first part of my intent as a family group therapist, to work with the family, has been met.

WORKING WITH THE GROUP

The second element of my intent is contained in my use of the word *group*. I choose to see the family as a group. That is, once having declared this to the family as my mode of working, I adhere to it. Others, I know, mix up work with the family group and work with individuals, or will permit the group to change from session to session. I do not consider this mode of working as family group therapy. We may call it family therapy if we wish, but I restrict my definition of family group therapy to working with the chosen family as a group.

My reasons for this are not superficial but are based on a systematic philosophical position and on evidence about what has worked for me. Actually, I had experienced success in working with the group before I recognized the basic philosophical position to which my experiences were leading me. Once having identified the fundamental principles behind my work, I have more and more permitted them to direct me.

Let me explicate the kinds of ideas to which I now subscribe. Fundamentally they grow out of efforts to answer for myself the old philosophical question, "What is man?" I have tried to take seriously the wisdom of Pierce (1960), who said,

> Find a scientific man who proposes to get along without any metaphysics [i.e., inquiries into the fundamental nature of reality] and you have found one whose doctrines are thoroughly vitiated by the crude and uncriticized metaphysics with which they are packed [p. 129].

If one is trying to promote the humanity of man, may I suggest that one's beliefs about reality are even more important. Of these beliefs, one's convictions about the nature of man take precedence.

In order to deal with the problems I have encountered in the family group, I have been struggling gradually and with great difficulty toward proposals that sound like this:

> The primary human unit is social, persons in relation. The basic unit is not biological; though it is built upon organisms, just as organisms are built on matter. But just as matter does not define the organism, so the organism does not define man. The individual as a person exists as an aspect of his group memberships. This means that the self is defined by the process and character of its actions with others. The person cannot be defined except as an aspect of social relationship. The ego does not exist except as an extension in one direction of a self-other relationship. The primary human dimension is a social unit in action, action that only exists in social processes, the sharing of aims, efforts, ideas, and experience.

These are old ideas, but they are now being filled out, extended, and systematized. You will recall their anticipation in the writings of James (1905), Dewey (1925), and Mead (1932, 1934, 1938). You will recognize their partial formulation in religious terms in the "I and Thou" of Buber (1937) and in the writings of other existentialists, but they go beyond existentialism. You will find their most eloquent exposition in two tough books, *The Self as Agent* and *Persons in Relation* by my former colleague at the University of Edinburgh, the eminent Scottish philosopher, Macmurray (1957, 1961).

In its expanded logical analysis this social concept of man is incompatible with the material concept of man based on the natural sciences and represented in the older behaviorism and positivism in psychology generally; it also forces us to reject the biological concepts of the person that grew out of the life sciences. But most radically, the social concept of man confronts directly many of our fundamental ideas of personality. It no longer fits to talk of the whole person as though he existed in isolation, especially as though he were contained in the skin. We must be prepared to find man's identity only by seeing him in relations, inseparably related, nonexistent except in relations. To try to make it clear, we are not talking about an individual who meets another individual and then is seen in relation; we are talking about relations and about seeing persons as differentiated within but not separable from these relations. This is a Copernican shift in orientation.

In the family treatment situation we try to apply the practical consequences of these opinions. We fight the tendency to give a primary and isolated significance to an individual who is in front of us. No longer may we deal with his parents, brothers, and sisters as shadows, abstractions, stresses, rewards, and species, that is, as ideas, as we might have found ourselves doing in individual psychotherapy. No longer can we push the relatives, whom we might never have seen, into equivalence with the physical world which is the patient's environment. We acknowledge the theoretical and practical importance of relationships. We catch ourselves, or the family catches us, when we objectify and depersonalize a family member unwittingly, dealing with him as a case, a chapter in a textbook, or an article in a journal. We cannot operate on him or abstract him as we do when we are reflecting on him. We cannot any longer talk about our relations with him as *object* relations.

Having adopted the position that we shall find man and find ourselves in social interaction, we meet the family as a group. The most salutary corrective to tendencies to drop back into the old idealistic or physicalistic conceptions is to confront a group. If we forget that we and a patient in individual psychotherapy are *persons* in relation, we are less likely to commit this error when we meet a group. Even in regular group therapy, though, we may not be freed from this error, because we look on the group there as instrumental and the desirable end-result as changes in individuals, making it easy for us to resume individualistic conventions of thought. But when the natural group of the family is in front of you, you have no escape from the interdependence of each of the individuals. Jane speaks; and father, mother, and Jim relate. How they relate is determining who Jane is, how she will act, what she will feel, what she will long for, what she will become in front of you. Persons are acting, are in process, are happening, are becoming. Jane is fulfilling herself as a dimension of the social action of the group.

Group therapy has, of course, introduced us to this lesson, but facing the natural group of the family, a group that comes to us already developed as a group, a group that leaves our therapy hour and remains together as a group until the next session, a group that has no alternative but to go into the future as a group seems to leave us no option but to master the lesson of the interrelatedness within it.

I do not claim that the only way of affecting the relations of the family is through joining the family as a group. Individual psychotherapy and family life education provide proof that other methods may modify the family either directly or secondarily. If one aims primarily to affect the relations among family members, however, there are commonsense, philosophical, and experiential justifications for seeing the family as a group.

Furthermore, in functional terms, a relational perspective requires our recognition that any approach that modifies the nature of the self and of man's development as a person accomplishes its work through transformation of groups in which the person is a member. Inevitably the most inclusive and enduring modifications will occur in those groups which are natural and which retain ongoing functional importance to the persons who make them up, of which the family is the prime example. This leads us, then, to the conclusion that a professional person who would initiate change in individuals should activate relations with natural groups. But such professionally developed groups have only an instrumental aim, that is, to work for change. Having accomplished this, the groups have achieved their purposes; therefore they should be self-limiting and self-dissolving. They must not stand in lieu of more basic natural groups. The professional man commits himself to press on toward another end than to preserve indefinitely his relationships with those whom he would help. So my intent in working with the family as a group has its defined limits.

WORKING AS A THERAPIST

This brings me to the third element of my intent in family group therapy. I intend to engage in *therapy*. As an agent I have the responsibility of defining my aims here also.

There are many differing forms of therapy. Obviously, I do not intend to work beyond my professional training and competence; for example, I shall not attempt to treat conditions that are best explained by mechanical or biological causes that I am not trained to understand. Insofar as a man's difficulties may be seen in his relations with his family, and insofar as the man asks my help with problems that are best conceived as issues in this social unit, I intend to join him and his family in trying to reduce or eliminate the troubles. If we find it an advantage to think of the problems as illness, then it is appropriate to apply the term therapy to what we do. I use the term, but I might have used another. The main consideration is that I intend to function professionally in relation to the family's problems. Family group *therapy* is the product of this intent.

This presumes, then, some ideas about the crises with which I shall deal and the methods that might be effective to resolve them. I am purposely oversimplifying the nature of the characteristic emergencies brought to me when I restrict my attention to the social realm. I have reduced their complexity even further when I report that, in my experience, the typical frustration in the family is isolation, the separation of an individual from those to whom he should be nearest and most real and with whom he should be able to function most vitally. This is not the unique quandary of the physically isolated but equally of those who are among their own, their families, as well as friends, co-workers, and neighbors, among those with whom they should find others and especially find themselves. They move among their families as ping-pong balls in a bingo machine, touching one another, identifiable by their numbers, but virtually unaffected by one another except mechanically.

It is not much wonder that the cause has been seen as a breakdown of communication: difficulty in speaking and a block in listening or hearing. It is this, but not in the sense that communication is a technique. The problem goes much deeper. It relates to the way in which all human groups become trapped in automatic ways of interrelating, habits that are so firmly entrenched that the group does not act. Nor does the group know any longer, except through anxiety, depression, and a sense of meaninglessness, that it has ceased to act. Interrelating that started out as immediate, functional, agreed upon, becomes dulled through usage into futile relics of relationships, satisfying no one and destroying the group. What a burden of hostility the family then carries!

If by some technical skill someone opens the communication, what danger! Yet to live among others is always dangerous. Ortega (1957) expressed this most transparently:

> Every other human being is a peril, is dangerous to us—each in his way and in his particular measure. Do not forget that the innocent child is one of the most dangerous of beings—it is he who sets fire to the house with a match, he whose playing with it fires the shotgun, he who pours nitric acid into the stew, and, worst of all, it is he who is constantly putting himself in danger of falling from the balcony, breaking his head against the corner of the table, swallowing a wheel from the toy train he is playing with—thereby subjecting us to the most serious inconvenience. And if we call this being "innocent," that is, "not harmful," imagine what those who have lost their innocence will be! [p. 159].

Ortega goes on to elaborate that the danger is not only in the unpredictable acts of the other but precisely when the other acts deliberately:

> . . . the other coincides with me, he collides with me, negates me. These active negations that are discharged from him to me "make" my living with him a constant collision . . . [p. 161].

Further on, he raises himself out of his Spanish pessimism to add, however, that:

> This collision with him in this, that, and the other thing makes me discover my boundaries, my frontiers, dividing me from your world and you [p. 161].

When the therapist identifies the family problem as one of communication, he is exposing the group to all the dangers, risks, negations in daring to communicate. This is one way of describing the intent to engage in therapy. The therapist will enter the group sufficiently to put its members up against the hazards of nearness. He wants to produce change in their intercommunication. He chooses with them to meet the risks when they come to hear each other say: "act, act, act; change, change, change." He wishes to uncover and share with them the hostility that expresses itself in the demand that the other must change, and he protects each against excess anxiety when others are defining his nature and his limits.

The therapist shares the danger with the family, but he is also the family's escape from danger. If he is skillful, he will help them to face the danger in assimilable doses; if he is careless or inexpert, he may then be used by the family as a scapegoat.

If he handles it right, a remarkable chain of events transpires. The family begins to release the hostility locked up in worn-out routines. Each person explodes because each has the conviction that the others are the source of his pain: "I hate you because you hurt me." At loggerheads in this battle, the family cannot see the way out, but it is already forthcoming. If there is reciprocity in their dedication to finding the way out, each begins to act toward the solution and to define the other in terms that may come to be acceptable to him. The dimensions of each act permissible in the family group are stretched or compressed. In due course the family self for each member is padded out or whittled away. How each may act within the family, and that which must be reserved for outside the family, is delineated. The crisis of the need to change yields before group resolution to change, to compromise, to reconcile, to unite, to push on into the future, to act.

The elements of the plot are always the same, as in some interminable TV series. But the characters change, the conflicts they bring vary, the evidences of group paralysis differ, the ways they communicate contrast, the intensities of their wranglings are dissimilar, their demands on one another are diverse, and their solutions for their group life are original and to a measure unpredictable.

In the very precision with which the therapist structures and holds to his own action, he promotes the dynamic sequences in the changing family groups. It is by his courage in taking the initiative as an agent that he starts the chain reaction. It is not that he is immune from danger. He may slip out of the present into the past. He may have to fight against being driven into himself and out of touch. He may have to suffer for irresolution. But the risk is less for him. He has the protection of defined ways of acting. He learns and holds to the principles that govern his work. He discovers and knows the forms of acting that we call technique. With his initiative, his directness, and his freedom from ambiguity, he challenges the family members to join with him in action. But thereafter his function comes to an end. Then the family takes over; then the father, mother, and children decide the next steps for their family, the functions they would perform for one another, the patterns and values to use with one another, the goals toward which they will move.

Not all the problems are solved, nor can they be. Man still must wrestle with his physical environment and with the ways he keeps complicating it by industry and business. Man still must meet the demands of the community and the nation. Man's body must still get its sop. The Ethiopian still cannot change his skin. Death will still diminish a man's family and the family of man. But I have learned that carrying my intent as a group therapist into action with a family can lead to change, can reduce isolation, can free communication, can deepen trust, can promote fun, can lead to fulfillment, can unfold the ego, and through it all promote a most singularly important group for any man: his family. [2]

Part Three

EXTENSIONS

Chapter VII

Implications of Emphasis
for Family Units
on Theories of
Child Psychopathology

Within the last two decades the interest of child development experts has extended to intensive study of the family as a social unit. Prior to that time they tended to look on the rest of the family as an environment within which a child developed. More recently, however, they have also defined the family as a *total unit* within which the child is a functioning member. The impact of this developing concept has been widespread.

Among the areas where we find the concept has an observable and widespread impact, none seems more important than the area of child psychopathology. The following sets forth some implications of the ideas about the unitary family for understanding of children who are disturbed.

PATHOLOGY AS A CIRCULAR PROCESS

Already the study of the total family has had profound effects in amplification of social theories of the etiology of disorder. One of the most important consequences has been revision of overemphasis on the child's behavior as a response to parental influences—parental pressures, inefficiency, maliciousness, indifference, brutality, or other forms of impact. The study of the total family has not made obsolete the body of theory that came to the fore earlier. It has offered a complementary way of looking at behavior disorder and a supplementary body of evidence and theory. The earlier orientation to behavior disorders in the child as a product of family influence continues to suggest important areas for study. Family unit theory has proven beneficial, however, in proposing that we regard the development of pathology as a circular process wherein impact of child on the parents is given equal significance to the impact of the parents on the child.

SYMPTOMS AS EXPRESSIONS OF FAMILY GROWTH

This circular process is observable in relation to many symptoms. They occur as a normal part of the growth of the family, as an aspect of a particular phase in the family's interaction. This is equivalent in some respects to the typical interpretation of "phases" in child development. As yet we understand little about developmental sequences of total family interaction beginning, perhaps, from the time of courtship and marriage of the parents through to some arbitrary time points such as departure of the children from the family, death of one or both of the parents, or some other specified point of termination.

DISORDER AS FAMILY RIGIDITY

Behavior disorder is seen also as an effort to disrupt a rigidified system in a family, to revise patterns into which it has settled. It appears that the family goes through cycles of system rigidification and system modification. Behavioral pathology seems to occur especially when forces toward change cannot prevail against inflexible family patterns. Change is inevitable—the impacts toward it will come from outside the family, from events which affect individual members, from the changing demands of persons as they mature, or from other changes in the family such as a crisis of illness.

DISORDER AS FAMILY CONSERVATION

On the other hand, the circular process wherein pathology develops is sometimes described also as an effort to restore patterns which have been disrupted, the result of family efforts to regain a stable or homeostatic balance in the interrelationships among family members. Some of the literature on the family as a unit seems to overemphasize the breakdown of family homestasis as a cause of behavior disorder and the restoration of the homeostatic balance as an objective of therapeutic efforts (Jackson, 1959; Satir, 1967). In correction to overvaluation of homeostatic balance, more attention needs to be paid to the adaptive value of behavior disorder, to its importance as evidence of motivation to change family interrelationships. Under such circumstances, the therapeutic objective would be modification of family patterns rather than the restoration of old ones.

DISORDER AND FAMILY DYNAMICS

A fifth important contribution to theory has been the understanding of the functional value of behavior disorder in terms of family dynamics. To give a concrete illustration we might point to the use of a scapegoating mechanism (Spiegel & Bell, 1959). Pathology elsewhere in the family, in individuals or in part-family relationships, is reduced or eliminated by the creation of a scapegoat who carries, in effect, the pathology for the total family. Ancient lore developing around the *black sheep* in the family has received much support from the analysis of the scapegoating that frequently causes emotional and behavioral disorders in individuals. The child who is selected to be a scapegoat is not, however, thereby removed from the family unit but takes on the role specified in the total family interactional economy.

This illustrates only one kind of functional use of disorder that becomes apparent when one sees the whole family.

Mention has already been made of the change-inducing purpose of symptoms. These may be efforts of a total family unit to effect change, as well as efforts stimulated by a particular individual who bears symptoms. In the former case the child with problems often is used as the representative of the whole family to gain entrance into systems of help for the family. Referrals to a child guidance clinic, to a hospital, or to a school counselor may be methods by which a family draws its total organizational and functional problems to the attention of helping persons. When agencies accept the child as the patient without sufficient examination of the functional necessity of referral for the total family, and thereby ignore the basic motivation for seeking help, they may fail to provide the required help.

FUNCTIONS OF SYMPTOMS

A sixth area in which family unit studies have extended theory relates to the communication value of a symptom for the child who carries the symptom, and for those who relate to him. Psychoanalytic theory has contributed much information on the purpose and meaning of symptoms as language—as body language or in verbal communication. Group psychotherapy extended the understanding of the meaning of symptoms in communication from a psychoanalytic perspective because the social processes within which a symptom was functioning as language became more evident. Reference has been made earlier to studies of the communication implied in behavior disorders within the family. Much work remains to gather further basic data about these phenomena in the family. We have been introduced, however, to methods of approach to newly discovered complexities in the symbolic meaning of symptoms.

DIFFERENTIATION AMONG DISORDERS

A contribution to prior understanding of behavior disorders comes from evaluation of the consequences of family group therapy. Family therapy has not always proven successful in removing symptomatic behavior in children. Some children presented to clinicians as emotionally disturbed have been relieved of their symptoms as a consequence of efforts to change the whole family. Other children have not been helped at all by such efforts. Others have been helped in part by efforts to change the whole family, and still others have emerged from family therapy with an accentuation of their symptoms. To make some sense from these various outcomes, it has been suggested that symptoms may be demonstrated to have been caused variously by family factors.

Some symptoms, it appears, are so primarily the product of disordered family interaction that changes in the family may actually lead to symptom elimination. This explanation might account for many of the successes in family therapy. It would appear also that where symptoms are basically derived from family relations we might explain at least some instances in which symptoms have been accentuated; here the family may have reinterpreted the meaning and importance of the symptomatic 'disordered behavior, seeing it anew after analysis of their interactions; so, as family policy, it has become acceptable to allow and accentuate the symptoms.

It has also been proposed that the reduction of some pathology, but the inability of family therapy to remove the basic symptoms, could be accounted for when difficulties in family interaction are secondary to primary disorders. The causes of disorder would in these instances be primarily intrapersonal and thus most readily amenable to change through efforts directed to the child. Such primary disorders commonly have a secondary disruptive effect on the family interaction; then we might expect that family therapy would at least ameliorate some of the destructive consequences of the primary disorder within the family interaction.

Another observation from family therapy indicates, however, that behavior which appears pathological or deviant to a professional person may not be a matter of concern to the family. Thus the family would not orient itself to modifying the symptomatic behavior; their value-orientation would direct their concern to other problems than those of seeming import to the therapist. Detailed and extensive study of cases in which family therapy has been wholly successful from the point of view of the family and of the professional, of instances wherein family therapy has been partially successful, and of instances wherein it seems notably to have been a failure should contain the information to develop increasingly complicated theoretical systems about causes of symptoms in family members.

FAMILY SUB-SYSTEMS

A final area to which the family unit approach has contributed has been in the expansion of our understanding of family subsystems, such as a marital pair, a mother-child pair, a father-child pair, or siblings. The whole family in action has shown us new interpretations of the significance of these sub-systems. It has become less relevant than before to attempt to identify one parent as more significant than the other in the development of pathology in a child. While the mother-child relationship continues to be interpreted as an extremely important influence in early child development, the quality of this relationship is more visibly the consequence of the parental interrelationships than had appeared earlier, although family theory had allowed for this. Now the importance of the father in the period of the child's infancy has become a central point of investigation. The study of sibling rivalry, so important two or more decades ago, has been reduced in its significance by the direct observation of siblings in action within the family system. Here they are often seen as directly acting out parental conflict or other parental patterns. This means that the understanding of conflict between siblings is extended while the significance of the conflict as a primary source of behavior disorder is reduced. These interpretations have not been inconsistent with earlier theory, but have been supported now by direct observation.

Chapter VIII

Reducing Tensions
through the Group
Process

It is nearly three decades since the end of World War II. During this period, psychological medicine and the mental health movement have promoted change with a burst of creative invention. One of the most imaginative and necessary changes in technique was to use groups for psychological treatment. For nearly the whole time, it has been a primary method to construct groups as instruments of psychotherapy with many kinds of disordered persons.

Shortly after devising group therapy, we began to work with natural groups, of which the whole family is a fine illustration. Thus oriented, we initiated professional interventions in natural groups in diverse ways. Much later we experimented with therapy involving multiple-family units. We observed advantages in combining the naturalness of the family with the artificiality of bringing several family units into a single group. Consultations within business, industry, social welfare, health and educational agencies and groups have increased the scope and impact of the professional person. My own most recent work which is concerned with family-hospital relations seems to be opening the way for professionals to promote interinstitutional change. Thus it seems not unreasonable, although audacious, to predict a role of growing importance for us and our professional descendants in modifying families, communities, our country, and international relations.

Such a prospect may not be so remote as we might choose. The demands on us may easily outrun our knowledge, skills, and confidence. But we may entertain some of the possibilities in the hope that we may be deconditioned out of timidity.

Who could feel equipped to lead the way? I feel ill prepared, though I have had 40 years at various forms of counseling and individual therapy, over 20 years to puzzle about the problems of total families, 12 years of solid work for the National Institute of Mental Health in promoting community mental health, a field trip of several months' duration in Africa and Asia where I met around-the-world contrasts in some of the most vital and internationally strategic of the developing countries.

In Khartoum I had the unique experience of a two-hour conference in the State Palace with the first psychiatrist to become president of his country—Dr. Tigani el Mahi, Regional Consultant for the World Health Organization, who was called back from Alexandria to the Sudan in a constitutional crisis to head the provisional government. I had the distinct impression he was relieved to talk about mental health after 10 days of round-the-clock political negotiations.

It moves near to an extreme evaluation of our mental health professionals when they are thrust into such national prominence. It also suggests that before long numbers from our midst might be cast into positions of political responsibility where they will be called on to use their skills for leadership and getting a job done rather than for therapy—a prospect that may not entirely please them. But against this contingency and the increasing scope of our responsibilities, we are looking at a synoptic panorama—"the use of groups in the reduction of tension—family, community, and world." Let us examine the components of our theme.

THE THEME

First, "use." Surely that refers to the work of professionals. Does it not imply a deliberate effort on their part to do certain jobs and achieve goals specified in advance? "Use" presupposes purposes. It connotes efforts that can be organized in programs, examined in theory, polished in practice, and evaluated in consequences.

Secondly, "groups." I would suggest this means bringing the professional into relations with others in more than an accidental fashion, the purposive bringing together of people whether or not they have been related before. If they have not been in previous functional relations we then have the chore of constructing the group; if they were a functioning group before we met, we have, as our first job, to develop our professional relations with it. Increasingly as we move into work with very large groups we shall be talking about using groups composed of representatives—spokesmen, power figures, indigenous leaders, standing in for themselves and for the others on whose behalf they speak, plan and act.

Third, "reduction of tension." I struggled with this, for while it specifies a purpose, I am not sure it points toward unambiguous goals. Tension is a necessary condition of human physiological and social processes. On the one side it preserves, improves, motivates, restores, and gratifies man and the groups within which he lives and works. On the other side, however, it ravages, paralyzes, offends, pains, debases, wastes, and destroys. It may be a precondition for improvement; or it may be a step toward harm. To reduce tension may equally promote or obstruct human welfare.

On many occasions, I have observed that the reduction of tension is essential for continuity of personal and group functioning.

I have felt it in myself. I hesitate to generalize from myself as one case, but I know that I am not alone in reaching a point of inner tension when there is a sense that something has to give inwardly or

outwardly to save one's self. The breaking of the tension may reconstitute one's self, or it may destroy the past, permitting one to change;
whatever the outcome there follows a sense of relief and a feeling of
re-creation. This may take place spontaneously and it has happened to
me, too, by the intervention of professional persons. It occurs also by
knowledge that resources are available if needed, a sort of therapeutic
hour with the therapist in absentia. It results, too, from the welcome
experience of being home, being in familiar surroundings and among
those others where one has learned to live securely and at peace.

So also you and I have known the reduction of tension in groups,
between groups, and in the larger social organisms of community and
world; and when we say that, we are referring to what we have
earnestly longed for.

But we also know instances where human good in a new and
broader sense is accomplished only by living with or increasing the
tension.

For instance, in segregated South Africa, I visited a private hospital founded by East Indians who are numerous all up and down the
east coast of Africa. The Europeans there call them "colored." The
chairman of the hospital board, our host, a cultured and distinguished Indian lawyer, invited us to his home in the evening, making
sure when he picked us up at our hotel that his wife was firmly seated
beside him in the front seat, lest one of us would move in beside him
and make him subject to arrest. He warned us that his entertaining
us was illegal, and that at any moment the police might knock on the
door to take him to jail where he had been before for similar reasons.
Tension there was, but simple reduction of the tension could not
have been the goal for any of us. We would not have sought relief for
the tension without an assault on the basic inhumanity that provoked
it.

We are brought full circle back to the term "use," back to a
requirement that we define our task in terms of the human conditions we would seek, the values we would profess, rather than in the
techniques we would employ. We are given the family, the community, the world, and asked what kind of life we will help to create for
them, that is, for mankind—what an arena!

When we confront the discussion of such comprehensive values we are exactly at the point where some are tempted to become preachers, to promote those values previously learned, solutions that have proven effective for them, and their wishes for how other people would deal with them. This is the impulse that, carried to its extreme, ends in demagoguery. This is why perhaps the most important word in our title is "group"—for here may be the corrective to self-seeking, to urges to use power like a giant for personal gain, for domination, rather than service for all.

I am of the conviction that no individual, professional or otherwise, no matter what his training, no matter how altruistic, no matter how wise, no matter how experienced, no matter how powerful can sustain efforts for the welfare of others unless he learns from them, unless he has mastered the art of listening and accepting the ideas that others advance. The secret of effectiveness of group processes is their mutuality, their elevation of individuals from positions of abasement to places of equality and worth. Thereby the range of social relationships is extended; thereby individual potentialities are maximized; thereby the interactive balances can fluctuate, be corrected, increase in functionality, and optimize resultant gratifications.

But here's the real difficulty; here's the problem of the centuries, and one that seems to be increasing in its complexity rather than simplifying itself—although that may not be the case. How can we reconcile concentrations of power and responsibility necessary for getting jobs done and at the same time magnify enough the small remote voices? The question reappears in many variations: How can we promote leadership and at the same time preserve and increase scope for the follower? How can we achieve the gains that come from group cohesion and allow for the differentiation of individuals? How can we use the technological and social processes that keep pushing toward sameness and conformity and at the same time accentuate individuality and freedom? This is the same question that in its intellectual form has been called "the problem of meaning"; but our activist youth keep us alert to the fact that the issue is the more earthy one of participation and that meaning is derived only from evaluation of acts. As specialists in group processes, we would claim competence to deal with such questions in microcosm. The daring proposal is that we take on the world. I can only take you a little of the way.

THE ISSUES

Let me concretize the issues as I see them by sharing with you the aspects that I am now wrestling with and some of the background that led up to them.

My own professional development as a clinical psychologist began with a preoccupation with personality theory, individual diagnosis, and psychotherapy. Tension, in such processes, had a more negative than positive connotation. To reduce tension, by reducing internal conflict, by strengthening ego processes, somewhat less by reducing external stresses, seemed laudable goals. Tension was seen as precipitating undesirable defenses, psychosomatic disorders, and, if extreme, the psychoses. To reduce tension meant in those terms, substituting advantageous and more functional defenses, for example, sublimation rather than repression, sanctioning the socialized release of energy in primary drives, ameliorating the distress of unacceptable symptoms, and maximizing the internal experiences of well-being. Composure, gratification, peace of mind, guilt reduction, freedom from anxiety were catchwords that epitomized therapeutic goals.

The shift to group therapy did not modify the goals extensively, but increased focus on the issue of tension in interpersonal relations. It threw the spotlight on the problems of relations with strangers. Later as each group progressed in its development, we were able to see these same individuals reflect parts of their relations within the established community groups of which they were or had been members. The range of their interhuman responses was increased thereby, providing in many instances both the relief of undesired personal tensions and potentialities for the modification of the tension-level in extra-therapy groups—family, work, friends, neighborhood, and so on. By analogues in the therapy, the patients dealt with aspects of the relations in the natural groups to which they belonged, and as a consequence often transferred new found interpersonal skills to such groups.

We must acknowledge that individual and group therapy did not always result in a decrease in tension level in these natural groups: not infrequently the opposite occurred. Many a marriage foundered because of the signs of change. Employee-employer tensions increased and new vocations were necessary. These outcomes may have been desirable or undesirable, purposive or not. The breakup of the marriage or the new job could be good or bad functional adjustments for a patient. The increase in group tension which precipitated them could in retrospect be found advantageous in some cases, destructive in others.

With the shift at the beginning of the 1950's to working with natural groups, of which the family is the most representative in current practice, concentration on tension as an *intra*personal matter was reduced. Confronted with the whole family—arguing, teasing, fighting, struggling, pushing, and shoving—one had the experience of watching a tense drama, where there was so much interaction that one had little time to attend to the finer points of what was happening inside individuals. Also, technically it proved advantageous to reduce the closeness of therapist-individual relations and to accentuate the therapist-group processes. Tension came to be seen primarily as a matter of *intrafamilial* rather than intrapersonal dimension. One could, if he chose, shift for theoretical and practical reasons into the individual orientation so well known from earlier training. I found myself choosing to do so less and less, as I worked to develop the most disciplined, economical, and beneficial techniques I could achieve. Gradually I found I was using myself in changing ways, ultimately to assist groups rather than individuals to work out their own salvation.

When I started family group therapy I thought I had a fairly clean conception of the appropriate interactions for normal child development and family health. In retrospect, I see that I was seeking for the most part to achieve my own goals, to eliminate the undesirable factors that I thought promoted pathology. Many sources provided the ideas that made up the consistent formulae I advanced for how father, mother, both parents together, and children should act and interrelate. These notions stimulated me to ritualistic analyses of family interaction and prescriptions for rectifying it. The treatment worked to the satisfaction of many families and me, but that is not confirmation of theory nor of my goals. As Oscar Wilde said, "A thing is not necessarily true because a man dies for it." But the families

taught me my own limitations. They showed me that working out
their lives together is a complicated matter that must not be oversim-
plified. It fails if only a few ideas about one's self or about another in
the family take over and become the prevailing assumptions behind
action. The error in our earlier notions of the family seemed more an
oversimplification than a misinterpretation of available facts. We
made generalizations from the limited data at our disposal; then, in
order to facilitate change, we slipped into regarding our conclusions
as norms for all families; we translated scientific abstractions into
moral imperatives. To generalize about family life in America, or
end-of-the-century Vienna, or among the Yoruba of Nigeria, or the
Moslems of Pakistan is desirable. But these abstractions give us no
simple prescriptions for father-mother-child interrelations. They are
only one order of information that has to be taken into account by a
family. Adjustment may depend on flying in the face of family custom.

Let me illustrate: A psychiatrist we visited in a West African
country was in a jubilant mood on the Monday morning we met him.
On his recent return from professional training and a long spell of
practice abroad, he was told by his father that, after the family
custom, he must continue to educate his brothers and sisters. These
were the progeny of his wealthy father's simultaneous marriages with
three wives. For a year, he struggled to do it and at the same time to
educate his own adolescent children. Finally in desperation he dared
the unconventional and challenged his father's authority. He called a
family council, a prerogative reserved for his father. It had been held
the day before our meeting. About 30 family members attended. The
ice between his father and him was long in thawing, but by the end of
the day the whole group, in concert, had decided who, including the
father, would support each son and each daughter. Not much wonder
the psychiatrist was jubilant.

The solutions of family problems are not necessarily those that
contravert authority or fly in the face of customs, but this must be
one of the many possibilities. More typically, of course, the solutions
to problems accord with community expectations: families are usually
well indoctrinated about community norms for individuals and
families as a whole. Usually they work to achieve a reconciliation

between them and the community and culture. Such agreement seems to lead to the reduction of tension.

FAMILY TENSION

Tension in the family has a new meaning for me, though, since my work with the family unit. Two basic propositions helped to order my thinking and observation:

1. I caught reflections of the family fluctuating in its natural life between periods of turmoil, stress, dissatisfaction, and scatter, and periods of interpersonal harmony, solidarity, and mutual gratification. These seemingly universal sequences appeared functional in breaking up antiquated adjustments that had lost their functionality and in exposing and consolidating patterns more responsive to the needs of the family group and the individuals who made it up. Periods of tension seemed phasic, with periods of accommodation. Families appeared to vary greatly in the intensity, frequency, and duration of these shifts, but as long as they maintained group identity they seemed to occur. Tension may be extremely painful, but it has the process meaning that the old is being destroyed and the way is being prepared for the new.

2. Within the therapy conferences, there were also periods of tension. These seemed somewhat related to the family life but not entirely explicable in these terms. They were too predictable. They came as part of the sequence of stages in the treatment and appeared of the following types:

The tension at the beginning of treatment when the guardedness of the individuals is more visible than their openness.

The closely-associated tension in the relationship with the therapist particularly as the individuals and group test out his requirements, expectations, soft-points and firm, limitations and strengths. Tension is shown in battles over authority in the therapeutic hour and in efforts to clarify who and what the therapist is and will be in the treatment setting.

The tension of the recurrent periods when anger prevails and the thematic content concerns attributions of blame to others.

The tension of the impasse, when the way out of problems seems unclear, when the moods are of discouragement and depression.

The end of treatment is usually marked by a reduction in tension in the conferences and reports of similar changes at home. This is no prophylactic against future tension, however. It may change the techniques of the family for dealing with tension in the future, but it cannot and should not prevent its occurrence.

The emergence of group treatment with several families at once parallels in many ways the shift from individual to group therapy. The therapist is developing skill in dealing with increasingly complex groups. Little enough is known as yet about the tension in multi-family groups, but we can expect it to be manifest in and among all the participants—therapist, family members, separate family units, interfamily units and thus the whole group. We shall know more about using ourselves in group processes and about taking functional advantage of groups for therapeutic goals as we increase our mastery over this adaptation of family group therapy.

Paralleling this period of technical advance has been the growth of procedures for dealing with groups in institutions where many of our professional colleagues work. In passing, may I simply refer to the therapeutic community and to the sensitivity training of staffs as important and common methods of handling intrainstitutional tensions toward therapeutic goals.

Looked at in this panorama we can congratulate ourselves on the rapid expansion of our willingness to work with groups and on the creativeness applied to enlarging the coverage of our theory and technical interventions. We have been learning to understand, use and control the processes that form groups, that propel them into conflict, that assist them in resolving the conflict, and that govern the part we and other individuals play in the groups.

INTER-INSTITUTIONAL TENSION

Even more is ahead. We are taking on increasingly complex assignments. My own most recent work, the center of my present research, illustrates a new and minimally explored extension of group techniques. For the past ten years, I have been trying to devise methods for reducing the distance between two cultural institutions, as it were, for dealing with inter-institutional tension. In specifics, at my own request I was placed by the National Institute of Mental Health in charge of a project to explore the sources of problems between the institutions of the family and the hospital where a family member is hospitalized. I was directed to work on uncovering principles and methods by which the family, the patient, and the hospital may be articulated effectively and productively.

Before describing enough details to give you an orientation, let me point out how somewhat parallel processes are being studied and engineered in the community. Many are busy working out interagency agreements and methods for providing continuity of patient care in community mental health centers. We observe mental health professionals negotiating, consulting, arbitrating, studying, theorizing, formalizing and documenting their efforts to move freely between institutions, and work out ways for them to operate together for the sake of treatment, and for community development aimed at the prevention of disorder.

Let me return to the matter of the family and the hospital. This research program grew out of the persisting isolation of significant numbers of mental hospital patients from their own families, even though the home is in some proximity to the hospital. It also started from recognition that institutionalization may in itself promote a disorder on top of a psychiatric disease. To prevent the breakdown of community-hospital reciprocation promises to be the ultimate solution for isolation and institutionalization.

As an aside, we agreed that there is a significant proportion of hospital patients who have been living singly, who have been removed from family associations for such a long period before hospitalization that for them the family is unlikely to be a functional community group in the future. For them, as for all alienated persons, groups have to be devised and fostered.

To reduce institutionalization, the patient has to keep his group memberships alive or has to be helped to develop functional memberships in new groups outside the hospital. We are convinced this is best done *while* he is in the hospital, not just as he faces discharge and rehabilitation, lest the hospital becomes his community.

Solving the problem of family-hospital articulation has proven a worthy occupation. Think of the scope of it. One faces on the one side a highly structured organization; memorialized in concrete and equipment; governed by formal policies, written rules and procedures; shackled by traditions, some going back centuries; mobilized to support professional and subprofessional roles and investments; patterned in its ways of looking at and dealing with patients: hemmed in by business, administrative, clerical, statistical, legal and public relations operations and other strictures on adaptability. On the other side, we have a small institution, the family, also highly structured, but from unit to unit markedly idiosyncratic. While we talk about family-hospital articulation, we are actually talking about the intercommunieation of a hospital with many and varied family units.

The patient as he is hospitalized makes a transition—he sets out from one institution, the family, and enters another, the hospital. In some instances, he is the only bridge between the two. Frequently, though, hospital-based staff, such as social workers, become bridges in the reverse direction.

I cannot take the time to give details of our progress to date, but you may be interested in the method and stimulated thereby to watch for progress reports. We set out to learn about this problem and about proposed steps we might take from those hospitals in other countries that permit or require full-time attendance on the patient by family members. Previously, no one had studied this practice in a systematic way, although it is referred to anecdotally in a variety of publications. Notable examples occur in Africa and Asia where I was sent to study them. It was my purpose to examine them for their own sake, and for whatever they might teach us about family-hospital relationships here, where full-time attendance on adult patients by the family is virtually unobservable except in the case of presidents, gypsies, and persons in extremis. Even in pediatric wards, it is found too occasionally.

In this country, we tend to ignore the tension that exists between families and hospitals. When the family is there in the hospital full time, it can never be overlooked. Hence the relatedness of this study to our theme today. A few illustrations about tension:

In a little mission hospital in Rhodesia, a mother staying on the pediatric ward fed her child an herb supplied by the local witch doctor, and the child became desperately ill. The American doctor who had tolerated the mothers up to that time became so furious that he threw them all out, and has refused to let them stay in since, though they camp on the grounds and cluster around the windows to watch their children.

A British nursing sister sent out by her government in colonial days to a hospital in Nigeria embarked immediately on a campaign to clean out the relatives. But the families were stronger than she was, they refused to budge, and she finally left in desperation.

There is virtually no family participation in mental hospitals and leprosaria. In each, the public contact with one's family is broken. Here the tension and the break has occurred before institutionalization. But the relationship is underground. Secret channels of communication are kept open so that if a patient dies, the family may claim the body and return it home for burial.

It was reported in many instances that the quality of nursing improves when the family is there, even though there is much about the system that the nurses despise. The relatives demand more, and serve also as models for how the nurses might handle patients. But, in the nurses, this promotes conflict over the dictates of their own training as against impositions by the family.

Tension is there and it is confronted in one way or another, so that the family, patient, and hospital work together. In hospitals in our country, tension exists, too, and if we address ourselves to it as a social problem we are led into the next goals of our study, to devise ways to use professionals to promote family-hospital liaison.

See how we are expanding our sights and at the same time meeting a whole new series of questions. Where do we intervene? In the hospital? With the patient? In the family? In the community, to modify its attitudes and sanctions? Can the professional person solve these problems and accomplish the desired changes by his own effort as an individual? Has he now undertaken such a complicated social enterprise that he must work in a team? For the near future, will his greatest contribution be in working with the team in order to help it to solve its own working relationships, or does he have the competence to be the leader?

Learning information and skills here will make all of us more ready for the community and the world, areas where some intervene effectively now, but all have much to learn.

TENSION IN THE COMMUNITY AND BEYOND

The problems in the community and its larger extensions to the limits of the world seem so immense. Where do we start? How do you tackle the world's language problems? How can you bring the hundreds of tribes of Africa or India into communication with one another? How for that matter can you bring the east side and west end in our own cities together? How can we move the developing nations toward our level of living at a faster pace than the growth of our national standard, so that the world is not divided into haves and have-nots; we have horrible and repeated reminders in Los Angeles and elsewhere that we have made only a start in dealing with the same issue right in our own country. Having rid the world of the colonial problem, how will we deal with the tensions between nations and tribes, largely invisible until independence removed the masks that permitted domestic hostility to parade as anti-imperialism? How do we bring sufficient health and welfare services to those countries around the world where half the babies die in the first year of life? How do we outlaw war and the proliferation of nuclear devices? How do we control population on a massive enough scale to rule out the possibility that adults will starve to death or sell their dying babies for 50 cents? How do we learn in our own country to respect, emulate, and use India's tolerance of human differences, the gentility of the Thais, the social expressiveness and discipline of the African family and village, the Japanese aesthetic in art in nature, the philosophies and religions of China and other ancient cultures?

Where are we as professionals in response to these and hundreds of like questions? Toward what ends will we use ourselves? How will our knowledge of groups, the solid ground from which we start, enable us to function and provide a base for expansion of our work? These are the horizons toward which we are being stretched. These are the charges set before us today and for the future. These are the matters in hand for us to talk about now. These contain issues of such immensity, such perplexity, such struggle, such urgency, such extremity, that we can all start profitably by acknowledging our need for one another. We are in good fortune that we have one another available so we may learn from each other, plan together and profit from our collective wisdom. The group we shall use today for tackling the problems of tension is ourselves. Tomorrow, our steps promise to take us inexorably toward family, the community, and the world.

Chapter IX

Family Group Therapy[1] in the Treatment of Juvenile and Adult Offenders

Efforts to apply family group therapy in work with offenders led to some interesting advances in the use of the treatment. Here I shall describe some aspects of this work within two settings: in the community, in relation to pre-institutionalization, probation, or parole; and in the institution, whether in juvenile hall, or in state or other correctional institutions.

WHY FAMILY THERAPY?

It might be questioned first, however, why we work with the families of offenders. The fundamental reason is that the family

247

remains the most important small social group to which individuals, even offenders, belong. This is not necessarily dependent on the quality of the family in providing what we might describe as a good life for the individual. I am putting to the side consideration of those who are deprived of a family during years of childhood and youth or who are completely alone in adult life. Most youth have a social investment in the family that is capital with which we work in their socialization. Adults who are married, and even more, are parents, also have such an investment. If we are aiming for increases of individuals' socialization, we are not starting from scratch when we meet them within a family.

Second, we believe that the family may be, and frequently is, a primary source of the disorder that leads to anti-social behavior. We do not find the best explanation of *all* delinquency on that basis, but know that much of it is related to the family life. Even where other factors seem more relevant, the family is important. The family disturbance leads to delinquency and the delinquency itself has repercussions on the family. These in themselves may accentuate tendencies to delinquency and magnify the seriousness of the correctional problem.

Third, since the life of the family will persist into the future, and continue to influence its members, anything that can be done to improve the quality of the family will work toward the reduction or elimination of pressures to behave anti-socially. Working with the family may prevent offenses in the future or lessen their seriousness.

Fourth, working with the family may multiply the motivation and strengths available for redirection and control of the offender. We have access not just to an individual, but to a social system. Both the individual and the system may have been regarded as reservoirs of pathology. But they may be mobilized to become reservoirs of support, solidarity, sanctions and limits. Just as the social system of the institution provides a milieu which may have a therapeutic influence, so also the social system of the family may become a milieu for growth.

Practically speaking we have solved many of the technical problems in working therapeutically with the whole family. We may not and need not claim complete understanding and control of the treatment process, but we know how to use ourselves and the consequences we may expect. Family group therapy has been applied in many settings. Correctional programs, particularly with juveniles, have begun to use it extensively. There is insufficient time to give you the necessary details. But at least, we may talk briefly about the overall conceptions of what takes place.

In family therapy we are operating on the assumption that we shall use ourselves to intervene in the functioning of a family system. Toward changing an individual among those who make up a family, I take this position: family changes will result in secondary changes in each of the individuals who compose a family. Others argue that changes must be sought by working with the family as a group, and simultaneously and separately with an individual member. In practice, two other approaches, at least, may be observed: first, working with an individual in the presence of the family group, that is, with the family as an audience; and, using several therapists to conduct simultaneous individual and separate therapy with each person in the family. A variation of the last is found where each family member is placed in a different group for therapy.

I am in favor of therapists having the option to do what each thinks he can do best. I believe, also, that for the freedom to do that he must oblige himself to evaluate critically whether he is offering himself for the sake of clients in an optimal fashion. I have yet to be convinced by the advocates of mixing approaches, that the impact on the family and on any individual is more potent, more economical, and more therapeutic. On the contrary, and this is a major point, I believe that, if one is to work with the family, the most rapid, most manageable, and most functional impact is made when one works only with the whole family as a group and concentrates on the interpersonal actions rather than on processes within an individual.

SHALL WE ABANDON INDIVIDUAL TREATMENT?

Does this mean then that we should throw out our efforts to work with individuals? Let us examine this. What opportunity is there in individual treatment to bring about a change in the family interaction? Are our chances greater through family work than through work with the individual patient? Here are questions we cannot answer absolutely, but at least we can examine some of the processes involved to see if there are any clues as to the range of the answers.

Here is a 14-year old boy who is in trouble with the juvenile court. Pressure has been brought by the court to assure that the family finds psychiatric help for the boy, and he has been brought to a clinic. The family members themselves have been troubled by this youngster for a long period, so they bring him to the clinic and the staff takes him on. What are the processes by which, in working with this boy, we are going to bring about changes in the ways in which father or mother interacts with him, or in how they all interact with each other? Have we any way of conceptualizing how this may be done?

We know that the therapist and the boy are in relations with one another wherein the therapist has an impact on the boy which results in change in him. The therapist is not working directly with father, mother, or siblings, however. So somehow changes in the boy must induce changes in his interactions with his family. So we have two steps in the process: the therapist produces change in the boy, and, then, the boy in turn produces changes in the relations with the family. Is this an efficient process?

There may be advantages in working in this fashion. For one thing, when the therapist is alone with the boy, ostensibly he can have a strong impact on him, so this may offer an edge in this kind of approach. But there are some things here which may work against the possibility of changing the family. For one thing, to take this boy on for treatment means that one had adopted the father's, mother's, and siblings' scapegoating of this youngster, as well as affirming the action of the court. One may be supporting the family in continuing to hold their present attitudes against the boy, by the very act of taking him on as a patient. Correlatively, one may be supporting the family's defenses against changing themselves. If it is an advantage for this family to have this boy as a scapegoat, it will be very hard for him to change their ways of looking at him, even though the therapist's efforts result in changes.

Another thing that happens when one has this kind of situation is that the family members, who are on the outside of the boy's relations with the therapist, will move in one of two directions in regard to the therapy. They will try to join the therapy relationship, shown, for instance, in curiosity about what is taking place there. If the boy, on his part, values this private relation, he will put blocks in the way of his family's efforts to learn what is going on. This only leads the family members to try further to find out what is happening, to seek out the therapist, and to try to build ties with him.

If the family is blocked by the therapist and the boy, then its only alternative is to isolate them. What we can not join, we fight. As the treatment is progressing, if a family does not feel that it is getting an opportunity to relate there, it may actually seal itself off from it, downplay its effectiveness, and resent its results. Such isolation from the therapy accentuates unresponsiveness of the family to the boy.

To counteract these difficulties in individual work, we have developed a singleminded focus. It says first that the whole family needs to change. We are not subscribing to the view that the delinquent is the source of a family's difficulties and that he is the one who needs to be changed. Preoccupation with an individual may be seen on its two faces as occurring through the initiative of an individual who takes on this role of the scapegoat, or through the pressures of family members who force it upon him. The delinquency of an individual is transmuted into justification for any interactional difficulties and for imposing the need to change upon the individual. This usually has the effect of undermining progress that is being made, and strengthens the status quo in the family.

Secondly, we are not setting up a private relationship with any individual in the family, which would divide it into two or more parts, one part related to a therapist and the others excluded from that relation. We are saying we work with the whole group. We are firming up the boundaries around the whole family. We are restricting the family's escape into matters extraneous to their relations with one another. They may engage in evasion by attending to matters that are in essence outside the family.

Working with the whole family seems especially pertinent for helping a family member who has been adjudged delinquent or criminal. In relation to him, there are strong tendencies for some family members, especially adults, to fluctuate between family and community roles. Now they take the role of the mother or father, and now they play the part of the judge, the court, the probation officer, the teacher, or, alternately, of community promoters of anti-social behavior. Their relations in the family sessions may become indulgent or punitive, because they function within outsider as well as family roles.

In relating to the outside, they may seek to force a therapist out of his family orientation, and push him to deal with questions such as, "Don't you think the judge was unfair?" or, "Why should they single out my child when there are so many others who do the same thing and are excused or never picked up?" The person in trouble with the law has provided the members of his family with an easy way to classify him. So the family can limit the ways they will look at him as a person and a family member and justify themselves when they look at him from a community perspective. The therapist has to check this. He does this by centering the family's attention on itself and by pointing out that relations in the community have to be bypassed in treatment when there is no way by which discussion in the family can directly change anybody outside the family.

PROBLEMS WITH FAMILY TREATMENT

Statutes and Tradition. There is a peculiar problem about family work in the correctional field, however. Our laws and traditional procedures require individual work with offenders, as exemplified in probation, institutional placement, or parole. We do not place the family on probation, we do not institutionalize the family, and, consequently, it is never on parole. Correctional relations with individuals are written into statute. No questions need to be asked about, "Where does society expect the change to be produced?" In most instances the law would say we want to see change in an individual, and the correctional officer, by his position of authority and his assignments from society, has to work with the individual. Practical measures to enable us to fulfill these requirements are publicly supplied. It would be equally apt to say that professional persons in the field recognize the importance of family change. However, to engage the family in treatment has to be engineered. Strangely, by virtue of the laws, these approaches may be incompatible. The sharper the differentiation that can be made between them, the greater the likelihood that they may go on concurrently and effectively. Thus I propose the conscious, public divorce of probation and parole as they are now established, from family treatment. If the same individual officer must conduct them both, I fear it is only theoretically possible that he will succeed.[2]

Family Boundaries.   Another major point about family treatment: the success and speed of the treatment depends on as clear definition as possible of the functions that will be performed by the therapist, and of those that will be expected of the family members. All of these individuals, including the therapist, are human beings, frail, disorganized, unable to control themselves, anxious, emotional, self-seeking, at least at times. We cannot turn therapists into angels, but we can warn them to expect complications if they slip into joining the family—if consciously or unconsciously they become a "parent" or "child," and especially if they become "delinquent" or "anti-delinquent" in the process. The line between the therapist and the family group wavers in its visibility. When the line is clearly seen by both the therapist and the family, the containing and strengthening boundaries around the family are at their firmest. When the line is only dimly seen, even by the therapist, then he may not know if he is shoving somebody outside the family and breaking down its solidarity. The therapist's work is the therapy, producing change in the family: getting it started, seeing that it is kept going, anticipating and accepting its termination, and getting out. The family's work is to change during the time with the therapist, but it has a whole lot of other ongoing functions too. Usually it will choose on its own or find itself promoting change elsewhere in its life, that is, outside the conferences. That is its own business. We have no right to try to exceed the agreed contract involved in the treatment conferences, that the therapist will work to help the family to change itself within the therapy sessions.

Therapist's Contract.   Another aspect of the clarity of the therapist's functioning concerns the limits he will impose on himself and uphold in front of the family. He will know that he has knowledge, skills, and other resources beyond those he "professes" as the therapist. He will not contract with the family to exceed his own resources, obviously. At the same time, he will know he can arrange with others to help the family in ways he could not. He could secure help from others for counseling, intervening in public agencies on behalf of the family, advocacy, assembling resources needed for family and personal sustenance, and so on. He may be tempted to extend his contract by functioning personally in these other areas, or by securing the help of others. He can legitimately do so, if he engages the family in the decision for that, and if he takes the responsibility for what this will do to the therapy.

Roles for Other Specialists. The family problems extend into so many operations at home and in the community, it may seem unduly restrictive to be only a therapist. To express willingness to enlist others to help in meeting the urgent needs of a family is not out of line with a therapist's use of himself. To advance offers, however, that may obligate the family to accept help in dealing with problems beyond the scope of the therapy, may overextend the therapist's role. Engaging in matters extraneous to the direct work of the therapy conference, may undermine the clear and authoritative role of the therapist in conducting his own functions, where he must accept responsibility.

Since family group therapy does not attempt to work through all problems, it is unrealistic to expect that it will solve them all. There is ample room and necessity for others to be involved—correctional officials, teachers, medical personnel, welfare workers, clergy, employment and rehabilitation counselors, recreation workers, lawyers, and persons of other professions. The place for others, however, who are following their specialized professional roles, is not to bring operations based on those roles into the family therapy that is focused toward solidifying internal functional relations in the family.

Therapy Goals. Another issue, about which we must achieve a position, is that of change "toward what"? This is the question of the values promoted in the therapy. These may be drawn from many sources. Persons in the field of corrections seem biased especially toward the value of socializing behavior of individuals and families. Their jobs seem to require this inclination. The family therapist probably has such a goal implicitly. He may be oriented toward family harmony and have a lot of other personal values that accord with those of the person in corrections. But some he may not share. His value commitments are not necessarily the same as those of the correctional officer, although by virtue of his profession he has proclaimed a precommitment to function ethically within that profession. A third set of values that may impinge on the family therapy are the

values of the court. Finally, we have the family's own value conceptions and commitments. There is plenty of room here for conflict
among competing ethical and moral systems.

In developing his own role, the family therapist has to take some
position on the matter of therapy goals. Some therapists have decided
for themselves that they know best what is good for families and that
the end of therapy is attested when families accept the therapist's
values and use them to govern the ways they will interact and conduct themselves in the community. Others say they have decided that
the family knows already the values appropriate for its own family life
and is dealing with the problem of attaining what it knows as right,
rather than of learning it. Doubtless there are middle positions;
doubtless, also, there are phases of treatment when one approach
may seem more suitable than another. It is relevant to consider that
there is room for a variety of therapists to take up independent points
of view in directions that will lead them to teach, preach, and order.
There is more consensus that the therapist should work with the
values that the family advances for itself, and that is my own position.
For another therapist or a correctional officer to adopt that position
because it is common, is less advantageous for him, than for him to
make up his own mind and seek consistent behavior in accord with
his own decisions.

Family, Offender, and Institution

Now a brief word about the family, the institution, and the offender there. Family therapy, as developed, has been an outgrowth of
efforts to help individuals in families who live together in the community. It was not designed for the family separated into two segments, one in an institution, the rest in the home. We have found it
somewhat possible to adapt the outpatient techniques to family work
in institutions, but not without the conclusion that family therapy is
done better in the community. The fact remains that for many
reasons offenders and lots of others are institutionalized. They come
from families, they will return to families, but for the present, they
are separated from them. During the separation, the family fre-

quently reorders its life in terms of the absence of the offender. We all know the difficulties, then, in reincorporating one who has been institutionalized into the family.

The inmate comes back after a period of absence, is a stranger with his own family. They have developed their own ways of getting along without him, their own new activities, new values, and often resent the necessity to disrupt their present life in order to integrate a returnee. This is a perfectly normal process, but not always seen to be so by the family, who may feel guilty because they are not more enthusiastic to have the person back. The result is only a natural consequence of the situation that sets two groups in opposition to one another.

The institution and the boy have become one group, and the rest of the family, a second. While there may be advantages in terms of the intensity with which the institution can work with the youngster, the staff, at the same time, may be setting up forces indirectly that work against the changes that would benefit the youngster and the rest of the family when they are reintegrated. This does not reduce, but perhaps increases, the importance of working with the family.

The overall relations of institutions to families are very confused. I could anticipate what you would find if you were to go into each of the institutions in any state in the country—juvenile halls, camps, schools, centers, prisons, jails, and so on—to ask where the family is in the institution. You would arrive at a most inconsistent picture of the ties between correctional institutions and the family. Specific institutions would have clean-cut positions, policies, procedures; others would not know how to answer the question; others would have a variety of relations; but among them all there would be diversity. We know also that what is said and what is operating may not be in accord. For instance, are we really oriented toward the return of a delinquent permanently to the family in the community, if the long-term consequence of institutional treatment is developing an inability to live outside an institution?

Being caught up in an extended study about family relations with hospitals, a not dissimilar matter, I believe I can at least point out some of the problems in family-institution relations, and some of the places where we may examine the possibilities for change toward a true family emphasis.

First, let me point out the tug-of-war that goes on between a family and an institution: When a person leaves a family and becomes an inmate, he lives as a member of two groups. These groups are in competition for his loyalty; each may try to close the other out. The physical opportunity is with the institution; the emotional may remain with the family. The institutionalized person may be on the bridge between. As one who has commuted across a bridge each morning for years, I can assure you that being stuck out in the middle is seldom what anyone would choose. The tendency is to head for one end or the other. But, we are really talking about groups of people —and processes of belonging or being cast out. Most people will choose to belong, even without much to offer or receive. The effect of institutionalization is the development of belongingness there—and a common corollary, resigning, or being pushed out, from the family.

Keeping the family relationship alive and improving while the person is in an institution should be our aim if we want him to return to a strengthened family in the community. All our activities, policies, procedures, opportunities should energize this. But we do not really seem to know how to do that, or to know if we really want to know.

But I think I can tell you some things to look at:

We have to examine the extent of family privacy; the extent to which an institution permits families to live together, full-time, part-time, occasionally, without the need to share any of their thoughts, feelings, and activities with others outside the family.

We need to look at the extent to which the *valuable*, old, everyday family roles and functions are being allowed to continue. The more a balance between the old and the new, shifts toward the new, with a correlative depreciation of the valued and worthwhile old, the more we promote inner tension and the break-up of the family. Take the case of a domesticated wife or mother, who has her status in the family by feeding, washing, and tidying up. When she comes to the institution, she has to relate to her family members as a dressed-up person with nothing to do but visit. We have stripped away her status, her comfort, and her contributions. She will take it out on her family; she will take it out on the institution; or she will try to find a group, perhaps the rest of the family, who will allow her to continue in her customary and comfortable roles, functions and activities. An institution can quickly strip away family strengths.

We need to study the extent to which the program or an institution has a sincere purpose to work with the whole family, and the extent to which programs are organized for and actually achieving the purpose. Those institutions that see in the presence of the family a fine opportunity to educate family members about health, nutrition, family development, safety and sanitation, recreation, and many other useful things to know are likely to support families. Relations with families are more successful than in institutions that have not taken advantage of such an opportunity. Those institutions that seek the help of families to supplement insufficient staff, and then work out complementary roles for staff and family members, are successful in family relations; those who have families present, but keep being competitive about who does what, promote institution-family discord and separation.

We need to assess what we are doing in relation to the expressions of family solidarity that are now being made by families who come within the institution's boundaries. In the Moslem countries a man's status is often measured by the size of the entourage that accompanies him when he leaves home. He wants this preserved, but so also does his family and the others around him. When he goes to an institution, the entourage tries to go too. They would not think of other possibilities. Fifty may crowd into a small room to continue the respectful relation. The institution must allow for this, or else—.

When a youth or an adult is institutionalized in our country, his status is supported by those who depend on it. They will attempt to continue it. We may observe this in the family. But what do we do to family gestures toward an inmate? What do we do with their reaching out to the institution, the patient, and to the community on his behalf? I know what often happens. The institution tries to turn the family out of doors, choking off the very motivation for family solidarity to be sought later when the inmate is ready for discharge. I am not romantic about families. I know they subvert the work of the institution. But I know also that it is not impossible for an institution and a family to join forces toward common ends.

These are only a few of the matters to be pondered. If we are to plan for family therapy in the field of correction, we are attending to only one part of the planning if we see it in the outpatient setting. The next progressive steps beyond that are to engage the family, offender and *institutions* in articulations aimed at treating the family, alleviating its problems, and promoting its functioning on behalf of all its members, including offenders. Though we may use family group therapy in selected cases in an institution setting, we need new group approaches to the family by institutions. Such approaches become possible only through new mind-sets based on stringent criticism of present family-institution disarticulation.

Chapter X

Contrasting
Approaches in Marital
Counseling

In case it seems strange to be talking about marital counseling in a book on family therapy, let me explain that my purpose is to deal with theoretical issues about family therapy. To simplify study of the therapist-family relations I shall talk about the smallest family group, a married couple. This small group is a paradigm of the family. I shall not extend what I say about marital therapy to therapy with larger families. For the most part such extensions will be feasible to accomplish by substituting "family" for "marital couple." In a sense we are playing a mathematical game, saying that T (therapist) + $2P$ (patients, or marital couple) is analogous to $T + (2+n)P$, where n represents however many members beyond a marital couple might be found in any family.

My aim, then, is to look at the therapist-marital couple (or therapist-family) relationship as a social system, and from this perspective to outline some aspects of the differences between treating a husband or a wife as an individual patient and treating them together as a marital couple. At the same time, this gives me a chance to say some things on my mind about the treatment process with marriage partners.

I will try to differentiate individual treatment and treatment of the marital pair on two dimensions: their respective use as sources of data about the marital relations, for both therapy and research, and their potentialities for changing the marital interaction.

SOURCES OF DATA ABOUT A MARRIAGE

In individual therapy of one of the marriage partners there are two essential ways in which we learn about the marriage. To begin with, the patient reports to the therapist facts and fantasies about his life with his partner. He tells about his attitudes to his mate, his feelings about her, his past experiences with her, his conjectures about her, and other events in their relationship. Depending on the patient, this reporting may range from full and rich to sparse and vacuous.

There is much variability in the quality of data, but essentially there are four major factors that limit them. The *data* depend on the competence of the patient, intellectually and verbally. The *report*, structured by the selective ways in which the patient sees the marriage, is biased because it is a partial report of what the patient could tell us, and because it is one-sided in that it reports about the marriage only from the perspective of the patient. The *content* is dependent on the amount and kind of opportunity in the therapist-patient relationship to recall and report. The *reporting* is abstracted in time from the immediate and actual relationship between the husband and wife, that is, the patient in the treatment room is out of the marriage temporarily. Everything that is reported has passed; it is abstract in its reference to the present, and it is theoretic in terms of its bearing on what will go on when the patient and his mate are together in the future.

Thus, while patient reports about the relationship are potentially fruitful, there are inherent limitations in the nature of the data they provide.

A second source of information about the marriage exists in the action between the therapist and the patient. When the therapist acts in the same manner as the mate in the marriage, we may expect the patient to act as he does in the marriage. That is, at times the therapy relationship is analogous to the marriage, and the patient participates in comparable ways. Mostly this occurs accidentally and sporadically rather than through the therapist's deliberation and planning, but occasionally a therapist may initiate an action with the intention of eliciting patterns used in the marriage.

Again, we may identify limitations on the data available through this source. In the first place, the data are mingled with other data obtainable from the therapist-patient relationship. It is difficult to identify when the patient is acting as he does in the marriage and when he is acting in ways foreign to that relationship. Second, if we can be certain that the behavior is actually an analogue of marital behavior, we have no criteria by which to judge its representativeness within the marriage, that is, whether the behavior typifies how the patient acts toward his mate or if it is rare. Evidence to permit us to judge how typical the behavior is does not normally accompany these glimpses of the marriage. Third, if the therapy situation has called forth patient action analogous to that appearing in the marriage, we have no evidence on how frequently comparable situations to evoke such action might occur there. The behavior may typify a response but the stimulus situation may be common or rare, and we seldom have information by which to estimate its singularity. Last, the therapist is at a disadvantage in observing analogous behavior because he is both in action with the patient and observer of the action. The therapist as a partner who called forth the action has limits on his distance for observation, particularly about those aspects of his own action that have stimulated the patient to act as he does. The therapist's actions with the patient and his functioning as an observer of his own action are not possible simultaneously. Since they can only occur sequentially, he must drop out of action for observation of himself. When this occurs it may be at the expense of anxiety and hostility in the patient, which he might wish to avoid. Since his knowledge of the patient cannot be independent of his observation of himself, and he may restrict his withdrawal into observation for therapeutic ends, he further limits the data available to him.

In summary, in individual psychotherapy we find two sources of such information—patient reporting and action analogues within the therapist-patient relationship. Both of these sources restrict in specifiable ways the accessibility of knowledge about the marriage.

Turning, by way of contrast, to the treatment system where the marital partners are seen together, we have here, also, limited types of data available to us which come from three characteristic sources of information.

First, the therapist is able to observe directly action occurring between the marriage partners at the moment of its occurrence. He can observe the communication patterns, especially the significant nonverbal communication, the decision processes, the modes of handling problems, the joint reactions to outside stresses, and so on, as they take place. This opportunity is not afforded in individual therapy. Such information is restricted, however, in that the marital action in the treatment session is always occurring in the presence of a third party. We lack knowledge to decide what distortions are created by the therapist's involvement.

We do know that how the man and woman love, fight, budget, entertain, do the chores, parent their children, manage the in-laws, plan their future when they are at home and out of the therapist's gaze may vary significantly from the samples of the relationship given in the treatment conference. We also know that there are characteristic stages in the development of any three-person group. The behavior of the marital couple as well as the therapist will be representative of these stages. Unless the therapist is conscious of the ways in which behavior is formed in the group, he might falsely attribute the group process to the marriage itself. The earlier in treatment such errors might be developed the greater the risk, for they have more opportunity then to direct the therapist's attention to behavior which will confirm them and away from contradictory evidence. In addition, the therapist might promote unwittingly the behavior that would confirm his conclusions.

The treatment situation also removes the couple from the immediate pressures that precipitate some of their interactions at home and structures action in relation to revelation of problems and anticipation of their solution. Having somewhat the demand to focus on the past (problems) and on the future (solutions) there is an abstraction from much in the present. This is shown in a heightening of the activities of evaluation, intellectualization, and verbal communication; we can assume a commensurate reduction of the immediate function-oriented action characteristic of the home environment. It is especially to be noted that the treatment situation accentuates verbal interaction between the partners and reduces the nonverbal, the language that is the preeminent basis of operations in most natural groups. Therapists learn the information that depends on words more easily than that which is unspoken and unspeakable.

In this three-person treatment situation the therapist is limited as observer as in individual treatment, although we may conjecture that the impact of his withdrawal into the observer role will differ from a similar withdrawal in a two-person system. We would know more about how these effects differ if we had studied systematically the impact of an audience on a single individual as compared to its effect on him as a member of well established diads such as a marriage. Direct observation of the marriage relationship thus provides information of a different order than that available in individual treatment, but it is not without definable limits.

A second source of information in the three-party system is through reports by one or both of the marriage partners. Obviously the reports about the marriage made in the presence of one's mate will differ from those given in privacy. The partner's presence will add significance to the reporting of some facts and diminish the importance and freedom for articulating others. The likelihood of immediate qualification by one's mate structures what one may choose to tell or how one may say it. One-sidedness is lessened but new biases enter into the reporting, e.g., withholding what is jointly regarded as private, and stating what is safe or advantageous to report. A particular limitation in this kind of reporting is the reduction of historical and developmental information. If such information is relevant to the immediate interrelations it will come out; if it is not, the therapist has less freedom for exploration. He cannot afford the preoccupation with the individual that such investigation involves if he seeks the most economical use of his time for therapeutic gain.

A third source of information occurs in the therapist's relationships, either with the man or woman in the presence of the other, or with the couple together. The therapist, as an outsider in the marriage, obviously can gain information about the couple's reactions to at least one outsider. Perhaps this is analogous to reactions to others outside the marriage, but we have little chance to test how much the therapy relationship manifests the range of relationships with outsiders. So here we face one type of limitation of the data gained in the relationship with the therapist.

The man's or woman's reactions with the therapist may show facets of actual marriage behavior. Sometimes we are even told this is so, as when a husband said, "You see she is doing exactly the same thing with you that she does with me." On the other hand, we might not have more advantage here in judging representativeness, or the likelihood of the behavior taking place outside the therapist's office, than we would have had in individual treatment.

We cannot use the therapist's relationship with an individual as a source of data about the marriage in the same way in the three-party situation as in individual treatment. In the three-party interaction, a relationship with an individual is always in the presence of a third party. It may for purposes of analysis be seen as abstracted from the three-person group, but in action it is not isolable. The third person pushes, competes, judges, protests, intrudes, supports, evades, or in other ways keeps acting with the group. This produces a different kind of information than that available from the therapist-individual relationship. Nor are the problems inherent in being a participant and an observer less pertinent here than in any other observation situation.

I am sure I have gone into enough detail to illustrate that there are important differences in the data provided in these two approaches to marital counseling. Each has its opportunities for gaining information, as well as its predictable and irremediable limitations.

AFFECTING THE MARITAL RELATIONSHIP

I shall now discuss the social processes in treatment by which the interrelational aspects of the marriage are affected. Please note that I am not talking about individual change, but about the changes produced in the marriage under the same two forms of treatment —treatment of one of the marriage partners individually and treatment of the two partners together—where the defined goal is to change the patterns of interaction in the marriage. We do not have enough information at this time for a definitive comparison, but we have to begin where we are.

To modify a marriage through individual treatment involves these processes:

The therapist enlists the patient, whom I shall refer to as being male, in action beyond that which occurs in the marriage.

Out of new modes of action learned with the therapist, and reinforced old actions exterior to the marriage, the patient develops new intentions for action within the marriage.

He attempts to act according to these intentions with his mate.

The mate enters the new action, producing changes in the ways she acts with the patient.

The new actions are consolidated and become part of the repertoire of their joint actions.

The therapist determines the extent to which the patient is engaged in new action and the extent to which the patient's intentions for the marriage are modified; the capacities of the patient to introduce change into the marriage depend on himself and the action of his mate. The therapist is the force in initiating change in the patient; the patient is the force instituting change in the marriage—the same kind of process as was described previously in treatment of the individual offender.

Change is not accomplished easily in any social relationship, however, let alone where there are entrenched patterns of interaction. To state the above steps makes the process sound simple. Prac-

tice shows that this is an excessive over-simplification which under-
states the matter. Some qualifying considerations that limit change
both within the treatment and within the marriage can be noted.

The patient is simultaneously a member in two social groups
—the therapy group with his therapist, and the marital group with his
mate, both two-person groups. Changes in one group create reciprocal changes in the other because of their overlapping membership.
When both these groups agree about the appropriateness of the
changes there is no conflict or bar to change, but let the mate resist
the changes promoted with the therapist and we are in for trouble.
Under these common conditions, the more intensely the patient relates to the therapist, the more the mate is distressed and tries to
intrude on or destroy the therapy relationship. This occurs because of
the tendency of overlapping groups either to coalesce into a larger
single group or to split and close the boundaries between them. Thus
the more forceful the patient's action with the therapist, the greater
the likelihood that his mate will attempt to join it or to disrupt it.

Obviously the therapist seeks the advantage to treatment of developing as vigorous a relation with the patient as possible. This is the
route to a major therapeutic impact on him. But the risks in the
marriage are great. Efforts to preserve it from intrusion by the
therapist will reinforce its old patterns, particularly through action of
the mate who is on the outside of therapy. Against this pressure the
patient is expected to carry the burden of the counter pressure that
will result in change. Not much wonder it often takes a long course of
individual treatment to help a patient to restructure his marriage, or
that so many marriages founder as a result of individual treatment.

If we think that the individual patient must find himself first, we
must not neglect to recognize that until we accomplish this we may
be promoting the therapy at the expense of the marriage. The most
apt way of describing the social process by which one finds one's self
is to elaborate how in action with others he learns to differentiate
himself from them. If the therapist advocates that his patient must
find himself in a relation outside the marriage, as in therapy, he is
discounting the marriage, thereby undermining the very forces which
work for ameliorating action within it.

The individual therapist depends on the intensity of his action
with a single patient to accomplish change in him, in his marriage,

and in other social groups. When the patient may have been driven into therapy by these selfsame groups, we are counting on his being able to gird himself with double power—first, to cancel his captivity to them, and second, to lead his captors to change.

When the therapist chooses to see the couple together, we have a different prospect of change. Here the therapist establishes a three-person group by expanding the two-person natural group of the marriage, which was previously organized around functions much different than treatment. Change produced in the marriage through action in the three-person group is the process of the treatment.

The first step is to establish the three-person group. There are few problems if the marital partners jointly seek the help of the therapist, and come to him at the beginning with confidence in his competence and a mutual desire for his help. Seldom do we have this ideal situation, however. More commonly we have a disparate motivation on the part of the man and woman, which predisposes one to establish a unilateral positive bond with the therapist and the other to counteract this or withdraw. Under these circumstances the therapist is thwarted in carrying on his work unless he can bring the partners into some equivalent but controlled relations with him, and ultimately transform these two parallel relations into a relation that is best described as between the therapist and the marital pair.

Assuming establishment of such a three-person group, by what manner is change effected? Obviously the therapist is the primary agent of change. He intends that the action in the marital subgroup will be modified. Insofar as the man and his wife keep acting with one another, the change is inevitable. No action of the marital partners can be the same in the presence of the therapist as it is at home. This introduces the new, the changed.

The tricky problem for the therapist is to keep the marital pair interacting with one another and to prevent their retreat into private associations with him. As they function together, revision in their action will take place; when as individuals they seek out relations with the therapist they are evading the marital interaction and driving their partners out of the relations.

This is a reversal in many ways of the practice of the therapist in treatment of an individual, where the intensifying of the relations with him is the basic technique. In the joint conference he must establish, but especially control, the relations at the same time. His action and his use of himself is disciplined in such a fashion as to prevent the accentuation of individual ties with him. In a sense the patient is "the couple" rather than either of its members as individuals, and the relations may be intense with the couple, but must remain limited with the individuals who make it up.

Consequently there are certain problems and limitations imposed by this method of approach. The old saw that "Two's company, three's a crowd" has more than surface validity. It is extremely easy in the three-person group to allow a series of diads to form, define themselves, and thus gain identity. It is extremely hard to maintain the sense of direction that keeps the marital pair in action with one another and the therapist relating to them only in terms of his therapeutic operations. Let us not so negate the human qualities of a therapist as to imagine that he can easily resist the separate advances of one or the other of the marriage partners or prevent himself from responding in kind to the hostility of the mate who observes and resents this cohesion. Unfortunately the longer the treatment goes on, the more information the partners have about how they can manipulate the relations with the therapist, and the more intensively the therapist has to work to keep relating to the couple. The more successful he is in this, the more rapidly change takes place.

Is there any protection for the therapist? Obviously there must be, or else the consequences could not be therapeutic. The insurance rests in the following:

The reactions to his becoming overinvolved with an individual are so pronounced that in most instances the alert therapist can quickly institute corrective counter-relationships. But there is always a risk here. Fortunately the mate's counter-responses become obvious so speedily that if the therapist is on his toes he can act to prevent their becoming entrenched. In effect this advances change in each of the partners or, more accurately, in their action with one another.

The therapist is also protected because he learns a defined role to fit into as a therapist. The more clearly his position in the three-person group is structured and the more specific are the principles according to which he acts, the less likelihood of his inadvertent departures from his role, disrupting the smooth flow of the treatment. His conception of the limits on how he will act in the group, the distance he will maintain, and the application and integrity with which he will pursue therapeutic aims all come to be part of his operating intentions. He can communicate these to the marital couple, and he can demonstrate principles in action. His consistency in following his instructions to himself becomes a power in forcing the man and wife to interact and in reducing the force of their efforts to use a relationship with him to disrupt that action.

Another protection rests in the consistency between the therapy situation and the home relationships. A husband and wife can less easily project their difficulties on the therapist when they are in joint treatment with him, although this does happen. In individual treatment, where the therapist is in direct relationship with one and is primarily a fantasy figure to the other, there is more play in the marriage for externalizing problems to the treatment and promoting anti-therapist action. This same projection may occur when the couple is seen together, but the freedom for it is lessened. Further, the therapist has a more immediate and telling opportunity to expose and rectify the projection and its consequences.

On the other hand, by the very nature of the social situation, working with the couple jointly has its disadvantages, some of which are inherent and some which can be overcome in time.

If one works on the marital relations, to achieve the best solutions as quickly as possible one should confine attention to that relationship. This requires reducing the efforts to solve problems outside the marriage. This disadvantage may be lessened somewhat by the spread of change into other groups, since the marriage is always an open social system. It is possible, however, that change in the marriage will mobilize resistance to change in the other groups. Individual treatment is not necessarily the alternative, though. The content of problems discussed there may be greater and we may have an illusion that the problem-solving is more universal, but, in fact, the changes taking place in the patient there depend on a single two-person relation, that between him and the therapist. As we have seen, change must spread from that into other social groups, just as it spreads from the marriage into other groups.

A second disadvantage in joint treatment stands in its challenge to what we have learned through formal training and experience in individual therapy. A direct carryover of the knowledge and techniques of individual therapy into joint treatment is self-defeating, not because it criticizes the pertinence of what we know for individual treatment, but because it confronts us with what we do not know about joint treatment. The consequence is that we have to adopt an experimental frame of mind and relinquish the comfort of being able to rest on authority—that of our own experience and that borrowed from others. An additional problem here grows out of our cultural bias to concern ourselves with individuals. We have a true bias here, in that this is not an adopted posture. We often do not know when our predispositions to think about individuals impel us into actions that disrupt therapeutic work with couples.

A third disadvantage is professional. As yet we have fewer opportunities for learning about joint treatment than about individual treatment. The pool of knowledge is less; the chances for communication through meetings and publications are reduced; the courses in universities, the supervisors to train, the consultants to advise have mostly to be developed. But none of these is beyond possibility. An additional professional problem has been that working in the field of marital counseling has only recently begun to assume respectability.

The social situations of individual treatment and joint treatment of a marital couple provide us with chances to know, to understand, and to affect marriages and to assist in solving marital problems. Categorical statements about the advantages of an individual approach over a conjoint approach, or vice versa, are not supportable. Each approach has its specific techniques, its advantages and disadvantages. Neither is so clearly preferable that we are left without choice; both are sufficiently applicable that we must choose. But having made our choice we have to accept the election of disadvantages as well as opportunities. Otherwise our expectations will exceed our accomplishments, and our promises to patients, implicit though they may be, will lead them to false hope.

Part Four

EXPANSION

Chapter XI

The Future of
Family Therapy

Having become used in my work to thinking of families as social institutions, it became for me a natural expansion of my work to move beyond the family to other institutions in the community; and to move from treating the family to investigations into how to intervene "therapeutically" in other social institutions. My initial identity with studies of the family made it seem natural at the beginning to concern myself with family relations other than those in the family therapy setting—the family in the hospital, in correctional institutions and other helping services.

Gradually I became convinced that the perspective of the family allowed me to see some kinds of community institutions freshly, especially when the family was not particularly evident within these institutions. The remainder of this book will record some of the experiences toward which I was motivated, some of the observations I have made, and some of the practical applications that followed.

FAMILY THERAPY AS A TECHNOLOGY

In an effort to order my ideas, I attended first to the fact that family therapy is a technology, an assemblage of methods to improve the possibilities of solving family problems. Technologies go through recognizable historical courses. I see parallels, for example, with the field of projective techniques that I had a part in developing and saw wane in its general importance. Individually we are at different points in the history of family therapy as a movement, and therefore the past and the future for each of us is individual; collectively we seem to be in a period characteristic of mid-life in the histories of technologies. We have no overall prevailing theories of family therapy, but much agreement, as well as many points of contention. We have not been as systematic as possible in our applications of technology, but there has been a spreading of the efforts to use family therapy. We have not been as orderly in evaluation of family therapy as hard-headed scientists would demand of us, but this has been consistent with most therapy technologies. Our journal, *Family Process*, represents one form of incorporation and institutionalization of the field. So far, we have resisted developing an organization, a step which may be ahead, but which we may choose not to take. Some grudge the investment of time in increasing institutionalization of our work, lest it orient us more toward conservation than toward expansion in new directions. Others prefer to work toward preservation of what we have achieved.

My own preference is to advance into the solution of family problems through new insights and methods yet to be discovered. I have accepted the fact that family therapy as we know it today will lose its mystique, its significant separateness as a technology, and the ardent backing of its exponents and promoters. I do not find this chilling; I think it is exhilarating, holding forth the promise that family therapy as the progenitor will find a new identity and value through its offspring.

While some therapists and investigators will spend their efforts in reaching out to work with families quite like those in their practices and will polish our tools, others will extend themselves to meet consistently with families quite different from those most of us have known in our work. This will confront them with new kinds of therapeutic problems and lead them to devise new techniques. Much is possible to us in the future in the wider application of family therapy. So, as far as the technology of family therapy as we now know it is concerned, perhaps the most significant developments in the future will come from the spread of effort broadly throughout the families in our communities.

Practitioners and the public in general will grow in tolerance for many forms of family organization and life. The picture postcard representation of the family as healthy, young parents of three lively children, petting the family dog, joyously indulging in a life that is more leisure than work, setting out on Sunday morning hand in hand for church, conscientiously attending the meetings of the PTA, happily visited by grandmother and grandfather, will be consigned to some kind of antique family album. This mythical ideal has never adequately represented the many actual forms of family that were hidden behind it. Now the variety is coming out into the open.

There is a diversity in the families in our society far beyond that revealed in the family therapy literature. Many cultures wonderfully enrich our national life and develop the striking and magnificent individual differences that characterize us as a people. In all these diverse families there are problems, and potentials for help through some form of intervention. I think we can discover how narrow we have been as we ask such questions as the following. How many of us have been struggling with the matriarchies presided over by grandmothers in our Black ghettoes? How many of us have been coping with multi-families created by repeated divorces and remarriage? How many of us have been torturing ourselves over the problems of the grossly disorganized family units living on welfare? How many of us have been taking seriously the refugee status of families shunted here and there across our nation by business and industrial reassignments? How many of us are able to live again some of our past, by working with the extended family units we still find clustered in the farming communities of our rural states? How many of us are using our skills to help the families of the new youth breaking out of suburbia into highly experimental forms of family living, sometimes in experimental communities such as Synanon? Individuals could report work with each of the kinds of families in this and a much

longer list. The semi-institutional nature of our field would be
quickly revealed if we asked them to sanction these efforts as being
family therapy. But the future of our field will be in technical experiment as much as in canonization of past practices and theories.

If we think transculturally as well, the potentiality for expansion
of family therapy and understanding is overwhelming. During a
unique opportunity to visit almost every country in Africa south of
the Sahara, the countries of the Middle East and several of the major Asian countries, I saw dramatic evidence of the bonds that link
family members together and an overwhelming variation from country to country in the ways in which families were organized and
related. I was stimulated to think what family therapy might be in
Ghana where they say "you need to know a thousand people to know a
man's family." I remember a journey with a Ghanaian driver into an
ancient coastal city, explored and colonized by the Portuguese long
before Columbus came to America. When we were searching out the
guest house where we were to spend the night I asked the driver
about his own arrangements. He said, "Oh, I'll stay somewhere." We
pursued the matter in order to be confident that he was provided for,
and he assured us he did not need our help because he intended to
stay with his family. We continued, asking innocently whether this
was a brother, sister, or some other close relative. He said, "I won't
know 'til I've met them." In accordance with the laws of West African hospitality, he knew he was free to eat at the table and spend the
night with even his most distant relatives. In the old days he would
have recognized his family by some scarification of the face; now it
took questions, asked without anxiety. I do not suggest that we could
begin to undertake therapy with a family of one thousand. Neither
could we enter the establishment of one of the Moslem sheiks in the
northern part of Ghana to bring together his four wives and their
many children. What could be the shape of family therapy in Ghana?
Already we know that sitting in an office bringing a single family or
several families together into therapy, is good, but not enough. We
will be tested and challenged as we are called on to help families
patterned after the Black matriarchy in Harlem, the tribal family-
community in the African bush, the Indian mother gripping her baby
close as the Wounded Knee buildings burn, the family memorialized
in Samoan *fales* by the village talking chief, the monogamous family,

now emerging in Moslem countries because it is too expensive to keep four wives and all the children who survive beyond the first year of life. We may not know how to help now, but some will learn; and in one form or another, family therapy is being practised in an increasing number of the developing countries. Wait until we are quiet enough to listen and humble enough to learn from them—how our eyes will be opened by the secrets of family living they will share with us.

This will be doubly important, for we shall find families among us adopting aspects of family organization and relations from diverse cultures across the face of the globe. Some youth here are no longer looking on these families as exotic curiosities, but rather as possible models for and useful distillations of human experience. There are still many who hold to the parochial view that "our own family is best, and all others should be like us." But our young people are not insulated. In this international era they travel everywhere. They are showing more and more curiosity about new family possibilities, for they are lonely and needful like all of us. Our youth are reaching out for the wisdom of other cultures; they are experimenting with what they are learning.

Perhaps we are especially aware of this in California where our young people are turning to the Orient, adopting Eastern religions and music with great enthusiasm, idolizing the leaders and cultural heroes of Japan, Indonesia, India, and journeying to Kathmandu. The tolerance for diversity and capacity for assimilation of an ancient and heterogeneous country like India is now being applied to changing attitudes among us. And the laws and their interpretations are becoming more permissive, which facilitates experimentation.

Family possibilities that did not formerly have social approval are now being tested; some are being tolerated; and some are strongly sanctioned. Because of this, the family is now less easily definable. An hypnotic young "guru" can gather about him a tribe, a harem of young girls, and wander over the deserts of the southwest and into the deserts of our inner cities, as though he were a bedouin from the Middle East—this is not new, but it is now American. Several young families can gather up their children, move together to a homestead and live in a commune—this is not Russian, this is American. An African doctor said to me, "There is no difference between your families and ours, a man here has four wives, except he has them all at once instead of one after another"—there are young people in our university communities and elsewhere who live openly in multiple marriages, without even the sanction of a common law. These youths will be among the youth majority in our population in almost no time. They will speak from experience and not myth. They will reject stereotyped moralizing. And they will help shape our national family policies. And the family practitioner will act in responsive ways.

I expect also that in the future we will take advantage of the opportunities to coordinate the vast amount of clinical information that will be secured from families. Attaining this broad perspective, we will be able to face more critically the outcomes of our work. At the beginning of my own work I felt a necessity to convince other people that therapy with the whole family was even possible, to reduce their fears about relating to the whole family. I knew early that there were some families where the results were more impressive than others, even though the success with all seemed quite outstanding. Accidental selection factors may have enhanced my experiences with the techniques or my own effectiveness.

Does it depreciate the usefulness of family therapy to face now that there are many families with whom our techniques do not work or where success is at best partial? Have we limited ourselves by rather blind devotion to the concept that psychopathology is a derivation of family processes and thus socially determined? Looking critically at the variance in our therapeutic success, moderate accomplishment, or failure, how productive are the explanations other than our inadequacy as therapists to account for the failures in family therapy? I ask these questions because I believe we can, should, and will change our failures into assets by encouraging additional explanations for them.

As a quick illustration, consider how we might test hypotheses to account for partial success with a family. If we assume that the partial success results from having affected the family interactions, then we may hypothesize the total disorder in the family included more than malfunctional interpersonal relations. We may hypothesize further that beyond the intrafamily disorders are those resulting from (1) intraindividual psychoorganic causes, and/or (2) those consequent on extrafamilial social stresses, such as from work situations, schools, community groups, peers with whom children play, and economic deprivations. It would be unexpected by many professionals that family therapy could illumine organic disturbance or shift the perspective on broad social problems. But the future could bring such gains if we are not too quick to explain away therapeutic failure in terms of therapist inefficiencies. More may be at stake in partial or total failure than we have guessed. So family therapists by spreading application of their techniques will increase their professional impact, discover new methods of working and learn more about family processes and their concomitants.

I think, then, as my first point that the future will lead us to look at and attempt to apply family therapy to the units of person and family across many spans, such as those of socio-economic levels, races, geographical locales, employment levels, evidences of deviance of members. In each, because we are interested in and concerned about change, we will work at different points in time, or over varying time spans, to measure the changes taking place.

FAMILY THERAPY IN NEW SETTINGS

Family therapy has taught me well to see the setting within which I am working in order to understand and manage what I do. So I am not necessarily thinking about matters unrelated to my first point when I predict, secondly, that family therapists will carry their work into many new settings and be much affected by them. But in the process we will learn to effect changes in the services where we will work, to improve the welfare of families. In turn, this will change mightily the nature and scope of family work.

Family therapy as we have known it has been grounded solidly in the traditions of personal health services, primarily as a method for treatment in private offices and outpatient clinics. During the two decades when family therapy has been developing, however, there has been a rapid change in the overall program for the delivery of health and mental health services. New settings are being created where family therapy must be tried and learn to be effective if it is to survive. We have observed what has happened to the practice of psychoanalysis, which has also been primarily a method for the private office and other outpatient settings; this projects a possible fate for family therapy. Psychoanalysis is not less but more effective, yet it has been subjected to severe public criticism and has lost its position of preeminence as a prevailing treatment theory and mode of psychotherapeutic practice. Family therapy, in contrast, has been burgeoning but we cannot be sanguine about this, for the field has changed radically. Shall we predict the decline of family therapy in a manner analogous to psychoanalysis? This may contain no threat for those whose practices remain economically secure and built upon established reputations as therapists, but it might cause anxiety for those who are novices and pinning their hopes on careers in family therapy. I say this to confront us with the reality of new and future health and mental health services.

While this may seem a negative prediction for some family therapists, for others it may seem to provide an opportunity for change. I see it in the latter sense. I am excited by the chance to use family therapy as an experimental base for finding the place of the family in a whole range of medical services in our communities. The family may become the most important primary unit around which most medical services will be organized, although it will not be the only one. The action of the American Medical Association in recognizing a broad specialty of family medicine is too new to test that possibility. Family health services would not mean preeminence for the present specialty of family therapy, however. How we will work with the family is far from conception and even farther from realization. Change is so rapid that we will have to work close to or within diverse health services and with their creators and developers to ensure that they make full use of our knowledge. Perhaps even more important will be the dynamic contribution of motivation to work with the family.

This means that we shall be examining each component of the full community health programs to see where family therapy and its derivatives fit. We will have no problems in thinking about the private practitioner's office, the offices of those in group practice, and outpatient clinics. These primary entrance points into the emerging medical services program have been where most of us have worked. Fortunately, even there most have recognized that family therapy is only one of a variety of techniques for helping people who present us with emotional problems and have maintained flexibility through refusing to become family therapists exclusively.

It is when we get over into other community medical treatment centers that we find the need to think astringently about the place of the family. Without a doubt, our first obligation is to examine the hospital. Here we are up against a dilemma. The hospital has become increasingly a locale for expensive short-term acute treatment where testing new machines and other inventions of medical engineers has taken precedence over humanizing the services and the environment. Many, however (and I include myself in this group), have become so alarmed about the impersonality and computerized machine-like aspects of the hospital that they are trying to complement these physical developments with new methods to improve the social climate for the patient in the hospital. These efforts to keep alive and to facilitate family relations with patients have to take into account cross-rationalizations that hospitalization is so brief as to make what it does to the family of minor relevance. This idea is insidious and completely insupportable in regard to the hospitalization of most children, of dubious validity in the hospitalization of psychiatric patients, and probably inappropriate for the hospitalization of most other patients, even under severe surgical and other interventions. Fortunately, some signs such as the new relations allowed to fathers in maternity wards of some hospitals show that change is in the wind. As far as mental patients are concerned, I cannot help contrasting the institutionalized separation of patients and families with a most remarkable hospital at Amritsar in Punjab State in India; here the hospital was built of tents. As a patient was brought by his relatives, a tent was set up and the family moved in. All played a role in the treatment, learning by observing the administration and importance of drugs, holding the patient during shock treatment and the recovery period, taking part in group therapy and community meetings. The hospital was open 24 hours per day; all basic care was provided by the family; if they needed provisions, the family could all go together to the markets in the city—and on the average they returned to their homes in 14 days.

One aspect of hospitalization easy for hospital staffs to ignore concerns the crisis hospitalization creates for the rest of the family

beyond the patient. Even nurses, trained to work against social bar-
renness, may be offenders in this respect. Medical social workers, of
course, have for many decades been concerned with practical and
emotional problems of the families of patients. Clergymen, too, have
given a good deal of support to family members. Within the hospital,
however, the medical staffs have tended to regard care of family
members as optional and, where possible, to accept what members of
other professions have chosen to do for the family. Most family
members want more. They want the chance to open communication
and relationships between medical staff and themselves. They want
more than the artificial process possible during the visiting period or
when a telephone call is dealt with abruptly. They want to keep alive
as far as possible their basic family relations even through the
illness—but the role prescribed in the hospital for a patient is seldom
conducive to customary domestic relations. We in family therapy
know how basic to the family is the communication that takes place
through activity rather than speech. Taking this as our message we
have much to tell hospitals about how to provide a humane and
beneficial patient-family relationship there. We also have much to
learn about this from how family members enhance the warmth of
the hospital in the developing countries and in an increasing number
of hospitals in highly developed European countries. Pressures building up from below, even from the level of our most impoverished
citizens, seem to be changing hospital program priorities somewhat.
But there are other possibilities for active change. Who but those
working in family therapy have more potentially valuable counsel to
offer about patients, their families and the social relationship in
which help may be best offered?

Other components of comprehensive community health programs
require similar examination and modification. I dare say you have
been watching new motel-like facilities being built to provide inexpensive housing for patients en route to intensive hospital care or
back to the community, and to serve for hospitalization which does
not require the close supervision of nursing personnel, as during
diagnostic examinations. The striking thing is that those developing
these centers seem not to have recognized the strength of the motivation among family members toward being included on an active and
up to full-time basis in the patient's living situation. So two-bed

rooms for strangers are being built, perhaps because insurance plans have not yet learned the psychological and medical advantages of family help for patients who are ill. Surely family therapists and the public will not overlook the potential opportunity for a family program here.

One might move easily from considering such facilities to looking at still other units of the medical service program of a community —the chronic hospitals, extended care facilities, halfway and three-quarter-way houses, day hospitals, night hospitals, and home care. Family therapy as we now know it is not necessarily appropriate in each situation. It may be essential in some; it could be adapted in others; and elsewhere it could provide the theoretical system on which we can invent other creative approaches and services.

Medical facilities are prototypes of many correctional and protective agencies. I am thinking of prisons, jails, schools for the retarded, juvenile halls, foster homes, group living homes, domiciles for veterans, homes for the aged, and many specialized institutions for coping with particular personal and social problems. Behind each are aspirations to improve the lot of residents, but often the institutions and their programs create unintentional social and family deprivation. For example, I am greatly concerned with the necessity of rethinking the use of foster homes, of applying our knowledge of family therapy to the relations between foster parents and children and to improving relations between the children and their actual parents or other relatives. Each of the agencies or institutions mentioned is oriented essentially toward solving problems that typically have family implications. If in its future, family therapy provides the model, it could help these agencies to see how the family offers a logical unit for their work, how our techniques can be adapted or how methods can be originated to order their programs toward strengthening the family.

Since many of these institutions are based in law, and official rather than private, it pushes the family toward social action on a large scale. Does family therapy not clarify social policy? Are family therapists not able to contribute fundamental statements about social values in reference to the family? Most family therapists seem to have shown a reluctance to extend themselves into public political arenas even in activities growing directly out of therapeutic practice with families. Knowing that there are risks of violating confidentiality, of publicity and sometimes of notoriety, of distraction from activities where one is securely entrenched, and of economic sacrifice, many may shy away from political action. With the opportunity for family therapy to extend itself in these directions of influence before us, I hope mentioning this option will help some to fulfill my prediction that family therapists will grow in public influence. Those who find the office a prison have only to reach out into problem-solving institutions just beyond their immediate environment.

PREVENTION OF FAMILY PROBLEMS

The future of family therapy seems to suggest movement into still a third area of activity. I refer to the prevention of family problems. Many have given repeated lip service to the notion of prevention; many have the motivation to work for it. But there are few precedents to follow, only limited confidence that we can be effective, and much reluctance to flounder where so much is at stake. The whole field of prevention of family problems may be looked at more positively as the field of promotion of effective and satisfying family interrelations. Will family therapists take initiative in the development of preventive and educational programs? It might not happen. Therapists are used to moving from identified problems to corrective efforts. Prevention and education start from a different base. The initial motivation is towards the promotion of certain values. The primary method is education to propagate these values in human action. Most family therapists would have to take great steps to think in the terms of prevention and education and to orient professional efforts in these directions. Will many achieve this transformation? Perhaps it will come primarily from younger people starting with the advantages of our insights. They may be able to identify the values implicit in our work, to state clearly the practices requisite to their propagation, and to organize these creatively into preventive programs.

Preventive work is linked with professional groups which do not even have much prestige in the hierarchy of professions these days. I am not just thinking of college presidents! Clergymen, home economists, and family life educators do not necessarily call up professional images of high status. The rewards for using these professions as models seem extremely modest, especially if one is thinking in terms of audiences for his ideas or the economic rewards of a profession. But those are perhaps superficial reasons why therapists have not engaged more frequently in preventive efforts.

One major reason may be the feminization of the fields of prevention and family education. They have not seemed to represent the hard-headed thinking and masculine enterprises that medicine, psychology or even, in latter years, social work have represented. My off-hand impression indicates that the proportion of women to men teaching family life education at the high school level exceeds that in most other subjects in the high school curriculum. Premarital, maternity, and well-baby courses and clinics, which have an immense importance in development of the family, are typically addressed to prospective or actual mothers. Lack of involvement of the fathers characterizes these medical clinics just as it did the psychiatric clinics for children in periods before family therapy, before we were thinking courageously and expansively about the significance of the father in the family.

Our cultural demand for rapidity of action, change, solution of problems militates against programs of prevention and education which show their benefits mostly over long terms. These programs require length of commitment that may also be more basically oriented to the feminine ways of looking at life than to the masculine. Ten sessions of family therapy may build our personal confidence more readily than settling for remote possibilities which we may never live to see and which may never in fact occur.

There may be among colleagues, some who have the character, the intelligence, the patience, the vision, and the hardheadedness to bring us successfully into the field of family promotion and the prevention of family problems. I see potentialities for family promotion through systematic efforts to examine some of the basic institutions of our society in reference to their family relations and through efforts to change the systems composed of families in action with these institutions. Here I am using institution not in the sense of a service agency, but in the more generic sense of the broadest kinds of organization in our culture.

Let me give you one example. I think of business and industry. I know that personnel managers, labor leaders, and top executives are reminded constantly that employees come from families and return to families at the end of work periods. Anywhere in industry we can document the disarticulation of family-industry relationships. Personnel managers know many cases where industry hurts the family; they know the reverse, too, where problems in the family provoke problems in the industrial world.

We in family therapy have available to us a whole content area of knowledge to illuminate the family-industry interaction. We could use family therapy as the source of information about what might be done to prevent these problems. At a primary level we may help children and other family members learn about the roles and functions that parents play in the work setting. What young boy today sees his father at work, knows what is expected there, knows the kind of interpersonal relations his father is working within, knows the satisfactions and frustrations of father's work life? How can business or industry provide more effectively for a child's exposure to his father (or his mother) in the work setting, and so prepare the youngster more adequately for his own future in business and industry? How indeed can wives learn what their husbands do at work, or husbands learn about the jobs of working wives? Our progress is slow in devising activities to help out in this area because there are very serious problems to be overcome when one begins to plan a direct introduction of children and young people into a plant. The necessary kind of exposure is seldom made possible on an open house day. It can never be achieved by a house organ that identifies the family of the month. It can never be represented in the check coming home on pay day.

In quite a different way, though, we may facilitate prevention. The distress when families do not follow a superficial ideal of a family, now presented as a problem to be solved, is being alleviated by an increasing tolerance. We may promote family welfare by remembering that we have influence to temper the criticism of such families. If we do not so readily label them as deviant, we will not push them into anxiety, depression, community exclusion, conflicts at all social levels, concomitant physical illness, and obsessive thoughts that they are abnormal. Under new tolerance, families will be freed to test their capacities for creative growth, and to attain new heights of family actualization.

We shall also find that change imposes constraints. The *limits* on change that will be forthcoming will continue to become obvious and will balance spreading diversity. We can only conjecture what some of the forces toward change and some of the limits may be. In California, we are feeling the impact of the cost of land and consequent new types of housing. What will be the later effects of continued upgrading of education; the effects of limitations on childbirth; of the growing domination of behavior by peer judgments and advertising; of the expansion of powerful international industrial organizations and the military; of giving up dealing with the international tensions by war and substituting international law and some surrender of sovereignty; of new medical developments—organ transplants, genetic transformations, superb new technology; of potential elimination of death; of encounters with new intelligences far out in the universe. These and other changes will shape—but also limit—the family. If study of the family in the world is now important, I can only believe it will become even more crucial. To know what to do as professionals we will need to keep up the effort to understand people and families. To get the knowledge will become increasingly complex and urgent.

Our theoretical approaches in studying communication and systematic interaction in the family have equipped family therapists almost more than any other group of professional people for the expansion of efforts beyond the immediate scope of the nuclear family unit. All that is needed, is liberation from the confines of investment in therapy for the family. The time has come for some at least to venture into unknown areas of theory and action, free from thinking that has become traditional, exposed to risks of professional isolation, thrust up against unfamiliar organizations, ideas, and people, using the family as a starting point, stepping out toward diverse families in strange and demanding settings where, ultimately, we will learn new ways to solve family problems and to prevent rather than treat.

Chapter XII

Modes of Relating to
Families in Therapy:
Overview and Prospect

The direct inclusion of the family in psychological treatment has been increasing progressively. Historical reconstruction would probably tie this movement to many social, cultural, and philosophical changes during the same decades. Doubtless these broad influences have provided a shifting matrix from which the mental health professional has drawn his motivation, his techniques, his theories, and his responses to demands for his services. From the combination of changes in the family and in professional practice, a progression in the role of the family in treatment has occurred. A simple representation of these changes would show four stages of development, which continue into the present, and a fifth which is now emerging.

The earliest stage of theory and therapeutic intervention involving the family is identified by *individual psychotherapy*. Here the direct interpersonal relation is between the therapist and patient, but the family is there in theory, in its indirect influence, both historical and current, in the ways the therapist and the patient interpret the therapeutic relationship, and in the principles that determine technique. Figure 1 represents the individual therapy situation and its family involvement by strong lines between therapist and patient, by firm boundaries around the diad they form, and by a tentative indication of the family in the background.

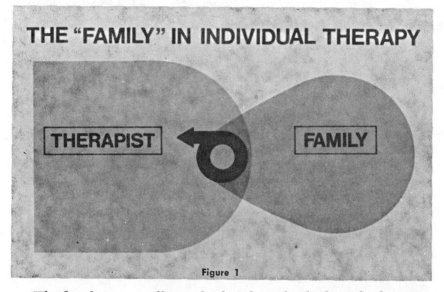

THE "FAMILY" IN INDIVIDUAL THERAPY

THERAPIST   FAMILY

Figure 1

The family is normally involved in the individual psychotherapeutic sessions only in the past and in the future: in the past, as the patient recalls his experiences, attitudes, fantasies, and other associations with family members; in the future, in terms of his purposes and expectations in relation to them. Time perspective is interesting in these sessions. The past may have been an hour ago, years ago, or as long ago as centuries; the future also is indeterminate in its exact time specification. Seldom is the family physically there and thus involved in present time. This makes the part of the family more intellectual than social. However, the increasing flexibility in clinical practice that permits and encourages occasional inclusion of relatives in individual therapy is modifying this description of classical treatment methods.

The second stage of theory and therapeutic intervention reached a zenith during the immediate post-World War II years. Reacting to the increasing demand for psychotherapy, responding to the growing understanding of small group behavior, attempting to devise economical ways to treat psychotic patients, many professionals turned their attention to *group psychotherapy*. This was a logical extension of individual psychotherapy. It continued emphasis on the treatment of individuals, although diluting somewhat the relations of the therapist with the individual while introducing the compensations of group membership. Group psychotherapy increased the roles within which the patient could function by allowing him to shift in and out of ego-supporting identification with the therapist and to become, erstwhile, an adjunctive therapist. It allowed him also to assume, or to function within, a variety of symbolic positions relative to other patients, often as surrogates for family members. But here, as in the earlier stage, the actual family is in the background. The family lacks

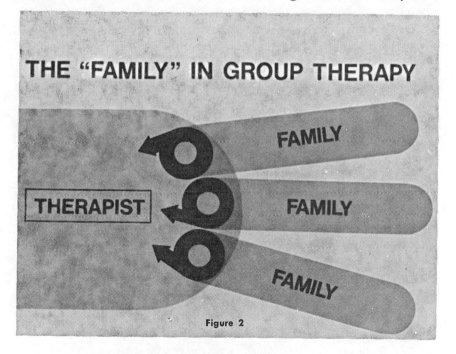

Figure 2

direct association with the therapist and enters the content of the treatment primarily by intellectual intrusion and only with a past or future time orientation. Group therapy resembles individual treatment in these respects, but the therapist was becoming more adaptable, was beginning to entertain new conceptions of his job, and was becoming comfortable in working with groups. These groups had the advantages of the laboratory although they were highly artificial, were constructed for the purpose of therapy, were only instrumental to treatment, and were valued not for permanence but for the possibility of dissolution. Experience with these groups helped therapists to understand and to prepare for working with natural groups, existent prior to the treatment, organized around functions other than therapy, valued for their own sake, and likely to persist into the future, whether or not a professional person intervenes to perform special functions such as psychological treatment.

The third developmental stage represented acceptance of the challenging notion that *group psychotherapy* would work *with natural groups*. As a therapist I accepted this challenge not so much in the abstract as in response to the problems of people in their families. Other therapists were working with various other kinds of natural groups—with industrial and business groups, with gangs, with social and recreational groups, and with leadership groups—all in their

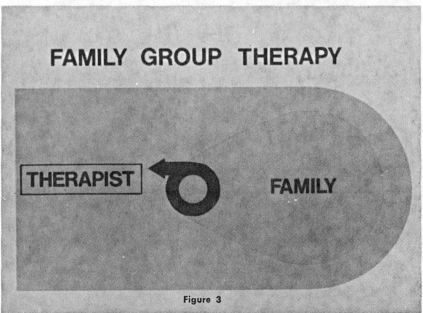

FAMILY GROUP THERAPY

THERAPIST   FAMILY

Figure 3

community settings. Therapeutic work was being illuminated by the
rapidly expanding sciences of social psychology and sociology.

The nature of the therapist's involvement with the family in this
relationship is quite different from that in individual treatment. The
family is physically present. The therapist learns to know the family
members, actually seeing the ways they act and hearing what they
say. He views and can evaluate their impact on each other. His
knowledge of them is from watching the drama take place before him,
not from report and reconstruction. His time orientation is toward
the present moment even though it is necessarily in the context of the
past and the future. As in a play, the action is only a sample of life,
affected by the setting in which it is played and by the therapist who
is the audience. In empathy with members of the family in their
problems and their gratifications, he struggles along with them to
solve the problems they are confronting together. Working with this
natural unit increases the therapist's range of treatment interventions. Experience has shown family group therapy to be productive in
accomplishing changes valued by patients and families.

The fourth developmental stage parallels the earlier one of group
therapy. It is found in the various recent efforts to assemble *groups of
families* and to work with a multi-family unit (fig. 4)—a social group
of great complexity, but a logical outgrowth of treatment of the

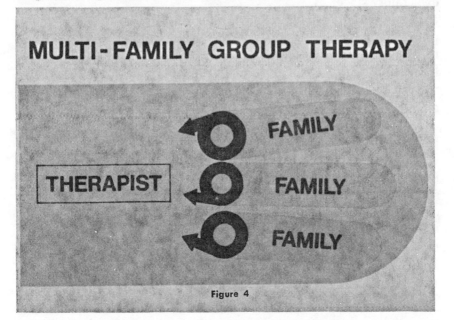

Figure 4

individual family. This method—variously illustrated in the work of
Detre, Kessler, and Jarecki (1963), Leichter (1962), Sculthorpe and
Blumenthal (1965), Laquer (1961, 1964; with associates, 1962,
1964[2]), and Owens—is expanding even further the potential types
of family contacts. Here the therapist, or group leader, brings together two or more families bound by some common problems and by
their willingness to work together toward solving them. Although the
group may gain social and educational benefits, its primary goal is
therapeutic, and thus the leader's attention is directed to using
himself and involving the families in relations that will achieve the
aims of therapy. These are identified with the individual families and
not with the group as a whole, which is temporary.

The parallels between this recent shift from therapy with a single
family to multifamily therapy and the earlier one from individual
psychotherapy to group psychotherapy are self-evident. We would
note similarities in the artificiality of the large groups, their instrumental nature, and parallels in the ways group participants relate to
one another and to the therapist. Multifamily therapy operates on
levels beyond group psychotherapy, however, for the individuals are
linked around the total group as persons *and* as family members
whose families are actually present. The various forms of multifamily
therapy and the appropriate therapeutic techniques are at an early
exploratory stage.

The types of family therapies developed to date have been adopted
primarily in outpatient settings, where each patient (if one is identified) is ambulatory and retains his domicile with the family, coming
from home with his relatives for treatment. The most recent developmental stage, only now emerging, sends therapists in a new
direction in family work with disturbed individuals. After having
experimented with seeing the family in the large artificial group
composed of several families, it was logical to move on to dealing with
the *family in natural relations with the community.* Abstract evaluation
is now being made of the links between the family and other natural
social units in the community. Therapists and social psychologists are
exploring the structured and the spontaneous interactions between
the family and other organized and institutionalized components of
the community, such as schools, factories, business, churches, hos-

pitals, labor unions, as well as courts, police, and other governmental agencies.

This has already shown itself in many operational changes within community institutions. General hospitals, particularly those associated with medical schools, have begun to teach medical practice from a family perspective, building upon the practical knowledge of the profession of social work, upon long-established patterns of family medicine in general practice, as well as earlier explorations in psychotherapy. Churches have always claimed a family orientation but in the past few decades they have segmented their programs to deal with each family member in his own age and interest groups. Now they are embarking on efforts to reconstitute family activities. Family courts have been organized to deal with legal, judicial, and casework approaches to problems. Business and labor have built personnel policies around family units. It was to be expected that the mental hospital would also show a related concern with the family, and this has been so. All these changes toward family involvement are in contrast to the strong continuing orientation to the individual in most of these institutions and to the divisive forces which impinge on the family in our society.

At the present stage of development of our psychiatric hospitals, isolation of many patients still exists; for them the consequence remains institutionalization, in spite of sincere staff objectives to accomplish rehabilitation. No one is now content to shut patients behind walls and doors and allow them to vegetate, but despite the good intentions, the experiments, and the new techniques, accomplishments in promoting family solidarity in regard to mental hospital patients are not impressive. Many of the patients were alienated from their families long before hospitalization, and for these the solving of their social problems has a singular urgency. For most of these patients there can be no expectation of involving their families in treatment nor of restoring them to their families in rehabilitation. For these patients, resocialization must be achieved by inventing approaches to using or forming social groups in the community apart from the family.

Many other patients whose relatives are near at hand are gradually absorbed into the hospital community, and the ties with home are weakened. Family solidarity is a central social value in our culture, but our mental hospitals have been organized and operated on the assumption that removal from the family and individual treatment are the best ways to improve the ultimate functioning of patients in their families. Hospitalization seems to have inadvertently promoted the isolation of patients from their relatives, which in itself may be antitherapeutic. As is represented in figure 5, the doors of the hospital close behind the patient and against the family, to open again when the treatment is done in the hope that the family will rush in to claim its own. Every social worker can testify, however, that in too many cases, unless the patient is released within a few weeks after admission, the family must be urged to take him back. Its circle has closed and must be breached if the patient is to be reassimilated. This is true especially with certain classes of patients, such as the aged, but it is by no means determined by any single variable such as age, sex, and distance from home.

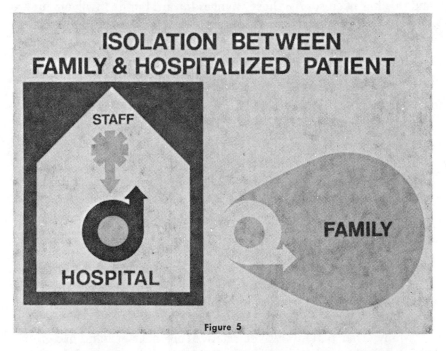

Figure 5

It is not necessary to restrict our attention to the mental hospital to observe family-hospital problems. It is equally true that we find many of the problems in relation to general hospitals. Thus we can speak generically about hospitals in analyzing the family-hospital interrelations, and we need to plan for development of these relations in general as well as mental hospitals.

The hospital takes its place as perhaps the most important component in total medical services. This is so, even though in many communities the hospital stands beside the offices of private medical practitioners as the place of entrance into medical help. While alternatives to the hospital, such as clinics, group practices, health maintenance organizations and extended care facilities, are being demonstrated and promoted, the hospital retains its primacy among medical settings, and in some communities has even taken on components of service that formerly were separately provided in the community. For example, in many communities the emergency rooms of hospitals, typically in the front line for provision of emergency services, function also as the intake point into medical services for patients with non-emergency illnesses.

The hospital is important for the intensity of its impact on the public whom it serves. The patients are hospitalized day and night; services are available around the clock; staff are concentrated and on hand at all times to offer whatever level of patient care is needed; they are backed up by extensive organization-maintaining operations and indirect services. In order to give its services, the hospital operates as a highly organized institution. This very organization, in its complexity and necessary rigidity, structures the relations and behavior of all individuals who come in contact with it. It is much more powerful in its impact on the total life of patients, and often of families, than most part-time services.

The hospital is important, too, as an institution on which to concentrate attention because it is a center for training, and thus perpetuates past ideas and practices, and shapes the future. Most typically the training does not include learning about relating to families. This is changing somewhat for physicians in training for the specialty of family medicine. Occasionally other professions have direct pre-professional or professional training about families. It must be noted, however, that the extent of such training is minimal throughout all the medical professions. Many from these professions find themselves motivated to work with families but are left unprepared for the complex demands this might place on them.

It must be remembered that families are present in our hospitals.

Staff relate in various ways with the families. In planning projects that involve the family in the hospital we must take into account the present activities of treatment staffs with families.

For some staff the families have primarily a nuisance value. "They are in the way." "They compete with staff for the time, attention, and emotion of the patient." "They add to the work load." "They ask stupid questions and make inappropriate and, at times, impertinent suggestions."

For other staff, families fade into the environment. The patients and their problems take such precedence that families do not often come into the center of gaze and regard. For these staff a priority on work for the patient moves toward exclusive preoccupation with that work.

Other staff show much variation in their implication with families. They relate to some and not to others. Among those to whom they relate, the patterns of relationship are not consistent but vary from family to family, time to time, patient to patient, according to the status of the hospital at the time, or in terms of factors totally outside the hospital that affect the staff member, patient, or relative.

Finally, some staff seem to have almost a preference for involving themselves emotionally and in action with the well family members rather than with the sick patients.

At the same time much has been written in the popular press and journals about the inadequacies of the hospitals as seen by patients and family members. Personal histories recounting the risks, horrors and depersonalization of the hospital touch a responsive chord among enough readers to sell newspapers and magazines. On the other hand, it would be as easy, although not so financially profitable perhaps, to develop stories about hospital personnel who show dedication to patients, and sensitivity, alliance, and concern with family members.

Frequently families are overawed by the organization, technology, and professional authority they meet in the hospital. They are intimidated by rules, regulations, laws, and procedures accreted over many decades and enacted daily without thought of their impact on families. Families hesitate to question these arrangements, and, if they did, might meet a parade of arguments and scientific citations to support their necessity and validity. Relatives are left to suspect that the issue is not the quality of evidence in support of many of the rules, but the respective importance of their enforcement as against the continuation and strengthening of family relations. At the same time families have to acknowledge, as staff do, that the hospital, by its defined purposes, is centrally oriented to the diagnosis and treatment of the ill.

Families are among those who foster a climate of discontent with hospitals; they join with others to engender growing public pressure for change. We read and hear statements by public-officials who are critical of deficiencies in the patterns for delivery of services. We find growing political efforts by dissatisfied groups who feel inadequately served, do not receive care, or are displeased with how they are dealt with as persons. They include many who feel discriminated against by reason of their minority status, those placed at distances geographically from medical services, and those in direct contact with medical persons who are reminded by the way they are treated that they are medically underpriviledged, as, for instance, many who are on Medicare. Their discontent makes its impact on all governmental levels and in the courts.

Health professionals, too, are concerned about the hospital situation, to assure the services inherent in professional training, accreditation, licensing, and quality surveillance, and to protect their own professional roles and functions.

Improvement in hospital practices as measured by family-patient interaction will not be achieved overnight, because family-hospital isolation is a complex social problem whose solution will demand careful exploration, systematic experimentation, creation of new techniques, convincing demonstrations, and wide-spread, consistent application of proven techniques. To affirm its necessity forces hospital personnel to examine whether there are not many cases where they could devise and apply techniques to preserve and possibly improve family solidarity even though a patient must remain hospitalized for a considerable period of time. In fact, that contingency may raise the problem to its most critical degree and offer the greatest challenge to invention.

The problem is worth tackling for its humane aspects alone, but beyond these it presents a sociological problem of great theoretical importance. This disarticulation between the family and hospitals has the advantage for research purposes of being of sufficiently limited duration that investigation of the total process from beginning to end is within a scope reasonable for research projects. The hospital, a large, highly structured, frequently monolithic institution can be observed in juxtaposition to the small, idiosyncratic, highly differentiable units that represent the institution of the family.

Interinstitutional disarticulation may be defined as a relationship that has changed one or both of the interacting institutions instead of achieving functional interaction in which the relating parts have been able to maintain their structure. The failure of the family-hospital articulation has been shown in the "institutionalization" of the patient, a secondary illness which has been recognized as having been promoted unwittingly by mental hospitals. Little attention has been paid to a corollary of this process, the inadvertent but profound intrusion of the hospital into the family. In extreme cases this has amounted to the dissolution of family groups, in somewhat lesser cases a regrouping of the family without the patient has resulted, and in the least disruptive form it has had the consequence of temporary family dislocation.

Because of the present minimal understanding of the factors that create disarticulation, effectiveness in improving relationships is limited. An obvious factor is the hospital's preoccupation with its intramural life. Administration tends to be impersonal, with its necessary but depersonalized talk of occupancy rates, purchasing, budgets, personnel policies and systems, square feet per bed, patient-staff ratios, fire and safety codes. Another factor in disarticulation is the individual-patient orientation of the professional staff, represented in the theories and practices of diagnosis and treatment.

Signs of the hospital's orientation to the individual, with its concomitant exclusion of the family, can be observed directly and indirectly. Take, for example, the standards for hospital programs and construction developed by various professional and governmental organizations. Scrutiny of them for the extent to which they give direct or even tacit recognition to the place of the family in relation to patients reveals almost no references to the importance of keeping alive the family relationships for the patient, the family, or the hospital. Even in the instance of standards for pediatric hospitals, where one might have anticipated an impact from the publications of the World Health Organization (Ainsworth, 1962; Bowlby, 1952), Robertson (1958, 1963), and others (Bergman, 1965; Fagin, 1966; Nuffield Foundation, 1963; Prugh, *et al.*, 1953; Spence, 1946), there is virtually no acknowledgment of the need to promote mother-child and family relations. There is a telling contrast between the importance given to sanitation and that given to the family.

Consider the infrequency with which hospital programs for families are discussed in professional and technical literature. The role of the family in home care, admission, and diagnosis is well recognized. The responsibility of the hospital in assisting the family in rehabilitation of the patient is amply represented. It is particularly in relation to the period between admission and release that there are gaps in program descriptions. There are articles describing occasional efforts to stimulate family participation in the hospital. There are professional articles discussing the role of the social worker in assisting the family outside the hospital to handle their problems and to prepare for the return of the patient, but in medical, psychological, nursing, occupational therapy, and other professional journals there is a notable paucity of concern with hospital-family relations. Discussions of patient-professional relations may contain references to the family context from which the patient has come and to the necessary therapeutic efforts to assist the patient in dealing with his family; only brief and occasional statements appear concerning the relevance of direct relations between the professional person and nonpatient family members, especially if these relations were conceived as going on intensively during the course of a patient's hospitalization.

A look at the arrangements for financing hospitalization shows that insurance programs, whether private or public, are essentially organized around payment for individual treatment and care. While fiscal agents might argue that it would be uneconomic to consider support for family members, the absence of discussion of such an issue in regard to hospital financing confirms the impression that medical programing is "individual-oriented." It is true that hospitals take some account of the presence of the family, for example, in providing canteens, either on a concession basis or directly, or in providing transportation, especially when the hospital is in an isolated location. But these are modest efforts compared to the wide range of services for families that would be required if an intensive program were launched to support family-patient relationships. Notably lacking are adequate provisions of space for the family throughout hospitals, and campaigns for raising funds seldom mention provisions for family participation. Hospital rules, government regulations, and professional training curricula offer additional confirmation of the nonfamily orientation of the hospital.

Although the hospital must carry a load of responsibility in the breakdown of its relations with the family, the causes extend far beyond. They will be found in the patients, in the families, in the communities from which they come, and in the cultures of which they are a part. The problem is complex, but there are enough hypotheses about it that detailed investigations can be undertaken even now to test the explanatory assumptions. Fortunately many of these hypotheses may be evaluated by observing actual efforts to modify the hospital-family disarticulation.

What needs to be accomplished is represented in figure 6. The patient is in the hospital involved in transactions with staff necessary to his treatment. He retains going relations with the total family. The hospital has opened its doors to receive the family, with whom the staff are also in active liaison. This interworking contrasts with the isolation that now troubles us when the walls of the hospital close

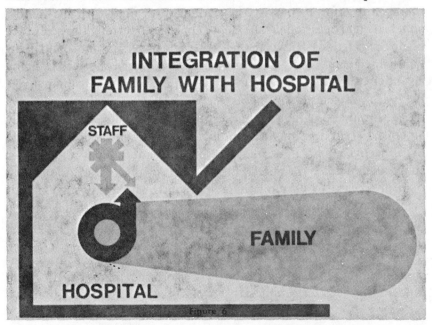

INTEGRATION OF FAMILY WITH HOSPITAL

STAFF

FAMILY

HOSPITAL

Figure 6

around the patient and others of the family are on the outside, removed from communication with patient and staff.

The technical problem of moving from disarticulation to functional interconnection between the family and the hospital is to determine the interventions required, who may best conduct them, and how they should be achieved. It appears that the answers will require enlisting a phalanx of professional and lay persons, possibly under the leadership of a person from one of the mental health professions trained in psycho-social therapies. I lean toward the point of view that a number of professionals from within and outside the hospital working together will be needed to keep the family tied closely to the patient and to bring its members into the desired constructive but temporary liaison with the hospital. Herein is the area of this newly-emerging stage of family-patient involvement in psychological treatment.

Procedures for the active incorporation of the family into mental hospital programs have been in development. In the past they have been initiated especially around entrance to and exit from the hospital, in relation to diagnosis, family orientation and education, preparation for discharge, and followup services during rehabilitation. Only a few efforts have been made in this country to engage the family consistently in the day-by-day treatment of the patient. Midelfort (1957) has described rather sentimentally such an experience. Bowen and his colleagues (Bowen, 1957, 1959, 1960, 1961; Brodey, 1957; Dysinger, 1959, 1961) brought a few families into hospital residence for research purposes. Grunebaum (1963), Weiss and others (1964) have hospitalized new-born babies with mothers suffering from puerperal psychoses; some other clinical centers, for example, the inpatient unit in the mental health program of San Mateo County, California, have tried the same procedure. Most general hospitals have arranged only part-time inclusion of the family, although a growing number of hospitals have welcomed the full-time participation of families in relation to some physical illnesses, such as leukemia, Hansen's disease, and certain forms of treatment of children.

We do not know at this time the most beneficial ways to keep the family, patient, and hospital functioning together. The general goal for the end of hospitalization is clear: to restore the discrete operations of the family and of the hospital with no more bonds between

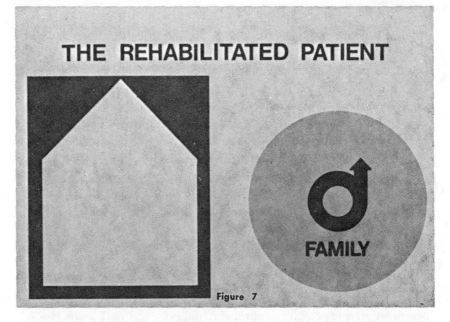

THE REHABILITATED PATIENT

FAMILY

Figure 7

them than characterize those between the average family and the hospital (fig. 7). That is, we are acknowledging that in the community there are always family-hospital connections, but of a remote and impersonal nature for the most part. The patient leaves these more abstract associations and becomes intimately and personally involved with the hospital during hospitalization, and so also may his family. Following treatment the expected and ideal relationship would require resumption of the impersonal and remote associations with the hospital.

Chapter XIII

Family Participation
in Hospital Care for
Children

During a National Institute of Mental Health study, previously mentioned, to examine the part played by the patient's family in care at about 150 medical facilities in what are known as "developing countries" in Africa and Asia, we found all levels of medical care and treatment for children. At one extreme a hut in the bush served as a makeshift hospital where there were not enough beds to give one to each child. The well-meaning but virtually untrained staff members supported their efforts to minister to the sick by raising baby gorillas to sell to zoos. At the other extreme, within a few minutes' travel time, teaching hospitals were so new that they fitted completely into a modern university. There highly sophisticated physicians of professional rank were applying the latest pediatric knowledge and techniques. But no matter what the level of medical care, we found nearly everywhere that the child had the security of the immediate love and care of his mother or other relatives for 24 hours every day.

Hospitals in Africa, South America, the islands of the Pacific, and many Asian countries are well acquainted with this practice. But Western scientists have paid it little heed. Our visits were made to learn whether the experiences in these countries might have any lessons for the West.

In each hospital we asked the question, "Where is the family in this hospital?"

We found members of the patients' families in almost all hospitals. Sometimes we found it helpful to rephrase our basic question to ask, "Where is the patient without his family?" The answer told us where we would find the points of real separation anxiety. For example, it was exceptional to find any relatives with the patients who were mentally ill, retarded, or who had Hansen's disease (leprosy). However, we did find children living with their mothers in a leprosy settlement in Biafra under the watchful eyes of an Irish missionary nurse and consultant physicians. Thus, if the patient was a mother with a nursing baby or an older child who could not be cared for otherwise, we would find the child with her.

To understand why relatives come or do not come to the hospital, it is necessary to look at the child, his family, the community from which the child comes, the hospital and its staff, and the complex interrelations among them. We are here restricting our observations mostly to situations in which the patients were children.

The Family

Let us look first at the family in the developing countries. In general, in such countries, families extend kinship relations further and more actively than do American families. With many relatives, there is no problem of having enough family members to spell one another at the hospital and to look after those left at home.

The few statistics available show that women more generally than men escort patients to the hospital but men more than women seek treatment in hospitals. In cities, however, women are increasing their use of hospitals, even for childbirth. A general hospital in Kinshasa in Zaire keeps up a steady rate of 3,000 deliveries a month. At noon the husbands stream in to bring the midday meal.

Many factors induce relatives to come to the hospital with patients. One is the pressure to carry on prescribed family functions —such as cooking, which is woman's work. Another is the custom of breast-feeding babies, so characteristic in these countries that an infant usually remains with his mother even when she is the patient. Many mothers bring their babies with them when they come to the hospital to look after their husbands or older children.

Pakistan is one of the Moslem countries in which many relatives must accompany a man to show his status in the community. A physician at one Pakistani hospital described such a troupe of relatives as "the bridal procession of the patient." In many African countries, a relative who is not at the bedside when a patient dies will be blamed for sorcery. This practice encourages members of the family to be present at the deathbed or to make strong efforts to bring a patient home to die. Some hospitals prefer that families take a dying patient home, because a death on the wards might be blamed on the staff and could lead to a mass exodus of patients.

Relatives often come along with patients to protect family secrets—an especially potent reason in Liberia, where secret society membership is a primary social obligation. Community pressures are strong to assume responsibility for the young, to revere the aged, and visit the sick.

On the other hand, sometimes the cost of keeping the patient at home is so great that the family abandons him. For example, in some areas families commonly reject children with burns or who have otherwise been handicapped or disfigured, fearing that they will be unable to get a job or to marry when they grow up. The family may also cast off a relative they regard as incurable, such as a leper.

Occasionally a nursing mother remains at home when one of the members of her family is hospitalized.

Distance seems of minor importance. Africans and Asians walk many hundreds of miles to be treated at a certain hospital or by a particular doctor; almost invariably a relative goes along. In India we found patients who had traveled 2,000 miles to reach a particular clinic. However, when a family lives close to the hospital, the relatives may spend less time at the hospital than when they have come from a distance. Much depends on the availability and the expense of transportation.

Hospital Policies

We found that the nature of the hospital is perhaps the most important factor in determining the presence or absence of the family. In many hospitals, including children's hospitals, the staff members welcomed the families of their patients. However, teaching hospitals built with foreign aid—attempting to qualify for international credentials, striving to be centers of research, and staffed extensively by Western expatriates—had limited family participation. In such hospitals we were often taken to see a magnificent laundry, a simulated ward for instruction, or some piece of laboratory apparatus.

What the teachings of such centers augur for the future of family relations in the hospitals in these countries remains to be seen. In India some teaching hospitals are being set up or remodeled in the style of the rural hospitals in which most of the medical school graduates will work.

Hospital policies and staff attitudes strongly determine how much the family participates in caring for the patient. Each hospital we visited had a family policy—either explicit or implicit. Sometimes this was dictated by the government. For instance, in Zambia, the government policy included payment not only for the child's hospitalization but also for his mother if her presence is judged essential to the patient's recovery. In another African country, using hospital resources to help family members stay in the hospital was prohibited, but hospital authorities often looked the other way.

Local hospital policy tends to be more powerful than national policy in any case. Often we discovered a hospital's policy by asking: "Where do members of a patient's family go in the hospital when they cannot be with him?" The attitude of the medical officer in charge usually explained the answers. For example, to keep mothers out of the wards, the physician-director of a hospital in Kenya set up a verandah for their use. The mothers found it cold, and—in spite of an occasional midnight raid by the staff—usually sneaked inside to comfort their children and to keep themselves warm.

The director of a hospital in Tanzania told us that the family policy "cannot be left to hit or miss. If it is thought through, the families create no difficulties." In Nigeria a hospital director told us, "It is important to have the role of the family in the hospital defined. The doctor must tell the family how far it can go . . . he determines whether or not staff trust family members and give them recognition."

One doctor planned to make his hospital rounds during the afternoon when he knew members of the families would be visiting. On the other hand, a few doctors ordered the families out.

In some hospitals, because a policy had not been set by the doctor in charge, we found open warfare between the families and the nurses. However, in many places we were convinced that the nurses had more influence than doctors in determining the policy toward the family. Indigenous nurses tended to give in to families; most nurses from the West had early in their tenure come to some resolution of the differences between their training and the local family and hospital customs. Some nurses saw the patient as their only responsibility; some saw the whole family as the hospital's clients. Some nurses seized the opportunity to teach good health habits to the patient's relatives and to treat them at the hospital.

Much seemed to depend on the nurse's differentiation between the roles she assumed and those she allotted the patient's relatives. The nurses reserved treatment functions for themselves and the doctors, but how they defined treatment varied from hospital to hospital, and depended upon their willingness and time to train mothers. We learned how nurses regarded the family when nurses told us what they alone should do, and what mothers were expected to do. In one hospital mothers would be given the tasks of giving the child his medicine at the specified time and taking and recording his temperature, while in another hospital even bathing the patient would be regarded as a part of the nurse's job.

Relatives' Roles

Relatives took on many tasks, however. In some places they only served as informants about the child at the time of admission. In others they provided full physical care: prepared food; fed, bathed, dressed, exercised, and toileted the patient; did laundry; cleaned the room; dressed the patient's hair; and watched over him. The relatives were effective communication links, keeping the nurse and doctor informed about the patient and other important matters, orienting the patient to the hospital, telling him about his illness and his treatment, sending news back home to the village, and bringing messages to the patient. In some hospitals, the staff even used the patient's relatives to instruct patients about their condition.

Problems arose only where mothers and nurses were allowed to compete, and where nobody took the time to define the separation of functions. Mothers could be as competitive as the nurses: some who did not like what the nurses were doing had no compunction about doing the work over. Occasionally a mother picked up her child and moved him to another hospital or took him to a native practitioner. Sometimes she persuaded all the rest of the mothers to leave the hospital in protest—a maneuver that greatly increased the sensitivity of staff to the personal feelings of the families!

Many hospitals did a great deal of improvising to make the families feel at ease. They kept newborn babies next to their mothers. In the wards for older children, a hospital in Kinshasa had built cubicles of glass, with bed, crib, wash basin, and storage space that separated each mother and child from the others on the ward. The point was to prevent cross-infection while keeping them from feeling isolated. At the College of Medicine, in Taipei, Taiwan, the beds were especially made so that mother and child—who normally sleep together at home—could be accommodated in the small rooms.

In some places porches, sheds, hostels, and villages were used to house the relatives of hospital patients. Even so, many relatives often made nests under the patient's hospital beds, sleeping on the floor as they did at home. We saw the "ultimate" in family participation: four relatives were sleeping on the bed, and the patient—who was frightened of the bed because he had never slept in one—was on the floor under it.

Many hospitals allowed their patients' relatives to build a kitchen where they could go to cook what they liked, to think things out, to gossip and laugh, or be together in crowds instead of being shut up in separate rooms. Other hospitals provided the patients' relatives with facilities for storing possessions, visiting, tending to sanitary needs, learning about health care, and playing.

Such efforts to give the members of the patient's family a feeling that the hospital is a natural part of the community helped overcome suspicion, anxiety, and timidity. As one German doctor said, the hospital then is "not cutting so much the roots." In contrast, handsome modern hospitals modeled on those in industrial countries often frightened the families away.

Premature Babies

Freedom for experimentation also promoted family participation. The program for premature babies at Baragwanath Hospital outside Johannesburg, South Africa, is an outstanding example. The hospital could not afford incubators, so Erich J. Kahn, M.D., later head of pediatrics at Harlem Medical Center in New York City, turned the whole ward for prematures into an artificially heated and humidified incubator. He daringly set up facilities for mothers in an adjoining ward and required them to live in and help care for their infants.

We arrived at Baragwanath just before lunch to visit one of two identical units that took care of 80 premature babies. Lunch was served to mothers on a porch where some of them slept. All the mothers were dressed in hospital clothes and wore white caps over their hair, even a woman with an immense woven coiffure. The head nurse rang a bell; the mothers scrubbed as if they were going into surgery. They put on masks and lined up at the door to the babies' room for a squirt of antiseptic on their hands. Then, happily, they filed into the room; each took up her station on a chair beside her baby, expressed her milk into a bowl and took it to the nurse who recorded the amount to be sure the mother was not trying to "dry herself up."

Each of these mothers had begun to take care of her baby from birth; she fed him by whatever method possible, and by the time he weighed 4½ pounds, he was put to the breast, even if he needed supplemental feeding. Through this experiment the death rate of the premature babies had been reduced from 70 percent to about 20 percent—a level equal to the rates in New York City and London.

Curiously, Dr. Kahn's efforts to duplicate his program in Harlem, where there is an unduly high premature birth rate, met a wall of resistance. Some opponents said they feared the babies would get second-rate care because no comparable model existed then in the best hospitals in this country.

Benefits

Although there are drawbacks in letting relatives have free access to patients in the hospital—as they have in developing countries—there are also many benefits: overworked staff members are able to use their time for professional functions; money can be spent for drugs and treatment instead of basic domestic provisions; and the quality of care is raised. For children who are protected by the rituals of family relations, regular continuing contacts with parents and relatives offer more psychological support than any contrived expressions of affection and concern or, any gift.

Where families are allowed freely in the hospitals, patients are more comfortable. They are insulated by their relatives when they need to be sheltered; when they are lonely their relatives help them have contact with other patients, with other members of their families, with the hospital staff, and the community at large. Psychologically they feel secure. We noticed how relaxed the children were: they seldom cried, banged their heads, or rattled the bars of their cribs. In fact, mostly they were on big beds that gave them comfort and scope. They could remain as active as was good for them under the watchful supervision of their mothers or other relatives. The noisiest children's wards were those in which mothers were not allowed.

Members of the patients' families grow in their understanding of illness and health. They learn how to monitor the patient's condition if they do not already know how. Being in the hospital around the clock, they are less likely to panic needlessly as changes occur in their patients. By the same token, the staff is more likely to take the patient's relatives seriously when they come to them in alarm. The hospital becomes a living school that trains agents to work for medical advancement, sanitation, and public health at home and in the community. If hospital staffs are not always enthusiastic about having families present, at least they usually acquiesce.

In our own country, when we increase our efforts to overcome the isolation of patients from their families, we shall be changing policies on a nationwide scale. We shall be forcing serious examination of existing policies about the place of the family in our national hospital and health programs. We shall be demanding changes in the laws and regulations that block humanization of patient care.

We shall be striking at the very foundations of professional careers and institutions in asking health insurance plans, group health schemes, union contracts, and Federal funding to support family participation in hospitals and care for the sick. We shall be calling for revisions in the standards for hospital safety, construction, and professional practice. We shall be asking hospital administrators to change their methods of accounting and record-keeping, their rules, and regulations. We shall be demanding that business and industries that profit from the technology of our hospitals develop the heart to invest in families.

Participation of the family in hospital care is not an exotic curiosity, but a natural expression of family conviction strongly adhered to in three-fourths of the world. The practice is followed because it is a humane response to the rights of children. We believe that access to the best in health care is a right for all the children in our country. In our minds, it follows that family access to children in hospitals is equally a right. Thus, we hope that professional persons trained to work with children in hospitals will join us in translating such rights into realities.

Chapter XIV

I Went to the Dentist's Surgery with My Wife

Here follows a simple story, describing a minor experiment—an attempt at a modest start in evaluating the place of the family in out-patient care. It is included because it shows one method of observation for criticizing procedures in the private medical office. I must admit, however, that the implications I drew are only suggestions, untested, as far as I know, in other than the one instance which I shall recount.

Since my wife and I expect and desire to share the pleasant and the painful in each other's lives, it seemed logical though not romantic that I go with my wife to the dentist. She had been referred for some oral surgery to a dentist whom she had not met before, and this was her first visit. My private intention went further than to sit outside in the waiting room while she had the surgery in an inner office. It is about what happened as I carried out this plan that I am writing. I need to say that it was not my original plan to write about what happened, but after it was over it struck me that some dentists and members of other professions, after having, perhaps, skepticism about the idea, might find here some new perspective on their work and relationships.

When an attendant leaned out a sliding glass window and invited my wife to come into the dentist's reception area, my wife was not unprepared theoretically for my accompanying her. She did turn to me and say, however, "You're not coming too!" but I affirmed that I was.

If the receptionist was slightly startled she managed to conceal it. In a cordial and somewhat matter of fact way she began to get my wife's name, address, physical status, reactions to anesthetics and drugs, and some other details. An advantage of my presence showed as my wife stumbled over the name of a prescription drug she takes daily. She had a try at naming it, then turned to me, feeling that the name was not quite right. I said, "That's not it," and together we pieced out the correct name.

The forms being completed, the receptionist showed my wife into one of the tiny rooms off a major corridor, and I followed. We were alone for a considerable time. I sat on a low stool beside the dental chair. After a while an assistant came in, put a bib on my wife, arranged some surgical instruments on a tray, thoughtfully behind my wife's head, and left.

As we chatted my wife, smiling, made two remarks that I registered: "Don't hold my hand." "Keep your hand off the arm of the chair." It ran through my mind that she was trying to separate from me for a relation with the dentist. Later she confirmed that such thoughts were in her mind. The dentist had to do his job, and it was something that I could never do for her. In recalling this time, she said: "I was afraid Dr. _____ would get mad at your being there and take it out on me. I was very definite, in my mind, that this was the time for me to relate to the doctor. I felt I had to be firm in my resolve, and concentrate on helping the doctor to get on with the job. In a way your touching my hand and leaning on the arm of his chair was pulling me back from my determination. The important thing was that you shouldn't interfere with the work of the doctor or upset him; in fact, that you be seen and not heard! Actually the remarks that the doctor made to the nurse seemed much more pertinent than his addressing himself to you.

"And yet, at another, deeper level, I felt your presence gave me confidence—and I much preferred your being there."

The dentist came in, gowned for surgery. He introduced himself to my wife, asked her what was to be done, and she explained. He said he would have to phone the referring dentist and started toward the corridor. My wife said she had a green slip in her coat. I knew where it was hung, and could recognize it easily. I went out to the closet in the reception area to get the slip, gave it to the nurse, and returned to the low stool. Soon the doctor came back, addressed himself to me, and asked me to leave. I knew in myself that this was a decisive moment. I braced myself, and said "I came to be with my wife," and continued, "I believe it is psychologically important to be with her." The doctor replied, "You can't stay in the surgery," and then he went out. I had the impression that he was confused, did not quite know what to make of the situation, and had not had time to become angry.

Anger followed. Back he came and spurted out, "You can't sit there!" Sensing that I would not be thrown out, I replied, "I don't want to be in the way." He continued, "You will be, there. You can stand over here—if you insist, uh, on staying." He pointed to a spot in a corner near the window. I soon learned that I had been placed strategically behind his back where I could observe little of the brief proceedings in the administration of the anesthetic.

There was a respite after this. The doctor and nurse left the room, my wife settled back in the chair to test the changes in her mouth; the only sensations she had were in the pounding of her heart and the shaking of her knees. These feelings I interpreted as signs of anxiety about the forthcoming surgery, but I realized later that this was only one reason. Perhaps more important was the tension that had been created in the dual relations she had been trying to handle—one with the doctor, one with me. She mentioned afterward her fear that there would be a big blowup, and that she would be in the middle. Such a possibility had crossed my mind but apparently I had not seen a showdown as so threatening as it seemed to my wife.

Talking about her tensions seemed to relieve her. Shortly afterward a nurse popped her head in the door and jauntily said, "Everything OK?", and before either of us had a moment to answer she continued, "Good," and dashed up the hall. "Reassurance!" said my wife, whose composure had been regained enough for her to show her amusement.

Soon the surgeon returned. I removed myself into my corner while he scrubbed and proceeded with the cutting and stitching. I could see very little, but caught my wife's eye occasionally. She seemed to be accepting the operation with equanimity, and it was soon over. The surgeon gave some brief instructions about after-care, and said the nurse would give us more on the way out. We could not tell whether it was a customary procedure for him to lead a patient out to the nurse's station and to remain there, taking part, while the nurse gave instructions. My wife clung to my arm as we stood, and I kept wondering why the nurse and doctor had not suggested a seat for her. Assuming that the time would be brief, I did not suggest it myself—but as the time became longer I regretted not having taken the initiative.

An interesting change in our relations took place. In the surgery the doctor spoke exclusively to my wife, except for the brief exchanges above. At the nurse's station he addressed all his remarks to me, and kept his eyes focused on me. I felt that he had eliminated my wife. The instructions for ice packs, aspirin, and other care were given to me, I was told when she was to return for the removal of the stitches, and in the goodbyes he shook hands with me and nodded somewhat perfunctorily to my wife. The relation may have been based on the equality of our heights, since we both were tall, while my wife is only slightly over five feet. But this seemed too simple an explanation. I can only speculate on what he might have been thinking—was he showing his relief that the episode was over, was he perplexed to understand why I was really there, was he responding to my solicitation for my wife, whose needs I was trying to concentrate on? Apparently following the doctor's lead, the receptionist gave to me the written instructions for my wife, and an appointment slip. I was embarrassed for my wife that they so ignored her.

Soon we were on our way through the waiting room. A thought that I might have been waiting there flitted through my head, but I did not have the time then to pursue it. I was busy opening doors and supporting my wife, who showed that she was tired.

Later, in my mind, I came back to the waiting room. If I had stayed there, renewing my acquaintance with an old issue of *Life*, or trying to find an article that I had missed when I first saw the edition of *Time*, what would have been different? For one thing, I would have been more worried, more curious, and more remote from my wife. I imagined what would have happened when she would have rejoined me after the surgery. I think first I would have questioned her, depending of course on how she seemed. I would have been asking, "Was he rough on you? Did you have a lot of pain? Was there much bleeding? When do you get the stitches out?" To quite an extent the answers would be less important than their deeper significance in overcoming the temporary break, and in restoring the relation. By contrast I realized that in what actually took place it was irrelevant to think of such questions. I knew the answers, and to have sought them again would only have distracted me from trying to help my wife. It was more important for both of us that I was able to concentrate on supporting her, on getting her home and cared for as quickly as possible.

It was only a few minutes until she was resting in bed. I needed no instruction from her to go to the refrigerator for two ice cubes and to put them in a plastic bag the way the dentist had said. I had heard it. I put the aspirin and the cup of water at the bedside. I could plan right away, with no more than nods of agreement or disagreement, for the next two or three meals that would feature the prescribed soft diet. On my own I could schedule time to provide transportation for the next visit.

The return visit was without strain. The climate had changed. When I went into the surgery with my wife, the doctor and nurse greeted us both cordially. The stitches having been removed, the doctor shook hands with us both and we were on our way.

This experience seemed to contain the basis for a number of questions this dentist and others might ask about their ways of relating to patients and their families. Many of them could be answered by simple changes in routines in the dentist's office. Such changes might ease greatly the various transitions for the patient, between leaving home for dental work and returning to it.

First, the dentist might ask how many patients are accompanied by relatives when they come to the office. A receptionist could easily keep a record.

Second, concentrating on this group, he might ask how much better the available admission data might be if the relatives took part in the interview. Since patients tend to be apprehensive before dentistry, and to focus their anticipation on the ordeal ahead, an admission interview may provide a useful and tension-relieving ritual of passage. Of course it may also be seen as a nuisance intrusion. If relatives, who would usually have less personal anxiety than patients, were included, might not the interview be accentuated in importance and acquire greater psychological and anxiety-management significance?

Third, for some patients and some relatives, being together with the doctor during treatment would be helpful all around. The doctor could have a more relaxed patient, the patient could feel more protected, and the relative could know the reality of the treatment rather than only his imaginings. The doctor would need to ask what preconditions would be desirable to accomplish this, though. Would he not need to structure clearly for the patient that he welcomes relatives and to orient them all to what the latter might do and where they might be? Might he not have to think through the spatial arrangements and the furnishings, and to determine that the changes would merit the expense and other complications? Would a relative being present, to fill periods when the patient would otherwise be alone, increase the doctor's freedom for keeping in motion the complex program of a busy practice? Would the nurse be able to concentrate more fully on treatment procedures and assistance to the doctor?

Fourth, would not instruction about follow-up procedures to both patient and relative tend to increase the care with which the procedures would be followed? By spreading the knowledge on which follow-up is based, patient and relative would seem to be better able to reinforce and support one another and to share the responsibility.

Fifth, since the waiting room is a vacuum for most relatives, even though current magazines might fill it, what are the gains in physically breaking the relative's relations with the patient, as against those that could be achieved through keeping them together?

From my point of view and experience, I would support the value of being with my wife. I will not speak for her and certainly not for the doctor. If I had been sure that he would not have rejected the idea absolutely, I would have preferred to warn him and prepare him for what I would do, and how I would regard my role. This would have helped my wife. But I am not sure that I would have been allowed to test out the idea if I had forewarned him. If this trial had gains for us, I know also that the ultimate test might be in repeating the experiment of including relatives with many other patients. Only then might the procedures and their application be developed to the point of minimizing problems and maximizing the benefits for dental practice, patients, and the patients' relatives.

Chapter XV

The Community as a
Medical Institution

During the past decade three important fundamental principles about medical services have come to the fore: a growing emphasis on the community as the base for health services; measuring the adequacy of health services by how comprehensive they are; affirmations that each individual in our nation shall have the opportunity for access to health services as a human right.

To provide comprehensive health services for all people in the community becomes then, the directive for national program development. To implement this requires expanding organization and institutionalization of services. They cannot attain the scope demanded without stressing the total organizational framework within which they are offered. This applies whether we are speaking about services directed to illness, to promotion of health, or to the prevention of disease. This applies whether we are talking about physical or mental illnesses. Accordingly we have to talk about institutions for health services and the community, as well.

The term *community* is used in many ways. We refer to a *place,* such as Palo Alto, as a community. We speak of community in a *social* sense. We may talk about any number of units of society in which people live, work, relate, and share a common fate, as communities. We may talk of bodies politic, *governmental* units, such as town, village, city or state, as community. We talk of small groups of people who *live together* and who relate to one another in functional ways, as community. We talk of those who belong in common to an *institution,* or business, as a community. We think in larger terms of the community of the *nation,* or a community of nations. We signify so many units by the word community that we could talk about many diverse ideas and operations involved in relating community to medical institutions.

Since *medical institution* and *community* are variously defined and used, we need to clarify the connotations involved with them. I hope to accomplish this, in part, by taking some remote situations to contrast with and reveal to us the ways we think, and the kinds of medical programs we plan, develop, and sustain in our own communities. In each of the remote illustrations involving medical services, the community concept is used in specific ways which are perhaps easier for us to identify because of their remoteness. In almost all, the family is of central importance in the success of the medical program.

COMMUNITIES AS MEDICAL INSTITUTIONS

In certain areas of Africa and Asia, the community, primarily a village, has emerged as a center for medical care. In both young countries and in special communities in more industrial nations, such use of communities has been heralded as a practical means to provide treatment for various kinds of patients, especially for the mentally ill.

Dr. T. A. Lambo, Professor of Psychiatry and Head of the Department of Psychiatry, Neurology, and Neurosurgery at the University of Ibadan, Nigeria, pioneered in applying the idea of the village as a medical institution to the treatment of the mentally ill in that country. He has become internationally known as a leading proponent of the concept, although others, notably Dr. Tajani el Mahi of the Sudan, endorsed and promoted it. Lambo has acknowledged his indebtedness to the town of Gheel, Belgium, where for centuries the mentally ill have been nurtured in the homes of residents while securing help, and to native Nigerian healers who for treatment have traditionally invited into their homes patients and their relatives who come from a distance.

I had the privilege of visiting Lambo, and was able to witness his creative experiments in the care of the mentally ill while I was studying mental and other hospitals in Africa and Asia. I also had the opportunity to visit many villages elsewhere that were providing care, treatment and rehabilitation to patients with mental and other ailments. This series of experiences, brief though they were, gave me a chance for comparative observation, and permitted me to analyze some ways to use villages in medical practice.

Such villages may be differentiated, first, on the basis of their history. Some existed as *indigenous* villages and were adapted for their specialized use, while others were *constructed* for medical purposes. This delineation does not necessarily correspond to a division of the villages into those which are truly independent communities and those which are medical institutions. Such a divison would provide a second way to characterize the ways in which villages are used. For the purpose of definition, I am calling the village *a medical institution if the ultimate authority in the government resides in a medical administrator or his designate.* Later application of this definition to some of the villages I observed will further clarify its meaning and importance.

Villages may be classified, further, by specifying their functions. Four types were identified:

1. The village as a treatment center for patients who are acutely ill.

2. The village as a place to live, in proximity to a hospital or medical facility.

3. The village as a transitional facility in patient rehabilitation.
4. The village as a locale for posttreatment independent living.

Each of these functional categories was observed directly, but as there was no initial expectation that we would study this issue, the data gathered were incidental and incomplete. However, enough information was collected to illustrate the various types listed above.

The Village as an Acute Treatment Center

The village of Aro, one of those used by Lambo in Nigeria, typifies villages in use as acute-treatment centers. The idea of classifying villages grew from my reflections on visits here, made in Lambo's company. Other villages had been seen earlier, and probably sharpened my attention to certain features of Aro, which in itself is one example among several villages which Lambo is developing along similar lines.

To understand Aro, one needs to return to its beginnings as a medical facility, to follow the stages of its development, and finally to make clear the nature of its present organization and function. Lambo points to three stages in the use of Aro, which is a prototype for his use of other villages.

Phase 1 may be described as a pre-hospital period. It began when Lambo was appointed in 1954 to the medical superintendency of a mental hospital in the process of being constructed near Aro, and appropriately called the Aro Hospital for Nervous Diseases. Since wards were not ready, Lambo urged residents in the nearby village to open rooms in their houses to patients. This was regarded then as a temporary arrangement.

It was the local custom that patients who were being treated by native practitioners would move nearby or into facilities provided by the healer. Not uncommonly, patients lived in the native doctor's home or in nearby homes, and were usually accompanied by relatives. To adapt this pattern to the practice he was establishing did not seem strange to Lambo nor to the patients and their relatives. He did not think it would be desirable to continue the practice after opening the new hospital, and no elaborate theory or procedures for the use of the village were set up.

By the time the hospital was opened in 1956, Lambo and his staff had obtained sufficient experience and success in treatment in a village setting to revise their earlier intention to abandon the village system. From that time until his appointment as professor at the University of Ibadan in 1963, the village of Aro and three neighboring counterparts were used jointly with the new, attractive hospital facilities and services. Within five miles there was another unit under Lambo's direction, Lantoro Hospital, essentially a domiciliary unit for chronic and criminal psychotic patients.

For the most part, the villages were used for temporary patient residence, with acute treatment offered at the hospital. Gradually, the villages assumed increasing importance in the area of treatment, becoming eventually "hospital wards." Each house was numbered and shown on a special map in the hospital superintendent's office; the number of patients in each house was posted, usually every day. Nurses detailed to each village provided daytime coverage, and kept notes on the condition of each patient. Doctors and nursing supervisors visited each village daily.

Occupational and activity programs were instituted in the villages based on African crafts and recreation—group story telling, games, and dancing. Native practitioners were among those employed to coordinate the village programs, to serve as counselors and guides for relatives, and to direct the social activities. Specialized treatments, such as "electro-convulsive treatment, electro-narcosis, modified insulin therapy, abreactive techniques, and various group psychotherapies and drug medication" were offered at the hospital.

Lambo (1965) described the relationship between the villages and the hospitals at that time:

We have now taken full responsibility for the administration, management, planning and public health of the villages surrounding Aro Hospital. Regular monthly meetings are held between the hospital staff and the village heads and their deputies. Loans are made available from the hospital to the people to enable them to expand and repair or build new houses to accommodate more patients. Among other things, we have paid for the installation of water-pipes and pit latrines and for a mosquito eradication squad.

At first, patients were selected carefully, according to their type of mental illness, for placement in village homes. But as the range of diseases handled in the villages increased with experience, no preselection was made. Treatment in the village and as outpatients at Aro Hospital became the basic program; hospitalization was made only when indicated by a patient's medical and social needs. The combination of residences and services offered at Aro and Lantoro Hospitals and in the villages allowed considerable flexibility, and proved most suitable for the treatment and care of the mentally ill.

Following his professorial appointment, Lambo revised the patterns of his practice. His successor at the Aro Hospital, Dr. T. Asuni, took over the complex of the Aro and Lantoro hospital facilities, and developed two new villages as temporary domiciles for acute patients. Lambo retained his involvement with Aro village and many nearby, and created a new pattern for their use. He now established villages as total treatment centers—medical centers without walls. He continued to encourage villagers to open their homes to patients with all kinds of mental illnesses, and through a central source, subsidized the landlords for their hospitality at the rate of 10 shillings ($1.40) per month per room. The subsidy was paid out of fees and research funds. Treatment was offered in a clinic in the village, which, in practice, expanded into a comprehensive public health clinic with the aid of medical school staff. In addition, relatives typically were accommodated along with patients to help with their care, bring them for treatment, report on the patients' status, protect them from danger, and secure help in an emergency. The ratio of patients to villagers was controlled (variously reported as 25-40%), to preserve the semblance of a normal community. In an area comprising 64 villages, four catchment areas were delineated, each with a village as a treatment and research center.

A major step was taken, however, to transform the four villages into institutions. Lambo, or his professional counterparts, joined the governing bodies of the villages, on the assumption that the welfare of the villages and the treatment of the patients required professional leadership. In concert with the village chiefs—elected for life by the villagers and paid five pounds sterling per month from funds available to Lambo—and their councils, the medical staff meet monthly to discuss village problems. In the hands of less benign and more dominating individuals, the governments might have become exclusively medical. But, in showing respect to village leaders, and continuous sensitivity to the status of their positions, Lambo achieved therapeutic village environments without destroying the essential character of village life.

Many changes have been wrought in the villages. Recently, specialists in agriculture and community organization have been introduced to promote village growth, land improvement and employment of residents. Village life has been upgraded from both external and internal perspectives, and has been organized to serve the goals of treatment.

The villages seem to be best adapted to the modern treatment of families with acutely ill patients, or repeated but relatively short-term hospitalization of the chronically ill. Whether or not these villages could provide comprehensive care for all mental patients without the support of an inpatient facility for the most severely disturbed is not known. It seems improbable that the villages alone can offer a setting for the treatment of the criminal psychotic and those rejected from a family and community because of insufferable behavior.

By the criterion of professional direction, we may say that Aro and the neighboring villages incorporated into Lambo's research program are indigenous villages become institutions. They have many virtues for treatment, and allow continuation of and improvement in the social skills basic to the life settings to which patients will return. Transitions into and out of the treatment settings are easy, informal, rapid, and natural. The development of these settings for treatment was a highly creative experiment worthy of the international attention and acclaim it has received.

The Village as a Domicile During Treatment

INDIGENOUS VILLAGES

The value of classification of the use of villages is perhaps well illustrated by the ways in which Lambo's successor, Asuni, uses the two villages now relating to the hospital. These villages, close to those used by Lambo, are essentially domiciles for patients and relatives who are receiving treatment at the hospital on a day basis, and as outpatients. The villages are only occasionally the locale for treatment. In general, they provide homes for a number of patients and their families in rooms rented by the villagers. This is a profitable business taken on enthusiastically by the villagers.

The homes and a village must qualify by attaining certain standards of furnishing and cleanliness. The village must develop pit toilets, a cleared area at its perimeter, an incinerator for rubbish disposal, and a road over which an ambulance can travel. A sanitary source of water might have been added as a standard, but villagers still use nearby streams to bathe, wash clothes, and provide drinking water.

Having met the suggested standards, the villages were then qualified to receive patients on referral. Patients and families negotiate their own financial arrangements, homeowners collect payments, and together they work out, if possible, the problems that develop between the patients and their landlords.

Some difficulties extend beyond the house where a patient lives. When patients are troublesome to the whole village, the problems are reviewed by the elders in the village council. They solve the problems, again if possible, in their own way. They may call in the psychiatric staff of the hospital as consultants, but the basic responsibility remains with the elders. If they cannot cope with the patient, which occasionally happens, they may recommend to him and to the medical staff that he be hospitalized.

The patterns for Asuni's use of these villages are distinguished from Lambo's in four respects. With Asuni (1964):

The village is a domicile rather than a treatment center.

The village and the home owners are independent in the development of their facilities and services for patients.

The government of the village is in the hands of the villagers and, in particular, their council of elders.

Professional staff are available essentially as consultants by arrangement.

The villages used by Asuni, then, are not treatment institutions, although they facilitate therapy and prove therapeutic in effect.

The drawing of this comparison with the villages used by Lambo should not be construed as an evaluation of their benefits for patients. In each instance, it is appropriate to say that the professionals are *using* the villages. The activities of the professionals in setting up clinics, taking part in village government, providing consultation, or performing other functions in direct relationship to villages brings them into direct and formal communication with the villages. The "Lambo" villages are total institutions; the "Asuni" villages are adjuncts to one of the more advanced African mental hospitals, part of a larger complex that includes Lantoro, the related but poorly developed chronic hospital. Asuni's use of the villages would not be supportable without the related mental hospital programs. Lambo's program for the village is required by his not any longer having ready access to the hospitals that he directed before. In other words, Asuni's program demonstrates one way to use an existing community while patients are being treated at a nearby hospital. Lambo's program illustrates how to use a similar existing community as a base for treatment when no hospital is available.

CONSTRUCTED VILLAGES

At the present time, the programmed use of already-existing villages as specified above or of their urban counterparts—the town or neighborhood—has been relatively infrequent. More typical, and often confused with the preexisting village, is the use of simulated or constructed villages. This is so common that it will be well for us to set forth a number of examples, not so much for the differentiation of types as for illustration of the ways in which the latter are employed.

Brief Domicile.   Across a field from the Firestone Hospital on the Harbel Rubber Plantation in Liberia is a camp for prospective mothers. It consists of a series of buildings that roughly parallel the multiple housing units set up in the company's plantation villages. About the seventh month of pregnancy, women whose homes are too far from the hospital for adequate prenatal and maternity care take up residence in the separate rooms of the buildings which are like row houses. They bring their children and other relatives with them if they choose, and are visited by husbands, especially on weekends. The camp is known among them as the "Belly Camp." Its accessibility to the Hospital allows for regular and frequent prenatal examination, for adequate medication or other treatments as needed, for supplemental feeding to combat the prevalent problem of anemia, and for immediate attention at the onset of labor.

When I visited the camp, the expectant mothers were busy husking rice—one of their staple foods—building cooking fires, drawing water from the central tap, and making purchases of foodstuffs, cosmetics and trinkets from the mammy trader. The women are characteristically proud to be pregnant, and showed off their living quarters, the utensils supplied by the hospital, their purchases, and the tasks they were doing. Those who had already delivered brought their babies to be admired.

I was told that the women were living here in a fashion and in facilities markedly similar to those at their own homes. The camp encourages semi-independence in a relatively familar environment. The family members retain their domestic functions and customary roles. The rhythm of daily life with its trips for water, fuel, food, its meal times, rest, gossip, sleep continues in essential form. The mammy trader comes with her wares on an almost daily schedule, as she does at home, if there is no market nearby.

The camp has the advantage that residence has a fixed but not arbitrary terminal date. Movement back to the home is never a matter of inclination; it does not come up as a question, it being so firmly understood that as soon as the mother can leave after delivery, she will be given transportation home and will resume full family and village life.

The camp receives only minimal attention from the hospital authorities. There is then much freedom, but not anarchy. The order and discipline of home villages are transferred by each mother into her relationships in the camp.

Perhaps the distinction between living at the camp and premdternity hospitalization should be described, in order to spell out why the camp is included as a village. During the period when the prospective mother is in the camp, she is related to the hospital as an outpatient. Her relationships with the obstetrician and other staff who assist her to prepare for the time of delivery are like those in a clinic. They resemble the relationships established by a mother whose home from which she comes for prenatal examinations is nearby.

At Harbel Hospital, the mother has a period as an inpatient. At the time of delivery, the hospital takes over the full responsibility for feeding, bathing, other general care, and medical treatment. In the maternity ward, the mother is not having a village experience.

I would further qualify the camp experience as distinct from that in the hospital by the fact that in camp the patient has self-determination over a significant portion of daily living. Furthermore, the camp can allow activity in usual social groups, such as the family, without professional interference to facilitate, impede, or control. Still further, in the camp, the resident undertakes employment. In this instance, she performs domestic duties, a direct carryover, or parallel, of employment that would be performed in her home and village.

For Permanent Residence.   Many leprosaria offer a second illustration of constructed villages. Since lepers pass through phases of their illness when they need hospitalization, and others where they may live outside a hospital, commonly a village type of life develops at such institutions. Villages have grown, also, as answers to the segregation of the leper, the limits of his physical capacity to engage in useful and economically productive work, and his social needs. Most family ties were cut on entrance into the leprosarium. Once there, many patients married others and started new families which could be housed more naturally in replicas of villages—in houses built by the patients themselves, according to traditional patterns and methods of building.

Many illustrations could be offered, of which the leprosy villages run by the Sudan Interior Mission about 10 miles outside Kano, in Northern Nigeria, are excellent examples. Clustering around the hospital and clinic where the administrative, management, educational, religious, and other central services and facilities are located, four separate villages have been established. Land was assigned, some materials were granted, and patients who had begun or intended to live as families were free to build as they chose. In addition, separate compounds were built for single women. A central well was drilled in each village by the mission, an area for village meetings, perhaps near shade trees emerged spontaneously, and a market and a mill, private enterprises, moved in.

The patients worked plots of land on the mission farm on a share basis, growing peanuts or guinea corn. A share of the harvest went to the mission to feed patients unable to work; the remainder was for the laborer to sell or store for personal or family use. The day I visited, the last threshing of the harvested guinea corn was being done collectively in a concrete pit, near which all grain is stored centrally. The following day, the animals, mainly goats, who had been penned in the family compounds during the growing season, were to be freed to glean the fields. There was a last-minute scurry to secure all vulnerable areas before the animals began to roam.

Some patients were weaving the matting used as fences around fields and houses. Others, especially those with trades, were working for wages paid by the mission. I saw several: the blacksmith repairing implements; the shoemaker making custom shoes for deformed feet; the carpenter planing wood; the cement worker, with the help of a number of laborers, constructing a toilet platform over a septic tank; the craftsmen making prosthetic devices of wood, metal, and plastic.

The women were busy, too. Some were hand-grinding corn with mortars and pestles, while others waited for their corn to be ground at the mill. Many were washing clothes at the well, drawing water, making fires, and cooking meals for their families, surrounded by pots, pans, and bowls spread out on the ground. Some were nursing infants. Even boys and girls were working members of the busy community. Only the very young were at play.

The government of the villages was a mixture of benevolent paternalism and self-determination. The overall responsibility was placed in an administrator, a steamfitter by trade, who, through his intelligence, personality, and sensitivity to people, was able to manage the medical institution and villages with sympathetic efficiency. He chose a headman to represent each village, and expected him to deal with local problems as far as possible. Each morning the village chiefs met in council with the administrator, who served as chairman. As many as 40 or 50 villagers usually gathered around, and each was free to enter the discussions. Most of the problems considered were interpersonal difficulties in families and the community, and the manager encouraged villagers to propose and carry out their own solutions.

In many ways, the sessions resembled therapeutic community meetings, although their function was government and not therapy. A major difference can be observed, however. For these residents, the village was not a place to stay temporarily—as far as they planned, they were to remain for the rest of their lives. They were not sheltered, then, from as many of the everyday problems as hospital patients, nor were they so readily able to deal with the issues of life in the abstract, from a distance established by the institution as a haven. They had to face the long-range future as presented in each day and complicated by the potential destructiveness of their illness. This they could see objectified in those nearby who were bedridden, or whose crippling prevented continuation of work, family life, physical and social mobility, and the intimacy so richly a part of the African's total life.

They lived much as they might have in their home villages. In terms of human satisfactions, they probably experienced many they might have known at home. In addition, they had the advantage of the clinic and hospital for maintenance of health, and treatment when necessary. Most had probably become unable, in fact, to readjust to living at their own home villages, as illustrated by unsuccessful efforts to rehabilitate patients from a somewhat comparable leprosarium in Ghana. The leprosarium there arranged escorts, transportation and follow-up services, and sent many patients for hundreds of miles from the south coast of Ghana to its northern frontiers. It was frustrating to find them back on the doorstep of the institution in a few weeks, begging to be allowed to stay. The advantages in the institution of the protected environment, the secure provisions, and shielding from social rejection outweighed the satisfactions in resuming early ties.

However, for all its benefits, professional authorities could now advance stronger arguments against the village system for the lepers. The villages were built on the propositions that leprosy is a chronic illness, and that the patients need permanent segregation and institutionalization. Medical advances have made these assertions obsolete.

For Protracted Residence.   A variant of the village as a domicile was that which allowed for residence within a hospital, as observed in many African and Asian hospitals. Few hospitals organized their space primarily for families. Instead, most had plants for medical and nursing activities in which families were accommodated somehow. A notable exception, unique in many respects was found outside Durban, South Africa. Perhaps the most unusual feature of all was the auspice under which it developed.

In 1939 five men of different race and background—two Indians, two Europeans, and an African—began meeting in Durban to discuss the problems of Indian citizens who had been brought to South Africa to work the mines and cane fields. Economic hardships; nutritional deficiencies; disease; illiteracy; chronic unemployment; overcrowded, unsanitary shanty housing; and segregation burdened their lives. Tuberculosis aroused particular public concern: in 1940, there were only 87 beds to treat 1400 diagnosed cases of tuberculosis among Indians in Durban.

Inspired by two outstanding Indians in South Africa, Ghandhi and Srinavisa Sastri, Agent General for the Government of India in South Africa, these five men formed "The Society of Servants in South Africa" and began meeting weekly to exchange information on problems facing Indians in Durban and Natal, where most of them lived. The society viewed its function as the stimulation of others, especially societies and official agencies, to perform needed services. It attributed its singular success, in part, to a firm rule that members' names were never to appear individually or collectively in any publication; thus they gave all credit to others.

Recognizing the urgency of the tuberculosis problem, and assuming that there must be hundreds of undiscovered cases, the Servants formed a subcommittee, named "Friends of the Sick." With the motto "one sick, one friend," the ensuing association soon became known by its initials, FOSA.

In June 1941 members of FOSA in Clairwood, a district of Durban, formed the first of 51 subsequent care committees. Now functioning for over 30 years, these committees, composed of anywhere from 3 to 25 members, seek out TB sufferers and their families, continuously supervise each family member until his health is assured, personally promote education on the subject of TB, its causes, prevention, and treatment, and serve as liaisons between patients, families, hospitals, official and social agencies. Regular training sessions for all Friends, and the requirement for annual membership renewal insures active committees, free of "deadwood."

Fund-raising for their work is accomplished by sponsoring dances, concerts, competitions and bazaars. Most receipts, however, come from regular collections in each neighborhood by members of a care committee. Individual contributions may be as small as a penny. In 1965, by this means, 719 active Friends, most of whom are poor people, raised, in dollar equivalents, $10,152 for relief, $1,072 for capital development, and $447 for rehabilitation.

As the original care committee began its work in 1941, its members quickly recognized the need to remove TB patients and their families out of the slums and into a healthier environment where healing and prevention could be supervised. A settlement was envisaged.

Two families donated 25 acres on a hillside at Newlands on the outskirts of Durban. On Christmas Eve, 1942, a tent given by a Natal University professor was erected on the site, and before New Year's Eve the first patient convalescing from TB moved in. Within a year 19 patients were under care at the FOSA settlement. Gradually, permanent buildings were constructed: a 72-bed hospital, 9 wards in separate buildings, 28 cottages, and over 20 other buildings, including an outpatient clinic which the government rents from the settlement at a nominal sum, and staffs to serve the whole district.

At the settlement gate, a sign on the building to the right advertises it as the store where foodstuffs may be purchased at cost by families of patients under care or in the process of rehabilitation, and by indigent families of the neighborhood.

Inside the gate, nearly 200 children rush by on their way to school; they have many of their lessons on the lawn, allowing the few classrooms to be used flexibly. The school and its facilities, leased to the government and operated by them, are not large enough for the community they serve, and must run on two shifts of 200 youngsters each day. Children of parents with TB are given priority in school admissions, whether they live with their families in the settlement, or have been brought to the settlement's Sunshine Home, a special residence for some children. When there is space, children from the community outside are admitted to the school.

Oddly shaped, roundish buildings with thatched roofs, among the earliest structures built in the Settlement, next intrigue the visitor. These "rondavels" are used as wards for small groups of patients with no families, and encourage high morale; from there the patient can watch the children at school, the weavers, the shoppers, the visitors and all traffic through the gates.

Nearby was a more prosaic structure, the weaving shed, since accidentally destroyed by fire. The shed housed the settlement's primary industry. On invitation to step inside, one found looms clicking and clanging as patients threw shuttles back and forth. I followed a young woman in a sari, her arms loaded with squares of many colors that looked like small pillow cases. She turned into a nearby building where other Indian women were ironing, sewing, folding, and packaging all manner of woven articles for sale in the FOSA store, or for distributing to gift shops. The subtlety of the patterns, colors and textures speaks of artistic planning and quality control, which, it was explained, represents talents among patients, staff, and especially volunteers who have worked together to make the products aesthetic and salable. The industry continues and is run by an efficient committee of six, a manager in charge of production, and salesmen on the road to promote distribution. It has to earn $1,680 (U.S.) per month in order to pay its way, and it more than does.

In the hot sun, the road from the gate winds up to the top of the hill where the hospital stands. The settlement's microbus is busy transporting patients. Steps lead up from terrace to terrace on each of which are built rows of cottages. Washing hangs on lines; a tricycle is on a front porch. Some householders have planted maize and beans; others, flowers; and a few have risked a gardener's disdain and planted nothing. A quarterly competition awards a cup to the most attractive cottage and garden.

These cottages, 23 of which are occupied by families of adult patients, were donated and built with funds and labor contributed by care committees. They enable impoverished families to secure adequate medical care, obtain job training, find employment and establish or reestablish a better way of living. As soon as a parent who is ill is no longer infectious, and is physically able to return to his family, he moves from the hospital into the cottage where they are living.

The cottages are maintained as private residences, and are not throughways for Settlement personnel. The public health nurse, however, is welcome, and visits each home, patient and family every day, primarily to dispense prophylactic drugs. Her headquarters are in a similar cottage which has been converted into a clinic. If on her rounds she finds anything amiss in the way of maintenance, she reports it to the administration. But there are few such reports. Knowing the houses are supported by sacrifices of poor people instills respect for property. Brother Albert, a layman who has been with the settlement since 1942, looks after the buildings.

There is considerable conflict about supporting the cottage system. The Natal State Health Department, which pays for patient treatment, frowns on funds for any aspect of the cottage life, although keeping a patient there is cheaper than maintaining him in a hospital bed. On the other hand, the welfare agency, which normally grants relief, is opposed, understandably, to using its grants for the cottage life as it may be regarded in the area of treatment. Complicated financial negotiations with authorities are part of a larger management problem, to meet the standards and audit requirements of 15 separate agencies.

The matron showed us through the Sunshine Home, a residence for 29 children whose parents had died in the hospital or had abandoned them, knowing that their illness would leave them unable to provide. Some preschoolers came down the path from their nursery school or from the playground on top of the hill. These facilities were placed near the hospital intentionally, so patients could watch the children. In the Home, older children had already seated themselves for lunch. Each of the youngsters was taking medicine to ward off TB. Their giggles and whispers at strange visitors bespoke health. The eagerness with which they welcomed the food further illustrated their vitality.

At the hilltop was the hospital, including surgery, wards, x-ray, treatment rooms, nurses, porches for sunning, shade for retreat, radios, two classes for child patients, a table for miniature golf, another for snooker—all spotless.

Viewed from the hospital porch, the Settlement spread out

down the slope of the hill has no institutional feel. It grew like a
village, as buildings were added gradually over 25 years with no
great evidence of preplanning other than conformity to the con-
tours of the land. It is a sharp contrast to TB facilities built elsewhere and later in South Africa, where the projects were conceived as a whole and laid out on a logical, regular, and perhaps
less intimate scale.

The romantic-looking rondavels were slated for razing. Mr.
Cory, the warden or lay administrator, known as Brother Basil by
staff and patients, said they would not rebuild such units if they had
to reconstruct the whole settlement. The concept of using them as
transitional facilities was excellent, but in practice they became
chronic wards whose dispersion around the Settlement made them
unmanageable for nursing supervision. But their passing is symbolic
of the future when no patients will be there to fill them; eventually,
the families will be so well established in the community, economically, socially, and physically, that the conditions fostering TB will be
ameliorated and infection will be prevented by prophylactic measures
and early treatment.

The whole settlement was a hospital and, at the same time, a
village. The children left their homes to go to school, the fathers
or mothers who were recovering and could work went to the weaving, those who were well went out to the city to their jobs. Like
families, most returned home at night to be together, to eat at the
family table, to enjoy one another and to sleep under a common
roof. But, one difference prevailed. The hospital-village was not
the end. There was a step ahead in the future, a move toward a
new home, job, school, temple, and neighborhood. The peculiar
advantages of this type of hospital were the opportunities for
evaluation of the total life of the patient, and for steps to proper
planning and progression through each necessary rehabilitative
step.

Yet the hospital is out-of-date. It is on the way to being phased
out. It illustrates a combination of hospital and community life
that may be desirable during one period in war against a disease
requiring long-term treatment and massive efforts toward rehabilitation. In our terms, it is a combination medical, welfare, and rehabilitation program with a good share of education thrown in. Its

success is told in its replication in many places in South Africa, in its being a model for treating TB, and in the closing of all such offshoots until the parent hospital-village alone remains. It will soon be gone, but perhaps its destiny is to live on elsewhere, as the idea behind an institution-village to combat other illnesses and restore other patients.

The Village as a Transitional Facility

For many patients, especially those with psychiatric illnesses, placement in a village following hospitalization would seem desirable as a step toward home. In reality, this practice seems relatively rare. No example of an operating program of this sort came to my attention in observations in 27 developing countries.

One hospital, however, offered a semblance of a village for partial rehabilitation for a few patients. On the outskirts of the city of Kinshasa in Zaire is a mental hospital, L'Institut de Neuro-Psychiatrie de Mont Léopold, housed in a plant more like a prison than an environment for healing. Outside the walls was a row of staff houses, left empty because staff resigned during turmoil in the country after independence. The World Health Organization, on request, sent an Argentine psychiatrist, Dr. J. E. Juan Alladio, now in Canada, to supervise the hospital. He saw an opportunity to restore family living for patients, and a chance to help them to resume life in the community. He converted these staff houses into patients' homes.

When a patient had a viable family, was able to live outside the walls, yet still needed to be near the hospital, Alladio arranged for the whole family to move in. This was probably welcomed by the family since the housing shortage in the city was critical. It was variously reported that the city had grown by 100%, 200%, or 300% following independence. Wherever the truth lay, some families were living under such difficult and distressing circumstances that the hospital houses must have looked luxurious. The experiment in using these homes had not been operating for long. Consequently, no evaluation had been made nor was a formal one intended. According to Alladio's report, the families were progressing adequately.

Although the staff houses could scarcely suggest a Zairean village, they did offer some similarities in the patterns of living and the freedom they provided while treatment continued.

Plans for a similar transitional village were under discussion in Zambia between Dr. B. Lind, Medical Superintendent of Chainama Hills Hospital, the national mental hospital; Mr. I. Yeta, Supernumerand Director of Social Welfare; and Mr. H. H. Ferreira, Director of Social Welfare.

Outside the capital city, Lusaka, where the hospital is located, is a small settlement of three blocks of buildings each with nine rooms. Originally built by the Labor Department to provide shelter to migrant workers, they were left empty when this purpose was over, and have since been used by squatters. They have deteriorated into slums and are now health and social hazards, but they cannot be emptied immediately as the present occupants must be resettled elsewhere.

The three officials proposed to use the buildings as temporary housing for mental patients and their families during a trial period in the community. The settlement was less than three miles from the hospital—far enough to give a sense of return to the community, yet close enough for treatment or followup visits by staff. A local bus service made connections with a bus to the hospital.

The plans were not complete. The Ministries of Health and Social Welfare were wrestling with basic policy decisions on the responsibilities of their separate agencies for the maintenance and support of the facility and its residents. In general the Ministry of Health, in addition to providing for the care of patients, acknowledged a clearcut obligation to care for nursing mothers, and mothers of young children who were expected to be with their children in hospitals. Responsiblity for care of relatives accompanying older children or adults, who were hospitalized, often far from home, had not been designated. The issue was to be decided by the National Cabinet. These matters had been brought to public attention and become of major importance since the settlement was being developed as a demonstration project, with the hope that success would inspire similar programs in other areas.

The aim was to move 18 to 20 patients out of the hospital and into the rooms of the hostels. Letters would invite relatives to Lusaka to stay with their family member for a period, and to assume responsibility for his care. From past experience, authorities knew that relatives would come, but could not predict what their relationship to the patient might be—brother, wife, mother, wife's aunt or another relative. To prevent unrelated individuals from moving in with patients to use the facility as a hotel, it was decided to restrict the number of attendants.

Residence in the hostels was to be limited to three to four weeks to guard against a gradual transformation from settlement to hospital annex. No single patients were to be transferred there, because in Zambia it is essential to rehabilitate patients to a group. The single patient might make the hostel his permanent home.

A warden would be placed in charge of the settlement; a social worker from the Department of Social Welfare, and staff from the Health Department would visit daily. The social worker would offer education, guidance, and relief funds of 10 shillings per person per week to buy food. The program was expected to save manpower; no one could guess whether it would save money.

Two features of this proposed program represent important conceptual contributions. First, the transitional facility is recognized as a multidepartment responsibility. Treatment continues as the province of the hospital. Housing, family care, and basic maintenance during rehabilitation have been accepted in principle by the Social Welfare Department, though details are not yet settled.

Second, rehabilitation is identified as a family problem, though only one member has been hospitalized. The integration of services for working collectively with the family unit is theoretically familiar, but difficult to actually achieve. In the face of crises in neighboring Rhodesia and other changing circumstances, the program may not yet have been instituted.

The Village for Rehabilitation to Independent Living

The final category applies to the village used for permanent placement of former patients where the goal is independent living—"to lose the patient in normal society"—even though there may not be complete recovery from illness. In many cases the rehabilitated patient might regard this village placement as better than his home village where he might continue to face rejection, or where he might face obligations beyond his capacity.

It may seem strange to make a category to cover one illustration. I have done this here, though, with a forward look. The particular village is the third constructed on the same principles, so that other examples exist. It has the potential to be a model for similar villages in many other rural areas, and has implications for rehabilitation in cities.

The village is called Amphur Li, and is the end product of a 10-year experiment in the rehabilitation of the physically and socially disabled in northern Thailand. The experiment was the realization of a set of goals of Robert Wulff, a highly motivated American veteran of the Pacific theater during World War II. Having lived in China and Manchuria during the war, he decided to return on his own to assist development of some part of Southeast Asia. He took me to visit the last of the villages he developed. It was my privilege to hear from him the underlying philosophy and procedures.

We set out from Chiengmai by jeep in early morning along the road to Bangkok, 400 miles south. Accompanying us was Wulff's assistant and probable successor in Thailand, Surin Chowapisit. I was wearing jeans and other clothes loaned by Wulff to protect against the clouds of dust thrown up by his jeep and other traffic. The road runs down a long valley, on either side of which one may see ridges of hills in the distance. Much of the countryside is populated; villages are marked by the brilliant "flame of the forest" and yellow cassia trees; cultivated fields occasionally give way to forests.

To construct a new village here requires land, which through negotiation became available from the government. It was deeded to the National Welfare Department and through them to the New Life Foundation, a Thai organization, sponsors of the project. Ultimately, the deed may be returned to the Welfare Department for subsequent granting to individuals.

The land was on the opposite side of the Li River from the road and a flourishing village; the nearest crossing was miles away, and here was the sponsors' first problem. Tractors, elephants, government workers and prospective villagers overcame this problem by building a wooden bridge.

Once over the river, Wulff's project staff cleared a road with a tractor gifted by the Lion's Club. Quick-growing plantain and bananas were planted down the shoulders for food to share and cuttings to start plantations. Plots of land about an acre in size were marked out roughly and the village was opened for settlers.

Certain goals were established at the outset: to create a village that had an appearance similar to others nearby; to remove within two years all outside assistance, other than that normally available to any village through local agencies; to avoid introduction of a deviant population in such a way as to attract a negative label to the village; to do nothing for any individual or group which could be done by themselves, and to offer only enough help to establish independence.

Settlers were assigned land to clear and plant, given a knife and a hoe, some seed, and the freedom to use the land. Land was ploughed by tractor the first year only. They were told that more land could be theirs if they used it, but that unused land would be taken away.

Crude shacks were thrown up and covered with thatch supplied by the foundation. After the first crop, the villagers were encouraged to cut timber, make their own thatch, and construct permanent homes after models in neighboring villages.

Since this was the third such village, and Wulff was confident of his principles and techniques, he was challenged but not uneasy when he was asked by the U.S. Overseas Mission in Thailand to establish and demonstrate that he could start this new community, and have it functioning and independent in two years. The deadline was imminent, three or four weeks ahead, and Wulff had taken passage for the United States, gratified that the demonstration was satisfactory.

He was leaving behind a fully operating village, where 46 homes were built and occupied, and a population of 200 were comfortably settled and caring for themselves. Eight were former mental patients (seven were single, one was married to a leper); lepers and their families accounted for 80; poor people with many children, another 80. Five former prisoners with their families completed the community. Citrus trees had been planted; pineapple was ripening; additional land was being cleared; lumber was being milled; a crop of garlic was ready for market; wells had been dug; children's toys had been carved or built; melons, bananas, chickens, goats, and a valuable community-owned ox were flourishing.

The ox, used to plough the fields and for transport, had been stolen during the previous night. The villagers were upset when we arrived. They had some suspicion that one of their number was implicated, but no evidence. Theft of animals is common in the country, and the loss was particularly great here, since money prosperity had not yet arrived, and the *baht* to purchase another ox were not easy to secure. The theft may have been the act of a villager, but it was always possible that someone had come in from outside.

The manner in which the crisis was handled shows the philosophy of the program. As soon as we arrived, the villagers began to report to Wulff, telling him what they had observed that might be useful in recovery of the animal. He carefully focused his attention on achieving four things. He encouraged the villagers to communicate with him, to inform him, in order to clarify for them the role he would take in regard to the problem. He urged the villagers to use the services of the police in solving the crime and recovering the animal, if possible. He proposed to them that they meet among themselves in whatever groups they chose, to develop their own solutions for the temporary problem until the animal came back, and, if he did not, the more difficult problem of securing another animal. Finally, he agreed to hear any requests for his help, but made no precommitment that he would help them.

With a tractor at his disposal, it might have seemed that the easiest way for him to meet the crisis would have been to work out a program to substitute it for the ox. But this would foster dependence. As he said later: "You always have to keep your mind on the goal of their standing on their own feet."

Preventing the village from being tagged with a hostile or depreciating label was not so simple. Every effort was made to keep the village and individuals in it from appearing to have preferential advantages, especially from an economic point of view. Those who worked hard began to prosper; those who did not were not overprotected from the consequences of their lack of success—they lost land, or they did not have so much food, or they lived in poor housing.

Residents were free to leave at any time. If they could not succeed, they might return to an institution, or move to another village, but they were not rewarded. A temporary boost might be given at a time of hardship, but long-term subsidization—economically, psychologically, socially—was not granted. Thus, the people who survived became independent, although their chances may have seemed limited at the beginning.

The heterogeneous makeup of the population reduced the chances of labeling, too. The village was not organized for one type of institutional population. Those settled there were not identifiable by a single category of illness, deviancy, or other handicaps. As a result, the village did not become known as a "leper village" or a "lunatic village" or by some other such pejorative name. Nearby communities called the village "Li."

No criteria such as age, marital status, or family status were imposed, in order to predetermine the composition of the community. Possibly that is not completely accurate, for it was hoped that the population of the community would be diverse. For instance, some single individuals moved in, as well as families, which were in the majority. Some aged were included along with children, youth and young adults.

One of the most interesting households in the village forced me to examine the rigidity of our conceptions of rehabilitation. In this house lived three single men—a leper under drug treatment and two chronic schizophrenics who had been hospitalized at the mental hospital in Chiengmai for 14 and 15 years before transfer to Amphur Li. None of these three single men would have been able to survive alone outside an institution. The leper's feet almost prevented his walking; he had lost sight in one eye; and his hands had lost fingers and were no longer useful in work. The schizophrenics were withdrawn, hallucinating, confused and without vocational skills. But, living and working together, these three were able to sustain themselves successfully in the village.

They built a primitive house, and looked after themselves simply. They were also independent economically. The leper conceived a plan to make charcoal for sale in the community. Though unable to do the physical labor, he could plan and supervise the felling of the trees, the burial of the major branches and trunks in the coking pit, the burning, the packaging of the charcoal, and its marketing. The schizophrenics had no administrative abilities, but they were able to saw down the trees, bring them back to the ovens, trim them, and carry out the rest of the assignments from their leper friend. As a trio, they were independent; as individuals, they probably would have been beyond rehabilitation. No program oriented to rehabilitation of the single person could have accomplished this successful, if bizarre, adjustment requiring no further services than those available to any citizen. No one suggested this was easy, however. Before this successful combination had been achieved, several groups were tried.

On the basis of his experience, Wulff has formulated some notions—but no systematic theory—for a successful rehabilitation village. He expresses these in a series of aphorisms; as we bounced along in the jeep, I jotted down the following:

"Most government programs give too much help for too long; they never phase it out. The staff becomes entrenched and perpetuates the project. Medical people use health supervision as their rationale—but there are medical problems in every village. If a demonstration project in health care is needed, it should be separated from village development, and be independently run for a limited time. So also with community development projects: a community must not be built around a project; a project must take place in and eventually be removed from a community.

"You can't treat everyone equally, or the village becomes an institution. Individuals have different goals and abilities. If you gear your program to the most ambitious, the rest of the land will be underused; if you gear it to the poorest, half or more of the villagers will not have enough land; if geared to the middle, there will be frustration all through. You must give each one opportunity, but no 'share' that belongs to him alone. You don't want residents thinking each one has a certain amount of anything coming to him. When you ask him to stand in line for the same towel, the same soap, the same pill, the same bowl of rice, you reduce him to a number, and he has no way to measure his own accomplishment and worth.

"If you think far enough ahead, one good thing will lead to another. When we required the villagers to cut down the weeds around their homes for health reasons (against rats, mosquitoes, flies), they had to build toilets because they had no place to hide.

"When two houses burned down because fire jumped the river from a farmer's field on the other side, the Foundation refused to restore the houses. One resident went to the police, and demanded that the farmer pay 1200 baht. The farmer agreed to settle for 650. The other family wanted 400 baht, and are still negotiating through the local authorities. There is a precedent now. When I am gone, they will have a mechanism for solving such problems. If there had been no settlement from the farmer, I would have helped out, but only if it would have made the difference between remaining or leaving, success or failure. I would never have given enough for a complete restoration.

"To develop the incentive to work is more important in rehabilitation than to appeal to the incentive for ownership. This is the basis of the distribution of land according to the extent of its use. (The resident has an advantage in that he does not pay taxes, though this may, in the long run, turn out to be a handicap if the village earns a special identity because of freedom from taxes. In that case, the residents would have to be given ownership.)

"Policies that promote village independence must be strengthened, and those that work against it abandoned. You can't always know in advance what will work, but when you do know, you must use that knowledge.

"The residents may need assistance at first in devising ways to do work for the village, beyond farming their own land—building roads, bridges, irrigation ditches, and a government." Wulff started the pattern of government by organizing a committee. Soon he introduced the idea of elections, and an elected committee was functioning before his departure. He also initiated village meetings to settle problems of community operations.

"Any villager can call a meeting, though no one has the authority to make the residents participate. If enough people attend, the meeting is official and its deliberations have the force of law in the village. If the problems to be solved at these meetings are of major importance, community pressure to attend naturally builds."

Finally Wulff set forth the rules for his own role in tackling and solving problems during the organizational period:

"Each problem is different and must be approached as such. It is tempting to use solutions that worked out before, but they may be wrong.

"Investigate the facts behind a problem. You cannot take the original statement or complaint as the primary concern; it often conceals a deeper issue that is the real source of difficulty.

"Confer among the staff; residents will play one staff member off against another, often claiming that promises were made when, in fact, they were not.

"Each solution is a precedent; you must think ahead to what you want as the villagers' own solutions after you have gone.

"Give problem-solving responsibility to the villagers wherever possible, for they will be alone soon.

"Stall, if you don't know what to do.

"Official agencies and channels in other villages and in the district should be used for the new village if possible, to promote equality and interdependence."

The villages I have described, from indigenous communities to those constructed *de novo,* closely related to or completely separate from treatment facilities, have played strategic roles in the care and treatment of patients and families. They have been categorized as treatment centers; brief, protracted, or permanent domiciles; transitional settings; and centers for independent living.

SOME IMPLICATIONS

The village concept has its counterparts and its contrasts in the United States, where the terms *community* and *milieu* might be used as equivalents to *village.* We have seen communities become institutions, and institutions become cities. Domiciliary communities have grown up around hospitals to house patients and their families. We have used communities, in both the social and physical sense, for treatment purposes within institutions, and for organized programs to place patients outside.

Much but not all use of the community in our country has been casual, rather than preplanned. We have tended to plan medical services around individuals, rather than around families or the total community. We have not generally defined the functions we expect a community to perform, except in general terms. Commonly, the services in the community have been directed by single professions, for example, by physicians, or by social workers. Commonly, also, the services in the community have been organized to serve limited groups of patients, sometimes, regrettably, in constricted ways.

By classifying some types of communities, some basic operational characteristics, and various uses to which they are put, I have hoped to sharpen our awareness of actual and potential functions of the community in medical care. I had not meant to advance an exhaustive list of types and purposes, but to provide a simple and frequently obvious frame which we can expand and on which we can fasten our own experiences and projects. My expectation is that increasing awareness of our professional use of communities will permit us to become more imaginative and, at the same time, more purposive in expanding the functions which we shall ask them to perform in relation to treatment.

To use illustrations from abroad and from societies very different from ours has permitted the distance necessary for analysis, but was not meant to promote direct application of all the ideas they presented. The cultural settings in which the villages developed are so foreign to ours that attempts at direct transfer would be unlikely to succeed. Nevertheless, translations, in which adaptations suited to our conditions would be proposed, might be feasible and desirable.

More valuable than modification of existing patterns, however, would be the effort to move from the principles underlying village programs abroad to formulation of concrete applications related to purposes intended in a designated setting elsewhere. Toward this end, then, some discussion of principles and issues that might form bases for creative program development would seem in order.

The Community as a Limit

Each of the communities (villages) abroad could be circumscribed geographically, and in terms of the people who resided there. Each community carried a name that specified its identity. From this has emerged the first principle, as follows: *A community* within which we shall offer medical services and for which we are planning *must be identified and delimited.* For ourselves, we must lift the concept of village, or community, out of its rural and foreign reference, and recognize that in our urban situation we may be talking about units as large as a megalopolis, and as small as two houses on a lane. We may think of town, neighborhood, suburb, inner city, school or health district, an institution, and various other geographical and population areas as community. And, just as the community may be described in terms of a place; so also, it can be seen in terms of relationships among people where the social links may be close, such as in a family or village, or remote as in a large apartment complex or on a main city street.

As we discuss the use of the community, we must think of the variety of units that it is possible to identify, and how program adaptations would be affected by shifts from one unit into another. For instance, to think of placement of individuals or families in the inner city for access to clinical facilities involves a different application of imagination than to picture their location in a suburban motel, or on a farm development near an institution. Ultimately, such reflections should lead to clear specification of the community within and for which medical service plans are being made.

Indigenous or Constructed Communities

The history of the origin of each community, at least in general terms, is readily apparent. Its uses for medical services relate strongly to that historical starting point. A simple proposition suggested itself. We have to *select between using an indigenous community or constructing a community* from inception. Program development will differ in each instance.

If we are to use an already existing community, we must learn about it, study and acknowledge its history and traditions, prepare it for our work, educate its citizens, utilize its developed motivations, reduce its anxiety, help it to solve its problems, deal with its government and leaders, and ensure its satisfactions. To accomplish these steps we relate to the people of the community and their leaders, especially through existing political instruments and persons.

If we plan to construct a community, we confront a markedly different set of factors. We have to determine the boundaries of the community, attend to the tension that will arise in relation to the people and organized groups or communities beyond, decide about the admission, orientation, and integration of individuals into the community, and, if intended, prepare for the release of members from the community and their rehabilitation elsewhere.

Some features of use are present whether the community is indigenous or constructed. Government is one example, since it is always necessary. There must be persons to govern, governing power, and mechanisms to wield it. The origin of the community may determine the manner in which it is governed, but that will not modify the necessity for government. Prior to the development of the medical services program, the nature and functioning of the government must be learned, or planned. The government will relate to the total life of the community; the medical services to those parts of the life of persons wherein such services are necessary for health, diagnosis, treatment, recovery from illness, and rehabilitation.

Whom to Serve

In some of the village communities all residents were being served medically; in other, only a portion were directly served, and others helped to make up the total community. In principle, we have to *determine the population we shall serve* medically. We have to predetermine those whom we shall choose to recognize for our medical programs. In general we shall move people into or identify them within a community.

The most obvious basis of choice would be to select an homogeneous population—all prisoners, all mentally retarded, all deaf, all juvenile delinquents, all cerebral-palsied. We think of other possibilities less frequently and perhaps too seldom—choosing the population by fixing the percentage of an homogeneous disturbed group in a normal population (a number of disturbed children in a normal classroom); a mixture of several deviant groups (mentally retarded, physically handicapped, emotionally disturbed, cerebral-palsied); a sprinkling of one disturbed population (chronic schizophrenics) in a large group of another (mentally retarded); a few normals (volunteers) in a large group of deviants (juvenile delinquents) and many other combinations.

One of the most difficult of all the steps that we take in choosing the population we shall seek to help is to break away from our stereotyped ways of finding and dealing with people. In our culture, we are so oriented toward the individual that we must discipline ourselves to think of people in groups and mixtures. Who would have chosen to throw a leper and two chronic schizophrenics together in rehabilitation? Yet from a social point of view, there is profound identity—they are among the most rejected and removed of men. We need to seek those links that bind men together in need and purpose, regardless of traditional categories and labels. Through the search for these elusive bonds, strengths may be accentuated and weaknesses overcome—and we may find new modes of access to the people for whom we are planning.

It became obvious, especially in constructed communities, that the medical authorities allowed to grow, or provided, an environment within which persons satisfy primary life-sustaining requirements from moment to moment. Characteristic of each community is that it works out a pattern of interaction within which people meet their basic human needs, and seek to enrich the quality of life, as through using medical services. The ways in which food, shelter, cleanliness, health, sexual gratification, reproduction, security, sleep, recreation, work, self-preservation, group memberships, learning, worship, dying are handled become articulated into an organic whole that gives each community its identity. To initiate and continue a community *basic human needs must be met.*

This leads to another simple proposition: There can be no perfect community in respect to the satisfaction of all human needs. A community's vibrancy comes, in part, from the tensions created by its inadequacies. These may not pass a certain point, however, without threatening a community's existence. Some efforts to create communities, too, never succeed because they cannot convince people that enough basic deficiencies will be overcome to preserve a balance weighted on the side of gratification.

In measuring gratification, the force of custom is strong. Indigenous villages have an advantage in this regard, because a familiar, though not complete, pattern of life achievement has been worked out historically. Where a community is being constructed, attention must be given to the relationships between the community in which a person lives at the present, and the communities in which he has lived before, especially in childhood. If one has moved to a new community, the transition is easiest if the communities are alike in most essentials, as when the lepers construct villages like those from which they are exiled. The community from which one comes is a standard for the evaluation of subsequent ones, and one usually seeks to recreate communities he has known.

After living in an alien community long enough to work out a way of life, one may find the return to a former community difficult. This is the basis of institutionalization or acculturation. The speed of the process is related to the satisfactions in the new setting, and also to the length of exposure. To facilitate rehabilitation from an environment rich in rewards, the time in a community should be brief. Otherwise, after a long period in such a community, the rewards for transfer beyond it must be extremely strong.

Thus, the use of the community must take into account the basic needs it will serve, the ways they will be met, the integrated whole created thereby, and its relationships to the known past and the anticipated future.

Medical Service Goals

Each observed community provided the base for a medical program. No program was limitless. Each set out to achieve certain goals, some specified in advance of services, some emerging as programs developed, and some taken for granted and not brought to the level of being named. This leads to the obvious principle that we must *define the goals for the medical services.*

This is not hard if we set up such goals as "total cure," "complete recovery," "return to normalcy," "full rehabilitation," where we are moving toward aims that are somewhat global and are left unqualified so they approach absolutes. The particularly difficult decisions are in regard to partial goals. To select them requires a recognition of one's limitations, and one may not care to accept these, even when honest about what can be expected reasonably. One may fear, also, that limited aims may result in reduced accomplishment. Often one may find himself saying in retrospect that he did not really believe he would achieve more. To move from after-the-event realism to before-the-event anticipation would be a significant gain, permitting orientation of the program in the direction of limited goals, perhaps more precise determination of procedures, greater economy in practice, and, thus, more surety of results. It could provide criteria for selection of the population to be served, more rapid recognition of progress or failure of individuals to achieve our aims for them, and earlier attention to the development of alternate plans for those who fail to profit.

But, medical programs will vary in the possibilities of prediction of the impact of treatment programs, depending on the particular illnesses and symptoms. For example, in the mental illnesses, prognosis is still a most imprecise art. For those who have illnesses where changes of patient status are frequent, often the best that can be done is to plan treatment in advance for a brief period, and adjust the plans on the basis of ongoing evaluations, even though broad outlines for a long-term treatment program may seem desirable. For those whose status changes slowly, long-term plans seem advisable.

The Functions of the Professional

In each community visited, the professional persons had been assigned, or had taken, certain roles, and were performing a definable set of functions that differentiated them from other persons in the community. This led to still another principle: The *roles and duties of professional persons* among people in the community *must be specified and developed.* If a professional identifies with the others in the community as a citizen, he has given up his professional role. A characteristic of the professional is his specialization of functions in regard to others. He sets forth (professes) some qualities, skills, proficiency, learning and motivation that distinguish him. Colloquially, "he hangs out his shingle."

The range of specialization is a matter of training, experience, or demand for his services. It also relates to his decisions about the methods and scope of his activities. Villages abroad have shown how some professionals take over more and more direction, government, and power in the total life of the village; or, in the converse, withdraw progressively from authority, responsibility, and activity. The decisions the professional makes about what he will do, how, when, and for how long, are not made apart from the goals he sets before him.

If the professional is striving for the maximum control over the factors in an individual's life, and in the corporate life of the community, he will transform it into an institution, as Lambo has tended to do. In an institution, the professional role allows and sanctions assumptions of governing powers. If a professional chooses to promote maximum independence of the community and its citizens, well and ill, he will keep his professional role clearly separate from roles appropriate for community members. If, for purposes of demonstration, he has taken on the functions of a nonprofessional member, he will progressively withdraw, leaving the job of meeting people's needs as far as possible to others, as Wulff did in Amphur Li.

Insofar as the professional's functions are consciously determined, and they may be to a major extent, he will seek to structure the possibilities for himself as finely as possible, and complement his use of himself by the ways in which a community, itself, serves those within it.

The Organized Program

To organize a program of medical services is usually complex. Medical programs are fluid as they adapt to changing needs, populations, goals, techniques, personnel and other resources, and the history of accomplishments in each community. It was possible, nevertheless, to determine in each community visited that there existed a formed program within which services were being provided.

Sometimes this program was described in writing, but more often it was defined in a regular pattern of operations. Stating this observation as a principle, one may say: In using the community as a base, a *program for medical services must be organized.*

If one transfers an individual from a community into a private office, where the professional deals with him alone, the multiple variables of community, population, goals, professional functions can be established into a program relatively easily. This *clinical* approach to program development is never removed from influences in the community, although it may function as if independent of them, and may not need constant adaptation to community factors.

In contrast, a program of medical services consciously established in and for a community seems massive, messy, and unmanageable. It requires a quantity and quality of organization that challenges some, and frightens others. Not every clinician would make a good community program director, a good superintendent of a hospital, or a good public health officer. Nor does training for clinical practice necessarily prepare a professional for the intellectual, volitional, interpersonal, and managerial aspects of community programming. However, the qualities needed in clinical work are not necessarily alien to the community practitioner, nor are the activities in using a community in professional ways beyond the potential skills of the clinician, no matter how foreign they may seem.

What has to be accepted is that program development requires a multiplicity of informed decisions—all oriented to the goals which must be specified. These decisions may not be absolute or final, for, once they have been made and acted upon, the conditions change. Evaluation and new decisions follow. Temperamentally, the professional in the community must be able to endure, if not enjoy, change. He must find rewards and excitement in action processes, as well as in the achievement of goals. But, he must also find time for the reflection, criticism, and planning that follow and precede steps in action.

The Rewards

It seems appropriate to talk about rewards, although this is a matter which is often ignored. The consequences of the professional use of the community may and must be *benefits for* the *community,* for particular *individuals and groups within it, and* for *the professional* himself. But rewards for each of these many parties may vary and be in opposition to those of others. The professional who is pleased when his patient can go home may arouse the ire of the family—frequently reported in Africa after a child's illness had left him disfigured or handicapped. A family that is delighted that an ancient member is admitted to an extended care facility, may become subject to criticism from the aging person's friends. The community group that has worked for years to open a clinic, may be more than dismayed that those who need its help do not come to its doors. Nevertheless, to the extent possible it is important to see that the people affected in medical programs find gratifications for their involvement. Typically, the outcome in some manner balances satisfactions and frustrations. When all are pleased, a rare combination of rewards has been attained.

Summary

Generalizing from a series of observations of villages, several commonsense principles for use of a community for medical services were formulated. They are not highly original, but, rather, general statements of precepts to bear in mind in planning practical programs and steps in organizing and using medical services in a community. In review, they are:

A community must be identified and delimited.

We have to select between using an indigenous community or constructing a community.

We have to determine the population to be served medically.

Basic human needs must be met.

We must define the goals for the medical services.

The roles and duties of professional persons must be specified and developed.

A program for medical services must be organized.

Benefits for the community, individuals and groups within it, and for the professional himself, must be attained.

SUMMARY TABLE

To suggest how the above statements may be related to the communities described earlier, a schematic summary table follows. Because of its schematic nature, it is not possible to indicate minor qualifications that would modify the characterizations of the communities. For example, in the case of the last community, Amphur Li, a new resident moving there in the future may also receive basic provisions initially, though basic provisions are no longer provided in any way for the general residents. To clarify the tabulation for any community, it would be necessary to refer back to the earlier description.

Summary Table

Characteristics of Community Medical Programs

Community	General Program Goals	Origins		Population Served		Basic Provisions		Duties of Professionals		Locale for Medical Services	
		Indig.	Constr.	Part	Total	From Community	From Medical Program	Med. Services	Govt	In Community	Out of Community
Aro (Lambo)	Acute treatment; domicile (temp.)	X		X		X	X	X	X	X	
Aro (Asuni)	Domicile (temp.)	X		X		X		X	X		X
Belly Camp	Domicile (temp.)		X		X	X		X			X
Kano Lepros.	Treatment; domicile (perm.)		X		X		X	X	X	X	
FOSA	Treatment; domicile (perm.)		X	X			X	X	X	X	
Institut, Kinshasa	Transit. to rehab.		X	X		X		X			X
Transit. Fac. Lusaka	Transit. to rehab.	X	X	X		X		X	X		X
Amphur Li	Rehab. (perm.)		X	X Initial	Final	X Final	X Initial		X Initial		

Chapter XVI

The Family in
Clinic, Hospital,
and Community

In conclusion, let me speak autobiographically, putting the ideas, activities, interests, and convictions I have set forth here into the framework of their development. No presentation of a field of study and work, such as I have tried to record in this book, is far removed from the author's self.

At this point in time, I am impressed by signs that the family is being taken into account in new ways in many places in our nation. Within recent years the American Medical Association established a specialty of family medicine. Over 10 years ago, the American Bar Association developed its Section of Family Law. This stimulated the modernizing, improvement, and planning for the future of family courts and laws about divorce, marriage, and children. The Group

365

for the Advancement of Psychiatry (1970, 1970), has issued two important publications on the family. Family destroying features of our welfare system are being purged out of legislation and regulations. The provisions of programs for public development of housing, inadequate as they are, include increasing attention to their effect on families, their location, and relocation.

I note little attention, as yet, to issues about the family in the official councils of professional organizations such as the American Psychological Association where I have found my primary professional affiliation. Nevertheless, there has been a growing recognition that behavioral scientists will be called on increasingly for expert opinion in this field. For example, Foster (1969), writing on "The Future of Family Law" in the Annals of the American Academy of Political and Social Sciences, concluded by saying:

> The family law of the future will be more responsive to the insights and theories of behavioral science, and should become increasingly humanistic. . . . The relevant theories and findings of psychology, psychiatry, and sociology will find a more favorable audience in legislative halls and courtrooms where decisions are made regarding the regulation of human behavior. . . . Assuming that we survive on this planet, the family law of the twenty-first century should have evolved according to the progress of behavioral science and the felt needs of our people. (pp. 143–44)

Toward increasing the involvement of psychologists with the family, I have felt a special obligation to share what families have taught me, to put into words matters that lie close to me and that may be useful to psychologists and the public as a whole. But the family is also of central importance to many other professional associations, with some of which, in public health, maternal and child health, family education and research, and pastoral counseling, I have identified.

PRECURSORS OF FAMILY RESEARCH

The center of my research for nearly a quarter of a century has been on the family. The interest in this group did not arise *de novo* when I began to develop family group therapy. I have often tried to analyze the early childhood factors that may have been crucial in my choice to work with the family. It had its origins partly in my own family life in Canada, and possibly lives out many values represented in the Canadian culture, at least of those days. In my brief career in the active ministry, after a spell in mining camps in the frozen north, part of my responsibility became parish-visiting associated with the largest church in western Canada. I had the unique privilege of meeting and being in the homes of nearly 4,000 families representing all levels in a city of 50,000 people. Such an experience with normal families is seldom available to psychologists. I knew the most needy and the wealthiest; the youngest and the oldest; the healthiest and the most ill; the powerful and the weak. I knew them under all circumstances, at work and play, at birth, marriage, illness, and death. They are presented to you in my work with the family.

Training in clinical psychology and the first 10 years of my practice in psychotherapy (before I began to experiment with family therapy) fostered my interest in and concern about the family environment, out of which disturbed people were coming to me. In sorting some ancient papers recently, I unearthed a series of talks that I gave on the radio in the 1940's, based on child pathology and treatment. I was interested to observe the extent to which my remarks revealed identification with the parents and sympathy for their plight. Primarily, however, I showed concern about the children. In psychotherapy I was concentrating my efforts on the child. I was following the fashion of attributing most of the child's problems to inadequacies of his parents. This was before the concept of family therapy had entered my mind.

THE FAMILY IN THE CLINIC

In 1951 the idea of seeing the whole family as a group came into focus. As indicated earlier, family group therapy did not start in the form in which I now think of it. The family was brought together, but the therapeutic effort was directed toward the child referred for help. At that time, the parents were seen somewhat as an audience for the therapy drama, somewhat as co-therapists. The aim was to

deepen their understanding of their child, and to give them background for planning appropriate steps toward a solution of their
child's problems. The major shift in my work, then, was to include
the family members physically in the treatment. This centrifugal expansion of my contact with and around a patient allowed me to study
a variety of new experiences, some based on problems, some on
achievements. These drew my attention to the family as a whole
group, and began to challenge the ways I explained psychopathology.

A SHIFT IN PERSPECTIVE

As the first chapter in this book shows, when I read the first
paper on family group therapy in 1953, I did not present the concept
of relating to the family as a unit. I was already defining many of the
techniques that have stuck with me in my clinical work since that
time. Conceptually, I had not arrived at the point of recognizing that
I could deal primarily with the total unit of the family seen as a
gestalt. I was still conceiving that the child was the primary unit in
the larger context of the physical presence of the family.

Two years later, at the time I wrote the manuscript for the second
chapter I was saying: "The method of therapy emerges from one basic
assumption differentiating it from individual therapy: *the family is the
unit to be treated.*" The period before writing that publication demonstrates well how firmly bounded I also was in ways of acting and of
structuring interpretations of my relationships in psychotherapy, for
it took me three or four years to learn to put the new idea of the family
as a group alongside the idea of the family members as individuals.
Now it seems easy for me to shift back and forth in my mind between
these two ways of seeing the family—on one side as a conglomerate,
on the other as a total unit. It is just as easy to see diads, triads, or
other multiples. The families taught me how. They showed me how
each event reverberated within the whole family, within each individual, and beyond the family where it touches the community. Since
the whole system is so interrelated and complex and since I became so
embedded in it, I had to learn that I was selecting out what I was
seeing, and knowing that, to recognize that I was free to choose what
I would look at.

At the time I did not realize what an intellectually releasing experience this was. Now I can give a name to the shift back and forth that became possible—I had moved from the exclusive dealing with a statistical concept of behavior where, because I was a clinical psychologist, the "n" normally stood for the number of "whole" persons, to using also a biorganic systemic mode of looking at behavior. According to the latter approach, behavior then became observable and explicable in terms of the unit I chose to carve out of its surrounding environment with which, in fact, it was always in relation.

THE THERAPIST IN THE GROUP

Corresponding with this point of view grew the recognition that in the family therapy sessions, I was as firmly integrated into the situations as were the family members. Thus, statements I might make about the behavior of the family now became for me what I said when I chose to look upon them as though functioning in isolation from me, or to look upon what was happening in the larger group of which I was inescapably a member. Now I knew the limits of pronouncements made about the family by those speaking as though they were outside the sphere of the family's relationships. But I also learned at firsthand the hazards of trying to observe one's self in a group with family members, achieving a new kind of realism for evaluating the statements of individuals or informants about family members and their significance: I could accept what was said at face value; I could question what might have been said if an individual and another person were each telling his story to the other; and I could speculate what might happen if they were both together with me.

VARIATIONS IN FAMILIES

During this same period of growth I came to learn and cope with the tremendous range of variation in family organization and functioning that families found acceptable and desirable to themselves. The statistical norms produced by family sociologists and other social scientists or the Census Bureau and other such organizations, emerged not as messages about stereotypes but as frameworks within which diversity could be revealed. Mathematics of permutations and combinations should have prepared me somewhat for this; the psychology of individual differences and personality should also have alerted me; but during the early days of direct exposure to the family unit, I required of myself a tight ordering of my growing knowledge. Only later did I learn to accept that American families live together by choice in many divergent ways, seemingly as disparate as the separate cultures across the world.

FAMILY TIES

Further, I learned about the bond within families and its importance for personal individuation. When I worked in the New York School for Boys at Warwick in 1940, I noted how frequently runaways were brought back immediately, because the officers had the good sense to check at the boys' homes. No matter how disordered the family, how brutalizing the environment, most young escapees headed home by the quickest route. I often recalled this when families were discussing the hellish side of their home-life in therapy hours. It kept reminding me that there were firm walls surrounding the turmoil, anger, and disorganization. And, I experienced over and over how the exposure of the hostility and hurts cleansed the family and allowed concealed affection, love, dependence, and respect to shine within the same walls.

PERSONAL INDEPENDENCE

An intriguing question in regard to this family bond was posed at the first professional report on my work. I remember that a close friend, psychologist Pauline Vorhaus, raised a highly pertinent issue in the discussion period: if family therapy were resulting in firming up the positive bonds in the family, what would happen with teenagers who, more than anything else, needed to learn to assert their independence and gain their freedom? I do not remember how I answered the question then, except probably to report that the teenagers seemed to gain freedom instead of entrapment. The question kept plaguing me, but gradually I arrived at a position to explain the seeming paradox that the more visibly positive and close the family bonds, the greater the freedom.

I developed no fancy theory but a firm conviction that has become a prevailing moral position with me—that every person, to progress toward the filling out of selfhood, must belong firmly and closely to at least one *small* group of others, and that selfhood is not achieved in isolation, but by action in relations where self is affirmed. I found immense support for this position in the contributions of philosopher John Macmurray, my colleague in leading the weekly seminars held jointly by the Departments of Philosophy and Psychology at Edinburgh, when I was teaching there. Later, in publications (1957, 1961), he elaborated his position that interpersonal action has primacy and that selfhood is derived from relations—a rebuke to the self-preoccupation of the existentialists and some humanists.

THE CHANGING FAMILY

The idea was later to prove particularly helpful to me in accepting diversity in families and in avoiding the bias that family members are doomed to pathology—social, familial, personal, and even somatic —unless the parents relate in conformity to an idealized or a statistically normal picture of a marriage, and bring up their children in predefined "mentally healthy" ways. Family therapy brought the relevance of the family and the multiplicity of its forms and ways of functioning out into the open. It prepared me for the idea that the family is changing significantly, and will continue to change. It pointed out for me, though, that what is described as the "changed" family is to quite an extent the picture that has emerged from public acceptance of diversity present all along. In other words, what has changed has not been the structures or operations of families so much as public exposure of what existed and greater general tolerance for what has been revealed.

In one way, though, it seems to me there is an increase in experimental family living, through conscious and open rejection of common family forms, and deliberate adoption of variant family patterns. I am impressed in California with the extent to which interactional patterns from families in other cultures are being incorporated into the way young families are living. However, much of this is dramatic posing, likely to catch the public eye and thus to lead to extreme statements in public, such as "The family is dead"—a few years ago it was "God"—or, less extremely, "The family is deteriorating and on the way out." I don't personally believe that. The proportion of adults who are now married in our country is higher than it has ever been—and many of those who are not officially married are living in familylike groups—even identifying in these groups the persons who play roles of mother, father, or dependents. Even if the family so changes that it becomes archaic to use the term "family," it surely is of human nature to develop in groups, to belong to groups, to need small groups, and as Harlow has proposed and Hebb has shown, to perish in isolation.

THE VALUE OF THE PRACTITIONER

It became plain to me, also, that man never lives in groups without turmoil, whether the group is family or some other. It is relevant that there should be practitioners who seek to unravel the interpersonal conflicts, to help people together to decide the ways they wish their interrelationships to develop, and to assist them in trial, error, and accomplishment of their plans. Thus family therapy has seemed to me a sufficiently important activity to lead me to spend many years in its promotion and improvement. It led me also to concern about the indications of failure in some attempts to use the therapy.

THE FAMILY IN THE HOSPITAL

I became increasingly conscious that family therapy, effective and instructive in outpatient settings, had not yielded comparable benefits in the inpatient settings of the hospital. It had been tried by many therapists in hospitals. As reports of efforts to use family therapy techniques there began to come in over succeeding years, it grew on our awareness that it was effective only in occasional instances. My concern about this shifted the direction of my research career in 1963.

REASONS FOR FAILURE

As I began to analyze the reasons for the difficulties in using family therapy in the hospital, I concentrated on what happened to the family as a unit during hospitalization. I saw a contrast with the clinic setting. The family came to the clinic from living together at home and staying in the same place geographically, even though not necessarily in effective interaction. In the hospital, the patient was physically with the family only on occasion, as when the relatives came to the facility, or when the patient might be out on leave. We were dealing with a group disrupted in the physical and time sequences of their interrelations. The patient was housed in a building away from home. He was expected, by staff in the hospital, to become actively and intensively engaged in relations with people who seldom had more than superficial contact with the rest of the family members. To come to the therapy session he came from his ward; the rest of the family came from home. At the end of the session, the patient returned to his ward and the relatives went their own way. Nothing could more vividly show the dislocation of the family, nor the extent of labeling of the patient. Nothing could more vividly direct the attention of all those in the therapy session to the patient's problems, to the patient as a problem, and sometimes to the patient as the only problem. Nothing could make it harder to convey the concept that the family was the unit under treatment. The progress of the therapy was slowed. In the outpatient setting, the greater part of the therapeutic work had been found to take place in the hours and days between sessions, rather than during the conferences themselves. Of course, this was not possible for the separated family group.

Other reasons were developed to account for the failures with family therapy in the hospital. I thought of such matters as the nature of the patient's illness, the competence of the therapist, the antecedents of the decision to hospitalize, but these I did not expand in my own thought. Rather, I soon found myself looking at the whole issue of family-hospital relations, expanding the unit of my attention from the family to the family-hospital articulation; in effect, seeing the family and the hospital as a single unit. Such a unit is unbelievably complex, and perhaps I was foolhardy to attempt an approach to describing and understanding it.

THE FAMILY-HOSPITAL UNIT

As I went to the literature to discover what was known about this unit, I discovered a relative dearth of report and a virtual absence of any scientific analysis of its nature. A few authors had described programs in which they had observed a close family-hospital interaction. In 1948 Main (1958), in Britain, began to allow family members to live in with patients at the Cassel Hospital. In India, at the Vellore Mental Health Center, Kolmeyer and Fernandes (1963) found a small mental hospital where family members were required to accompany patients; they described their observations at the Toronto meeting of the American Psychiatric Association in 1962. Some pediatric hospitals had moved to active inclusion of parents during the hospitalization of children—more so in Britain than on this continent—but there was virtually no major research to analyze these family-institution relationships. I read, however, a number of interesting anecdotes showing that relatives attend patients full-time in hospitals in almost three quarters of the world. I found that no one had systematically studied these relationships.

A STUDY

When I proposed a study of the family-hospital unit to the Director of NIMH, he accepted its potential importance for suggesting models by which the isolation of patients from their families during hospitalization might be diminished and by which institutionalization could be reduced. He agreed also, that rehabilitation to the home might be speeded up and accomplished much more efficiently, if family-hospital relations were better understood. This set me forth on a project which has resulted in a recent book (Bell, 1970). The publication reports an investigation of a large number of hospitals of different kinds in the developing countries. To place this study in the context of my professional career may perhaps make public in another way the unfolding of my work.

When I had the opportunity to study situations in which it was commonly a practice for family members to be in full-time attendance at the hospital, many factors, that facilitate or deter family participation there, were uncovered. For example, in these hospitals family members carried over from home those roles and functions that were typical of normal domestic relationships. They did not come to the hospital as guests of the patients, but to do family work. Both families and hospitals prevented disruption of the customary family relations.

IMPLICATIONS IN DEMONSTRATIONS

Such an observation opened a whole new way of thinking about professional intervention in family-hospital relations. Now we have designed a number of demonstrations where verbal therapy is no longer the basic pattern for professional assistance to hospitalized patients and their families. A simple illustration might illumine this point: In the California mental hospitals there is an unduly high rate of hospitalization for Mexican-American patients. The family relations among the Mexican-Americans are very close, and the motivation of family members to visit and take part in the patient's life at the hospital, is high. Nevertheless, relatives tend not to be more obviously involved with their patients than families of Blacks or other population groups. At the same time, we know that there is frustration among many of the Mexican-Americans over dietary changes imposed on them at the hospital They miss their tacos, chile, beans. It did not take much imagination to suggest a role for family members that would be easy, inexpensive, and deeply significant, namely, feeding of the patient by the prearranged periodic bringing of meals to the hospital. We have assumed the experiment did not need to be based on total provision of a Mexican diet, since even occasional feeding could symbolize the whole domestic life. The design of the experiment was the easiest part.

To implement it has introduced difficulties which we have not yet been able to overcome. One of them that offers especially difficult problems is that the State Hospital Code specifies that "a diet consisting of a variety of foods of good quality shall be provided . . . not less than three meals shall be served daily." This is obviously a sensible specification from the points of view of survival, nutrition and sanitation. But some hospital superintendents interpreted this code as restricting the bringing of food into the hospital, even though the State Department of Public Health has always regarded the regulation as permissive. We are pushing ahead to revise this misinterpretation. From a humane point of view, I trust that a change here will be as significant for the welfare of the patients as promoting family therapy with a whole series of Mexican-American families. I do not denigrate the latter—I use the illustration to point up how the shift of my focus to the family-hospital unit led into new insights and action.

FAMILY HOPTEL, CHILDREN'S HOSPITAL AT STANFORD

Some time ago, in my class on *The Family in the Hospital* at the Stanford Medical School, we made a class project out of another opportunity for affecting the family-hospital field. At the nearby Children's Hospital at Stanford, the director had planned to convert an abandoned residence for nurses into a family live-in unit, to allow children who are ill, but do not require full-time nursing care, to benefit from the familiar care of the mother and father, rather than from staff who do not know them so well. Such children would include those who were visiting a clinic for an extended period of diagnosis, follow-up examination, or out-patient treatment. The unit was also proposed as a temporary domicile for the relatives of children who are in-patients. My class worked hard to define some of the program possibilities that should be kept in mind by the architect in remodeling the building. To bring the plan into operation took three years, primarily in order to secure the necessary funds. When the Hoptel finally opened on April 1, 1973, the first occupant of a room was a patient's father on welfare, who had slept in his car on previous visits.

Eight rooms of the projected 16-bed unit were opened, and all were full by the end of the first month. Since that time reservations normally extend into the succeeding few weeks. Various family combinations have used the rooms—patient with a parent, most frequent; parents together; relatives other than parents, such as a grandmother; and parents with well siblings of long-hospitalized patients.

Mostly the rooms contain two beds, but one room has four. The rates are kept low so as to encourage family members to come; rates are adjusted to family income. A breakthrough in financing occurred recently when the State Crippled Children's Service authorized payment for room and board for a parent and child, when the latter is able to live in the Hoptel and receive medical services as an outpatient in the Hospital's clinics. Linen and some housekeeping services are supplied. The building has a common living-room next to a small snack kitchen. Most guests eat in the hospital cafeteria; but occasionally some eat at nearby restaurants. An automatic washer and dryer are provided. Schooling is available for children who stay longer than one week.

Staff are looking ahead to a systematic evaluation of the impact of the Hoptel on the program of the hospital, where a parent has long had the chance to sleep right on the ward or in the room where his child is an inpatient. Staff have been impressed by the demand for Hoptel rooms, and are anticipating its forthcoming expansion to complete the original plan. They have become convinced that, for families who can be housed in this unit, the hospital will ensure a quality of living and an environment that will almost always exceed the very humane inpatient services now provided by a sensitive staff. They would find it hard to argue with one mother who said: "After all, a nurse's skill cannot mend a child's broken heart, only a mother can do this, because there is nothing in the world like a mother's love, when a child is ill and upset" (MacCarthy & MacKeith, 1965).

FAMILY FOCUS, STANFORD UNIVERSITY MEDICAL CENTER

Another project, Family Focus, ensued on planning by Katherine F. Shepard, an instructor in the Division of Physical Therapy in the Stanford School of Medicine. When she was my student, early in our first class session I asked, "Where is the family in physical therapy?" She replied, "It isn't, at least very much, but it should be!" This shaped her project assignment for the quarter, to plan how to put the family in physical therapy. An outstanding program plan led to a successful application for a grant to fund an innovative five-year training project, now into its fourth year.

The goals of the project, with which I have been proud to be associated, are to train physical therapy students to expanded professional roles in patient evaluation, treatment planning, collaboration and consultation with other health personnel, and working with families. This last objective is being realized by providing opportunities for students "to obtain knowledge and develop skills in providing transfer of the essential elements in continuity of patient care to the family and in effecting reintegration of the disabled patient back into his family setting, specifically:

1. To recognize the importance of and obtain knowledge in training the family to assume carryover of physical therapy skills needed to maintain the health status and functional independence of the patient;

2. To understand the impact of physical disability on the patient and his family and to obtain knowledge in assisting the patient and his family to cope with the physical, psychoemotional, and interpersonal ramifications of physical disability *before* the patient leaves the hospital setting.

A distinctive feature of the project has been the establishing of a training laboratory in a modular home on the grounds of the Medical Center near Hoover Pavilion, one of the Stanford hospitals. The home sleeps six without bringing in additional cots. It consists of a living room, family room with eating area, kitchen, bedroom, and bath. A second bedroom, adjacent to all rooms except the family bedroom and bath, was converted into an office for the project and observation room for students.

Three days before a planned discharge, a handicapped patient receiving physical therapy treatment is transferred into the home. He remains as an in-patient, occupying an officially designated in-patient bed, and has nursing and other medical services as needed during his stay. As he moves from the ward, his family comes from home to live with him. Some families who have hired a housekeeper to help the patient at home have arranged for the housekeeper to stay at the house also. This allows her and the patient a trial period to explore their compatibility and a chance to test the demands of the relationship. Families provide physical care, learn to carry out the physical therapy, nursing, dietary, and other treatment procedures that will be their responsibility soon, when they all return home.

During training sessions for physical therapy students, and others, the family opens the drapes on their side of the one-way mirrors, and plugs in the microphones for sound, so students may observe treatment and family problem-solving procedures. On many occasions, advanced physical therapy students conduct the treatments while observed by their instructors and family advisers, who later lead seminars discussing the treatments, interpersonal relations, and family-specific functional methods of coping with their difficulties.

The impact of the training in this homelike setting on the physical therapy curriculum has been immense. It has helped to lift student attention from concentration on physical techniques to sensitive concern and assistance for the people being treated and for the relatives who must adjust in major ways to the patient's new status as a person with a handicap. Close work with the relatives makes realistic the strengths they possess and the difficulties they must overcome to help successfully in the patient's daily living at home and in rehabilitation.

Although it had been hoped that patients of all ages would be seen in the house, the greater number of those transferred there have been older adults, some of whom have had terminal illnesses. Staff have gradually come to acknowledge an advantage here. Students have been helped to identify with and relate to geriatric patients and their families. They have lived through crises, perplexities, disappointments, frustrations, and death with the families. They have come to admire the families' inventiveness, capacities to learn, and motivations to overcome problems. They are better prepared, as a consequence, for the projected demographic shift toward a higher proportion of older adults in future populations. The advantage of exposure to older patients may change however, for there is an increasing acceptance of the Family Focus program throughout the whole hospital, and transfer of younger patients to the house is becoming more frequent.

Controlled evaluation of the effect of the period in the house on patients and their relatives is being conducted through follow-up visits to the homes of experimental and control patients and families. Only clinical impressions of the effects of the time in the house are now at hand. It is common that moving to the house confirms the prospects of returning home. The first night in the house is often a time of much anxiety, however. The demands on family members for care and treatment seem frightening and the fear of an emergency (for which tested procedures are well developed) leads them to pay especial attention to instruction about how to get help. Requests for help are infrequent, considering that the patient is adjudged to need still the services available during full hospitalization; most family members find ways to deal with difficulties that arise. Sometimes, however, they must have the feeling expressed by one of the students that being in the house is "like all being shipwrecked together," a feeling that probably would have been intensified had the patient been sent straight home from the hospital.

Relatives are often uncertain that they will be able to pick up the techniques for managing the patient (turning him in bed, helping him to a wheelchair, transferring him to a commode or a chair, bathing him, managing a colostomy, and so on) or for building his capacities to overcome his physical limitations. Teaching by individualized oral explanation, especially in response to questions by the patient or his family, and by demonstration are carried through usually to the point where techniques are successfully mastered by family members. The particular problems that are troubling the patient and other family members are brought out into the open: What if I fall to the floor? Can I get her from the car up the stairs into our home? Will I be able to do my own hair? Can we manage the respirator? How will we ever remember the times and how many of all these pills? Will he ever be able to get out of bed? What about sex? How will I get help?

Clinical physical therapists and students contrast this method of developing competence with methods used in other settings where family members are expected to learn skills for home treatment and care—where sometimes they have a chance for only a brief observation of a physical therapist conducting a treatment, or short, verbal generalized instruction prior to the patient's discharge.

Students see at firsthand and are sensitized to how important family relations are in affecting patients, how hard they may work to help themselves, and how willing they are to be helped. Students remember how one patient relaxed when his spouse began to pick up new ways of helping; how another tensed up and continued more easily able to respond to staff than to a family member. Ways by which family members support or irritate one another become readily visible. Individual differences in patient and family skills and learning are dramatically revealed; students analyze the differences to capitalize on teaching methods that work best to circumvent blocks or slowness in learning. When a crisis occurs for the patient or family, the student sees the impact of the crisis on all of them, and learns how to assist at that time within a refined sense of the occasion.

Physicians who have arranged for their patients to continue their treatment in the house have not always done so for the sake of preparation for rehabilitation. In a few instances they have brought the patient and his family together in the house to demonstrate to the relatives that they cannot handle the patient and should not take him home. In these cases, so far, the experience has strengthened the families' determination to return home, and they have turned the tables on the physicians, proving their competence for taking care of the patient in a homelike setting. In some future instances, like these, we expect to find the physician's judgment supported, and the experience in the house a help to the physician and family in realistic planning for the patient's placement in an extended care facility.

When patients and family members return home, students make the follow-up visits with an instructor. In these home visits, a common experience for many community-based physical therapists, the students have a chance to evaluate the families' progress in using the treatment methods they have learned and in adapting to new family circumstances. Instructors who accompany the student have contrasted these home visits with those they have made where there has not been an intensive relationship with all family members. They report that in this latter instance it is common for family members to slip into the background when evaluation and treatment activities begin. In contrast, after Family Focus, the family members remain involved with the clinician who places central importance on their further education so they may improve or expand their efforts in necessary treatments. Not infrequently the family uses this occasion, too, as a chance to work on solving some interpersonal problems. Thus physical therapists see themselves developing new functions as clinician-teachers to family members.

Students thus gain intensive and supervised experience in interpersonal relations within which patients live and like those with which the students will be working directly or indirectly when they become professionals. They learn the interplay between application of techniques and the social and behavioral contexts within which application is made. They enlarge their awareness and use of themselves as persons who are mastering and deploying skills in evaluation and treatment.

One further and last benefit of the program has been the expansion of the physical therapists' contacts on the hospital wards and in the house with a wide range of professions who serve on the total medical team. Students accompany the clinical instructor, who visits patients and family members on the wards and in the house with a wide range of professions who serve on the total medical team. Students accompany the clinical instructor, who visits patients and family members on the wards to orient them to what they might expect in the house. During this time they confer with physicians, nurses, occupational therapists, consultants, dietitians, administrators and many other staff who may have information that needs to be taken into account in planning the program at the house. This augments patient-oriented experience in working as a member of the medical team. Those students who have previously had much of their hospital and clinic experience restricted to working with physical therapists, find the awareness of the larger staff context for their work beneficial. Students meet some of these same members of the medical team at work in the house after the patient is transferred, and they find that the homelike environment and absence of distractions eases and personalizes their collaboration.

REHABILITATION-TARGETED PATIENT PROGRAMMING

More recently, a program for hospitalization, specifically targeted from the time of admission, to facilitate return of older patients with multiple problems to carefully pre-selected placements in their communities, has been conceptualized and partially implemented in the Intermediate Care Service, Palo Alto Veterans Administration Hospital. Each patient, his family, if he has one, and the hospital staff coordinate their efforts at the time of admission to decide where the patient is to be placed after treatment, even though hospitalization may last for many months. Their plans are registered in written "agreements." If the placement is to be in the patient's own home, elements of his hospital program are coordinated with the home placement objective. This will affect such program elements as where and with whom he lives on a ward, the possessions he brings with him, the chores the family does for him, the ways in which the staff integrate family members, the frequency of home visits or of family visits to the hospital, the assistance to solve family as well as patient problems, the occupations and recreation encouraged, and the specific medical treatments. The program is appropriately different for a patient whose illness or needs for care are of the nature that hospitalization until death is the planned placement. Or, a patient who is to live with other discharged patients in an apartment in the community, will be provided with a hospital environment, social relations, activities and treatment that will speed his preparation for and placement in a living-group.

PRE-PLANNED INTERDEPENDENCE REHABILITATION

Simultaneously attending to the problems of those who no longer have viable family support systems, I have taken the idea represented in the home of a leper and two schizophrenics in a Thai village (see p. 349), and formulated a new principle for rehabilitation. These three men, long institutionalized, pooled their personal skills to achieve an interdependent way to overcome their handicaps, and to establish a productive life of work and group support in the village. The previously-unformulated fundamental principle is that chronically institutionalized persons with various illnesses, and varying handicaps and strengths, can so complement one another, if the right mix of patients can be found, that they can live independently in the community.

A sizable minority of hospitalized patients no longer have continuing relations with their families. Among those whose ties with families have been broken, we find neuropsychiatric patients, many who are chronically ill with physical diseases, and others who are severely handicapped physically. The patient may not be able to make long-lasting and intensive relations within the hospital, he may not be well enough to acquire, easily, close relations with persons outside the hospital, and he may not have the capacities to function independently in the community to build these relations.

For such patients two social processes must be made possible:

1. When the patients are in the hospital, links must be built with actual families, or family-like social groups must be created for them.
2. Groups as substitutes for families must be invented, into which patients are so assimilated on an intensive basis that they may leave the hospital and return to community living.

The Pre-Planned Interdependence Rehabilitation (PIR) Project concerns the latter process; it tests a model method for constructing a surrogate family group. It has the objective of allowing the maximum number of chronically hospitalized patients to be rehabilitated to living outside a medical institution and in the community.

The most common method for grouping patients for rehabilitation programs is to take those with the same diagnosis—all *neuropsychiatric,* all *mentally retarded,* all *blind,* all *cancer* patients, and so on—and bring them together in a community-based setting such as a residence, workshop, club or other kind of social organization, or treatment program. In some respects this is advantageous because there can be easy continuity between treatment setting and community base, often involving the same professional persons; there can be simplification and specificity about the programs to be offered, and funding can be secured on a categorical basis. However, there are weaknesses in this type of organization. Not the least of the weaknesses is the risk that individuals will be seen as prototypes of an illness category rather than as persons. When this happens a patient finds it difficult to escape a label, status handicaps, and social restrictions.

Reflection on the Thai prototype household convinced me that we tend to think of rehabilitation in terms of a single class of patients or by separate individuals. Our thought patterns may have stood in the way of our conceiving potentialities for community living within carefully structured, interdependent groups assembled in such a way that the mix of individuals provides strengths to compensate for the limitations of each separate person. In no sense does this idea undervalue what has been accomplished through group placement of single classes of patients. It suggests, rather, that deliberate pre-planned placement of mixed groups of patients in the community may extend the range of possible patients who may be placed, and enrich living for each.

A modest test of this principle is in progress. We are building on the base of an already successful program for vocational placement and structured social living units in the community. The Veteran's Workshop, Inc., a private non-profit corporation located at the Menlo Park Division of the Palo Alto Veterans Administration Hospital, operates a number of employment programs: contract work in a sheltered workshop, a service station, house renovation, landscaping and garden maintenance, and placement in private industry. The Workshop arranges and supervises the moving of groups of from four to six chronic *neuropsychiatric* patients into houses purchased by the corporation, or into apartments. Patient-managed group homes are established. The total program has received international attention; it provides an outstanding illustration of what may be achieved through the placement together of patients from a single category.

The new program is utilizing components of this existing program and will augment it. The demonstration has attempted to combine together a group of not more than five patients who represent a variety of illnesses. They were carefully selected, with analysis of how the limitations of each patient are balanced by competencies in other members of the group. They moved together from the Veterans Administration Hospital into one of the Workshop residences. Since they had no supporting family ties, chronic patients of varying diagnoses—diabetes, severe brain injury and epilepsy, schizophrenia, alcoholism and psoriasis, spinal cord injury—have been given a chance to move together out of the hospital into the house in the community, deliberately without live-in staff. Not all of those who were placed were able to remain, but a group of four patients has stabilized into a functioning, mutual-help unit. Together they plan and carry out their home life, shopping, food-preparation, laundry, cleaning, personal care, recreation—with ups and downs but successfully. Strikingly, through pooling finances from various private and public sources they are virtually self-supporting, a significant saving for the hospital. Their way of living is modest but after institution life they are gaining immense satisfactions out of simple decisions, such as choosing their own food, selecting their own TV programs, and turning out the lights when they want.

Each of the men is employed by the Workshop. Noticeable movement toward independence has resulted for three of the former patients. One has progressed in his employment to responsible work in a service station. He is near to financial independence. He joined Alcoholics Anonymous and regularly attends meetings. At his own request, antabuse has been prescribed to help him resist impulse drinking. Further, he has resumed communication with his family, and met for the first time his child, who is now an adolescent.

A second patient is venturing on his own into community relations, responding to an invitation from a visit to his home by a member of a local church. He has become a regular participant in weekday and Sunday services. In addition, he has set forth successfully on short trips, which he finances from his new bank account, growing as a consequence of his work. The achievement this represents is reflected in the recollection that until a few months ago all his affairs were managed by a conservator.

The third patient is beginning to plan for eventual return to his home community, although he is far from solving the problems of employment and restoration of family relations.

THE FAMILY IN THE COMMUNITY

DERIVATIVE UNITS

I will let you expand the ideas as to where such attention to the family-hospital unit might lead. I am pursuing the same issue and greatly stimulated by the mental health possibilities. Having learned to see the family and hospital as a unit, it is easy to move to looking at family-institution units throughout the total medical service program of a community. The research crop that can be harvested from the bio-organic selecting and shifting of units for scientific work, is illustrated still further by the way in which the family-hospital unit pointed up for me analogues in many other community helping facilities and agencies. So my colleagues and I thrust ourselves into family-community relations that were new to scientific effort. Out of this emerged a whole series of fresh ideas for research and action projects involving the helping institutions.

FAMILY-BASIC INSTITUTION UNITS

We continue to be acutely conscious of the fact that the family-helping institution relationships are complemented by the family relationships with the basic institutions in our society—the school; business and industry; church and synagogue; shopping center; theater; centers for art, sports, recreation; police and the courts; the army; and the state. We are moving to develop understanding of the complex relations between the family and basic institutions, and of problems in these relations, hoping ultimately to learn how to prevent some of these problems.

In none of these projects are we yet far enough advanced to report extensive findings. Part of the significance of mentioning them is to demonstrate again the identification of new units for study, to gain courage and help in developing modes of entrance into this and similar fields, and to learn methods of data collection and analysis to cope with their complexity.

Time often seems too short to pursue the many exciting possibilities. To expose them is perhaps a suggestion as well for other professional persons to enter into similar studies. Their major importance will be their yeelding the kind of knowledge that will help us to intervene broadly in efforts to prevent family erosion and disarticulation. These efforts will correct the simple, widespread notion that personal problems can be explained in terms of family relations. We shall substitute more complex theory from which we shall increasingly gain the base of knowledge from which we can produce change in individuals, families, institutions, and the community as a whole. If the reconstruction or new shaping of the relations in the family-institution untts can be accomplished, the scope of our public service moves definitely from clinical to preventive spheres.

SOME RESULTS

A Family-School Program. I can present a statement on two studies that are not yet reported in the literature, but which confirm that we may not be unduly optimistic. By careful attention to the family-school articulation, we backed a group of families and helped them to achieve their ambition to create the only successful nursery school in the country under OEO auspices, started and operated by parents at or near the poverty level, mostly Black. We saw them incorporate, learn what bylaws mean, work within them, hire and fire staff, develop an exciting program, maintain their commitment to integration against militant efforts to make the school "all Black," gain community cooperation in planning an architecturally-daring building, raise $11,000 toward its construction, and survive and grow through crisis after crisis. Basic to this program was keeping constantly in mind the family-school unit.

Unfortunately this creative school eventually foundered as the securing of operating funds became increasingly difficult. The memory of the successful early years and the spirit that made them successful persist, but reconstitution and reopening of the school now seems unlikely. The staff is dispersed, and the mothers who were leaders have lost some of their initiative and commitment as their children have advanced into the elementary school years.

A Family-Church Program. Also, we completed a pilot study and implemented a program by which churches could create substitutes for extended families for the isolated individuals and nuclear families so commonly found in communities. In the pilot phase, two groups of five families were formed by canvassing every tenth member on a church roster. Families agreed to spend two hours together with the other families each week, for nearly three months, at whatever activities might emerge fro collective group decision. Families were brought together who did not necessarily like one another any better than relatives do, and we have seen them work on ways to secure new experiences, knowledge, fun and interdependence among themselves. They have challenged, thereby, the church programs that segregate every age into its own compartment, and begun to develop a model that is transferrable widely to other religious institutions. A teenage boy reported in the evaluation of one of the groups that, to his memory, this was the first time his whole family had ever been together with any other family. A father reported that he had never realized before how helpless he was in trying to do things with children, and that he had learned to have fun with his own kids.

The impact of these pilot programs on programming in one church resulted in organizing multi-family groups to meet once a week for six weeks in Lent each year. These groups were composed in such a way as to continue the principle of bringing together families who were not necessarily close to one another. In the fourth year of this program, fourteen groups are meeting, encompassing 70 families, nearly the whole congregation, and spanning ages from infancy to the nineties. Other churches in the vicinity are now following the same model, and forming groups to substitute for or supplement the extended family.

IMPLICATIONS

I have shared with you these constructions by which I have looked at my world, the history of their development, and by indirection at least some of the values that have motivated me. I would like to think that there are implications for others who are also at work in the public arena, though I hesitate to point up lessons from myself. For me it has seemed productive to keep seeing the persons who make up the public from various and shifting points of view: now as individuals, now as family members, now as citizens in the community, now as participants in the basic and the helping social institutions. I have found it valuable but difficult to get away from looking at the individual to see the unit of the family in the clinic, and beyond this, to create seemingly arbitrary but rational units such as that of the family and hospital. It has helped me to break out of stereotypes. It seems to have suggested new potentials for research programs and services, and new definitions on which public policy could be based. It seems also to have provided a standing point from which it has been possible to sharpen the critique of disarticulated and malfunctioning programs. Were I a politician, perhaps my personal life might have reflected these developments in legislation to change old programs and to authorize new ones for the benefit of the public. As a scientist, I would hope that my development of understanding and experimentation by seeing myself and others in varying unit frames, will help others to formulate more publicly relevant social change.

Notes

(Notes in italics were extracted from original publications.)

PREFACE

In appreciation, the author wishes to credit the following publishers with granting permission to reprint portions of previous publications:

Family Process, the Mental Research Institute, Inc. and the Nathan W. Ackerman Family Institute, Inc. for reprinting from:

Family Group Therapy—A New Treatment Method for Children. *Family Process*, 1967, 6, 254–263.

A Theoretical Position for Family Group Therapy. *Family Process*, 1963, 2, 1–14.

Contrasting Approaches in Marital Counseling. *Family Process*, 1967, 6, 16–26.

The Future of Family Therapy. *Family Process*, 1970, 9, 127–141.

Pergamon Press and the Editors of the *Journal of Child Psychology and Psychiatry* for reprinting from:

Recent Advances in Family Group Therapy. *J. Child Psychol. Psychiat.*, 1962, 3, 1–15.

The International Journal of Group Psychotherapy, for reprinting from:

The Family Group Therapist: An Agent of Change. *Internat. J. Group Psychother.*, 1964, 14, 72–83.

Aldine-Atherton, Inc., for excerpts from:

Rie, Herbert E. *(ed.) Perspectives in Child Psychopathology.* Chicago, New York: Aldine-Atherton, 1971, *pp.* 342–346.

Appreciation is also expressed to:

The National Institute of Mental Health, Public Health Service, Department of Health, Education and Welfare, for initial publication of:

PHS Monograph No. 64, Family Group Therapy: A Method for the Psychological Treatment of Older Children, Adolescents, and their Parents, 1961.

The Family in the Hospital: Lessons from Developing Countries, 1970.
The Office of Child Development, Department of Health, Education and Welfare, for initial publication of:

Family Participation in Hospital Care for Children. *(with,* Elisabeth A. Bell). *Children,* 1970, *17,* 154–157.

Chapter I

1. Before I could ask for details, the topic of conversation shifted, and I took away a misapprehension of what Dr. Bowlby was doing. I assumed he was using contact with the whole family as his sole way of meeting the problem child, or the problem adolescent, and was working out the treatment of the child through having the whole family come to each therapeutic session.

I discovered only much later through reading articles by Dr. Bowlby and a personal meeting with him, that the family approach he had used included only occasional conferences with the whole family. These conferences were adjuncts within the typical mode of dealing with children and their parents where one therapist sees the child and another the adult (usually the mother).

But on the ship returning to the United States just after my visit with Dr. Sutherland in 1951, I began to think through the technical implications of meeting the whole family as a group. Although I had spent much time in reflecting on the transformations in technique that might be required to work with a whole family, I made no mention of this idea in a comprehensive review of my summer travels presented to my colleagues at Clark University. Re-reading my notes for that presentation reminded me of my reactions to the 13th International Congress of Psychology in Stockholm, and of my own youth. The "distinct impression—a troublesome one—was that of the arrogant domination of European psychology by the older men. Not that every one of the older representatives was personally arrogant—but there seemed to be little room for youth!" Perhaps my identification with youth (scarcely brash) held me back from sharing my newest ideas, but, more probably, I regarded the ideas as private until tested.

I speculated that the children would need to be 9 years of age or older, on the assumption that children younger than 9 might not be able to verbalize easily their insights into their own difficulties and the situation of the family. This assumption has since received considerable support in practice, although the inclusion of some 8-year-olds with well-developed verbal skills has also proved possible. My attempts to include even younger children have been unsatisfactory, but others have begun to work out a methodology for family group work with young children and their parents.

Shortly after my return to the United States, a case came to my attention that gave me the opportunity for trying out the method as a therapeutic device. As a result of its apparent success with this case, I extended use of the treatment method.

2. *After preparing this manuscript, I became acquainted with the work of Dr. R. Dreikurs, of the*

Community Child Guidance Center of Chicago. In close study of his articles (1948, 1949 [2], 1950, 1951), I did not discover that he was using the technique described here, although he emphasized the need of simultaneous treatment, partly in groups, of all the members of a family, and of others in the community, such as teachers, who are linked to the family.

3. Read at a meeting of the Eastern Psychological Association in Boston, Massachusetts, at 8 a.m. on April 24, 1953, to an audience of about 20 persons, mostly personal friends and students. Wilson Shaffer of Johns Hopkins University was the chairman.

Following the meeting, Chester C. Bennett, of Boston University Graduate School, wrote a letter inviting me to give a special reading of the paper for broadcast on WGBH-FM. I had mixed feelings about this, not knowing who might hear it, or how effective the communication would be without the opportunity for hearers to ask questions and make comments. At the same time, I was pleased that my paper had been selected, and my wife prevailed on me to accept the invitation. The reading was broadcast, and heard by a number of professional people who told me their reactions.

This led almost immediately to invitations to speak, one of which stands out in my mind. The Mental Hygiene Clinic of the Boston Veterans Administration Outpatient Clinic was directed by Morris Adler, a psychoanalyst with a reputation for authoritarian direction of his staff. He sat in the front row during staff meetings and after hearing a speech set the tone for discussion by responding first. Protective staff members had warned me in advance that Adler might be ruthless in condemnation of my work because of the orthodoxy of his psychoanalytic views. After reading my paper, I was anxious as he rose to his feet. He proclaimed, "This is the most significant event in American psychiatry since Freud's visit to Clark University in 1909."

More than any other early reaction, this support confirmed me in my work and encouraged me to speak in professional circles. I held back the publication of the paper to incorporate experiences with additional cases. The paper was not revised, and I did not publish it until 1967, when I was persuaded that it had gained some historical moment, and allowed it to appear in *Family Process.*

4. At the beginning, I was very reluctant to share my ideas with professional associates. This reflected something of the climate in which psychotherapy was conducted at that time. There were some who so strongly advocated separation of children and family members during treatment that they would not allow themselves to meet any other than the one with whom they had a therapy relation. I knew I was defying a taboo, but relatively quickly gained confidence in my work.

My first official written mention of family therapy appears to have been in a letter dated November 10, 1952, to R. B. Liddy, Head of the Department of Psychology at the University of Western Ontario, in London, Canada. We were planning a speaking engagement, and I was asked to take part in a round table or panel discussion. I replied, "I will be glad to fit in with the plans for the round table or the panel discussion if they are developed around topics to which I might be able to contribute. Or, I might be willing to give a lecture entitled *An Experiment with Family Group Therapy*. I think I would prefer to participate in a panel."

The next identifiable written reference to family therapy was in a letter of December 2, 1952, to Noble H. Kelley, Secretary and Treasurer of the American Board of Examiners in Professional Psychology, Inc. I had been asked to comment on written examinations I had recently completed. I suggested that essay questions be made relevant to the particular type of clinical experience of the examinee, and continued: "While I have worked diagnostically with a wide range of subjects, I have a limited experience with group therapy, and with groups of an unusual nature, that is, family groups, composed of father, mother, a problem child, and siblings."

Eight days later, I forwarded to the Eastern Psychological Association Program Committee Chairman, Douglas Courtney, an abstract of a paper I proposed to deliver at the meetings of the Association in Boston during April, 1953. About the same time, I sent an abstract to the American Orthopsychiatric Association, suggesting the possibility that a paper on family group therapy be included in the 1953 meeting of the Association. Because of deadlines, this suggestion was rejected.

Soon others were beginning to hear of my work and were in correspondence about it. For instance, I was writing to Margaret Lowenfeld in London, England, telling her about use of the World Test with Peter, the five-year-old child in one family.

5. This was the first family with whom I worked. I had met frequently with sub-groups of the family during weekly sessions for a year and a half. At the last conference the father became so angry that he walked out, saying he would never return. The rest of the family and I were stunned.

In the preceding session, the son had been full of fury because his father would not let him have the family car whenever he wanted it; he went into the irrational way (to him) that his father had dealt with control of the car. The girl was much concerned about her father's drinking, and full of hostility about how he behaved when he had too many cocktails before dinner. The wife almost choked with complaints against her husband. The whole session was turned over to bringing out bitterness against father. All went away feeling grand. But father came back the next week, and when his family picked up where they had left off, it was too much. In the middle of the session he stood up and walked out.

Chapter II

1. I should have said that the sequence of these stages is not so clearly identifiable that each transition point to a succeeding stage can be identified and marked. In the social process of the therapy, behavior changes often begin with small anticipatory and experimental movements that become firmly established only after tentative exploration and trial confrontation with their consequences. Thus the stages are abstractions of interpersonal processes prevailing during time intervals in the therapy, rather than absolute and to-be-expected stages.

2. Repeated efforts to publish the McAndrew case over the five years after it was written in 1955 were totally unsuccessful. When a prospective publisher referred the manuscript to Nathan Ackerman for review, he recommended rejection since it would be a competitor with his own proposed publication, "The Psychopatholgy of Family Life." Other publishers were reluctant to venture on a short volume about a new treatment method running counter to prevailing practices. The manuscript circulated in dittoed form during intervening years prior to publication in 1961, and won enthusiastic endorsement from Dr. J. McV. Hunt (who tried energetically on my behalf to find a publisher). Other professional and non-professional friends, and colleagues in the National Institute of Mental Health, such as Jerry W. Carter, Jr., Pearl Shalit, and Warren Lamson, helped to promote early distribution and the ultimate publication.

Against this background, I wrote the following:

I wish to express my appreciation to the friends with whom I have discussed this work and whose enthusiasm has emboldened me in times of discouragement; to colleagues in Scotland, especially the staff of the Child Guidance Clinic of the Royal Hospital for Sick Children, who made it possible for me to further the experiments on which this report is based and who stimulated much thought about the therapy by their intelligent questioning; to the families who have permitted me to enter their personal living to witness both the pleasures in the companionship there and the distress occasioned by problems; to my wife, Elisabeth, whose penetrating insights into family life are bound into the fabric of which family group therapy is fashioned; and to the "McAndrew" family, who generously gave permission for the use of quotations from the transcribed record of their treatment to illustrate the text.

3. Consistent with the theoretical notions about treating the whole family group as a unit, developed later when I consolidated ideas about: the importance of emphasizing in the therapy the boundaries within which the members of the family cohere; the importance of an emphasis by the therapist upon the interactions among family members, rather than upon inferred inner psychological processes.

4. These are not insuperable difficulties, as I learned; but they are of sufficient difficulty to require extension of the therapy in time. Believing that it is especially important to make therapy as brief as possible, I would still subscribe to the principle of no pre-therapy relations with individuals of a family. I have stated this principle categorically from time to time, after the experience that the therapy can be conducted expeditiously by adhering to the principle and

that the therapy is slowed by mixing total family sessions with interviews with separate members or subgroups of the family.

5. Contrast the child-centered approach here with the family orientation reached by 1960, and mentioned on page 1130. The orientation of the children here has a family base which is intermediate between the methods of 1953 and 1960.

6. Certainly an important goal, but now I would regard this as intermediate—a process goal rather than an ultimate objective. At the beginning, I do not know the end goals for the family, these must emerge out of the family's own situation, evaluated according to their own value systems. Communication for its own sake may justifiably be pursued in an encounter group composed of unrelated individuals. In a family, however, the basic functions of the members as individuals as well as a group are under review, and goals relative to such functions will emerge and become for the family the dominant goals of the treatment.

7. This anticipated by several years my full comprehension of Macmurray's priority on action in interpersonal relationships and my relating this to the development of insight (see Chapter V). Doubtless, the extent of my commitment to Macmurray's position grew out of our colleague relationship at Edinburgh during 1954-1955, as well as out of his statements in the Gifford Lectures at Glasgow, which seemed to provide philosophical underpinning for the clinical structures and operations that I had found functional.

8. Although this sounds sensible and potentially productive, I later ceased to offer the possibility of sessions with individuals. They had been functional but time-consuming. However, it was especially the working through of total family repercussions following a conference with an individual that dissuaded me from continuing. Without improving the total benefits, the sessions with individuals appeared primarily to prolong the treatment.

Others advocate private sessions; I find that these therapists are often more concerned with hearing, analyzing, and reporting on the *content* of individuals' contributions to communication than with studying and affecting the interactional processes in the family. There are certain things that can never be learned about a family unless one has private sessions with its individual members. Of course, a therapist's curiosity will be aroused about information that is inaccessible. Knowing that content is not necessary or useful, however, if your goal is to achieve changes in the interaction among family members. The material which is essential for change in the whole group will come out there if you insist on no private sessions, and you will not know many things about the family. You cannot afford the price for satisfying your own curiosity unless you are deliberately doing so for some scientific purpose.

Let me give you an illustration. I was invited to a conference to confer with a therapist about a family he was carrying. This involved the case of a young man who had been hospitalized for two years and had reached a point in his treatment where he was well enough to return to the community. His father and mother were blocking this, saying "He's not well enough." "He can't go back to his job." "He'll only break down again." Over and over they were putting barriers in the way of rehabilitation. The psychiatrist in charge decided it would be best to bring the whole family together. He tried an approach, however, which doomed the treatment to failure. He said, "I'll just simply invite the father and mother to come in and instead of my working alone with the boy, as I've done for the last two years, I'll see all the family together." This kind of transition is never calculated to succeed easily, because one cannot undo the previous relations with an individual. That always stands as a barrier to the therapist's relations with the people who are newly introduced.

In this particular case, there was an additional problem. Before the son became an inpatient, the psychiatrist had separate conferences with the mother and father. At the conference with the mother, she told him a secret involving a pre-marital problem, something neither the patient nor her husband knew. She secured a pledge that the therapist would keep this confidential and especially not reveal it to any of the family members. By this little maneuver of the first session she had the therapist "under her thumb." When he had the whole group together, he knew it would be important for her to reveal this secret, and on several occasions he sensed that she approached its disclosure. Yet the psychiatrist was prevented from moving into this area, even to support the mother, by the fact that she kept backing off. She would develop a headache, she would have to go out to take aspirin, or she would call up the next week and say, "I'm sorry, I'm ill. I can't come to the interview." The therapist knew he was on a spot, for she became the controller of the therapy process, rather than him. If you allow these private communications, you are lost; you cannot use them and you cannot get rid of them.

9. Shortly after writing this, I began to concern myself primarily with the interactive events and *what* was happening, more than why. The question of causality pushes attention to the past—whether the past of a moment ago or of many years. The therapy, an action taking place in the present, is shown to progress in the change of actions as the treatment continues. Experiencing these changes, reflecting on them, and attempting to understand why they have taken place is a common consequence in each family member and in the therapist. But directing attention to these inner processes and seeking to affect them by interpretation appears not so productive of interactional change as might be anticipated from theories of individual and group therapy. Thus I have now given up communicating to families my formulations of the causal factors behind their interactions.

10. I would not now call this "connective," nor my interventions, "interpretation." One of the most useful methods of facilitating change is to point out links (sequences) between acts. For example, I would now say, "I noticed when you are doing that, your family (or an individual) is doing this." Such a statement keeps a person's behavior in its interactive framework and prevents him from withdrawing into himself and forcing the rest of the family to cohere into a group that excludes him.

11. I was struggling here to combine educational efforts with those that I called therapeutic, or, as I soon came to say, problem-solving. Having been associated with educational enterprises all my life, I continue to hold good education in high regard. Within the therapy situation, over time I have become less and less of an educator, preferring to leave educational activities to various family specialists in the community. This separation of roles came about as I struggled with issues of effectiveness of various kinds of therapist interventions. I found great difficulty in predicting the varying readiness of each person in the family to receive instruction, and marked variability in each individual's responses to it as family members were wrestling with one another about how to solve their problems. Unless ideas presented to them in the aim of extending knowledge seemed to have pragmatic value to each one in the present moment of their interaction, the educational effort proved to be divisive of the group, disruptive of its interaction, and antitherapeutic. Thus I have concluded that educational efforts are probably more useful in settings other than in crisis therapy, and commonly more useful for individuals or part-groups of the family than for the family as a whole.

12. The idea of "balance of forces" parallels somewhat the concept of *homeostasis* as used early by Jackson (1951, 1959) and some of his associates (Bateson, 1956, 1958, 1964; Haley, 1959; Satir, 1967; Weakland, 1958, 1960). My internal picture of "balance of forces" came from my undergraduate days in physics, one of my major subjects. I had a mental picture of a large plywood, multisided form on which we determined the center of gravity when weights of different sizes were attached to various points around the edge. I found this somewhat analogous to the effects of the seeming weight exerted by each individual in determining the state of the family at any one point in time. I did not regard "homeostasis" as a normative state to be sought; I thought of it rather as a condition of any moment in the family, which had to be disrupted in order for therapeutic change to take place.

13. Compare this traditional approach to the relations between thinking and "acting" with the position elaborated later, in Chapter V.

Chapter III

1. Based in part on presentations at the following meetings:

Fourth Annual Western Regional Meeting of the American Group Psychotherapy Association, Hotel Statler, Los Angeles, California, November 19, 1957.

Invitational lecture, Menlo Park Division, Palo Alto Veterans Administration Hospital, May 29, 1958.

Tri-City Conference of School Social Workers, Chehalis, Washington, April 2, 1960.

Conference on Family Therapy, sponsored by the California Youth Authority, Nelles School for Boys, Whittier, California, October 20–21, 1960.

Conference on Family Therapy, sponsored by the Eastern State Hospital and the District Chapter, NASW, Spokane, Washington, February 16–17, 1961.

Invitational lecture, New York Society of Clinical Psychologists, New York City, New York January 22, 1962.

2. Later experiences proved that this was an unduly optimistic point of view. More perspective taught me later to utilize failures in family therapy for learning (see page 280).

Chapter IV

Based in part on presentations at the following meetings:

Invitational address, Residential Weekend, Child Psychiatry Section, Royal Medico-Psychological Association, St. Andrews, Scotland, June 25, 1960.

Tri-City Conference of School Social Workers, Chehalis, Washington, April 2, 1960.

Conference on Family Therapy, Nelles School for Boys, Whittier, California, October 20–21, 1960.

Conference on Family Therapy, Spokane, Washington, Feburary 16–17, 1961.

New York Society of Clinical Psychologists, New York City, January 22, 1962.

Chapter V

Adapted from presentation at symposium on "More Imaginative Approaches in Consulting Psychology," Chairman, Gilbert C. Wrenn, Annual Meeting of the American Psychological Association, Philadelphia, Pennsylvania, August 29, 1963.

Chapter VI

1. Invited address at Fourth Annual Meeting, Los Angeles Group Psychotherapy Society, Los Angeles, California, March 16, 1963.

2. Discussion by Saul Brown, M.D., Chief, Department of Child Psychiatry, Mt. Sinai Hospital, Los Angeles, California:

Bell believes in change; when he forwarded his paper prior to this meeting, he wrote that what he would say might differ considerably from the written draft. The change is not great. Obviously, change for Bell does not mean chaos or disorder. His conception of change seems quite restrained. But from his remarks, it is clear that he is not content to wait for it to occur. He believes in acting so as to bring it about.

Bell's role is definable, as he himself suggests, in relation to others. In relation to me, he is an enlightened liberal. To some of you, he may be quite a radical. This reciprocity of relationship arises out of our individual action. My own action has been to explore seriously the method of family group interviewing during the past year and a half. I have found it meaningful, provocative, often enlightening, often productive, and never once totally unuseful. So there would seem to be little to argue about, but I would like to express some implications.

I would suggest that Bell has introduced us to both the temptations and the dangers of a certain relativism. His purpose is to reduce stagnancy in intrafamilial existence. There are innumerable clinical terms that could be used here: sadomasochistic families, leaderless families, constricted families, noncommunicating families, double-bind families, etc. Less clinically, and paraphrasing the existentialist dramatists, we might speak of "families of despair." Through the reduction or the dissolution of stagnancy, individual personalities are freed to become what they can become, and what they can become, once freed, becomes a matter for group forces and group opportunities beyond the family: social and professional groups, cultural groups, economic groups, political groups, and so on. Bell limits himself to doing just so much of the job, that is, the release of the dammed-up family function. He makes the following observations: "I recall what I have observed, that no individual is necessarily more significant in the family than another." "The individual . . . exists as an aspect of his group memberships. "The primary human dimension is a social unit in action that only exists in social processes, relations with others, communication, the sharing of aims, efforts, ideas, and experience." Furthermore, in functional terms, a relational perspective requires our recognition that any approach that modifies the nature of the self and of man's development as a person accomplishes its work through transformation of groups in which the person is a member." "Insofar as a man's difficulties may be seen in his relations with his family, and insofar as the man asks my help with problems that are best conceived as issues in this social unit, I intend to join him and his family in trying to reduce or eliminate the troubles."

I call this a kind of relativism because implicit in it, some might find a disregard for certain of the norms around which we professionals have become so accustomed to talking with each other. These include statistical norms and behavioral standards like masculinity-femininity scores, aggression indices, achievement percentiles, intelligence quotients; and within psychoanalytic phraseology, genital character, productive character, ego integration, successful sublimation, etc. Are we to question, now, what we have so laboriously evolved? Are we about to discover that we have been ensnared and even deluded by a system of measures and criteria the locus for which lies only and insufficiently in the *individual personality?* Are we being asked to conclude that everything is relative to the family in which the individual lives?

The American mythology holds that if a thing cannot be fixed as good as new, it should be turned in for a new one. This may be an illusion.

The European tradition states "We know it's old and creaky, but the parts are well worn to each other; a few repairs here and there and it will do just fine.": This too is an illusion. But is this what family therapy asks us to be content with?

Those who have worked psychoanalytically are only too familiar with how deeply entrenched and how relentlessly recurring certain behavior patterns are, how slowly insight is achieved, how long the working through process requires. In our studies of very young children, we see how tenacious certain psychopathology can be even by the age of four or five. Are we to be content with a therapy that seems to sidestep these realities with an implicit claim that, through a reordering of certain mutually reinforcing defense systems, the family members can move along to something better? Is this not simply defying the facts? And is this not a dangerous relativism that in effect uses no measure save adjustment within a given family?

If I sound like I am accusing Dr. Bell of a crime, I myself stand accused with him.

My own defense is to return to the empirical data and to proceed from there. The empirical data lie in a long historical chain by now. Within this chain are not only the revelations of psychoanalysis but its limitations; not only the excitements of the drug therapies but the disappointments; not only the promise of child guidance but its boundaries; not only the enthusiasms of group therapy but its frustrations; and not only the exaltations of the individual and his freedom but the realization of his fantastic vulnerability and his infinite dependency.

For each situation of emotional distress there are more optimal and less optimal therapies. One hopes that therapists will become free enough *and* wise enough to offer or to lead those who are distressed to the therapy that is optimal for them.

To Bell's thesis that family therapy is a therapy of choice, I would add my own view that it is a treatment of choice *to be used in a variety of ways.* Bell may view this addition as muddying the waters; and, in truth, if we take a therapy model, whatever it is, and adhere strictly to it, as I believe Bell does, we may more quickly learn about its idiosyncratic nature. In our clinic, however, we have been inclined to use the procedures of family interviewing for a variety of objectives.

Bell speaks with simple eloquence about a kind of therapy that has its own prerequisites in terms of patient's needs and therapist's competence. He invites therapists to learn this special competence and he proposes that we all, through empirical study, attempt to define just what those patient needs may be that fit this particular therapy.

I join him with enthusiasm.

A Rejoinder:

In my opinion, Dr. Brown has illustrated reification of the individual, typical of the philosophical traditions against which I have directed my criticisms. I have no quarrel with the validity of norms, scores, measures, or the systematic methods by which such data are secured and analyzed. I have no quarrel with diagnostic categories in psychiatry, or with personality descriptions of psychoanalytic patients. But I have developed a position with regard to the interpretation of these "objective" data, and the appropriate actions to take in therapy as a consequence of these interpretations.

My judgment now tells me that data about individuals and the objectified individual in psychotherapy are being seen as though they were independent of the social relations in which they originated, exist, and are transformed. I am sure that any skillful diagnostician would be acutely aware of the impact of the examiner on the data secured, and of the social developmental processes behind the existence of the phenomena being measured. I am equally sure that a skillful therapist such as Dr. Brown would be the first to confirm that psychoanalytic successes are the product of a therapist-patient social process, and that specific changes in the patient (ideas, values, goals, ways of acting, self concept, etc.) are products of their interaction. Such ideas are in the direction of, but not as radical as, my position.

I return again to the basic assumption in my thought and work: "The primary *unit* is social, persons in relation." This does not lead to the assumption, as Dr. Brown implies by his term "relativism," that all other units than social are non-existent, or contextual. Rather, it gives to the social unit a primacy which requires then that other units be singled out of this primary social unit, perhaps to be examined as though they existed independently. But no matter what the findings, they must be reexamined in the final analysis as within the primary social unit. This metaphysical challenge is difficult to grasp, and more difficult to sustain, because it has to displace the prevailing and deeply entrenched positivist tradition that keeps saying that any unit exists for its own sake and independently.

Chapter VII

From Impact of Emphasis on Family Units. Chapter 9 in Rie, Herbert E. (*Ed.*) *Perspectives in Child Psychopathology*. Chicago, New York: Aldine-Atherton, 1971, pp. 344–348.

Chapter VIII

Keynote address, Thirteenth Annual Conference of the Group Psychotherapy Association of Southern California, Inc. Conference Theme: "Tension Reduction in Group Process: In the Individual, Family, Nation, and the World." Los Angeles, California, May 22, 1966.

Chapter IX

1. Read at 36th Annual Conference, California Probation, Parole, and Correctional Association, San Diego, California, May 26, 1966.
2. This paragraph created a storm of protest from probation officers who cited cases of successful family work. I always meant to pursue the issue of how their techniques compared with my own, but I have not yet had the opportunity. It was my impression, though, that some took advantage of their authority as officers to gain entrance to the family, to keep the family in treatment and in some instances to direct change. I was intrigued by the admixture in one person of the authority of the corrections agency and the authority of a therapist, as well as the apparent acceptance of the officers as constructive and benign agents.

Chapter X

Presented at the Symposium on Family Therapy, Eastern Pennsylvania Psychiatric Institute, Philadelphia, Pennsylvania, September 1, 1963.

Chapter XI

Adapted from:

Concluding Address, Don D. Jackson Memorial Conference, Asilomar, California, March 2, 1969.
Conference Theme Address, Concluding Dinner, Symposium LXXXVIII, Geigy Symposia Series, Hartford, Connecticut, June 11, 1970.

Chapter XII

Based in part on Chapter II in *The Family in the Hospital* (Bell, 1970).

Chapter XIII

Keynote Address, Annual Conference, The Association for Child Care in Hospitals, Ann Arbor, Michigan, May 8, 1969.

Chapter XVI

Based in part on Presidential Address of Division 18, Division of Psychologists in Public Service; presented at Annual Meeting of the American Psychological Association, Miami Beach, Florida, September 5, 1970.

Bibliography

Ackerman, N. W. Group dynamics 1. "Social role" and total personality. *Amer. J. Orthopsychiat.*, 1951, *21*, 1–17.

———Interpersonal disturbances in the family: Some unsolved problems in psychotherapy. *Psychiatry*, 1954, *17*, 359–368.

———Psychoanalytic principles in a mental health clinic for the pre-school child and his family. *Psychiatry*, 1956, *19*, 63–76.

———A changing conception of personality: a personal viewpoint. *Amer. J. Psychoanal.*, 1957, *17*, 78–86.

———An orientation to psychiatric research on the family. *Marriage Fam. Living*, 1957, *19*, 68–74.

———*Psychodynamics of family life: Diagnosis and treatment of family relationships.* New York: Basic Books, 1958.

———Toward an integrative therapy of the family. *Amer. J. Psychiat.*, 1958, *114*, 727–733.

Ackerman, N. W., and Behrens, M. L. Child and family psychopathy: problems of correlation. In *Psychopathology of childhood.* Hoch, P. H. and Zubin, J. (eds.). New York: Grune and Stratton, 1955, pp. 177–196.

———A study of family diagnosis. *Amer. J. Orthopsychiat.*, 1956, *26*, 66–78.

———The family group and family therapy: the practical application of family diagnosis. *Int. J. Sociometry*, 1956, *1*, 52–54.

———The family group and family therapy. Part II. The practical application of family diagnosis. *Int. J. Sociometry*, 1957, *1*, 82–95.

Ackerman, N. W., and Neubauer, P. B. Failures in the psychotherapy of children. In Hoch, P. H. (ed.). *Failures in psychiatric treatment.* New York: Grune & Stratton, 1948.

Ackerman, N. W., and Sobel, R. Family diagnosis: an approach to the study of the preschool child. *Amer. J. Orthopsychiat.*, 1952, 22, 744–752.

Ainsworth, M. D. The effects of maternal deprivation: a review of findings and controversy in the context of research strategy. In *Deprivation of maternal care: a reassessment of its effects.* Public Health Papers, No. 14. Geneva, Switzerland: World Health Organization, 1962, pp. 97–165.

Asuni, T. Community development and public health by-product of social psychiatry in Nigeria. *West African Medical J.,* 1964, *13,* 151–154.

Bandura, A., and Walters, R. H. *Adolescent aggression: A study of the influence of child-training practices and family interrelationships.* New York: Ronald, 1959.

Bateson, G. Cultural problems posed by a study of schizophrenic process. Presented at the American Psychiatric Association, Conference on Schizophrenia, Honolulu, 1958.

Bateson, G., and Jackson, D. D. Social factors and disorders of communication. Some varieties of pathogenic organization. *Res. Publ. Assoc. Research Nerv. Mental Dis.,* 1964, 42, 270–290.

Bateson, G.; Jackson, D. D.; Haley, J.; and Weakland, J. Toward a theory of schizophrenia. *Behav. Sci.,* 1956, *1,* 251–264.

Behrens, M. L., and Ackerman, N. W. The home visit as an aid in family diagnosis and therapy. *Soc. Casework,* 1956, 37, 11–19.

Bell, J. E. Family group therapy: A new treatment method for children. *Amer. Psychol.,* 1953, 8, 515 (T). Also privately published. Reprinted in *Family Process,* 1967, 6, 254–263.

————Family group therapy. *Public Health Monograph No. 64.* Washington, D.C.: U.S. Government Printing Office, 1961.

————Recent advances in family group therapy. *J. Child Psychol. Psychiat.,* 1962, 3, 1–15. Reprinted in Rosenbaum, M., and Berger, M., *Group psychotherapy and group function.* New York: Basic Books, 1963. Also in Howells, J. G., *Theory and practice of family psychiatry.* Edinburgh and London: Oliver & Boyd, 1968.

————A theoretical position for family group therapy. *Family Process,* 1963, 2, 1–14. Reprinted in Ackerman, N. W. (ed.), *Family process.* New York: Basic Books, 1970; in Mahrer, A. R., and Pearson, L. (eds.), *Creative developments in psychotherapy. Vol. I.* Cleveland, Ohio: Press of Case Western Reserve University, 1971.

————The family group therapist: An agent of change. *Internat. J. Group Psychotherapy*, 1964, *14*, 72–83.

————Counseling with families. *Mental Health Research Inst. Bull.*, 1961, *3*, 31–33.

————Contrasting approaches in marital counseling. *Family Process*, 1967, *6*, 16–26.

————Hospitalization—A crisis for the family. *Seventh Annual Training Sessions for Psychiatrist-Teachers of Practicing Physicians—1966*. Western Interstate Commission for Higher Education, 1967, 26–32.

————*The family in the hospital: Lessons from developing countries.* Washington, D.C.: U.S. Government Printing Office, 1970.

————The future of family therapy. *Family Process*, 1970, *9*, 127–141.

————Impact of emphasis on family units. In, Rie, H. E. (ed.). *Perspectives in Child Psychopathology*. Chicago: Aldine-Atherton, 1971.

Bell, J. E., and Bell, E. A. Family participation in hospital care for children. *Children*, 1970, *17*, 154–157.

Bell, N. W.; Trieschman, T.; and Vogel, E. A sociocultural analysis of the resistances of working-class fathers treated in a child psychiatric clinic. *Amer. J. Orthopsychiat.*, 1961, *31*, 388–405.

Bergman, T. *Children in the hospital.* New York: Int. Univ. Press, 1965.

Bodin, A. M. Family interaction, coalition, disagreement, and compromise in problem, normal, and synthetic family triads. *Dissertation Abstracts*, 1967, 28 (3-B), 1184.

Bowen, M. The family as the unit of study and treatment: I. family psychotherapy. Workshop, 1959. *Amer. J. Orthopsychiat.*, 1961, *31*, 40–60.

————A family concept of schizophrenia. In Jackson, D. D. (ed.), *Studies in schizophrenia.* New York: Basic Books, 1960.

Bowen, M.; Dysinger, R. H.; and Basamania, B. Role of the father in families with a schizophrenic patient. *Amer. J. Psychiat.*, 1959, *115*, 1017–1021.

Bowen, M.; Dysinger, R. H.; Brodey, W. M.; and Basamania, B. Study and treatment of five hospitalized family groups, each with a psychotic member. Read in the sessions on Current

Familial Studies, at the annual meeting of the American Orthopsychiatric Association, Chicago, Illinois, March 8, 1957.

Bowlby, J. The study and reduction of group tensions in the family. *Human Relat.*, 1949, 2, 123–128.

————*Maternal care and mental health. Second edition.* Geneva, Switzerland: World Health Organization Monograph No. 2, 1952.

Brodey, W. M., and Hayden, M. Intrateam reactions: their relation to the conflicts of the family in treatment. *Amer. J. Orthopsychiat.*, 1957, 27, 349–355.

Buber, M. *I and thou.* (Trans. R. G. Smith.). Edinburgh: T. & T. Clark, 1937.

Clausen, J. A., and Yarrow, M. R. Mental illness and the family. *J. Soc. Issues*, 1955, 11, 3–5.

Clausen, J. A.; Yarrow, M. R.; Deasy, L. C.; and Schwartz, C. G. The impact of mental illness: research formulation. *J. Soc. Issues*, 1955, 11, 6–11.

Detre, T. P., Kessler, D. R., and Jarecki, H. G. The role of the general hospital in modern community psychiatry. *Amer. J. Orthopsychiat.*, 1963, 33(4), 690–700.

Dewey, J. *Experience and nature.* Paul Carus Foundation Lecture. Chicago: Open Court Publishing Co., 1925, pp. 166–207.

Dreikurs, R. *The challenge of parenthood.* New York: Duell, Sloan and Pearce, 1948.

————Counseling for family adjustment. *Indiv. Psychol. Bull.*, 1949, 7, 119–137.

————Psychotherapy through child guidance. *Nerv. Child*, 1949, 8, 311–328.

————Technique and dynamics of multiple psychotherapy. *Psychiat. Quart.*, 1950, 24, 788–799.

————Family group therapy in the Chicago Community Child Guidance Center. *Ment. Hyg.*, 1951, 35, 291–301.

Dysinger, R. H. The family as the unit of study and treatment. *Amer. J. Orthopsychiat.*, 1961, 31, 61–68.

Dysinger, R. H., and Bowen, M. Problems for medical practice presented by families with a schizophrenic member. *Amer. J. Psychiat.*, 1959, 116, 514–517.

Fagin, C. M. *The effects of maternal attendance during hospitalization on the post hospital behavior of young children: a comparative study.* Phila.: F. A. Davis, 1966.

Fleck, S., et al. The intrafamilial environment of the schizophrenic patient. II. Interaction between hospital staff and families. *Psychiatry,* 1957, *20,* 343–350.

Fleck, S.; Freedman, D. X.; Cornelison, A.; Terry D.; and Lidz, T. The intrafamilial environment of the schizophrenic patient—V. The understanding of symptomatology through the study of family interaction. Read at the annual meeting of the American Psychiatric Association, May, 1957.

Foster, H. H., Jr. The future of family law. *Annals Amer. Acad. Polit. Soc. Science,* 1969, *383,* 129–144.

Glasmann, R.; Lipton, H.; and Dunstan, P. L. Group discussions with a hospitalized schizophrenic and his family. *Int. J. group Psychother.,* 1959, *9,* 204–212.

Group for the Advancement of Psychiatry. The case history method in the study of family process. *Report #76.* New York: Group for the Advancement of Psychiatry, 1970.

————The field of family therapy. *Report #78.* New York: Group for the Advancement of Psychiatry, 1970.

Grunebaum, H. U., and Weiss, J. L. Psychotic mothers and their children: joint admission to an adult psychiatric hospital. *Amer. J. Psychiat.,* 1963, *119* (10), 927–933.

Guerney, B., Jr.; Stover, L.; and Andronico, M. P. On educating disadvantaged parents to motivate children for learning: a filial approach. *Community Mental Hlth. J.,* 1967, *3(1),* 66–72.

Haley, J. Control in psychoanalytic psychotherapy. *Progr. Psychother.,* 1959, *4,* 48–65.

Hearn, G. The process of group development. *Autonomous Groups Bull.,* 1957, *13,* 1–7.

Jackson, D. D. The question of family homeostasis. *Psychoanal. Quart.,* 1951, *31,* 79–90.

————Family interaction, family homeostasis, and some implications for conjoint family psychotherapy. In Masserman, J. (ed.), *Individual and family dynamics.* New York: Grune & Stratton, 1959.

James, W. *Principles of psychology.* New York: H. Holt, vol. 1, pp. 288–289, 298, 336; vol. 2, chaps 19, 21.

Johnson, A. M., and Szurek, S. A. The genesis of antisocial acting out in children and adults. *Psychoanal. Quart.*, 1952, *21*, 323–343.

Kohlmeyer, W. A., and Fernandes, X. Psychiatry in India: family approach in the treatment of mental disorders. *Amer. J. Psychiat.*, 1963, *119*, 1033–1037.

Lambo, T. A. Personal communication. 1965.

Laquer, H. P. Discussion of Part IV, II. In Greenblatt, M. *et al* (*ed.*). *Mental patients in transition*. Springfield, Ill.: C. C. Thomas, 1961, pp. 265–269.

———Multiple family therapy. In Masserman, J. H. (*ed.*). *Current psychiatric therapies, IV*. New York: Grune and Stratton, 1964, pp. 150–154.

Laquer, H. P. and LaBurt, H. A. The therapeutic community on a modern insulin ward. *J. Neuropsychiat.*, 1962, 3(3), 139–149.

Laquer, H. P. and LaBurt, H. A. Family organization on a modern state hospital ward. *Mental Hygiene*, 1964, 48, 544–551.

Laquer, H. P., LaBurt, H. A., and Morong, E. Multiple family therapy: further developments. *Int. J. Soc. Psychiat.* Special edition 2, 1964, pp. 70–80.

Leary, T. *Interpersonal diagnosis of personality: A functional theory and methodology for personality evaluation*. New York: Ronald Press, 1957.

Leichter, E. Group psychotherapy of married couples' groups: some characteristic treatment dynamics. *Int. J. Group Psychother.*, 1962, 12, 154–163.

Lennard, H. L.; Beaulieu, M. R.; and Embrey, N. G. Interaction in families with a schizophrenic child. *Arch. Gen. Psychiat.* (Chicago), 1965, *12*, 166–183.

Lidz, R. W., and Lidz, T. The family environment of schizophrenic patients. *Amer. J. Psychiat.*, 1949, *106*, 332–345.

Lidz, T. Schizophrenia and the family. *Psychiatry*, 1958, *21*, 21–27.

Lidz, T.; Cornelison, A. R.; Fleck, S.; and Terry, D. The intrafamilial environment of schizophrenic patients. I. The father. *Psychiatry*, 1957, *20*, 329–342.

———The intrafamilial environment of schizophrenic patients. II. Marital schism and marital skew. *Amer. J. Psychiat.*, 1957, *114*, 241–248.

Lidz, T.; Parker, B.; and Cornelison, A. The role of the father in the family environment of the schizophrenic patient. *Amer. J. Psychiat.* 1956, *113*, 126–132.

MacCarthy, D. and MacKeith, R. A parent's voice. *Lancet,* 1965, ii, 1289–91.

Macmurray, J. *The self as agent.* New York: Harper, 1957.

———*Persons in relation.* New York: Harper, 1961.

Main, T. F. Mothers with children in a psychiatric hospital. *Lancet,* 1958, *Oct.,* 845–847.

Mead, G. H. *The philosophy of the present.* The Paul Carus Foundation Lectures. Murphy, A. E. (ed.). Chicago: Open Court Publishing Co., 1932.

———*Mind, self and society.* Morris, E. W. (ed.). Chicago: University of Chicago Press, 1934.

———*The philosophy of the act.* Morris, C. W. et al. (.eds.) Chicago: University of Chicago Press, 1938.

Midelfort, C. *The family in psychotherapy.* New York: McGraw-Hill, 1957.

Nuffield Foundation. *Children in hospital: studies in planning.* New York: Oxford Univ. Press, 1963.

Ortega y Gasset, J. *Man and people.* London: George Allen and Unwin, Ltd., 1957.

Owens, W. E. (Community Child Guidance Clinic, Portland, Oreg.). Personal communication.

Pierce, C. S. *Collected works,* vol. 1. Hartshorne, C., and Weiss, P. (eds.). Cambridge: Harvard University Press, 1960.

Pollak, O. *Integrating sociological and psychoanalytic concepts: An exploration in child therapy.* New York: Russell Sage Foundation, 1956.

Prugh, D. G., Staub, E. M., Sands, H. H., Kirschbaum, R. M., and Lenihan, E. A. A study of the emotional reactions of children and families to hospitalization and illness. *Amer. J. Orthopsychiatry,* 1953, 23, 70–106.

Rie, H. E. (.ed.) *Perspectives in child psychopathology.* Chicago, New York: Aldine-Atherton, 1971.

Robertson, J. *Young children in hospitals.* New York: Basic Books, 1958.

Robertson, J. *Hospitals and children: a parent's eye view.* New York: Int. Univ. Press, 1963.

Ryckoff, I. M.; Day, J.; and Wynne, L. C. The maintenance of stereotyped roles in the families of schizophrenics. Read at the American Psychiatric Association Meetings, San Francisco, May, 1958.

Satir, V. *Conjoint family therapy.* Revised edition. Palo Alto: Science and Behavior Books, 1967.

Sculthorpe, W. and Blumenthal, I. J. Combined patient-relative group therapy in schizophrenia. *Mental Hygiene,* 1965, 49(4), 569–573.

Sears, R. R.; Maccoby, E. E.; and Levin, H. *Patterns of child rearing.* Evanston, Ill.: Row, Peterson & Co., 1957.

Sears, R. R.; Whiting, J. W. M.; Nowlis, V.; and Sears, P. S. Some child-rearing antecedents of aggression and dependency in young children. *Genet. Psychol. Monogr.,* 1953, 47, 135–236.

Singer, M. T., and Wynne, L. C. Thought disorder and family relations of schizophrenics. III. Methodology using projective techniques. *Arch. Gen. Psychiat.* (Chicago), 1965, 12(2), 187–200.

Spence, J. C. *The purpose of the family: a guide to the care of children.* London: Epworth Press, 1946.

———The care of children in hospitals. The Charles West Lecture, Royal College of Physicians, November 1946.

Spiegel, J. P. New perspectives in the study of the family. *Marriage Fam. Living,* 1954, 16, 4–12.

———A model for relationships among systems. In Grinker, R. R. (ed.), *Toward a unified theory of human behavior.* New York: Basic Books, 1956.

———Interpersonal influences within the family. In *Group Processes.* Third Conference, Macy Foundation, 1957.

———The resolution of role conflict within the family. *Psychiatry,* 1957, 20, 1–16.

Spiegel, J. P., and Bell, N. W. The family of the psychiatric patient. In Arieti, S. (ed.), *American handbook of psychiatry,* vol. 1. New York: Basic Books, 1959, pp. 114–149.

Spiegel, J. P., and Kluckhohn, F. R. Integration and conflict in family behavior. *Group for the Advancement of Psychiatry. Report No. 27.* Topeka: Kansas, 1954.

Vogel, E. F., and Bell, N. W. The emotionally disturbed child as a family scapegoat. *Psychoanal. Psychoanal. Rev.*, 1960, 47(2), 21–42.

Weakland, J. The double bind hypothesis of schizophrenia and three-party interaction. In Jackson, D. D. (ed.), *Studies in schizophrenia*. New York: Basic Books, 1960.

Weakland, J., and Jackson, D. D. Patient and therapist observations on the circumstances of a schizophrenic episode. *Arch. Neurol. Psychiat.*, 1958, 79, 554–575.

Weiss, J. L., Grunebaum, H. U., and Schell, R. E. Psychotic mothers and their children: II. psychological studies of mothers caring for their infants and young children in a psychiatric hospital. *Archives Gen. Psychiat.*, 1964, 11(1), 90–98.

Wynne, I. D.; Ryckoff, I. M.; Day, J.; and Hirsch, S.E. Pseudomutuality in the family relations of schizophrenics. *Psychiatry*, 1958, *21*, 205–220.

Index